T0213546

Communications
in Computer and Information Science   766

Commenced Publication in 2007
Founding and Former Series Editors:
Alfredo Cuzzocrea, Orhun Kara, Dominik Ślęzak, and Xiaokang Yang

More information about this series at http://www.springer.com/series/7899

Alessandro Piva · Ilenia Tinnirello
Simone Morosi (Eds.)

Digital Communication

Towards a Smart and Secure Future Internet

28th International Tyrrhenian Workshop, TIWDC 2017
Palermo, Italy, September 18–20, 2017
Proceedings

 Springer

Editors
Alessandro Piva (ID)
University of Florence
Florence
Italy

Simone Morosi (ID)
University of Florence
Florence
Italy

Ilenia Tinnirello (ID)
University of Palermo
Palermo
Italy

ISSN 1865-0929 ISSN 1865-0937 (electronic)
Communications in Computer and Information Science
ISBN 978-3-319-67638-8 ISBN 978-3-319-67639-5 (eBook)
DOI 10.1007/978-3-319-67639-5

Library of Congress Control Number: 2017952859

Printed on acid-free paper

This Springer imprint is published by Springer Nature
The registered company is Springer International Publishing AG
The registered company address is: Gewerbestrasse 11, 6330 Cham, Switzerland

Preface

Over the past decade, the evolution of the Internet has been characterized by the proliferation of mobile smartphones as dominant devices for accessing the network, and by the impressive growth of connected objects with sensing and actuation capabilities within the paradigm of the Internet of Things in different application domains, such as critical manufacturing, emergency services, energy, financial services, health care and public health, information technologies, and transportation systems.

The proliferation of data and connections is creating new opportunities to leverage knowledge and to manage systems in innovative ways, but is also introducing new risks due to the increased interactions between entities, in particular in the context of critical infrastructures. This leads to a variety of conflicting requirements and technical challenges for the Future Internet: On the one hand, it is required to improve the mechanisms to retrieve information, distribute contents, and manage knowledge; on the other, it is essential to deal with data protection, privacy, and access control.

The goal of the 2017 Tyrrhenian International Workshop on Digital Communications (TIWDC 2017) was to investigate emerging paradigms and solutions for the design of a smart and secure Future Internet: TIWDC 2017 offered to the scientific community an opportunity of exchanging results and perspectives about these challenging topics.

This volume gathers the contributions that were presented at TIWDC 2017 and collects the original results that were presented in the technical sessions that were devoted to the topics of biometric systems, multimedia forensics, software defined networks, emerging services with NFV, security protocols, and technologies for IoT. The contributions come from renowned international experts and researchers in the fields.

The editors would like to express their sincere and grateful appreciation to the Technical Program Committee co-chairs, Prof. Mario Marchese and Prof. Pietro Paolo Corso, and valuable members for their support and to all authors for their contributions.

Finally, the editors would also like to thank the members of the Organizing Committee for their valuable and committed work, which made an important contribution to the success of TIWDC 2017.

September 2017

Alessandro Piva
Ilenia Tinnirello
Simone Morosi

Organization

General Chairs

Ilenia Tinnirello   University of Palermo, Italy
Alessandro Piva   University of Florence, Italy

Program Co-chairs

Mario Marchese   University of Genoa, Italy
Pietro Paolo Corso   University of Palermo, Italy

Publications Chair

Simone Morosi   University of Florence, Italy

Technical Program Committee

Alessandro Armando	University of Genoa, Italy
Sebastiano Battiato	University of Catania, Italy
Giuseppe Bianchi	University of Rome Tor Vergata, Italy
Patrizio Campisi	University of Rome Tre, Italy
Mauro Conti	University of Padua, Italy
Haitham S. Cruickshank	Institute for Communication Systems, 5G Innovation Centre (5GIC), University of Surrey, Guilford, UK
Jorge Cuellar	Siemens, Munich, Germany
Franco Davoli	University of Genoa, Italy
Tomaso de Cola	German Aerospace Center, Wessling, Germany
Isao Echizen	National Institute of Informatics, Tokyo, Japan
Marcos Faúndez-Zanuy	Tecnocampus, Mataró, Spain
Yanick Fratantonio	University of California, Santa Barbara, USA
Pierluigi Gallo	University of Palermo, Italy
Fabio Garzia	Wessex Institute of Technology, Ashurst, UK
Stefano Giordano	University of Pisa, Italy
Chang-Tsun Li	Charles Sturt University, Sidney, Australia
Emanuele Maiorana	University of Rome Tre, Rome, Italy
Lorenzo Mucchi	University of Florence, Italy
Fernando Peréz-Gonzalez	University of Vigo, Spain
George Polyzos	Athens University of Economics and Business (AUEB), Greece
Soodamani Ramalingam	University of Hertfordshire, Hatfield, UK
Anderson Rocha	University of Campinas, Brazil

Contents

Biometric Systems

On the Use of Time Information at Long Distance in Biometric
Online Signature Recognition 3
    Carlos Alonso-Martinez and Marcos Faundez-Zanuy

Automatic Face Recognition and Identification Tools
in the Forensic Science Domain 8
    Angelo Salici and Claudio Ciampini

Biometric Fusion for Palm-Vein-Based Recognition Systems 18
    Emanuela Piciucco, Emanuele Maiorana, and Patrizio Campisi

Emerging Services with NFV

Availability Modeling and Evaluation of a Network Service Deployed
via NFV 31
    Mario Di Mauro, Maurizio Longo, Fabio Postiglione,
    and Marco Tambasco

Definition and Evaluation of Cold Migration Policies for the Minimization
of the Energy Consumption in NFV Architectures 45
    Vincenzo Eramo and Francesco Giacinto Lavacca

A Lightweight Prediction Method for Scalable Analytics
of Multi-seasonal KPIs 61
    Roberto Bruschi, Giuseppe Burgarella, and Paolo Lago

Multimedia Forensics

A Copy-Move Detection Algorithm Based on Geometric Local
Binary Pattern 73
    Andrey Kuznetsov

A Dataset for Forensic Analysis of Videos in the Wild 84
    Dasara Shullani, Omar Al Shaya, Massimo Iuliani,
    Marco Fontani, and Alessandro Piva

Illumination Analysis in Physics-Based Image Forensics:
A Joint Discussion of Illumination Direction and Color 95
    Christian Riess

Random Matrix Theory for Modeling the Eigenvalue Distribution
of Images Under Upscaling   109
    David Vázquez-Padín, Fernando Pérez-González,
    and Pedro Comesaña-Alfaro

Security Protocols

A Security Evaluation of FIDO's UAF Protocol in Mobile
and Embedded Devices   127
    Christoforos Panos, Stefanos Malliaros, Christoforos Ntantogian,
    Angeliki Panou, and Christos Xenakis

Delay Tolerant Revocation Scheme for Delay Tolerant VANETs (DTRvS). . . .   143
    Chibueze P. Anyigor Ogah, Haitham Cruickshank, Philip M. Asuquo,
    Ao Lei, and Zhili Sun

Impact of Spreading Factor Imperfect Orthogonality
in LoRa Communications.   165
    Daniele Croce, Michele Gucciardo, Ilenia Tinnirello,
    Domenico Garlisi, and Stefano Mangione

Software Defined Networks

A Network-Assisted Platform for Multipoint Remote Learning   183
    Alfio Lombardo, Corrado Rametta, and Christian Grasso

A De-verticalizing Middleware for IoT Systems Based on Information
Centric Networking Design   197
    Giuseppe Piro, Giuseppe Ribezzo, Luigi Alfredo Grieco,
    and Nicola Blefari-Melazzi

Technologies for IoT

Measuring Spectrum Similarity in Distributed Radio Monitoring Systems. . . .   215
    Roberto Calvo-Palomino, Domenico Giustiniano, and Vincent Lenders

Green and Heuristics-Based Consolidation Scheme for Data Center
Cloud Applications   230
    Alessandro Carrega and Matteo Repetto

Implementing a Per-Flow Token Bucket Using Open Packet Processor   251
    Giuseppe Bianchi, Marco Bonola, Valerio Bruschi, Luca Petrucci,
    and Salvatore Pontarelli

Author Index   263

Biometric Systems

On the Use of Time Information at Long Distance in Biometric Online Signature Recognition

Carlos Alonso-Martinez and Marcos Faundez-Zanuy

ESUP Tecnocampus (Pompeu Fabra University), Av. Ernest Lluch 32, 08302 Mataró, Spain
{calonso,faundez}@tecnocampus.cat

Abstract. In this paper, we investigate the possibility to improve biometric recognition accuracy taking advantage of in-air movements at long distance in online handwriting signature. In-air movements at long distance appear when the distance from the tip of the pen to the paper surface is higher than 1 cm. In this case, the computer can only know the time spent in air because the distance is too high to track the x and y coordinates of the movement. In this paper, we tried several strategies and we checked that the most suitable approach consists of filling the gaps in the acquired signals replicating the last acquired value. In this paper, we check that in air-long movements are three times more frequent in skilled forgeries (1.59%) than in genuine ones (0.48%).

Keywords: On-line signatures · Dynamic time warping · In-air movements

1 Introduction

Signature recognition can be split into two categories [1], off-line and on-line. In the former case, just the result of the signature is known because it is acquired after the realization process. On the other hand, online signature consists of acquiring the signature during the realization process. This provides a larger set of signals:

a. Absolute spatial coordinates (x, y) of the tip of the pen.
b. Pressure exerted on the surface. Of course, this value is zero when the pen is not touching the surface.
c. Angles of the pen: altitude and azimuth.
d. Time stamp of the moment where the previous values have been acquired.

When pressure is different from zero the movement is considered to be on-surface and the whole set of information described before is acquired. When pressure is zero, the movement is considered to be in-air. If the distance from the tip of the pen to the paper surface is below one centimeter the whole set of information described before is acquired with the unique exception of pressure, which is always zero. However, when the distance is higher than 1 cm the track between the tablet and the pen is lost and no samples are acquired. This means that the previous described information (a) to (d) is not acquired. However, as soon as the pen touches the surface, samples are acquired again. Working out the difference between consecutive time stamps we can detect the time spent at this long-distance movements.

© Springer International Publishing AG 2017
A. Piva et al. (Eds.): TIWDC 2017, CCIS 766, pp. 3–7, 2017.
DOI: 10.1007/978-3-319-67639-5_1

2   Experimental Results

In this paper we will use BIOSECUR-ID database [2], whose main characteristics are: it is a multimodal biometric database, that includes speech, iris, face (still images and videos), handwritten signature and text, fingerprints, hand and keystroking; with respect to handwritten text, this database defines five different tasks: a Spanish text in lower-case, ten digits written separately, sixteen Spanish words in upper-case, four genuine signatures and one forgery of the three precedent subjects. The database comprises 400 subjects and four different sessions where the different tasks were recorded.

Using this database, we have evaluated the percentage of movements done at different distances: on-surface, in-air short and in-air long where for on-surface movements pressure is different from zero and for in-air movements pressure is zero. At short distance the tablet can track the movements in air and provides x and y coordinates while for long distances (higher than 1 cm) no samples are acquired. Table 1 summarizes the percentages of time spent in these situations.

Table 1. Percentage of time at each distance for genuine and skilled forgeries.

Signatures type	On-surface	In-air short distance	In-air long distance
Genuine	79.60%	19.92%	0.48%
Skilled forgery	68.54%	29.87%	1.59%

Considering that in-air long movements have been lesser studied we investigated its distribution and found the histogram (see Fig. 1). We use a subset of 40 subjects for this study.

Looking at Fig. 1 and Table 1 we observe that skilled forgeries tend to pass more time at in-air long distance than genuine signatures thus it is worth to investigate the possibility to use this information for improving recognition accuracies. We will use a Dynamic Time Warping classifier (DTW) and as a base line our previous work [3]. We use session 1 genuine signatures for training, session 2 genuine signatures for random test and whole 12 skilled signatures (three for session).

A signature of a user extracted from its file (see Fig. 2) and our first attempt to include in-air long distance movements in the signature signal (see Fig. 3). It consists of filling up the signature with zeros, as many zeros as lost samples (the tablet does not acquire while the pen is at long distance). It can be seen that a discontinuity appears. We repeat the process of filling up the gaps using a different strategy (see Fig. 4). Rather than filling up with zeroes we replicate the last available value in order to avoid the discontinuity shown in Fig. 3.

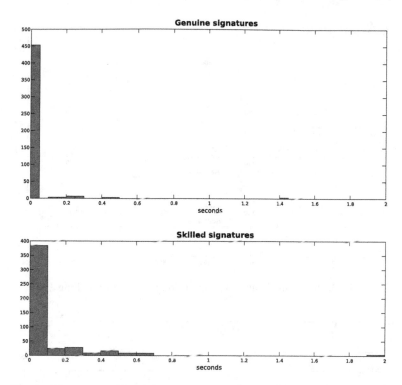

Fig. 1. Histograms of in-air long movements for genuine and skilled forgeries.

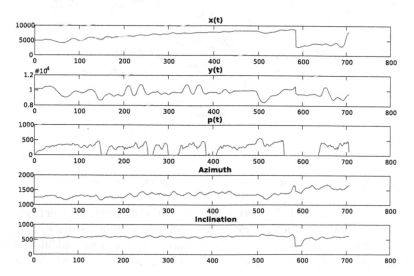

Fig. 2. Signature features without in-air long distance

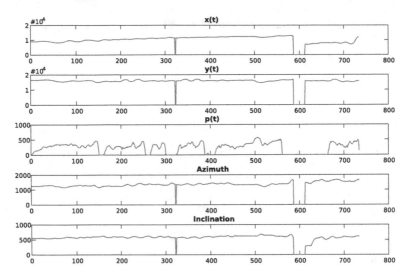

Fig. 3. Signature features with in-air long distance zero filling

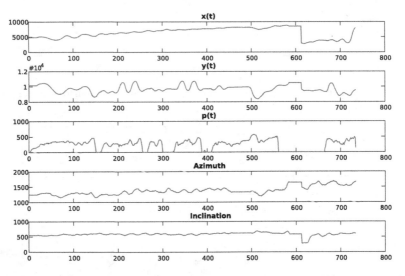

Fig. 4. Signature features with in-air long distance last value filling

Table 2 shows experimental results of DCF (detection cost function) for random and skilled forgeries and identification rate under different conditions: using on-surface information only, including in-air near distance information and with addition of in-air long distance information filling gaps with 0 and with repetition of the last tracked value.

Table 2. Experimental results filling up with 0 and with repetition of the last value

	Random DCF	Skilled DCF	Identification
On-surface information only	3.189%	5.833%	99.375%
In-air near distance	1.795%	3.021%	98.750%
In-air long distance with 0	15.32%	9.896%	84.375%
In-air long dist. with 0 ignoring gaps < 0.15 s	2.716%	3.750%	98.125%
In-air long distance with rep.	2.043%	3.229%	98.750%
In-air long dist. with rep. ignoring gaps < 0.15 s	1.797%	3.229%	98.750%
In-air long dist. with rep. excluding outliers	1.995%	3.229%	98.750%

3 Conclusions

In-air long distance gaps imply the loss of track of the capture system and can be observed as gap in timestamp values for signature files. Skilled signatures present longer values of in-air long distance times than genuine ones but nevertheless, using popular and well-known DTW classifier do not improve results. On the contrary, the most abundant gaps with duration lower to 0.15 s reduce the DTW accuracy dramatically when gaps are filled with 0 s. It can be observed that using last tracked value instead of zeros, improves results.

Outlier values, gaps with duration above $Q3 + 1.5\,IQR$, where IQR is the interquartile range, and Q3 is the third quartile. These values have less impact in results because there are few of these values but a slight improvement can be achieved.

In future works, study of in-air long distance influence on another verification methods like HMM, VQ will be tested.

Acknowledgement. This work has been supported by FEDER and MEC, TEC2016-77791-C4-2-R.

References

1. Faundez-Zanuy, M.: Signature recognition state-of-the-art. IEEE Aerosp. Electron. Syst. Mag. **20**(7), 28–32 (2005)
2. Fierrez, J., et al.: BiosecurID: a multimodal biometric database. Pattern Anal. Appl. **13**(2), 235–246 (2007)
3. Faundez-Zanuy, M.: On-line signature recognition based on VQ-DTW. Pattern Recogn. **40**(3), 981–992 (2007)

Automatic Face Recognition and Identification Tools in the Forensic Science Domain

Angelo Salici[✉] and Claudio Ciampini

Raggruppamento Carabinieri Investigazioni Scientifiche, RIS di Messina,
S.S.114 Km 6,400, 98128 Messina, Italy
{angelo.salici,claudio.ciampini}@carabinieri.it

Abstract. This paper describes an experimental work executed by Carabinieri Forensic Investigation Department (Italy) to explore the performance of the automatic face recognition systems in forensic domain. The main goal of the research is to survey the recognition ability and identification performance of these tools. The experiments are carried out using three commercial automatic facial recognition platforms. In our work we compare the difference between the forensic experts' way of manual facial comparison with the machine outcome in two different scenarios; the first is a training and certification environment, a facial image comparisons proficiency test to verify the recognition capabilities. The second is a daily forensic caseworks scenario, formed by 130 real cases successfully investigated by forensic experts, to analyze the identification achievement.

Keywords: Face recognition · Automatic · Identification · Forensic · Likelihood ratio

1 Introduction

In the forensic science world, the identification of the subject from the trace evidence he/she leaves is the main goal. People can be identified by their fingerprints, by traces of their DNA from blood, skin, saliva, hair, by their teeth, by their walk with a gait analysis and by their voice. Anyway, frequently these data does not exist or does not suffice to guarantee a successful identification. In these cases facial recognition from photo or video recording can provide many benefits.

Images or video recordings are often available for investigation and also for these reasons face recognition systems have recently received significant attention. Image or video may come from a witness camera or surveillance system and can show the face of a perpetrator. If we had not a suspect to compare, then we need to provide a manual search in a police database to solve and correlate the crime. This represents a long and difficult job like in other cases where it is necessary to analyze hundreds of hours of video to search the excerpts in which faces are visible.

For these reasons in the last period, thanks to more than 40 years of research that produced feasible technologies, we have seen a wide range of commercial and law enforcement applications to realize an automatic facial identification.

© Springer International Publishing AG 2017
A. Piva et al. (Eds.): TIWDC 2017, CCIS 766, pp. 8–17, 2017.
DOI: 10.1007/978-3-319-67639-5_2

In our paper, we focused attention on the forensic aspects of automatic face recognition and describe a small scale experimental work carried out by Carabinieri Forensic Investigation Department (Italy) which explores the performance of three commercial automatic face recognition system in forensic domain. We compare the difference between the forensic experts' way of manual facial comparison which the machine results in two different scenarios; the first is a training and certification environment, the ENFSI-DIWG 2013 facial image comparisons proficiency test (FIC test 2013), and the second is a daily forensic caseworks scenario, formed by 130 real cases successfully investigated by forensic experts. In Sect. 2 we introduce some related works. In Sect. 3 we describe the principle and the methodology of our approach. In Sect. 4 we present our experimental results. Conclusions are presented in last section.

2   Related Works

In this section we briefly survey the existing literature on face recognition and describe the current state-of-the-art in Automatic Forensic Face recognition systems analyzing the main existing platform and evaluating their main features.

The history of the face recognition dates back to the advent of photography and the researches in automatic face recognition started in the 1960s. In [1] the authors carried out a review in the field of facial recognition and automatic human face detection describing the significant progress that has been achieved in the years. In [2] W. Zhao et al. provide a critical survey on face recognition categorizing recognition techniques and presents detailed descriptions of representative methods within each category. Face Recognition has become a very popular application in several fields and the interest on it is broad interdisciplinary ranging from biometrics and security to psychology and neuroscience. An overview on the wide range of face recognition practical applications is described in [3]. Face recognition has long been a goal of computer vision and a lot of work has been done on this subject to report the new developing techniques and methodologies or to tackle biometrics problem. On the other hand there are very few published works which describe automatic face recognition in forensic domain. The matching score from a biometric face recognition system is not directly suitable for forensic applications where a fundamental requirement is to evaluate the weight of the recognition evidence in a scientific framework. With this goal in mind Aitken and Taroni in [4] explore the use of statistical and probabilistic approach in forensic science to allow evaluation and interpretation, according to the evidence where there is an element of uncertainty. In [5] Tauseef et al. review famous works in the forensic face recognition, report on attempts to use automatic face recognition in forensic context and develop a framework to use automatic face recognition in the forensic setting. In [6] Peacock and Goode describe a pilot study carried out by the Forensic Science Service (UK) through a specific software package (Image Metrics Optasia™ [7]) which explores how reliable and under what conditions digital facial images can be presented as evidence. This work lays a foundation for how face recognition systems can be evaluated in a forensic framework.

A methodology and experimental results, carried out through a system based on AdaBoost algorithm [8] and Cognitec FaceVacs [9] commercial face recognition system, for evidence evaluation in the context of forensic face recognition are presented in [10]. The proposed approach presented in [10] is in accordance with the Bayesian framework where the duty of a forensic scientist is to compute Likelihood ratio (LR) from biometric evidence which is then incorporated with prior knowledge of the case by the judge or jury.

3   Experimental Materials and Methods

The first scenario analysed in our work was the ENFSI-DIWG 2013 Facial Image Comparison Proficiency Test [11]. FIC 2013 Test was set-up and created by Salima SBIA of the Central unit of Belgian Federal Judicial Police – Forensic Science Directorate in Belgium [12]. The SKL (Statens Kriminaltekniska Laboratorium) [13] acted as organiser and have also written the final report. The test has been sent out to the members of the European Network of Forensic Science Institutes (ENFSI) Digital Imaging Working Group (DIWG) [14] as being the annual proficiency test regarding facial image comparisons (FIC). The test contained one to one single image comparisons where the subject sometimes (approximately in twenty image pairs) was wearing some kind of concealment such as a cap, scarf or other type of headwear. Thirty image pairs were of male and ten image pairs were of female subjects. In total forty image pairs were included in the test. The participants were asked to report their answers according to the conclusion scale based on the standards for the formulation of evaluative forensic science expert opinion discussed in [15] and shown in Table 1.

Table 1. Conclusion scale used and LR equivalent.

		Likelihood ratio	Log_{10} LR equivalent
+4	The observations **extremely strongly support** that it is the same person	>10000	>4
+3	The observations **strongly support** that it is the same person	1000 to 10000	3 to 4
+2	The observations **support** that it is the same person	100 to 1000	2 to 3
+1	The observations **support to some extent** that it is the same person	1 to 100	0 to 2
0	The observations **support neither** that it is the same person **nor** that it is different persons	1	0
−1	The observations **support to some extent** that it is **not** the same persons	1 to 0.01	0 to −2
−2	The observations **support** that it is **not** the same persons	0.01 to 0.001	−2 to −3
−3	The observations **strongly support** that it is **not** the same persons	0.001 to 0.0001	−3 to −4
−4	The observations **extremely strongly support** that it is **not** the same persons	<0.0001	<−4

The second scenario analyzed was a collection of 130 real forensic study caseworks successfully investigated by forensic experts. These daily forensic caseworks contained images of perpetrators extracted from video surveillance footage. Mostly images were in very low resolution and a wide variation exist in pose of face, lighting conditions and facial expression. In these images some kind of "concealment" such as a baseball cap to hide the frontal hairline, glasses and/or scarf was also present. The comparison of these subjects was carried out with a suspect image acquired from a database containing only frontal images with a small variation of pose, light and expression conditions. The time gap between these reference images and the images of perpetrators range from several months to several years.

These reference suspect images and the reference images from ENFSI-DIWG 2013 FIC Test were included in a database of 1829 images, which were used to configure the automatic face recognition systems tested. All images in the database are frontal with only small variations in pose, but variations in order of lighting conditions and facial expression exist.

The automatic facial comparison was conducted with three different commercial software. For every image pairs comparison the automatic face recognition systems provide a similarity score (a numeric value or percentage value) if the images were processed or return a message indicating the failure to process the image. When the images were processed, every system provides also a ranked matching list from the internal database. In Fig. 1 are shown two different examples of ranked matching lists and similarity score values provide by an automatic facial comparison software.

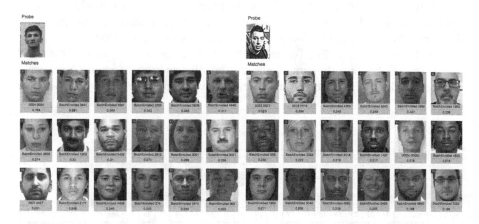

Fig. 1. Examples of ranked matching lists and similarity score values of two different cases.

The score is not directly suitable in the forensic domain. The automatic systems suggest a threshold to decide between two categories, (positive or negative match) but in the forensic world this is unacceptable.

Today, the standard way to report the value of the forensic evidence is based on the Bayesian interpretation framework (or the likelihood ratio framework). A general description of this framework in the forensic context can be found in [16].

4   Results and Observations

Both the two scenarios were engaged with an automatic approach and compared with a typical forensic experts' way of manual facial comparison. The typical forensic face recognition approach is based on the judgement of trained persons and so, in our experiment, we consider the judgement of forensic experts in facial comparisons field. In the first scenario, we analyzed the conclusions of the forensic experts of the 23 European law-enforcement participants at ENFSI-DIWG 2013 FIC Test. In the second scenario, we take into account the conclusions of the forensic Italian Carabinieri experts. The criteria used in the typical investigation from the forensic Carabinieri experts are the same used in the ENFSI-DIWG 2013 FIC Test presented in Table 1. To compare the results of the typical face recognition approach the responses on the upper side (from +1 to +4) of the conclusion scale were considered as a positive match, the responses on the lower side (from −4 to −1) of the conclusion scale were considered as a negative match. To compare the results of the automatic face recognition systems we considered the placement in the candidate rank list and the score provides by every automatic system. About the placement we considered a positive match if the automatic tool evaluated the correct comparison image in the first three positions with a consistent score. If the automatic systems evaluated the correct image in fourth position or on the upper part we considered a negative match. We considered also a negative match if the systems placed the comparison image in the first three positions but with a very low similarity score value. The threshold score value used was dependent by the automatic system tested. Only in the identification context of the second scenario we considered also an inconclusive zone to describe the circumstance where the automatic identification tool finds a match from fourth to fortieth position or not processing the image.

The ENFSI-DIWG 2013 FIC Test results [17] of the forensic experts are summarized in Fig. 2. The results show the sum of corrects (positive and negative matches), sum of zeros (sum of class 0 in Table 1), sum of errors (wrong positive and wrong negative matches).

Forensic Experts Results for FIC test 2013

IMAGE PAIR NO.	1	2	3	4	5	6	7	8	9	10	11	12	13	14	15	16	17	18	19	20		
SUM OF CORRECTS	18	11	4	22	23	19	22	12	17	13	19	14	23	19	14	19	18	18	16	20		
SUM OF ZEROS	3	6	7	1	0	3	1	6	4	9	4	7	0	3	4	3	5	3	7	2		
SUM OF ERRORS	2	6	12	0	0	1	0	5	2	1	0	2	0	1	5	1	0	2	0	1		
IMAGE PAIR NO.	21	22	23	24	25	26	27	28	29	30	31	32	33	34	35	36	37	38	39	40	MEAN	% TOT.
SUM OF CORRECTS	11	19	11	12	23	22	19	19	22	19	23	15	16	22	22	22	15	23	20	14	30,9	77,17%
SUM OF ZEROS	7	3	3	6	0	1	3	2	1	3	0	7	7	1	1	1	5	0	2	7	6,0	15,00%
SUM OF ERRORS	5	1	9	5	0	0	1	2	0	1	0	1	0	0	0	0	3	0	1	2	3,1	7,83%

Fig. 2. Results of laboratory participants for ENFSI-DIWG FIC 2013 test.

The results of our experiment on the same test with the three automatic face recognition systems are shown in Figs. 3, 4, 5. For every image pair test comparison, the table value indicates the position on the candidate rank list provided by the automatic tool. A summarized of the results is shown indicating both the sum and percentage of the correct answers (for positive and negative match) and error made.

Automatic Face Recognition Systems no.1 — Results for FIC test 2013

IMAGE PAIR NO.	1	2	3	4	5	6	7	8	9	10	11	12	13	14	15	16	17	18	19	20
POSITIVE MATCH CORRECT				1	1		1		1				1		3		1			1
NEGATIVE MATCH CORRECT			> 25			> 25		> 25		> 25	> 25			> 25		> 25		> 25		
ZEROS - NOT PROCESSING		NP										NP							NP	
POSITIVE MATCH ERROR																				
NEGATIVE MATCH ERROR	> 25																			

IMAGE PAIR NO.	21	22	23	24	25	26	27	28	29	30	31	32	33	34	35	36	37	38	39	40	SUM	% TOT.
POSITIVE MATCH CORRECT	2				1		1					1		1		1	1		1		16	40%
NEGATIVE MATCH CORRECT			12	> 25		> 25		> 25		> 25	> 25		> 25					> 25		> 25	17	42,5%
ZEROS - NOT PROCESSING		NP							NP						NP						6	15%
POSITIVE MATCH ERROR																					0	0 %
NEGATIVE MATCH ERROR																					1	2,5%

Fig. 3. Results of the 1st automatic recognition systems tested on ENFSI-DIWG FIC 2013.

Automatic Face Recognition Systems no.2 — Results for FIC test 2013

IMAGE PAIR NO.	1	2	3	4	5	6	7	8	9	10	11	12	13	14	15	16	17	18	19	20
POSITIVE MATCH CORRECT	1			1	1		1		1				1				1		1	2
NEGATIVE MATCH CORRECT		20	13			32		365		463	361	> 524		274		18				
ZEROS - NOT PROCESSING																				
POSITIVE MATCH ERROR																		3		
NEGATIVE MATCH ERROR															8					

IMAGE PAIR NO.	21	22	23	24	25	26	27	28	29	30	31	32	33	34	35	36	37	38	39	40	SUM	% TOT.
POSITIVE MATCH CORRECT	1	1			1		1		1			1		1	1	1	1		1		20	50%
NEGATIVE MATCH CORRECT				494		342		113		> 524	> 524		322					326		495	17	42,5%
ZEROS - NOT PROCESSING																					0	0%
POSITIVE MATCH ERROR			1																		2	5%
NEGATIVE MATCH ERROR																					1	2,5%

Fig. 4. Results of the 2nd automatic recognition systems tested on ENFSI-DIWG FIC 2013.

Automatic Face Recognition Systems no.3 — Results for FIC test 2013

IMAGE PAIR NO.	1	2	3	4	5	6	7	8	9	10	11	12	13	14	15	16	17	18	19	20
POSITIVE MATCH CORRECT	2												1				2			1
NEGATIVE MATCH CORRECT			>50	>50		>50		>50		>50	>50	>50		>50		>50		>50		
ZEROS - NOT PROCESSING																				
POSITIVE MATCH ERROR																				
NEGATIVE MATCH ERROR				>50	21		>50		>50						>50				13	

IMAGE PAIR NO.	21	22	23	24	25	26	27	28	29	30	31	32	33	34	35	36	37	38	39	40	SUM	% TOT.
POSITIVE MATCH CORRECT							1		2					1					3		8	20%
NEGATIVE MATCH CORRECT			>50	>50		>50		>50		>50	>50		>50				>50		>50		19	47,5%
ZEROS - NOT PROCESSING																					0	0%
POSITIVE MATCH ERROR																					0	0%
NEGATIVE MATCH ERROR	>50	30			>50								>50			>50	25	10			13	32,5%

Fig. 5. Results of the 3rd automatic recognition systems tested on ENFSI-DIWG FIC 2013.

A summarize table reports the percentage values of the results for forensic experts and automatic systems are shown below in Fig. 6.

No. 1-23 = Laboratory participant FIC Test 2013   -   I,II,III= Automatic Face Recognition Systems no.1, 2, 3

	1	2	3	4	5	6	7	8	9	10	11	12	13	14	15	16	17	18	19	20	21	22	23	I	II	III
% EXACTS	92,5	100	87,5	82,5	82,5	92,5	80	67,5	17,5	80	92,5	82,5	82,5	87,5	80	72,5	67,5	52,5	82,5	60	70	77,5	85	82,5	92,5	67,5
% ZEROS	7,5	0	7,5	5	5	0	12,5	25	82,5	10	2,5	12,5	7,5	7,5	5	17,5	25	40	5	37,5	25	2,5	2,5	15	0	0
% ERRORS	0	0	5	12,5	12,5	7,5	7,5	7,5	0	10	5	5	10	5	15	10	7,5	7,5	12,5	2,5	5	20	12,5	2,5	7,5	32,5

Fig. 6. Comparisons between forensic experts and automatic systems results.

Two of the three automatic systems performed a superior total results than the mean of the forensic experts. The recognition ability of the automatic systems is very high with a good images quality. Also the similarity score is commensurate with the placement, high rank position corresponded with an high similarity score.

The performance of the automatic face recognition tools in the second scenario is shown in Fig. 7. The research has pointed out that the ability of the automatic tools to identify the correct candidates seems to decrease because of the different pose, light conditions and image quality. Instead, all the automatic systems showed steadiness and tolerance with regard to the mutation of facial expression, the concealment and the age variation.

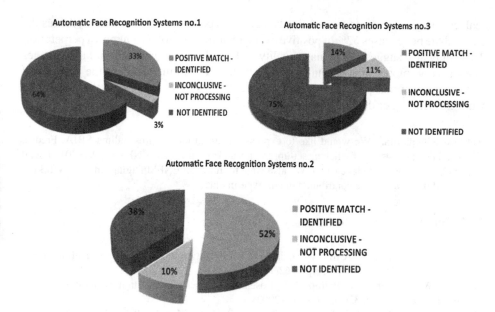

Fig. 7. Identification performance of automatic tools in real forensic cases.

A lot of work has been done to tackle the problem of face recognition across ages. An empirically study on how age differences affect recognition tasks is shown in [18].

Our experiment confirms that the image quality plays a very important role also in automatic facial image comparisons.

The effect of image quality in facial image comparisons have examined in such previous study that suggests that poor image quality leads to more accurate conclusions. How differences in image quality affect the performance of forensic experts and untrained persons is described in [19].

5   Conclusions and Future Works

The present study tested automatic face recognition systems ability to perform a forensic investigation in recognition and identification context. The results show that these systems are ready to support a forensic image comparison laboratory. In face recognition context the study shows a very important feature from a forensic point of view: a very little number of forensic experts, probably with more experience, gave conclusions with less errors and most correct answers. Furthermore the high rate of correct answers of the automatic systems is more than acceptable and makes the automatic tools very important to support the forensic expert decisions. For a complete application in the forensic domain these automatic tools should provide directly a Likelihood Ratio value and not only a similarity score, according to the ENFSI guideline for evaluative reporting in forensic science [20]. In face identification context the experiment shows encouraging and very promising results to adopt these systems in law-enforcement investigation cases where there are not enough suspected candidates. Although our experiment used real test images, in very low resolution and different pose and light conditions, the results showed the better cases 52% of positive match identification of the unknown perpetrator. This study also suggests that image quality and the choice of databases of facial images plays a very important role. Future research should take into account the Likelihood Ratio computations performance to evaluate a threshold similarity score value and working with larger database of facial data.

Acknowledgements. We would like to express our gratitude towards Salima SBIA, Fredrik Eklöf and Peter Bergström for having set-up, created and organized the ENFSI-DIWG 2013 Facial Image Comparison Proficiency Test. We also want to thank all ENFSI Digital Imaging Working Group and those who have contributed in our experiment.

References

1. Patil, C.S., Patil, A.J.: A review paper on facial detection technique using pixel and color segmentation. Int. J. Comput. Appl. **62**(1) (2013)
2. Zhao, W., Chellappa, R., Phillips, P.J., Rosenfeld, A.: Face recognition: a literature survey. ACM Comput. Surv. **35**(4), 399–458 (2003)
3. Senior, A.W., Bolle, R.M.: Face recognition and its application. In: Zhang, D. (ed.) Biometric Solutions. The Springer International Series in Engineering and Computer Science, vol. 697, pp. 83–97. Springer, Boston (2002). 10.1007/978-1-4615-1053-6_4
4. Aitken, C.G.G., Taroni, F.: Statistics and Evaluation of Evidence for Forensic Scientists, 2nd edn. Wiley, New York (2004). ISBN: 978-0-470-84367-3
5. Tauseef, A., Raymond, V., Luuk, S.: Forensic face recognition: a survey. In: Face Recognition: Methods, Applications and Technology. Computer Science, Technology and Applications, vol. 9. Nova Publishers (2012). ISBN 978-1-61942-663-4
6. Peacock, C., Goode, A., Brett, A.: Automatic forensic face recognition from digital images. Sci. Justice **44**(1), 29–34 (2004)
7. Image Metrics Optasia™. www.image-metrics.com
8. Freund, Y., Schapire, R.: A decision-theoretic generalization of on-line learning and an application to boosting. J. Comput. Syst. Sci. **55**, 119–139 (1997). Article No. SS971504
9. http://www.cognitec.com/facevacs-dbscan.html
10. Ali, T., Spreeuwers, L., Veldhuis, R.: Towards automatic forensic face recognition. In: Abd Manaf, A., Zeki, A., Zamani, M., Chuprat, S., El-Qawasmeh, E. (eds.) ICIEIS 2011. CCIS, vol. 252, pp. 47–55. Springer, Heidelberg (2011). doi:10.1007/978-3-642-25453-6_5. ISSN 1865-0929
11. http://forensicscience.eu/fic-test/
12. http://www.polfed-fedpol.be/org/org_dgj_en.php
13. http://skl.polisen.se/
14. http://www.enfsi.eu/about-enfsi/structure/working-groups/digital-imaging
15. Association of Forensic Science Providers. Standards for the formulation of evaluative forensic science expert opinion. Sci. Justice. **49**(3), 161–164 (2009)
16. Evett, I.: Toward a uniform framework for reporting opinions in forensic science casework. Sci. Justice **38**(3), 198–202 (1998)
17. Fredrik, E., Peter, B.: Results and presentation of the ENFSI-DIWG 2013 facial image comparisons proficiency test. SKL Intern rapport. Dokument-och informationsteknikenheten 2014:08. http://media.forensicscience.eu/2014/05/FIC-test-20131.pdf

18. Ling, H., Soatto, S., Ramanathan, N., Jacobs, D.W.: A study of face recognition as people age. In: IEEE 11th International Conference on Computer Vision (ICCV 2007), Rio de Janeiro, 14-21 October 2007, pp. 1–8 (2007)
19. Norell, K., et al.: The effect of image quality and forensic expertise in facial image comparisons. J. Forensic Sci. **60**(2), 331–340 (2015). doi:10.1111/1556-4029.12660
20. ENFSI Guideline for evaluative reporting in forensic science. European Network of Forensic Science Institutes, 8 March 2015 (2015)

Biometric Fusion for Palm-Vein-Based Recognition Systems

Emanuela Piciucco$^{(\boxtimes)}$, Emanuele Maiorana, and Patrizio Campisi

Section of Applied Electronics, Department of Engineering, Rome Tre University,
Via Vito Volterra 62, 00146 Rome, Italy
{emanuela.piciucco,emanuele.maiorana,patrizio.campisi}@uniroma3.it
http://biomedia4n6.uniroma3.it

Abstract. In this paper we investigate the impact on performance of biometric fusion techniques for palm-vein-based recognition systems. In more detail, feature-level fusion, score-level fusion as well as decision-level fusion approaches are applied in a biometric system exploiting patterns of palm veins for user recognition, and both local binary pattern and local derivative pattern features for template generation. The obtained results show that a significant performance improvement can be achieved when the aforementioned feature extraction approaches are jointly taken into account, compared to the case where no biometric fusion is performed.

Keywords: Biometrics · Palm vein recognition · Biometric fusion

1 Introduction

Designing and having available a secure and reliable system for people recognition is an issue whose interest for is more and more increasing during the last decade. Recognition can be based either on what we know, such as a PIN or a password, or on something that we own, like a smart card, or, eventually, on what we are. In this last case, we talk about biometrics and we mean user's recognition based on physiological or behavioral characteristics [1]. Among the physiological characteristics used for biometric recognition, vein pattern is one of the most-recently-discovered biometric traits, with both industries and the research community intensively focusing their work on this kind of modality. This is mainly due to the several advantages the use of vein patterns show compared to other traditional biometric traits, such as face, iris and fingerprint. In detail, besides the fact vein patterns are able to guarantee very high recognition accuracy, they are very difficult to steal and duplicate, since veins are hidden under the skin and visible only through the exploitation of a near-infrared (NIR) camera and NIR illumination, and therefore allow to reach a high-level of system security. Moreover, liveness detection is easily possible since veins, and the blood they contain, represent the liveness itself of a person. Besides, being the vein inside the body, they are difficult to be damaged and modified. Finally, most of the existing devices used for vein pattern imaging are contactless, ensuring

© Springer International Publishing AG 2017
A. Piva et al. (Eds.): TIWDC 2017, CCIS 766, pp. 18–28, 2017.
DOI: 10.1007/978-3-319-67639-5_3

convenience for the biometric system's users. On the other hand, the acquired images are generally characterized by poor quality and low definition because of the employed acquisition devices and the different placement of the veins inside of the body. The issue regarding the low quality of the acquired images makes the feature extraction process a difficult task, and it can lead to a degradation of the recognition performance of the considered system.

Many solutions have been proposed in literature to overcome the impact on recognition performance of vein images characterized by bad quality. Among them, contrast enhancement techniques [6,7], adjustment of illumination distribution [8,9] and multimodal biometric systems [10–13] have been proposed. In this work, we propose biometric fusion for a palm-vein-based biometric system. In detail, in Sect. 2 an overview of the existing techniques for palm-vein-based recognition is given. Section 3 explains the employed palm vein recognition system, comprising the adopted template representations together with the exploited fusion techniques, while the obtained results are shown in Sect. 4. Some conclusions are eventually drawn in Sect. 5.

2   Palm Vein Biometric Recognition: State of the Art

Biometric systems based on vein pattern can rely on finger veins [14,15], palm vein structures [2,11] , hand dorsal vein pattern [16,17] and, eventually, wrist veins [18,19]. Different techniques aiming at the extraction of discriminative features from the network of blood vessels have been proposed in literature, and can be categorized into four different groups:

- **segmentation-based methods:** since veins can be seen as a network of dark lines on a brighter background, the vein pattern can be segmented through geometric-based algorithms and information as line shapes, minutiae or point information are taken into account as representative features of the users. Generally, the region of interest (ROI) where the vein pattern is contained is extracted, and some alignment steps are performed in order to reduce the errors due to misalignment during the acquisition step. This category of feature extraction methods suffers from negative impact on performance linked to image quality, as well as poor ability in discrimination of scaling, displacement and rotation variations;
- **subspace-based methods:** subspace coefficients computed though subspace-based methods such as principal component analysis (PCA), independents component analysis (ICA), linear discriminant analysis (LDA) or non-negative matrix factorization (NMF) can be considered as discriminative features;
- **local-invariant-based methods:** local invariant features are extracted directly from the original vein image. This kind of approaches is inspired by techniques employed in computer vision, such as speeded-up robust feature (SURF) and scale-invariant feature transform (SIFT);

- **statistical-based methods:** features are computed employing statistical information, such as moments and local binary histogram, extracted from the vein images. These techniques can be divided into local and global methods. Global- and local-statistics-based method differ in their behavior with respect in terms of invariance to scaling, translation and rotation. Specifically, global-statistics-based method are invariant to the aforementioned variation, while local statistics methods are not.

In the context of segmentation-based method, many works have been proposed in literature for palm vein recognition. Han and Lee [22] have applied texture-based feature extraction techniques based on Gabor filters to palm vein, with the obtained representation encoded in a bit-string representation, later employed in a comparator employing an Hamming distance as classifier. In [23] Zhang et al. have employed multi-scale matched filters to extract features and comparison scores are obtained through the hamming distance. Also Chen et al. [24] have exploited multi-scale matched filters for palm vein feature extraction, with comparison scores generated using the iterative closest point (ICP) algorithm. Some works about subspace learning applied to palm-vein-based biometric recognition have been proposed in the last decade. Wang et al. [11] used a Laplacian palm representation on fused palm vein and palm print images, exploiting locality-preserving projection (LPP) subspace, then using a k-NN classifier for comparison purposes. Zhou and Kumar [20] have designed an approach based on the Hessian phase that extracts the structure of the vessels by analyzing the second-order derivatives of the normalized palm vein images, and proposed a comparison approach based on the Hamming distance. Among local-invariant-based methods proposed for palm vein recognition, Ladoux et al. [25] have used SIFT descriptors as users' discriminative features, and Euclidian distance as employed similarity measure. A variant of the SIFT method, namely RootSIFT, has been proposed by Kang et al. in [26], with a hierarchical mismatching removal algorithm based on neighborhood searching and local binary pattern (LBP) histograms adopted to improve the accuracy of feature comparison. Statistical-based methods have been deeply exploited in the field of palm-vein-based biometric systems. Mirmohamad-sadeghi et al. [2] have used LBPs and local derivative patterns (LDP) operators to extract features and histogram intersection to obtain the comparison scores. Kang et al. [27] have proposed an approach based on mutual foreground LBP for palm vein identification, that is, the gradient-based maximal principal curvature (MPC) algorithm, with a k-means method utilized for texture extraction, and an LBP comparison strategy adopted for similarity measurements between the mutual foreground of grayscale images.

3   Employed Palm Vein Recognition System

The systems here considered for palm-vein-based biometric recognition is detailed in this section. Specifically, the setup employed for image acquisition during the carried out experimental tests is outlined in Sect. 3.1. The preprocessing performed on the available images is introduced in Sect. 3.2, while the features considered for comparison are presented in Sect. 3.3. The biometric fusion approaches investigated for improving the performance achievable with the considered representations are eventually presented in Sect. 3.4.

3.1   Data Acquisition

The employed palm vein database has been acquired using a device consisting of a NIR camera (Visiosens VFU-V024-M-H-C camera) and an illumination system consisting of an array of NIR leds (wavelength = 850 nm). The resolution of the camera sensor is 752×480 pixels with 8 bit gray-scale per pixel. The sensitive range of the employed CCD camera is between 450 and 900 nm, and an optical infrared filter is mounted in front of the cameras lens with the aim of eliminating the effects of visible light.

The device employed for the acquisition includes a docking device for hand placement and ROI extraction to reduce both misalignment and registration problems. In detail, pegs for a correct hand placement, and a window of the desired ROI size are included in the acquisition device.

3.2   Preprocessing

A square area of 240×240 pixels containing the palm vein pattern is extracted from the acquired images and taken into account as ROI. This latter is then preprocessed through a non-linear image enhancement technique in order to tackle the problem of uneven illumination and non-uniform background. In detail, 20×20 pixels overlapping blocks are extracted from the ROI, considering four pixels of overlap between consecutive blocks. The average gray level of each block is then computed. The background illumination is estimated by extending the obtained mean values through a bicubic interpolation. Finally, the obtained background illumination is subtracted from the considered ROI image, and the enhanced vein pattern is then obtained.

3.3   Feature Extraction

In our work, feature extraction methods based on local statistics are taken into account. In detail, LBPs and LDPs are employed to extract representative characteristics from the palm vein network.

Local Binary Pattern. The LBP operator is a texture descriptor relying on differences between gray levels of pixels [2,3]. Let us denote the target image as I and indicate with Z_0 the central pixel of a $R \times R$ neighborhood of P pixels extracted from I, as shown in Fig. 1(a). When the LBP operator is applied, the aforementioned neighborhood is thresholded by the value of Z_0, and the obtained

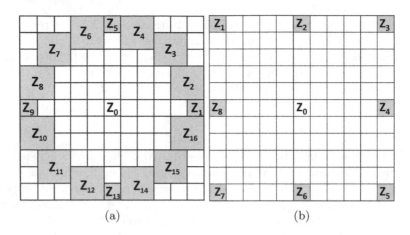

Fig. 1. (a) LBP neighborhood. (b) LDP neighborhood.

results is considered as a binary number or its decimal equivalent. Specifically the LBP code for each center pixel is obtained as:

$$LBP_{P,R}(Z_0) = \sum_{p=1}^{P} t(Z_p, Z_0) 2^{p-1} \qquad (1)$$

where Z_p is the p-th neighbor of Z_0, as shown in Fig. 1(a). In case of neighbors consisting of more than one pixel, the selected pixels are weighted average, with weights depending on the distance between Z_p and Z_0, and the obtained value is taken into account in the LBP code computation stage. The function $t(Z_p, Z_0)$ is called *thresholding function* and it is defined as:

$$t(Z_p, Z_0) = \begin{cases} 0, & \text{if } I(Z_p) - I(Z_0) < 0 \\ 1, & \text{if } I(Z_p) - I(Z_0) \geq 0, \end{cases} \qquad (2)$$

LBP codes, that is, binary numbers or its decimal equivalents, are saved by incrementing the corresponding histogram bin. Each obtained decimal number can be seen as a micro-pattern, and the bin of the histogram represents one type of pattern.

Local Derivative Pattern. The LDP operator is a high-order texture descriptor and it extracts information about the direction variations in derivatives, that is, a second-order information [2,4]. Different directions are taken into account when the derivatives are computed, namely $0°$, $45°$, $90°$ and $135°$, and the subtraction between neighboring pixels according to each direction is performed to compute derivatives. In detail, given a $R \times R$ neighborhood of the central pixel Z_0 of an image I, the first-order derivative in the four mentioned directions is computed as:

$$I'_{0°}(Z_0) = I(Z_0) - I(Z_4)$$
$$I'_{45°}(Z_0) = I(Z_0) - I(Z_3)$$
$$I'_{90?0}(Z_0) = I(Z_0) - I(Z_2)$$
$$I'_{135°}(Z_0) = I(Z_0) - I(Z_1)$$

$$(3)$$

where $Z_1, ...Z_4$ are the neighbors around the central pixel in the four considered directions, as shown in Fig. 1(b). Considering a direction α and a given central pixel Z_0, the LDP code for the neighborhood of Z_0 is obtained by concatenating the values computed taking into account each neighbor, that is:

$$LDP^2_\alpha(Z_0) = \{t(I'_\alpha(Z_0), I'_\alpha(Z_1)), t(I'_\alpha(Z_0), I'_\alpha(Z_2)), ..., t(I'_\alpha(Z_0), I'_\alpha(Z_8)),\} \quad (4)$$

with $t(I'_\alpha(Z_0), I'_\alpha(Z_j))$ being a binary coding defined as:

$$t(I'_\alpha(Z_0), I'_\alpha(Z_j)) = \begin{cases} 0, & \text{if } I'_\alpha(Z_0) \cdot I'_\alpha(Z_j) > 0 \\ 1, & \text{if } I'_\alpha(Z_0) \cdot I'_\alpha(Z_j) \leq 0, \end{cases} \quad (5)$$

and $j = 1, 2, ..., 8$ are the indices of considered neighbors. The decimal values derived from the conversion of the obtained codes are stored in histograms whose bins represent the occurrence of a given micro-pattern:

$$LDP_{R,\alpha} = \sum_{j=1}^{8} t(I'_\alpha(Z_0), I'_\alpha(Z_j)) 2^{8-j} \quad (6)$$

The LDP codes can be also computed considering $(n-1)^{th}$ order derivatives in the four direction, $n > 2$, thus obtaining the nth order LDP codes.

3.4 Biometric Fusion Approaches

Several limitations affect biometric systems which operate using any single biometric trait [1]. First, noise could be present in the acquired data, due to sensor's defects or unfavorable ambient conditions, leading to incorrect match between templates. Besides, biometric data could be characterized by a very high intra-class variation, that is, the enrolment and recognition templates are very different, resulting in problems during the comparison stage. Finally, the system can show intra-class similarities in the features set used to represent the users, restricting the discrimination capability of the biometric characteristic.

Some of the aforementioned limitations of the unimodal biometric systems can be overcome by exploiting *multimodal* biometric systems, that is a biometric system which integrate multiple information [5]. There are different modalities of fusion of the information that can be exploited by a multimodal biometric system. Specifically, the information fusion in a biometric system can be classified into several categories, that is:

- **sensor-level fusion:** data belonging to the same biometric trait are acquired from multiple sensors and then combined;

- **feature-level fusion:** a combination of different feature vectors is performed. The different features can be obtained by either data acquired from multiple sensors or by applying multiple feature extraction algorithms on the same biometric data;
- **score-level fusion:** a similarity score indicating the closeness between two compared features is provided by each biometric comparator. These comparison scores can be combined to assert the genuineness of the claimed identity of the user;
- **decision-level fusion:** the output of multiple classifiers relying on different feature vectors are combined in order to take the final decision.

Performing one or a combination of the different fusions listed before, the biometric system is expected to be more reliable because of the presence of multiple instances of the same biometric trait, and the performance achieved by the system are generally higher compared to what reached in unimodal biometric recognition systems.

In this paper, we want to give an example of the effects of different kinds of fusion applied to a palm-vein-based biometric system. Specifically, we exploit the feature-, score- and decision-level fusion approaches, and demonstrate that better recognition performance can be achieved exploiting such methods, when compared to what can be attained with a unimodal biometric system. Detailed results are given in Sect. 4.

4   Experimental Tests

The experimental setup, comprising further details on the characteristics of the employed palm vein image database, is described in Sect. 4.1. The performed tests are then outlined, together with the obtained results, in Sect. 4.2.

4.1   Experimental Setup

The database employed in our tests is collected thought a NIR camera and NIR illuminator, as detailed in Sect. 3.1. Palm vein images are collected from the right hand of 86 users and each palm is acquired 12 times, leading to a dataset having size of 86 users × 12 acquisitions = 1032 palm vein images. The users' palm is docked from the acquisition device in order to facilitate the ROI extraction. The ROI consists of an area of 240 × 240, and the vein width is about 2–8 pixels in the captured images. The ROI images are enhanced according to the procedure described in Sect. 3.2.

Representative features are computed from the enhanced images considering both LBP and LDP methods. In detail, when the LBP feature extraction method is taken into account, the considered image is divided in 16 non-overlapping sub-images of size 60 × 60 pixels and the LBP operator is applied on each sub-image.

LBP features are computed from sub-blocks of size $R = 8$ and $P = 16$ neighbors are considered; $(2R+1) \times (2R+1)$ overlapping sub-blocks are taken into account and histograms consisting of $P(P-1) = 240$ bins are obtained from each sub-block. The final descriptor of the image is the result of the concatenation of the histograms derived from each sub-block. When the LDP operator is applied, we consider the second-order derivatives computed on sub-blocks with radius of 5 pixels. The original image is divided in 16 non-overlapping sub-images of size 60×60 and for each one the derivatives in the four directions are computed for all the pixels. The histogram resulting from the application of the LDP operator to each block and for each direction are concatenated obtaining a histogram consisting of $2^8 \cdot$ *number of directions* $\cdot$ *number of blocks* $= 16384$ bins.

Being the employed templates histograms, the histogram intersection measure [21] is exploited to compute the comparison scores. Specifically, let us denote the two histograms to compare as h and g, the similarity measure can be defined as:

$$H(h, g) = \frac{\sum_j \min(h_j, g_j)}{\sum_j g_j} \tag{7}$$

4.2 Experimental Results

As a first step, the performance achievable when LBP and LDP feature extraction methods are applied, that is, when an unimodal biometric system is taken into account, are computed. Different kinds of fusion are then performed, namely feature-, score- and decision-level as explained in Sect. 3.4. When the feature-level fusion approach is applied, features extracted from the same image but exploiting both LBP and LDP feature extraction methods are concatenated and fused into a single feature. In case of score-level fusion approach, the scores derived from the comparison of the couples of templates extracted from the same image, but by exploiting the two considered feature extraction methods, are combined through the *max-rule* method, that is, the fusion rule that has shown the best performance in the performed experimental tests. Finally, a decision level-fusion approach is also carried out. In detail, the effects of the application of different decision rules are investigated, and the OR rule has shown to be the best option in our case.

The results obtained are shown in the detection error trade-off (DET) curve presented in Fig. 2. When LBP codes are considered as features an equal error rate (EER) of 3.81% is reached, while a EER = 3.17% is achieved when the LDP feature extraction method is used to extract discriminative characteristics from palm vein images. When the feature-level fusion approach is performed, the EER of the system decreases to 3.09%, while an EER of 2.96% is reached when the score-level fusion method is applied. Eventually, an EER of 3.07% can be achieved when the decision-level fusion approach is chosen.

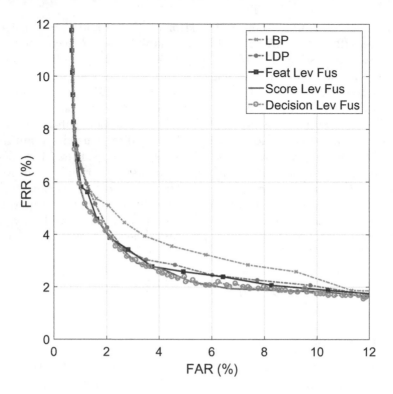

Fig. 2. DET curves obtained considering LBP and LDP feature extraction methods and the different adopted fusion techniques

5   Conclusions

In this paper we have investigated the performance improvements achievable when exploiting multi-biometrics fusion techniques in a palm-vein-based recognition system leveraging on statistics-based feature extraction methods such as LBP and LDP. The obtained results show that a noticeable reduction of the achievable EER can be actually guaranteed with multimodal approaches, with respect to unimodal ones. In the considered framework, score-level fusion approach has been highlighted as the best option to be followed when designing palm vein recognition systems based on more than a single template representation.

References

1. Jain, A.K., Ross, A., Prabhakar, S.: An introduction to biometric recognition. IEEE Trans. Circuits Syst. Video Technol. **14**(1), 4–20 (2004)
2. Mirmohamadsadeghi, L., Drygajlo, A.: Palm vein recognition with local binary patterns and local derivative patterns. In: 2011 International Joint Conference on Biometrics (IJCB), pp. 1–6. IEEE (2011)

3. Ojala, T., Pietikainen, M., Harwood, D.: Performance evaluation of texture measures with classification based on kullback discrimination of distributions. Pattern Recogn. **1**, 582–585 (1994)
4. Zhang, B., Gao, Y., Zhao, S., Liu, J.: Local derivative pattern versus local binary pattern: face recognition with high-order local pattern descriptor. IEEE Trans. Image Process. **19**(2), 533–544 (2010)
5. Hong, L., Jain, A.K., Pankanti, S.: Can multibiometrics improve performance? In: Proceedings AutoID, vol. 99, pp. 59–64, Citeseer (1999)
6. Djerouni, A., Hamada, H., Loukil, A., Berrached, N.: Dorsal hand vein image contrast enhancement techniques. Int. J. Comput. Sci. **11**(1), 137 142 (2014)
7. Yang, J., Shi, Y.: Towards finger-vein image restoration and enhancement for finger-vein recognition. Inf. Sci. **268**, 33–52 (2014)
8. Chen, L., Wang, J., Yang, S., He, H.: A finger vein image-based personal identification system with self-adaptive illuminance control. IEEE Trans. Instrum. Meas. **66**(2), 294–304 (2017)
9. Lee, Y.H., Khalil-Hani, M., Bakhteri, R.: FPGA-based finger vein biometric system with adaptive illumination for better image acquisition. In: 2012 IEEE Symposium on Computer Applications and Industrial Electronics (ISCAIE), pp. 107–112. IEEE (2012)
10. Wang, K., Zhang, Y., Yuan, Z., Zhuang, D.: Hand vein recognition based on multi supplemental features of multi-classifier fusion decision. In: Proceedings of the 2006 IEEE International Conference on Mechatronics and Automation, pp. 1790–1795. IEEE (2006)
11. Wang, J.G., Yau, W.Y., Suwandy, A., Sung, E.: Person recognition by fusing palmprint and palm vein images based on "Laplacianpalm" representation. Pattern Recogn. **41**(5), 1514–1527 (2008)
12. Kauba, C., Piciucco, E., Maiorana, E., Campisi, P., Uhl, A.: Advanced Variants of Feature Level Fusion for Finger Vein Recognition. In: 2016 International Conference of the Biometrics Special Interest Group (BIOSIG), pp. 1–7. IEEE (2016)
13. Veluchamy, S., Karlmarx, L.R.: A system for multimodal biometric recognition based on finger knuckle and finger vein using feature level fusion and k-SVM classifier. IET Biometrics (2016)
14. Miura, N., Nagasaka, A., Miyatake, T.: Feature extraction of finger-vein patterns based on repeated line tracking and its application to personal identification. Mach. Vis. Appl. **15**(4), 194–203 (2004)
15. Song, W., Kim, T., Kim, H.C., Choi, J.H., Kong, H.J., Lee, S.R.: A finger-vein verification system using mean curvature. Pattern Recogn. Lett. **32**(11), 1541–1547 (2011)
16. Kumar, A., Prathyusha, K.V.: Personal authentication using hand vein triangulation and knuckle shape. IEEE Trans. Image Process. **18**(9), 2127–2136 (2009)
17. Wang, L., Leedham, G., Cho, D.S.Y.: Minutiae feature analysis for infrared hand vein pattern biometrics. Pattern Recogn. **41**(3), 920–929 (2008)
18. Pascual, J.E.S., Uriarte-Antonio, J., Sanchez-Reillo, R., Lorenz, M.G.: Capturing hand or wrist vein images for biometric authentication using low-cost devices. In: 2010 Sixth International Conference on Intelligent Information Hiding and Multimedia Signal Processing (IIH-MSP), pp. 318–322. IEEE (2010)
19. Hartung, D., Olsen, M.A., Xu, H., Busch, C.: Spectral minutiae for vein pattern recognition. In: 2011 International Joint Conference on IEEE Biometrics (IJCB), pp. 1–7 (2011)
20. Zhou, Y., Kumar, A.: Human identification using palm-vein images. IEEE Trans. Inf. Forensics Secur. **6**(4), 1259–1274 (2011)

21. Swain, M.J., Ballard, D.H.: Color indexing. Int. J. Comput. Vis. **7**(11), 11–32 (1991)
22. Han, W.Y., Lee, J.C.: Palm vein recognition using adaptive gabor filter. Expert Syst. Appl. **39**(18), 13225–13234 (2012)
23. Zhang, Y.-B., Li, Q., You, J., Bhattacharya, P.: Palm vein extraction and matching for personal authentication. In: Qiu, G., Leung, C., Xue, X., Laurini, R. (eds.) VISUAL 2007. LNCS, vol. 4781, pp. 154–164. Springer, Heidelberg (2007). doi:10.1007/978-3-540-76414-4_16
24. Chen, H., Lu, G., Wang, R.: A new palm vein matching method based on ICP algorithm. In: Proceedings of the 2nd International Conference on Interaction Sciences: Information Technology, Culture and Human, pp. 1207–1211. ACM (2009)
25. Ladoux, P.O., Rosenberger, C., Dorizzi, B.: Palm vein verification system based on SIFT matching. In: Proceedings of the 2009 International Conference on Biometrics (ICB). Advances in Biometrics, pp. 1290–1298 (2009)
26. Kang, W., Liu, Y., Wu, Q., Yue, X.: Contact-free palm-vein recognition based on local invariant features. PLoS ONE **9**(5), e97548 (2014)
27. Kang, W., Wu, Q.: Contactless palm vein recognition using a mutual foreground-based local binary pattern. IEEE Trans. Inf. Forensics Secur. **9**(11), 1974–1985 (2014)

Emerging Services with NFV

Availability Modeling and Evaluation of a Network Service Deployed via NFV

Mario Di Mauro[1]([✉]), Maurizio Longo[1], Fabio Postiglione[1], and Marco Tambasco[2]

[1] Department of Information and Electrical Engineering
and Applied Mathematics (DIEM), University of Salerno, Fisciano, SA, Italy
{mdimauro,longo,fpostiglione}@unisa.it
[2] Research Consortium on Telecommunications (CoRiTeL),
Fisciano, SA, Italy
marco.tambasco@coritel.it

Abstract. The Network Function Virtualization (NFV) has been conceived as an enabler of novel network infrastructures and services that can be deployed by combining virtualized network elements. In particular, NFV is suited to boost the deployment flexibility of Service Function Chains (SFCs). In this paper, we address an availability evaluation of a chain of network nodes implementing a SFC managed by the Virtualized Infrastructure Manager (VIM), responsible for handling and controlling the system resources. A double-layer model is adopted, where Reliability Block Diagram describes the high-level dependencies among the architecture components, and Stochastic Reward Networks model the probabilistic behavior of each component. In particular, a steady-state availability analysis is carried out to characterize the minimal configuration of the overall system guaranteeing the so-called "five nines" requirement, along with a sensitivity analysis to evaluate the system robustness with respect to variations of some key parameters.

Keywords: Network function virtualization · Service function chaining · Stochastic reward nets · Reliability block diagram · Availability analysis

1 Introduction

The increasing demand for a dynamic and elastic deployment of network and telecommunication services is becoming a critical issue for the operators. As enabler of fifth generation (5G) networks, the Network Function Virtualization (NFV) [1] has been conceived to boost the deployment of new services by adapting the classical virtualization concepts to the network environments. Therefore, classical network elements (e.g. routers, firewalls, load balancers) are deployed in a cloud computing infrastructure by means of virtual machines running on general purpose hardware. The resulting architecture consists in a set of Virtualized Network Functions (VNFs), realizing novel services. A composition of VNFs is often referred to as Service Function Chain (SFC), and is typically governed [2]

© Springer International Publishing AG 2017
A. Piva et al. (Eds.): TIWDC 2017, CCIS 766, pp. 31–44, 2017.
DOI: 10.1007/978-3-319-67639-5_4

by the Virtualized Infrastructure Manager (VIM), namely, the key element of
the whole NFV architecture. The result is a system, referred in this work to as
Network Service (NS), composed by the VIM that plays a role of the manager
furnishing vital services for VNFs (deployment, fault control, network and storage resources tuning etc.), and by the SFC that provides the service itself by
means of its VNFs. This kind of deployment raises a critical availability issue,
since the fault of an individual block could compromise the whole functionality.
Thus, the purpose of this work is to characterize the NS availability aimed at finding the minimal configuration respecting the so-called "five nines" availability
requirement (no more than 5 min and 26 s system downtime per year) as invoked
in typical deployments, including cloud-based ones [3]. The availability analysis is performed by considering a hierarchical model that relies on two different
formalisms: *(i)* the Reliability Block Diagrams (RBDs), a combinatorial model
used to characterize the high level dependencies among the elements, and *(ii)*
the Stochastic Reward Networks (SRNs), a state-space model exploited to typify
the probabilistic behavior of the underlying system structure. The rest part of
the paper is organized as follows. Section 2 introduces the theme by referring
to some ongoing research. Section 3 offers a more detailed view about the NFV
reference architecture. An availability model of the whole system along with the
adopted formalisms is outlined in Sect. 4. Section 5 presents some experimental
results whereas, conclusions and considerations about future works are drawn in
the Sect. 6.

2   Related Research

The interest of scientific and technical communities in the reliability and availability issues related to the novel network architectures is growing recently. The
European Telecommunications Standard Institute (ETSI) has provided some
guidelines about the application of reliability concepts to new generation networks, and among which NFV-based ones [4]. Some research has been devoted
to characterize the high availability of OpenStack platform, a cloud computing
architecture implementing the Infrastructure-as-a-Service (IaaS) paradigm. In
[5], a reliable restoration method of virtual resources is provided by exploiting
Pacemaker, an OpenStack component able to detect physical server failures, and
Libvirt, a set of software libraries in charge of managing virtual resources. An
availability model of a IaaS based on a Continuous-Time Markov Chain (CTMC),
has proposed in [6]. A similar CTMC-based approach has been used to evaluate
the dependability of a virtualized server system in [7], and a cloud-based architecture in [8]. However some serious issues arise when Markov chains models are
applied to complex systems, as the state space rapidly reaches intractable sizes.
In order to counter this problem, we propose a model relying on the Stochastic
Reward Nets, which admits more compact representations of large models, by
identifying repetitive structures or model regularities. Inspired by some preliminary works concerning reliability and availability analyses of novel architectures
[9–11], in this work the authors offer, as an original contribution, an SRN-based

availability model of a Network Service in an NFV environment, that can help to select the best Network Service configuration that fulfills the "five nines" condition with a minimum number of deployed components.

3 Service Chaining Model in the NFV Deployment

Classical deployment of network services is typically tightly coupled to the underlying physical topology, resulting in a lack of flexibility to re-arrange the existent components and obtain new functions. On the other hand, NFV allows the creation of an SFC by a chain of VNFs traversed in a predefined order, that in the NFV context, can be interpreted as a VNF Forwarding Graph (VNF-FG). A VNF can be regarded as independent (often geographically separated from other VNFs) element composed by the following three modules:

- *software*: a module implementing a service functionality;
- *hardware*: a module aggregating all physical components (CPU, RAM, Power Supply etc.);
- *hypervisor* (often referred to as Virtual Machine Monitor - VMM): a software layer acting as an interface between hardware and software modules.

On the other hand, the Virtualized Infrastructure Manager is a part of the MANO (MANagement and Orchestration domain) [1] that performs some critical operations as managing a set of resources (storage, networking etc.) to be deployed on demand, mapping the virtual resources on the physical ones and managing the chain of VNFs. In accordance to a common implementation based on OpenStack, we consider the VIM (in a virtualized implementation) as composed by five modules: hardware, hypervisor (similar to those in SFC), and other three elements:

- *database*: devoted to store the critical data of the whole system (inventory of hardware resources, register of available VNFs and others);
- *HAproxy*: the High Availability proxy acts as a load balancer distributing the load among the redundant VIM nodes;
- *functional blocks*: a collection of sub-elements accomplishing several functionalities, such as nova-keystone (providing authorization and authentication mechanisms), nova-scheduler (dispatcher of computational requests), rabbitmq (allowing the communication among internal components).

4 Availability Model of a Network Service

The RBD [12] of a Network Service is reported in Fig. 1, where it has been emphasized that an SFC is a chain of VNF nodes. Being a series configuration, the NS is available (working) when each subsystem (VIM, VNF_1,..., VNF_k) is available (working). On the other hand, the high availability requirements obtained by redundant parallel elements, will be addressed by SRN [13,14], whose main features are presented in the following subsection.

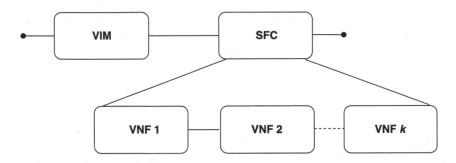

Fig. 1. RBD representation of the Network Service obtained by aggregating VIM and SFC. The latter is in turn composed by a sequence of VNFs.

4.1 SRN Formalism

An SRN model is based on a Stochastic Petri Net and is represented by a bipartite directed graph, where a *place* (drawn as a circle) accounts for a specific condition (e.g. a system element up or down) and can contain one or more *tokens*, namely a parameter value associated to a condition. The distribution of tokens (at a time t) is referred to as *marking*, and can be described by a vector $\mathbf{m} = (m_1, m_2, \ldots, m_k)$ where m_h is the number of tokens in the place h. A *transition* (drawn as a rectangle) accounts for a specific event (e.g. a system element that crashes), and lets a token to be transferred from a place to another one, resulting in a marking alteration. In particular, we discriminate between: *timed transitions* (drawn as unfilled rectangles), associated to the events whose times are assumed to be exponentially distributed random variables with a given rate parameter (*firing rate*), and *immediate transitions* (drawn as thin and filled rectangles), whose transition time is equal to zero. When the firing rate of timed transitions depends on tokens distribution in the SRN graph, we use the symbol (#) nearby the correspondent transition and we refer to as *marking dependent transitions*. A transition can be optionally controlled by a *guard function* (indicated by g) that assumes value 1 when transition has to be enabled. Besides, a transition can be inhibited by an *inhibitory arc* (depicted as a line with a blank unfilled circle nearby the correspondent transition). An SRN model is able to capture the dynamics of the system by analyzing the distribution of tokens as time elapses. In an SRN model, the *reward rate* is a non-negative random variable associated with certain conditions of the system, and its value is related to the particular measure (performance, dependability, availability etc.) we are interested to characterize [15]. For example, let $X(t)$ be the availability reward rate where $X(t) \in \{0, 1\}$ and $X(t) = 1$ when the system is working. The instantaneous availability $A(t)=P\{X(t) = 1\}$ of a system modeled by an SRN, can be computed by the expectation of $X(t)$ [13], viz.

$$A(t) = E(X(t)) = \sum_{i \in S} r_i p_i(t), \tag{1}$$

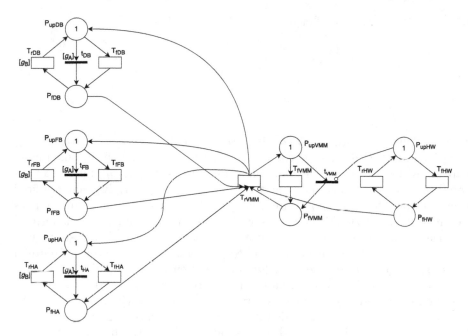

Fig. 2. SRN model of the VIM node. Such model follows the classical OpenStack deployment.

where S represents the set of possible markings, $r_i \in \{0, 1\}$ is the reward value associated to state i, i.e. $r_i = 1$ if system is working, and $p_i(t)$ the probability of system to be in state i.

For the sake of clarity, we analyze separately the SRN models of VIM node and SFC, respectively, and, finally, we combine the results by means of the RBD model in order to characterize the whole NS.

4.2 SRN Model of VIM

The SRN model associated to the VIM node is reported in Fig. 2. We want to remark that the VIM subsystem is composed by N redundant VIM nodes. Places P_{upDB} [resp. P_{fDB}], P_{upFB} [P_{fFB}], P_{upHA} [P_{fHA}], P_{upVMM} [P_{fVMM}] and P_{upHW} [P_{fHW}] indicate the conditions where the database, the functional blocks, the HAproxy, the hypervisor and the hardware of the VIM are up [down], respectively. The numbers in the places (tokens) represent the corresponding initial conditions. The transitions T_{fDB} [T_{rDB}], T_{fFB} [T_{rFB}], T_{fHA} [T_{rHA}], T_{fVMM} [T_{rVMM}] and T_{fHW} [T_{rHW}] model the time to failure [repair] of database, functional blocks, HAproxy, hypervisor and hardware, respectively. Let us now briefly discuss the dynamics of such SRN. We start by considering a fully working system (namely all the elements are up and running). As an exemplary case, we focus on the sub-model of the HAproxy (similar considerations hold for database, functional blocks, hypervisor and hardware modules). When

Table 1. Guard functions defined on the SRN model of VIM

Guard function	Value
g_A	1 if # $P_{fVMM} = 1$, 0 otherwise
g_B	1 if # $P_{upVMM} = 1$, 0 otherwise

HAproxy fails, the transition T_{fHA} is *fired* and the token removed from P_{upHA} is deposited into P_{fHA}. In the considered model we also introduce some immediate transitions to cope with common cause failures: t_{DB}, t_{FB} and t_{HA} (associated to database, functional blocks and HAproxy, respectively) that are fired when the transition T_{fVMM} is fired, meaning that a hypervisor failure implies the three virtual modules failure as well. Similarly, the immediate transition t_{VMM} accounts for a hypervisor failure as a consequence of a hardware failure. The *inhibitory arc* between P_{upHW} and t_{VMM} compels the hypervisor failure in case of hardware failure. The *inhibitory arc* between P_{fHW} and T_{rVMM} forbids the hypervisor repair in case of hardware failure. Besides, in order to formally describe the dependencies among hypervisor and the three virtual modules (the case of hardware failure is included in the case of hypervisor failure) we introduce two guard functions g_A and g_B described in Table 1. The guard function g_A enables t_{DB}, t_{FB} and t_{HA} when hypervisor fails, namely, when a token is moved from P_{upVMM} to P_{fVMM}. The guard function g_B, instead, inhibits the repair of the three virtual modules in case of hypervisor failure.

4.3   SRN Model of a Single VNF

In this model, we adopt the realistic assumption that the number of deployed VNFs can vary dynamically with the time, in accordance to a pay-per-use cloud model. In an exemplary scenario, we consider L replicas sharing a (time-varying) load, and M (extra) replicas needed to satisfy a certain availability requirement. Thus, when the load increases or decreases (as per day/night variations), the number of replicas L changes, resulting in a possible variation of the number of M replicas in order to preserve the desired availability.

Figure 3 shows the model of a single VNF. The place P_{upVNF} indicates the VNF working condition, implying that the hardware, software and virtual resources are correctly working. The token value inside P_{upVNF} amounts to $L + M$, namely, the number of initial working VNFs replicas. Let us analyze directly the evolution of such model. First of all we take into account the Scale-Out (S-O) and Scale-In (S-I) operations corresponding to a provisioning phase (deploying replicas) and a de-provisioning phase (un-deploying replicas) respectively. Thus, when an S-O operation is requested, t_{so} is fired and a token is deposited in place P_p, modeling the condition of a replica requested but not working yet, until the token enters P_{upVNF} after T_p is fired. It is worth noting that the *inhibitory arc* from P_p to t_{so} models the impairment of multiple provisioning stages. On the contrary, when an S-I operation is requested, t_{si} is fired

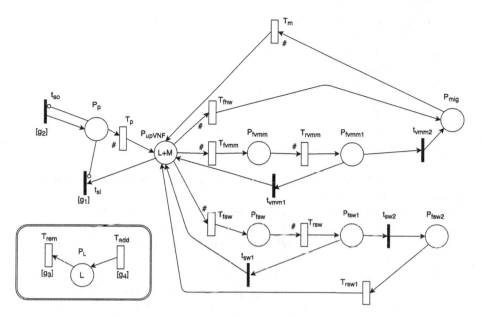

Fig. 3. SRN model of a single Virtualized Network Function.

and the *inhibitory arc* from P_p to t_{so} preventing S-I operations during provisioning stages. In case of an hardware failure, T_{fhw} is fired and a token passes from P_{upVNF} to P_{mig}, being the latter a place ruling a migration process (resources are transferred into another hardware platform with no state loss). Once T_m is fired, the migration is completed and the token can come back into P_{upVNF}. In case of a hypervisor failure, T_{fvmm} is fired and a token enters P_{fvmm}. The repair procedure is governed by T_{rvmm} that, when fired, lets the token move into P_{fvmm1}. In this place, two alternatives are admissible: *(i)* the VMM repair procedure is successful (e.g. a simple *reboot* solves the problem) with a certain probability p_{vmm}, resulting in firing transition t_{vmm1} and the returning in the working place P_{upVNF}; *(ii)* the vmm repair procedure is unsuccessful with probability $(1 - p_{vmm})$, the transition t_{vmm2} is fired, the token reaches place P_{mig}, and the migration process described previously is activated. In case of software failure, T_{fsw} is fired and the token is deposited in P_{fsw}; the repair process is ruled by T_{rsw} and the token passes into P_{fsw1}. Similar to the previous case, two options are allowed: *(i)* the software repair procedure is successful with a certain probability p_{sw}, thus t_{sw1} is fired and initial condition is gained; *(ii)* the repair procedure is vain with probability $(1 - p_{sw})$, hence t_{sw2} is fired and place P_{fsw2} (indicating a tough fault condition needing a repairman) is entered; once repair process is terminated, T_{rsw1} is fired and place P_{upVNF} is reached.

Finally, place P_L (see the boxed sub-model) takes into account the condition of L replicas that can be added (T_{add}) or removed (T_{rem}). We note that transitions T_p, T_{fhw}, T_{fvmm}, T_{fsw}, T_{rsw}, T_{rvmm} and T_m, depend only on the

Table 2. Guard functions defined on the SRN model of single VNF

Guard function	Value
g_1	1 if $N_{tot} > L +$ M, 0 otherwise
g_2	1 if $N_{tot} < L +$ M, 0 otherwise
g_3	1 if $L < L_{max}$, 0 otherwise
g_4	1 if $L > L_{min}$, 0 otherwise

number of tokens in their originating places, and their overall firing rates are proportional to those numbers.

The guard functions present in this model are defined as follows. Said $\#P_k$ the number of tokens in the place k[1], we define N_{tot} the number of VNFs replicas in the SRN at time t as: $N_{tot} = \#P_p + \#P_{upVNF} + \#P_{fvmm} + \#P_{fsw} + \#P_{fsw2} + \#P_{mig}$, where we omit the time dependence[2]. Guard g_1 inhibits S-I operations when N_{tot} undergoes the sum $L + M$. Similarly, g_2 inhibits S-O operations when N_{tot} exceeds the sum $L + M$. Guard g_3 prevents that L exceeds the maximum number of admissible replicas (L_{max}) and g_4 prevents that L could be lower than the minimum number of admissible replicas (L_{min}), as summarized in Table 2.

4.4   Availability Analysis and Model Combination

We now consider an NS, given by the combination of N VIM replicas and the $L + M$ replicas of the three VNFs arranged in a chain. As regards the VIM, let r_i be the reward value assigned to marking i and $p_i(t)$ the probability for SRN in Fig. 2 to be in marking i at time t; according (1) it is possible to express the instantaneous availability $A_{VIM}(t)$ as:

$$A_{VIM}(t) = \sum_{i \in I} r_i p_i(t), \tag{2}$$

where I is the set of *tangible markings* (markings where no immediate transitions are enabled). The instantaneous availability $A_{VIM}(t)$ in fact, is the probability that the VIM is available at time t and, being the markings mutually exclusive, can be expressed as the sum of the probabilities of all markings that at time t result in a working condition for the VIM subsystem.

The reward value r_i assumes value 1 for the markings identifying the VIM working conditions, namely all the operating conditions where at least two Database instances (as typical in many active-active configurations), one Functional Block and one HAproxy are active. For all the remaining states, r_i is set to 0.

---

[1] In Petri Net jargon, there is a little abuse of ($\#$) symbol that indicates either number of tokens, and marking-dependent transitions.

[2] Places P_{fvmm1} and P_{sw1} do not contribute to N_{tot} because the time spent in such places is zero.

Thus, the reward value can be written as:

$$
r_i =
\begin{cases}
1 & \text{if } \left(\sum_{k=1}^{N} \#P_{upDB}(k) \geq 2\right) \wedge \\
& \left(\sum_{k=1}^{N} \#P_{upFB}(k) \geq 1\right) \wedge \\
& \left(\sum_{k=1}^{N} \#P_{upHA}(k) \geq 1\right) \\
\\
0 & \text{otherwise,}
\end{cases}
$$

where k goes from 1 to the number of replicas N, and $\#P_{upDB}(k)$, $\#P_{upFB}(k)$ and $\#P_{upHA}(k)$, indicate the number of tokens in the "up" places of virtual modules, for the $k-th$ parallel element. The hardware and hypervisor "up" conditions do not appear, being included in expression when at least 1 virtual module is active. The VIM steady-state availability is given by (2) as $t \to \infty$,

$$
A_{VIM} = \lim_{t \to +\infty} A_{VIM}(t) = \sum_{i \in I} r_i p_i, \tag{3}
$$

where p_i is the steady-state probability of state i, i.e. $p_i = \lim_{t \to +\infty} p_i(t)$. A similar reasoning holds for the case of VNF. Let s_j be the reward value assigned to marking j and $q_j(t)$ the probability for SRN in Fig. 3 to be in marking j at time t. The expected reward value at time t for the VNF model corresponds to:

$$
A_{VNF}(t) = \sum_{j \in J} s_j q_j(t), \tag{4}
$$

where J identifies the set of *tangible markings* of the VNF model. In this case, the reward value s_j associated to the tangible marking j follows:

$$
s_j =
\begin{cases}
1 & \text{if } (\#P_{upVNF} \geq \#P_L) \\
\\
0 & \text{otherwise.}
\end{cases}
$$

The VNF working condition ($s_j = 1$) occurs when the number of total replicas (represented by the tokens in P_{upVNF}) is no less than the number of regular replicas (represented by the tokens in P_L). Thus, steady-state availability for a VNF is obtained by (4) as $t \to \infty$,

$$
A_{VNF} = \lim_{t \to +\infty} A_{VNF}(t) = \sum_{j \in J} s_j q_j, \tag{5}
$$

where q_j is the steady-state probability given by $q_j = \lim_{t \to +\infty} q_j(t)$.

Now, we are able to evaluate the steady-state availability of the whole Network Service, composed by the series of VIM and the 3 VNFs according to the RBD representation in Fig. 1.

The resulting Network Service availability A_{NS} can be expressed as the product of the availabilities associated with the VIM and SFC subsystems, namely

$$
A_{NS} = A_{VIM} \prod_{m=1}^{3} A_{VNF}^{(m)}, \tag{6}
$$

where A_{VIM} is derived by (3) and A_{VNF} is computed by (5), where m denotes the VNF m.

5   Experimental Results

An exemplary application of the proposed approach is now provided, where system parameters assume specific values suggested by the technical literature (e.g. [16]). The values of parameters associated to VIM and to VNF are reported in Tables 3 and 4, respectively. In order to respect the notation used in Figs. 2 and 3, we use uppercase subscripts for the VIM parameters and lower case subscripts for the VNF parameters. The present availability analysis has been carried out with the help of SHARPE [17], a tool that allows to analyze SRN availability models. According to elasticity concepts typical of cloud environments, we target two exemplary different operating conditions, namely c_1 and c_2 associated to a dynamically variable load managed by the system, that results in a different number of deployed replicas. We suppose that in condition c_1 (low load) VNFs share the load among two replicas ($L_{c1} = 2$), while in condition c_2 (high load) they share the load among three replicas ($L_{c2} = 3 \geq L_{c1}$).

Accordingly, we characterize the system in terms of the number of extra replicas M guaranteeing the "five nines" availability requirement, namely M_{c1} and $M_{c2} \geq M_{c1}$ in the two conditions of VNFs. We investigate also the influence of the number of VIM replicas N. We distinguish 6 settings $S_1, ..., S_6$ representing different configurations, as reported in Table 5 with their corresponding availability value A_{NS}. Figure 4 reports the main results where, for visual comfort, we show the steady-state unavailability of the Network Service $(1 - A_{NS})$ in said exemplary settings. By comparing S_1, S_2, S_3 with S_4, S_5, S_6, it is evident that an increase from $N = 3$ to $N = 4$ improves the NS availability. For $N = 3$, instead of considering greater values of N for $M_{c1} = M_{c2} = 1$ (setting S_1), it is possible to achieve the "five nines" requirement by deploying $M_{c2} = 2$ replicas (setting S_2). By incrementing M_{c1} (setting S_3), a negligible increment of NS availability is obtained. Similar considerations can be provided for the $N = 4$

Table 3. Input parameters for the SRN representing the VIM

Parameter	Description	Value [a]
$1/\lambda_{VM}$	Mean time to (DB, FB, HA) failure	3000 h
$1/\lambda_{VMM}$	Mean time to hypervisor failure	5000 h
$1/\lambda_{HW}$	Mean time to hardware failure	60000 h
$1/\mu_{VM}$	Mean time to (DB, FB, HA) repair	1 h
$1/\mu_{VMM}$	Mean time to hypervisor repair	2 h
$1/\mu_{HW}$	Mean time to hardware repair	8 h

[a] We assume the same failure/repair rate values (being deployed on similar VMs) for database, functional blocks and HAproxy.

Table 4. Input parameters for the SRN representing the VNF

Parameter	Description	Value
$1/\lambda_{hw}$	Mean time to hardware failure	60000 h
$1/\lambda_{sw}$	Mean time to software failure	3000 h
$1/\lambda_{vmm}$	Mean time to hypervisor failure	5000 h
$1/\mu_{sw}$	Mean time to easy software repair	7 min
$1/\mu_{sw1}$	Mean time to tough software repair	2 h
$1/\mu_{vmm}$	Mean time to hypervisor repair	10 min
$1/\alpha_p$	Mean time to provisioning	20 min
$1/\alpha_m$	Mean time to migration	20 min
$1/\alpha_s$	Mean time to scaling (S-I/S-O) procedures	12 h
p_{sw}	Probability of successful software repair	0.98
p_{vmm}	Probability of successful hypervisor repair	0.99

Table 5. Availability results of the whole network service

Setting	Redundancy level	A_{NS}
S_1	$L_{c1} = 2, L_{c2} = 3, M_{c1} = 1, M_{c2} = 1, N = 3$	0.99998444
S_2	$L_{c1} = 2, L_{c2} = 3, M_{c1} = 1, M_{c2} = 2, N = 3$	0.99999080
S_3	$L_{c1} = 2, L_{c2} = 3, M_{c1} = 2, M_{c2} = 2, N = 3$	0.99999084
S_4	$L_{c1} = 2, L_{c2} = 3, M_{c1} = 1, M_{c2} = 1, N = 4$	0.99998686
S_5	$L_{c1} = 2, L_{c2} = 3, M_{c1} = 1, M_{c2} = 2, N = 4$	0.99999323
S_6	$L_{c1} = 2, L_{c2} = 3, M_{c1} = 2, M_{c2} = 2, N = 4$	0.99999326

case (setting S_4, S_5, S_6). Given a "five nines" availability constraint, S_2 is the minimal cost setting in terms of deployed replicas.

5.1 Sensitivity Analysis

Generally, a sensitivity analysis concerns the robustness of the system with respect to deviations of some system parameters from their nominal values. We analyze the influence of two crucial parameters on the availability of the minimal cost setting S_2, such as:

- λ_{SW}, influencing the transition T_{fsw} of the VNF model reported in Fig. 3 governing the software failures;
- $\lambda_{VMM}(= \lambda_{vmm})$, influencing both the transition T_{fVMM} of the VIM model (Fig. 2), and the transition T_{fvmm} of the VNF model (Fig. 3) (since we assume the same hypervisor for both).

Figure 5 shows that the reciprocal of failure rate of the software part can be relaxed from 3000 h (nominal value) to 2500 h by still guaranteeing the

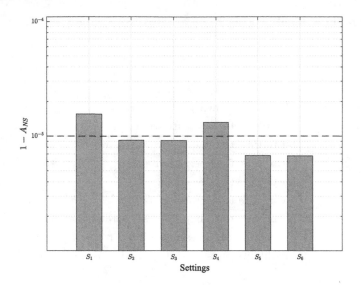

Fig. 4. Unavailability $1 - A_{NS}$ of the Network Service for 6 settings $S_1, ..., S_6$ representing various replicas arrangements. The horizontal dashed line represents the "five nines" requirement $(1 - A_{NS} = 10^{-5})$.

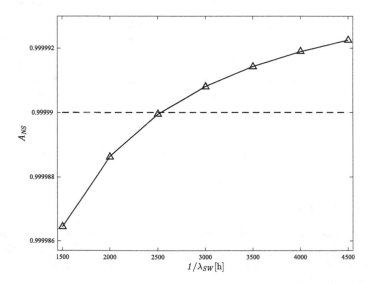

Fig. 5. Influence of the software failure rate on the overall system.

"five nines" requirement indicated with a horizontal dashed line. Similarly, Fig. 6 shows that the working value of 5000 h for $1/\lambda_{VMM}$ can be reduced to 4300 h with no side effects on the desired availability condition.

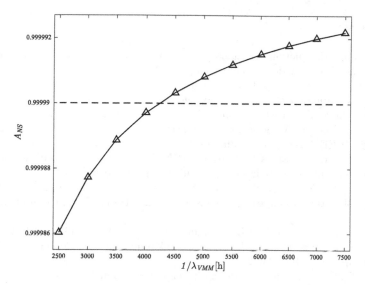

Fig. 6. Influence of the hypervisor failure rate on the overall system (same hypervisor for both VIM and VNFs).

6   Concluding Remarks

The NFV represents a cutting-edge paradigm in the telecommunication and networking industry, that allows to offer advanced communication services by deploying software-based network appliances, namely VNFs, replacing traditional physical equipments. The VNFs, and their interconnections, namely the SFC, are managed by the VIM, a critical element in charge of supervising the whole NFV environment and, at an higher level, the whole Virtualized Infrastructure. In this work we proposed an availability evaluation of a Network Service (NS), resulting from the aggregation of VIM subsystem and an SFC. Such a composition has been modeled by hierarchical approach where a Reliability Block Diagram represents the high-level interconnections between VIM and SFC, and Stochastic Reward Nets modeling each subsystem characterized by failure and repair events. A steady-state availability analysis, has been performed to evaluate different NS configurations. Besides, the robustness of the whole system with regard to variations of some critical parameters has been evaluated. The proposed availability and sensitivity analyses provide useful indications to network and telco operators about, the deployment of the number of component replicas satisfying a certain availability requirement, and perception about the influence of characteristic parameters on the overall architecture. Future works will be devoted at considering more sophisticated interconnections among components, including the virtual and physical links.

References

1. ETSI: Network functions virtualisation: an introduction, benefits, enablers, challenges and call for action. Technical report (2012)
2. Medhat, A.M., Taleb, T., Elmangoush, A., Carella, G.A., Covaci, S., Magedanz, T.: Service function chaining in next generation networks: state of the art and research challenges. IEEE Commun. Mag. **55**(2), 216–223 (2017)
3. Taleb, T., Ksentini, A., Sericola, B.: On service resilience in cloud-native 5g mobile systems. IEEE J. Sel. Areas Commun. **34**(3), 483–496 (2016)
4. ETSI: Network Functions Virtualisation (NFV) reliability; report on models and features for end-to-end reliability. Technical report (2016)
5. Yamato, Y., Nishizawa, Y., Nagao, S., Sato, K.: Fast and reliable restoration method of virtual resources on OpenStack. IEEE Trans. Cloud Comput. (in press, 2015)
6. Khazaei, H., Mii, J., Mii, V.B., Mohammadi, N.B.: Availability analysis of cloud computing centers. In: 2012 IEEE Global Communications Conference (GLOBECOM), pp. 1957–1962 (2012)
7. Zhang, X., Lin, C., Kong, X.: Model-driven dependability analysis of virtualization systems. In: 2009 Eighth IEEE/ACIS International Conference on Computer and Information Science, pp. 199–204 (2009)
8. Dantas, J., Matos, R., Araujo, J., Maciel, P.: An availability model for eucalyptus platform: an analysis of warm-standy replication mechanism. In: 2012 IEEE International Conference on Systems, Man, and Cybernetics, pp. 1664–1669 (2012)
9. Di Mauro, M., Postiglione, F., Longo, M.: Reliability analysis of the controller architecture in software defined networks. In: Podofillini, L., Sudret, B., Stojadinovic, E., Zio, B., Kröger, W. (eds.) Safety and Reliability of Complex Engineered Systems, pp. 1503–1510. Taylor & Francis Group (2015)
10. Di Mauro, M., Postiglione, F., Longo, M., Restaino, R., Tambasco, M.: Availability evaluation of the virtualized infrastructure manager in Network Function Virtualization environments. In: Walls, L., Revie, M., Bedford, T. (eds.) Risk, Reliability and Safety: Innovating Theory and Practice, pp. 2591–2596. Taylor & Francis Group (2017
11. Di Mauro, M., Longo, M., Postiglione, F.: Performability evaluation of software defined networking infrastructures. In: ValueTools 2016–10th EAI International Conference on Performance Evaluation Methodologies and Tools, pp. 1–8 (2016)
12. Kuo, W., Ming, Z., Modeling, O.R.: Principles and Applications. Wiley, New York (2002)
13. Muppala, J.K., Ciardo, G., Trivedi, K.S.: Stochastic Reward Nets for reliability prediction. In: Communications in Reliability, Maintainability and Serviceability, pp. 9–20 (1994)
14. Nicol, D.M., Sanders, W.H., Trivedi, K.S.: Model-based evaluation: from dependability to security. IEEE Trans. Depend. Sec. Comput. **1**(1), 48–65 (2004)
15. Muppala, J.K., Malhotra, M., Trivedi, K.S.: Markov Dependability Models of Complex Systems: Analysis Techniques. Springer, Berlin Heidelberg (1996)
16. de Matos, R., Maciel, S., Machida, P., Dong, F., Seong, K., Trivedi, K.: Sensitivity analysis of server virtualized system availability. IEEE Trans. Rel. **61**(4), 994–1006 (2012)
17. Sahner, R.A., Trivedi, K.S.: Reliability modeling using SHARPE. IEEE Trans. Rel. **36**(2), 186–193 (1987)

Definition and Evaluation of Cold Migration Policies for the Minimization of the Energy Consumption in NFV Architectures

Vincenzo Eramo$^{(\boxtimes)}$ and Francesco Giacinto Lavacca

DIET, "Sapienza" University of Rome, Via Eudossiana 18, 00184 Rome, Italy
{vincenzo.eramo,francescogiacinto.lavacca}@uniroma1.it

Abstract. In the Network Function Virtualization (NFV) paradigm any service is represented by a Service Function Chain (SFC) that is a set of Virtual Network Functions (VNF) to be executed according to a given order. The running of VNFs needs the instantiation of VNF Instances (VNFIs) that are software modules executed on Virtual Machines. In this paper we cope with the migration problem of the VNFIs needed in the low traffic periods to switch off servers and consequently to save energy consumption. The consolidation has also negative effects as the energy consumption needed for moving the memories associated to the VNFI to be migrated. We focus on cold migration in redundant architecture in which virtual machines are suspended before performing migration and energy consumption required for transfer of virtual machine memory is the main concern. We propose migration policies that determine when and how to migrate VNFI in response to changes to SFC request intensity and location. The objective is to minimize the total energy consumption given by the sum of the consolidation and migration energies. The obtained results show how the policies allows for a lower energy consumption with respect to the traditional policies that consolidate resources as much as possible.

Keywords: Network function virtualization · Migration Policy · Power consumption · Markov decision process

1 Introduction

Network Function Virtualization (NFV) is emerging as a new network architecture that uses standard IT virtualization techniques to consolidate many network equipment types onto industry standard high volume servers [10]. The service functions are virtualized and executed on Virtual Network Function Instances (VNFIs), that are Virtual Machines running in Commercial-Off-The-Shelf (COTS) servers. The virtualization makes service deployment more flexible and scalable. The efficiency of a network, however, closely depends on the placement of the VNFIs as well as the routing of Service Function Chains (SFCs), characterizing a set of service functions to be executed for a packet flow. For this

© Springer International Publishing AG 2017
A. Piva et al. (Eds.): TIWDC 2017, CCIS 766, pp. 45–60, 2017.
DOI: 10.1007/978-3-319-67639-5_5

reason efficient algorithms have to be introduced to determine where to instantiate the VNFIs and to route the SFCs by choosing the network paths and the VNFIs involved. The algorithms have to take into account the limited resources of the network links and servers and pursue objectives of load balancing, energy saving and recovery from failure [15]. The task of placing SFC is closely related to virtual network embeddings [9] and may, therefore, be formulated as an optimization problem, with a particular objective. The main proposed solutions are discussed in [15]. For instance Moens et al. [16] formulate the SFC placement problem as a linear optimization problem that has the objective to minimize the number of active servers. The optimization problem and a heuristic have been also introduced in [6] where the processing resource in terms of the number of vcores assigned to each VNFI is also evaluated.

In this paper we consider situations when VNFI placement needs to be changed as traffic demands change over time. Such change of placement, called VNFI *migration*, is desirable for several reasons. Function instances may be migrated to new locations to adapt to changing traffic patterns. We assume a static traffic scenario in which a given number of SFC is offered to the network with bandwidth varying over time. For this reason when the traffic handled by a VNFI decreases, a migration may be triggered in order to consolidate the VNFIs in as few servers as possible with the consequence to save energy. Such migration can be either *hot* or *cold*. Hot (or "live") migration [13] is performed while the network operation is on going. As such the main concern for hot migration is to minimize the QoS degradation that may be incurred while moving VNFIs. We have proposed a hot migration policy in [5] aiming at minimizing the total cost taking into account both the energy consumption and the reconfiguration costs characterizing the QoS degradation. We followed the same approach already proposed in [3, 4] in virtual network embedding problems.

In order to avoid QoS degradation and to obtain other benefits like recovery from failure, many network operators have decided to deploy redundant virtual machines so as to guarantee service continuity in the case of one server failure. In the redundant virtual machines scenario is not necessary to perform live migration but it is sufficient a simple *cold migration* [14] in which the virtual machines are suspended before performing migrations. This type of migration can be easier to perform, even if it can be quite disruptive for on going traffic. Here, due to the redundancy of the virtual machines, the main concern is not QoS degradation during migration but rather the *energy consumed during the migration* for transferring the memory associated with migrated virtual machines. For these reasons in this paper we define and investigate two migration policies whose aim is the minimization of the total energy. The first one, referred to as Global Policy, allows for the minimization of the total energy in cycle-stationary traffic scenarios and is applicable to the case in which the entire traffic profile is known. The second one, referred to as Local Policy, is applicable in traffic scenarios in which the knowledge of the current traffic only is assumed.

The paper is organized as follows. Section 2 introduces the problem of the energy consumption minimization in NFV architectures. The Global and Local migration policies are illustrated in Sect. 3. The evaluation of the consolidation and migration energies are reported in Sect. 4. The main numerical results are shown in Sect. 5. Finally the main conclusions and future research items are discussed in Sect. 6.

2   The Problem of the Energy Consumption Minimization in NFV Architectures

Network Function Virtualization (NFV) involves the instantiation of VNFIs in order to execute VNFs belonging to SFCs [7,12]. We assume the case in which each VNFI is executing one VNF of a given type (e.g., a virtual firewall, or a load balancer) and the resources (vcores, RAM memory,...) assigned to it are shared among more SFCs. The problem of SFC routing and allocation of resources to VNFIs has been investigated in [6] where the formulation of the optimization problem is given. Due to the complexity of the problem, the Maximizing the Accepted SFC Requests Number (MASRN) heuristic has been proposed whose outputs are the routing of SFC and the resource dimensioning of the Virtual Machines (VMs) associated to the VNFIs. At the end of the application of the MASRN, a logical network is identified in which the edges are the VNFIs and the links identify which VNFIs are interconnected. This logical network is embedded in the physical network and the MASRN establishes in which physical paths the logical links are routed.

We show in Fig. 1 an example of SFC routing and resource dimensioning in the case of the NFV site reported in Fig. 1 composed by sixteen servers, two switches and two routers. Two SFCs are considered in Fig. 1a. The first one shows that packets need to be processed through two functions: Firewall and VPN Encryption, in that order. The second one involves the execution of a firewall function only.

To support the two SFCs, two VNFI are instantiated by activating the VMs VM_3^{FW} and VM_{11}^{EV} in the servers S_3 and S_{11} respectively. We illustrate in Fig. 1b the routing of the two SFCs considered. The first one uses the memory and processing resources of VM_3^{FW} and VM_{11}^{EV} for the running of the FW and EV VNFs respectively. The second one uses the resources of VM_3^{FW} only. The memory amount and the number of vcores allocated to the VMs are also shown in Fig. 1b. In particular two and three vcores have been allocated for VM_3^{FW} and VM_{11}^{EV} while we assume that the ones available in each server are four.

In order to save energy, server consolidation procedures can be activated in low traffic periods when the needed bandwidth and processing resources decrease. As shown in Fig. 1c, this decrease may lead to the need to allocate only one and two vcores to VM_3^{FW} and VM_{11}^{EV} respectively. We illustrate in Fig. 1d how the migration of the VM_3^{FW} in server S_{11} leads to the advantage of switching off the server S_3.

VNFI consolidation, as shown in the above example, allows for energy consumption saving, unfortunately it involves reconfiguration costs. For this reason sometimes migration could not be recommended or only some migrations should be performed. The investigation of migration policy has been carried out in [5] in the case of hot migration of Virtual Machines. In this case the downtime is minimized with successive stop and copy operations [13] and the main requirement is the one of minimizing the QoS degradation due to the bit loss occurring during the downtime.

In this paper we investigate policies in the case of cold migrations where the virtual machine is suspended before performing the migration and high migration times are involved; in this scenario QoS degradation is not the main concern because this type of migration is applied in case in which the virtual machines are redundant and the switching off of one of them does not impact on the Quality of service. Conversely the main concern in this scenario is the energy consumption due to transferring the bit of the VM memory allocated. This energy consumption characterizes the reconfiguration costs to be taken into account when migration policies, minimizing the total energy cost, have to be identified.

3 Energy Consumption Aware Migration Policies

When traffic reduction occurs, the VNFI can be dimensioned with a number of cores lower than the one evaluated in [6] during the Peak Hour Interval and consolidation techniques can be applied by migrating VNFIs so as to occupy fewer servers and to save power consumption. The migration can be performed when the VNFIs are supported by Virtual Machines (VMs) but at the price of an increase in the energy consumption due to the moving of the memory associated to the VMs. Because this migration energy may impact the total energy consumption, VNFI migration policies have to be defined allowing for a minimization of the energy consumption and consequently a right compromise between energy saving due to consolidation and the energy consumption due to moving memory associated to VMs.

Before illustrating what we intend for optimal migration policy, we introduce the following notations:

- T_i ($i = 0, 1, \cdots$): traffic state in the period $[t_i, t_i + \Delta)$ of duration Δ; T_i is characterized by the bandwidth $\beta_{i,k}$ ($k = 1, \cdots, N_{SFC}$) of the SFCs offered and N_{SFC} is the number of SFC offered;
- $\mathcal{G}^{PN} = (\mathcal{V}^{PN}, \mathcal{E}^{PN})$: graph of the physical network where $\mathcal{V}^{PN}$ and $\mathcal{E}^{PN}$ are the sets of physical nodes and links respectively;
- $\mathcal{G}^{VNFI} = (\mathcal{V}^{VNFI}, \mathcal{E}^{VNFI})$: logical graph where $\mathcal{V}^{VNFI}$ represents the set of VNFI nodes and $\mathcal{E}^{VNFI}$ denotes the links between them.

A mapping Γ of $\mathcal{G}^{VNFI}$ in $\mathcal{G}^{PN}$ determines in which servers, the VNFIs are hosted and in which network paths the virtual links are routed.

A mapping Γ is admissible for the traffic state T_i when the node processing, memory and link capacity are not overloaded that is when the following conditions hold: (i) the sum of the vcores and memory amount of the VNFIs hosted in any server is lower than or equal to the total number of vcores and memory amount available in the server respectively; (ii) the sum of the capacity

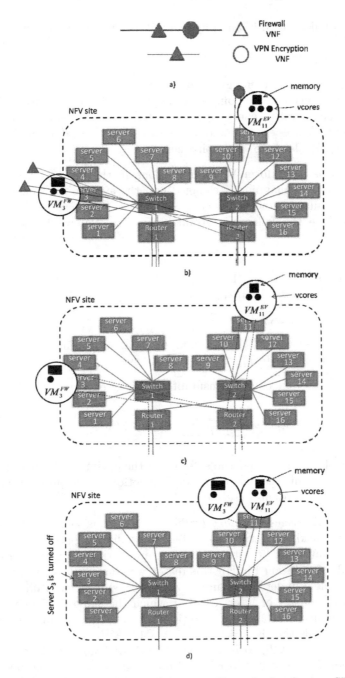

Fig. 1. An example of SFC routing and resource dimensioning for two SFCs (a) in a NFVI site composed by sixteen servers, two switches and two routers; memory and vcores allocated for the virtual machines VM_3^{FW} and VM_{11}^{EV} are shown in the peak hour interval (b) and when the traffic decreases (c); the consolidation application leads to the migration of VM_3^{FW} in server S_{11} (d).

of the logical links routed in any physical link is lower than or equal to the link capacity.

We also define:

- $E_{i,\Gamma}^c$: the consolidation energy defined as the sum of the energy consumption of the servers when the mapping Γ admissible for the traffic state T_i is applied;
- $E_{i,\Gamma_a,\Gamma_b}^m$: the migration energy defined as the energy consumption due to the moving of memories associated to the VNFI when the traffic condition change from T_i to T_{i+1} leads to a mapping change from Γ_a to Γ_b.

The objective is to perform VNFI migrations in the instants $t_i = i\Delta t$ ($i = 0, 1, \cdots$) so that the mapping is changed and the average total energy is minimized over infinite time horizon.

We introduce the following Optimal Mapping Policy Problem (OMPP) Formulation:

Given

- the traffic states T_i ($i = 0, 1, \cdots,$)
- the set Π of all possibles mappings;

Find the mapping policy

- $\{\Gamma_i, i = 0, 1, \cdots\}$ where $\Gamma_i \in \Pi$ is a mapping applied in instant t_i and admissible in the traffic state T_i;

Minimizing the average energy consumption E_{av} given by:

$$E_{av} = \lim_{K\to\infty} \frac{1}{K} \sum_{i=0}^{K} (E_{i,\Gamma_i}^c + E_{i,\Gamma_i,\Gamma_{i+1}}^m) \tag{1}$$

It is possible to prove that the solution of the optimal migration problem is NP-Hard [5]. For this reason we provide a solution of the problem introduced under the two assumptions described below.

- *Assumption-A: cycle-stationary traffic scenario.* It is well known that traffic matrices in backbone networks exhibit strong diurnal patterns and are typically cycle-stationary [5] with a 24 h cycle and with stationary characteristics in intervals of duration 1 h. For this reason we illustrate how we can solve the OMPP problem under the assumption of cycle-stationary traffic. We denote with N the number of intervals after which the same traffic characteristic occurs again; in this traffic scenario the same condition of traffic occurs every N time intervals that is $T_i = T_{i+kN}$ ($i = 0, 1, \cdots, N - 1; k = 1, 2, \cdots$) where we also assume that T_0 corresponds to the Peak Traffic condition.
- *Assumption-B: choices of a-priory determined mappings.* The mappings Γ_i ($i = 0, 1, \cdots, N - 1$) are selected in a restricted set Θ of possible mappings; the choice of these mappings is accomplished by applying suitable optimality criteria. The mappings of the set Θ are determined by applying the consolidation algorithm proposed in [5] and based on minimization of power consumption.

Under these assumptions the optimal policy, referred to as Global Policy and denoted as $\mathcal{D}^{glo}$, is characterized by the the the mappings Γ_i^{glo} ($i = 0, 1, \cdots, N - 1$) minimizing the total energy in a cycle-stationary interval, where Γ_i^{glo} is chosen to belong to the set Θ and it is admissible for the traffic state T_i. The mappings Γ_i^{glo} ($i = 0, 1, \cdots, N - 1$) can be determined by evaluating the optimal policy in a Discrete Time Markov Decision Process [4,11] and by following an approach similar to the one proposed in [5] in the case of hot migration of the VNFIs. The approach is briefly described in Appendix A. Another solution has been proposed in [2] by solving a least cost cycle problem.

We also introduce the Local Policy $\mathcal{D}^{loc}$, less complex than the Global Policy $\mathcal{D}^{glo}$ and adoptable when only the knowledge of the actual traffic is known. Its objective is to perform mapping changes so as to minimize the sum of the migration energy involved in the transition and the consolidation energy consumed by the servers when the new mapping is applied. The mappings Γ_i^{loc} ($i = 0, 1, \cdots, N - 1$) of the policy $\mathcal{D}^{loc}$ are established as follows:

- Γ_0^{loc} is the mapping belonging to Θ, admissible for the traffic state T_0 and with the lowest consolidation energy;
- the mapping Γ_i^{loc} ($i = 1, \cdots, N - 1$) is chosen from the set Θ, it is admissible for the traffic state T_i and it is chosen so as to minimize the sum of the migration energy involved in the transition and the consolidation energy of the mapping Γ_i^{loc} that is the following expression holds:

$$\Gamma_i^{loc} = \arg \min_{\Gamma \in \Theta} (E_{i,\Gamma}^c + E_{i-1,\Gamma_{i-1}^{loc},\Gamma}^m) \tag{2}$$

4   Evaluation of Consolidation and Migration Energy

In the evaluation of the consolidation and migration energy E_{i,Γ_i}^c and $E_{i,\Gamma_i,\Gamma_{i+1}}^m$ respectively, we assume that the main power contribution is due to CPU use because this component has the largest impact among all components [5]. We also assume a power consumption trend linear as a function of the load. As future research item, we will study the cases of more complex dependence [5]. We assume the following expression for the server power consumption P:

$$P = \left[a + (1 - a)\frac{A_s}{N_c}\right]P_{max} \tag{3}$$

wherein P_{max} is the maximum server power, a is the ratio of the baseline power to the maximum power, N_c is the total number of vcores and A_s is the average number of packets handled by the server.

Notice as the power consumption is given by the sum of the constant contribution aP_{max} and the one $(1 - a)\frac{A_s}{N_c}P_{max}$ dependent on the offered traffic. Next we evaluate the consolidation and the migration energies in the case of cold migration, which involves halting the VM, copying all its memory pages to the destination server and then restarting the new VM. We denote with D the migration time that in this case characterizes the downtime period in which the server stops the executions of the processes.

Next we report the evaluation of the consolidation and migration energies E^c_{i,Γ_i} and $E^m_{i,\Gamma_i,\Gamma_{i+1}}$ in Subsects. 4.1 and 4.2 respectively.

4.1   Evaluation of Consolidation Energy

In the evaluation of consolidation energy E^c_{i,Γ_i} $(i = 0, 1, \cdots, N - 1)$ in the traffic state T_i when the mapping Γ_i is applied, we introduce the following parameters:

- N_s: number of servers;
- $x^{\Gamma_i}_{i,j}$: parameters assuming the value 1 if the server j-th $(j = 1, \cdots N_s)$ is turned on in the traffic state T_i when the mapping Γ_i is applied;
- F: number of service function types;
- t^k_p $(k = 1, \cdots, F)$: packet processing time when service function k-th is applied;
- $R^{\Gamma_i}_{i,j,k}$: packet rate of the flows handled by the VMs running the service function k-th in the server j-th.

A consolidation energy is involved when the servers are active in runnings VMs executing the service functions. According to (3), we can write the following expression for E^c_{i,Γ_i}:

$$E^c_{i,\Gamma_i} = \sum_{j=1}^{N_s}(a + \frac{1-a}{N_c} \sum_{k=1}^{F} R^{\Gamma_i}_{i,j,k} \ t^k_p) \ x^{\Gamma_i}_{i,j} \ \Delta_j t \tag{4}$$

where $\Delta_j t$ is the time in which the server j-th is active and it is equal to the stationarity period Δt if the server has been not involved in a switching on process (the server it also turned on in the traffic state T_{i-1}), otherwise the migration time D must be subtracted from Δt. We can simply write:

$$\Delta_j t = \begin{cases} \Delta t & if \ \ server \ \ j-th \ \ is \ \ on \ \ in \ \ T_{i-1} \\ \Delta t - D & otherwise \end{cases} \tag{5}$$

4.2   Evaluation of Migration Energy

The migration energy $E^m_{i,\Gamma_i,\Gamma_{i+1}}$ is characterized by two components: the first one $E^{m,mem}_{i,\Gamma_i,\Gamma_{i+1}}$ is the energy consumption dependent on the total memory amount that has to transferred when a mapping change occurs; the second one $E^{m,ser}_{i,\Gamma_i,\Gamma_{i+1}}$ is dependent on the switching on or switching off of servers and characterized by the baseline power of the servers. Hence we can write:

$$E^m_{i,\Gamma_i,\Gamma_{i+1}} = E^{m,mem}_{i,\Gamma_i,\Gamma_{i+1}} + E^{m,ser}_{i,\Gamma_i,\Gamma_{i+1}} \tag{6}$$

For the evaluation of the energy consumption components we can introduce the following parameters:

- M_k: memory amount allocated to VM running the service function k-th;
- L_{agg}: packet length of the flows carrying the memory bits;

- t_{agg} $(k = 1, \cdots, F)$: processing time of the packets containing the memory bits;
- $v_{i,k}^{\Gamma_i, \Gamma_{i+1}}$: number of VMs migrating and supporting the service function k-th
- $s_i^{\Gamma_i, \Gamma_{i+1}}$: number of servers that are involved in a switching off or switching on process when the traffic state changes from T_i to T_{i+1} and the mapping change from Γ_i to Γ_{i+1} occurs.

$E_{i,\Gamma_i,\Gamma_{i+1}}^{m,mem}$ involves the energy consumption in both origin and destination servers for the transferring of memory bits of the migrated VMs. It is only dependent on the variable component of the server power consumption and can be expressed by the following expression:

$$E_{i,\Gamma_i,\Gamma_{i+1}}^{m,mem} = 2P_{max}\frac{1-a}{N_c}\sum_{k=1}^{F} v_{i,k}^{\Gamma_i,\Gamma_{i+1}}\left\lceil \frac{M_k}{L_{agg}} \right\rceil t_{agg} \tag{7}$$

Notice as the term $E_{i,\Gamma_i,\Gamma_{i+1}}^{m,mem}$ is independent of the migration time D as already observed by some experimental studies [13].

Conversely $E_{i,\Gamma_i,\Gamma_{i+1}}^{m,ser}$ is dependent on the baseline power consumption and it is simply given by:

$$E_{i,\Gamma_i,\Gamma_{i+1}}^{m,ser} = as_i^{\Gamma_i,\Gamma_{i+1}}P_{max}D \tag{8}$$

Finally by inserting expressions (7) and (8) in (6), we can evaluate the migration energy.

5   Numerical Results

We will verify the effectiveness of the VNFI migration policies introduced in Sect. 3. A given number N_{SFC} of SFC requests is generated, each one composed by three VNFs that is a firewall, a load balancer and a Virtual Private Network (VPN) encryption. We also assume that the load balancer splits the input traffic towards a number of output links chosen uniformly from 1 to 3. The execution order of the VNF is randomly chosen for the t-th generated SFC request. An example of graph for a generated SFC is reported in Fig. 2 in which u_t is an ingress access node and v_t^1, v_t^2 and v_t^3 are egress access nodes. The first and second VNFs are a firewall and a VPN encryption respectively; the third VNF is a load balancer splitting the traffic towards three output links. In the considered case study we also assume that the SFC handles traffic flows of packet with length equal to 1500 bytes.

In our analysis, we consider a three levels hierarchical network composed by five core nodes, five edge nodes and six access nodes in which the SFC requests are randomly generated and terminated. The network is reported in Fig. 3. Four NFV sites, as the one illustrated in Fig. 1, are connected to the network. Each of them is equipped with 16 servers. In this configuration, 40 Gbps links are considered except the links connecting the server to the switches in the NFV sites whose the rate is equal to 10 Gbps. The 64 servers are equipped with 48

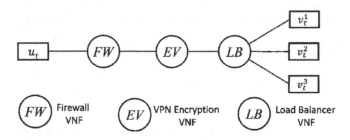

Fig. 2. An example of SFC composed by one firewall VNF, one VPN Encryption VNF and one load balancer VNF that splits the input traffic towards three output logical links. u_t denotes the ingress access node while v_t^1, v_t^2 and v_t^3 denote the egress access nodes.

vcores each one. We assume a vcore technology allowing for the packet processing times equal to 7.08 μs, 0.65 μs and 1.64 μs [1] for the firewall, load balancer and VPN encryption VNFs respectively.

The SFC routing and the dimensioning of the VNFI in terms of vcores is performed during the Peak Hour Interval (PHI) by using the Maximizing the Accepted SFC Requests Number (MASRN) algorithm proposed in [6]. We evaluate the effectiveness of the introduced VNF migration policies when the following case study is considered: (i) $N_{SFC} = 360$ SFCs are generated where the bandwidth $\beta_{0,k}$ of the k-th SFC ($k = 1, \cdots, N_{SFC}$) is uniformly distributed from 500 Mbps to 1 Gbps; (ii) the SFCs are routed in the PHI according to the MASRN heuristic; iii) we assume a cycle-stationary traffic scenario with $N=24$ intervals and where the bandwidth $\beta_{0,k}(k = 1, \cdots, N_{SFC})$ is modulated by the scale factor τ_i in the i-th interval ($i = 0, \cdots, N - 1$) chosen according to the classical sinusoidal trend and given by the following expression:

$$\tau_i = \begin{cases} 1 & if \quad i = 0 \\ 1 - 2\frac{i}{N}(1 - \tau_{min}) & i = 1, \cdots, \frac{N}{2} \\ 1 - 2\frac{N-i}{N}(1 - \tau_{min}) & i = \frac{N}{2} + 1, \cdots, N - 1 \end{cases} \tag{9}$$

where $\tau_0 = 1$ and $\tau_{\frac{N}{2}} = \tau_{min}$ denote the scale factors in the peak and least traffic conditions respectively.

The set Θ of mappings chosen a-priori and introduced in Sect. 3 is composed by the elements $\{\theta_i, i = 0, \cdots, \frac{N}{2}\}$ where the mapping θ_i ($i = 0, \cdots, \frac{N}{2}$) is evaluated by applying the VNFI Mapping Minimizing the Power Consumption (VMMPC) consolidation algorithm illustrated in [5] during the interval in which the traffic is characterized by the scale factor τ_i. The VMMPC algorithm, starting from the mapping evaluated by the MASRN algorithm, determines VNFI migrations so as to minimize the number of turned on servers and consequently the power consumption.

Next we evaluate the effectiveness of the policies $\mathcal{D}^{glo}$ and $\mathcal{D}^{loc}$ introduced in Sect. 3. We compare these two policies to the two classical Never Change and Always Change policies $\mathcal{D}^{nc}$ and $\mathcal{D}^{ac}$ respectively. When the $\mathcal{D}^{nc}$ policy

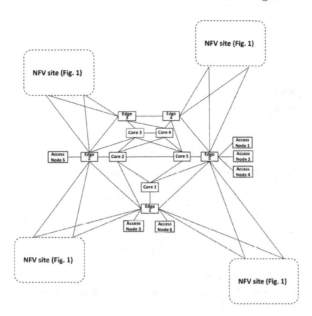

Fig. 3. The network topology is composed by six access nodes, five edge nodes, five core nodes and four NFV sites. Each NFV site is composed by two routers, two switches and sixteen servers connected as represented in Fig. 1.

is selected, the only mapping θ_0 is applied and the migration energy cost is absent. The mapping θ_0 is the one obtained by the application of the VMMPC algorithm during the PHI. It is admissible for all of the traffic conditions and for this reason it is chosen as mapping of the policy $\mathcal{D}^{nc}$. Conversely when the policy $\mathcal{D}^{ac}$ is selected the least power consumption admissible mapping is applied during each traffic state T_i $(i = 0, 1, \cdots, N-1)$. Notice how the policy $\mathcal{D}^{ac}$ allows for the minimization of the consolidation energy consumption at the expense of migration energy.

We report in Fig. 4 the total energy in a cycle-stationary interval of the policies $\mathcal{D}^{glo}$, $\mathcal{D}^{loc}$, $\mathcal{D}^{nc}$ and $\mathcal{D}^{ac}$ as a function of the memory size M associated to each VNFI. We have assumed the same size M for all of the service functions. The traffic profile is characterized by the factor scales expressed by Eq. (9) in which N and τ_{min} are chosen equal to 24 and 0.2 respectively. Finally the parameter a characterizing the ratio of fixed to maximum power consumption of the servers is set equal to 0.7, the migration time D is set equal to 10 s, the memory packet length L_{agg} is equal to 1500 bytes and the processing time t_{agg} of each memory packet is assumed to be 1.6 μs. From Fig. 4 we can observe how the proposed policy $\mathcal{D}^{glo}$ performs better than the policies $\mathcal{D}^{loc}$, $\mathcal{D}^{ac}$ and $\mathcal{D}^{nc}$ for all of the memory sizes and allows for a minimization of the total energy. For instance for $M = 460$ Mb the total energy values 21402 Wh, 23066 Wh, 23570 Wh, 29306 Wh are obtained for the policies $\mathcal{D}^{glo}$, $\mathcal{D}^{loc}$, $\mathcal{D}^{ac}$ and $\mathcal{D}^{nc}$ respectively. As expected

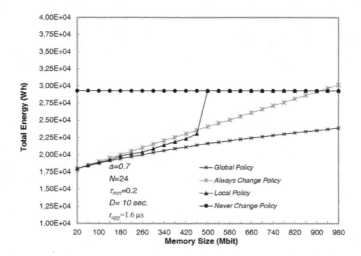

Fig. 4. The total energy of the policies $\mathcal{D}^{ac}$, $\mathcal{D}^{nc}$, $\mathcal{D}^{loc}$ and $\mathcal{D}^{glo}$ as a function of the memory size M associated to each VNFI migrating when $N_{SFC} = 360$, $N = 24$, $t_{agg} = 1.6\,\mu s$, $a = 0.7$ and $D = 10\,s$.

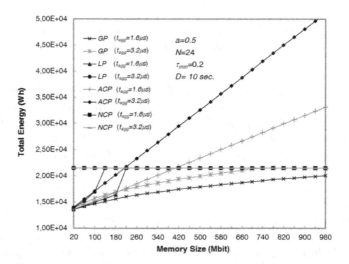

Fig. 5. The total energy of the policies $\mathcal{D}^{ac}$, $\mathcal{D}^{nc}$, $\mathcal{D}^{loc}$ and $\mathcal{D}^{glo}$ as a function of the memory size M associated to each VNFI migrating when $N_{SFC} = 360$, $N = 24$, $a = 0.5$ and $D = 10\,s$. The value of the aggregation processing time t_{agg} is chosen equal to $1.6\,\mu s$ and $3.2\,\mu s$.

the policy $\mathcal{D}^{ac}$ reaches the total energy value of $\mathcal{D}^{glo}$ only for low memory size M. In fact in this case the migration energy is negligible and the optimal policy is the one minimizing the consolidation energy that is $\mathcal{D}^{ac}$.

Next we show the impact of the packet memory processing time t_{agg} on the behavior of the proposed policies. In particular in the case $a = 0.5$ we compare in Fig. 5 the total energy of the policies $\mathcal{D}^{ac}$, $\mathcal{D}^{nc}$, $\mathcal{D}^{loc}$ and $\mathcal{D}^{glo}$ for the values of t_{agg} equal to 1.6 μs and 3.2 μs. The increase in t_{agg} leads to an increase in the migration energy due to the higher power consumption of the vcores involved in the migration process. For this reason when $t_{agg} = 3.2$ μs and the memory size M is larger than or equal to 660 Mb, the global policy $\mathcal{D}^{glo}$ is the one in which VNFI migrations are not performed at all and it is convenient to apply the same mapping solution in all of the traffic intervals as the policy $\mathcal{D}^{nc}$ makes. This is the reason for which starting from this memory value, the policies $\mathcal{D}^{glo}$ and $\mathcal{D}^{nc}$ have the same total energy.

6   Conclusions

The aim of this paper is to propose migration policies that establish when and where migrations of VNFI have to be accomplished so as to minimize the total energy characterized by the sum of the consolidation and migration energies occurring when the VNFIs are moved from the initial location. We have introduced two migration policies applicable in cycle-stationary traffic scenarios and when the possible mappings, characterizing where the VNFIs are instantiated, are a-priori determined. One of the two proposed policies, referred to as Global policy aims at minimizing the total energy consumption in the cycle-stationary period duration. We have compared the proposed policies to the Always Change and Never Change classical policies. The obtained numerical results have shown how the Global policy allows for the lowest energy consumption with respect to traditional migration policies.

Appendix A   Application of the Markov Decision Process (MDP) Theory for the Determination of the Global Policy

The proposed approach is based on choosing the solution in an a-priori determined and "good" possible solutions set. The assignment of the VNF nodes and links of the graph $G^{VNFI} = (V^{VNFI}, E^{VNFI})$ to server nodes and physical network paths respectively is defined as *mapping*. The global policy $\mathcal{D}^{glo}$ consists in choosing the mapping Γ_h to be applied in each traffic state T_h ($h = 0, 1, \cdots, N - 1$) so as to minimize the objective function expressed by (1). The proposed simplified approach consists in selecting the mappings Γ_h ($h = 0, 1 \cdots, N - 1$) applied in the traffic states T_h ($h = 0, 1, \cdots, N - 1$) by a set Θ; the choice of these mappings is accomplished by applying optimality criteria based on minimization of power consumption, minimization of reconfiguration costs, $\cdots$; not all of the mappings in Θ can be applied in any state T_h but only the admissible ones that do not lead to overcome the link bandwidth and the node processing resources. We denote with $\theta_{h,l}$ ($l = 1, \cdots, n_h$) the n_h mappings belonging to Θ and admissible for the traffic condition T_h ($h = 0, \cdots, N-1$); the state diagram reported in Fig. 6 represents the set of admissible mappings for each traffic state; it is organized in N levels where the $h-th$ ($h = 0, 1, \cdots, N-1$) level is composed by the n_h bi-dimensional states $(T_h, \theta_{h,l})$ ($l = 1, \cdots, n_h$). The objective is to determine a policy that establishes which mapping to apply when traffic changes happens. Formally a policy is characterized by the set of integer values $\mathcal{D} = \{d_{h,l} \ h = 0, 1 \cdots, N-1; l = 1, 2, \cdots, n_h\}$ where $d_{h,l}$ establishes that from the state $(T_h, \theta_{h,l})$, the mapping $\theta_{(h+1) \bmod N, d_{h,l}}$ has to be applied when the new traffic condition $T_{(h+1) \bmod N}$ occurs. Our objective is to determine the policy $\mathcal{D}^{glo}$ that minimizes the total cost in a cycle-stationarity period. We can determine the policy $\mathcal{D}^{glo}$ by finding the optimal policy in a Discrete Time Markov Decision Process (DTMDP) [8,11] whose Markov chain is characterized by the states of Fig. 6. The state and transition costs [8,11] in the DTMDP are as follows. Each state $(T_h, \theta_{h,l})$ is characterized by the consolidation energy cost $E^c_{(\theta_{h,l})}$ that is the energy consumed in the stationary interval T_h when the mapping $\theta_{h,l}$ is applied. Furthermore a transition from the state $(T_h, \theta_{h,l})$ to the state $(T_{(h+1) \bmod N}, \theta_{(h+1) \bmod N, k})$ is characterized by the migration energy cost $E^m_{(\theta_{h,l}, \theta_{(h+1) \bmod N, k})}$ that is the energy consumed to move the virtual machines involved in migration process.

The number of possible *alternatives* [8,11] in the state $(T_h, \theta_{h,l})$ is equal to $n_{(h+1) \bmod N}$ that is the number of mappings applicable when the traffic state transition from T_h to $T_{(h+1) \bmod N}$ occurs. The integer variable $d_{h,l}$ ($d_{h,l} \in [1..n_{(h+1) \bmod N}]$) codes the *alternative* chosen in the state $(T_h, \theta_{h,l})$ that involves the use of the mapping $\theta_{(h+1) \bmod N, d_{h,l}}$. When $d_{h,l}$ has been specified for $h \in [0..N - 1]$ and $l \in [1..n_h]$, a mapping policy has been determined. The optimal mapping policy $\mathcal{D}^{glo} = \{d^{glo}_{h,l} \ h = 0, 1 \cdots, N - 1; l = 1, 2, \cdots, n_h\}$ is the one that minimizes the expected total cost. To determine it we apply the policy iteration method [8,11] that needs the evaluation versus the *alternative* $d_{h,l}$ of both the transition probabilities $p^{j,k,d_{h,l}}_{h,l}$ from the state $(T_h, \theta_{h,l})$ to the state $(T_j, \theta_{j,k})$ and the cost $q^{d_{h,l}}_{h,l}$ to be expected in the next transition out of the state $(T_h, \theta_{h,l})$. The transition probabilities $p^{j,k,d_{h,l}}_{h,l}$ are reported in Fig. 6 for the *alternatives* $d_{h,l} = 1$, $d_{h,l} = k$ and $d_{h,l} = n_{(h+1) \bmod N}$. We can notice as the choice of the *alternative* $d_{h,l}$ involves only a transition with probability 1 from the state $(T_h, \theta_{h,l})$ to the state $(T_{(h+1) \bmod N}, \theta_{(h+1) \bmod N, d_{h,l}})$. Thus we can simply write:

$$p^{j,k,d_{h,l}}_{h,l} = \begin{cases} 1 \ if \quad j = (h+1) \bmod N, \quad k = d_{h,l} \\ 0 \ otherwise \end{cases} \tag{10}$$

For the evaluation of $q^{d_{h,l}}_{h,l}$ we observe that if the choice of the *alternative* $d_{h,l}$ in the state $(T_h, \theta_{h,l})$ leads not to change the applied mapping, that is $\theta_{(h+1) \bmod N, d_{h,l}} \equiv \theta_{h,l}$, the migration energy costs are not involved and only the energy consumption cost $E^c_{(\theta_{h,l})}$ of applying the mapping $\theta_{h,l}$ has to be considered. Otherwise when a mapping change occurs, also the migration energy cost $E^m_{(\theta_{h,l}, \theta_{(h+1) \bmod N, d_{h,l}})}$ from the mapping $\theta_{h,l}$ to the mapping $\theta_{(h+1) \bmod N, d_{h,l}}$ has

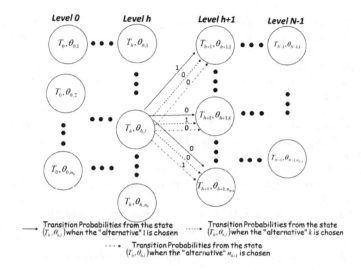

Fig. 6. Bi-dimensional Discrete Time Markov Chain in which each state is characterized by some possible *alternatives*; the choice of an *alternative* in each state determines a mapping policy.

to be added. Hence we can write:

$$q_{h,l}^{d_{h,l}} = \begin{cases} E_{(\theta_{h,l})}^c & if \;\; \theta_{(h+1) \bmod N, d_{h,l}} \equiv \theta_{h,l} \\ E_{(\theta_{h,l})}^c + E_R^m(\theta_{h,l}, \theta_{(h+1) \bmod N, d_{h,l}}) & otherwise \end{cases} \tag{11}$$

Once established the transition probabilities $p_{h,l}^{j,k,d_{h,l}}$ and the cost $q_{h,l}^{d_{h,l}}$ as a function of the *alternative* $d_{h,l}$ we can find the policy $\mathcal{D}^{glo} = \{d_{h,l}^{glo}, \; h = 0, 1 \cdots, N - 1; l = 1, 2, \cdots, n_h\}$ by applying the policy-iteration method [8, 11].

References

1. Dobrescu, M., Argyraki, K., Ratnasamy, S.: Toward predictable performance in software packet-processing platforms. In: 9th USENIX Symposium on Networked Systems Design and Implementation, pp. 1–14, April 2012
2. Eramo, V., Ammar, M., Lavacca, F.: Migration energy aware reconfigurations of virtual network function instances in NFV architectures. IEEE Access **5**, 4927–4938 (2017)
3. Eramo, V., Miucci, E., Ammar, M.: Study of migration policies in energy-aware virtual router networks. IEEE Commun. Lett. **18**, 1919–1922 (2014)
4. Eramo, V., Miucci, E., Ammar, M.: Study of reconfiguration cost and energy aware vne policies in cycle-stationary traffic scenarios. IEEE J. Sel. Areas Commun. **34**, 1–17 (2016). doi:10.1109/JSAC.2016.2520179
5. Eramo, V., Miucci, E., Ammar, M., Lavacca, F.G.: An approach for service function chain routing and virtual function network instance migration in network function virtualization architectures. IEEE Trans. Netw. **25**(4), 2008–2025 (2017). http://ieeexplore.ieee.org/document/7866881/

6. Eramo, V., Tosti, A., Miucci, E.: Server resource dimensioning and routing of service function chain in NFV network architectures. J. Electr. Comput. Eng. 1–12, April 2016. article ID 7139852
7. ETSI Industry Specification Group (ISG) NFV: ETSI Group Specifications on Network Function Virtualization, January 2015. http://docbox.etsi.org/ISG/NFV/Open/Published/
8. Fan, J., Ammar, M.H.: Dynamic topology configuration in service overlay networks: a study of reconfiguration policies. In: Proceedings of 25th IEEE International Conference on Computer Communications (INFOCOM), pp. 1–12. Barcelona (Spain), April 2006
9. Fischer, A., Botero, J., Till Beck, M., de Meer, H., Hesselbach, X.: Virtual network embedding: a survey. Commun. Surv. Tutor. IEEE (15), 1888–1906, July/August 2014
10. Gu, L., Tao, S., Zeng, D., Jin, H.: Communication cost efficient virtualized network function placement for big data processing. In: Proceedings of INFOCOM 2016, April 2016
11. Howard, R.A.: Dynamic Programming and Markov Processes. The Massachusetts Institute of Technology (1960)
12. Internet Engineering Task Force (IETF) Service Function Chaining (SFC) Working Group (WG), Halpern, J., Pignataro, C.: Service Function Chaining (SFC) Architecture, RFC 7665 (2015). https://datatracker.ietf.org/doc/rfc7665/
13. Liu, H., Xu, C., Jin, H., Gong, J., Liao, X.: Performance and energy modeling for live migration of virtual machines. Cluster Comput. 14(6), 249–264 (2013)
14. Medina, V., Garcia, J.: A survey of migration mechanisms of virtual machines. J. ACM Comput. Surv. 46(3), 1–33 (2014)
15. Mijumbi, R., Serrat, J., Gorricho, J., Bouten, N., De Turck, F., Boutaba, R.: Network function virtualization: state-of-the-art and research challenges. IEEE Commun. Surv. Tutorials 18(1), 236–262 (2016)
16. Moens, H., Turck, F.: Vnf-p: a model for efficient placement of virtualized network functions. In: Network and Service Management (CNSM) 2014 10th International Conference on. Rio de Janeiro (Brazil), November 2014

A Lightweight Prediction Method for Scalable Analytics of Multi-seasonal KPIs

Roberto Bruschi[1], Giuseppe Burgarella[2], and Paolo Lago[1,3(✉)]

[1] S3ITI National Lab, CNIT, Genoa, Italy
paolo@tnt-lab.unige.it
[2] Ericsson Telecomunicazioni S.p.A., Genoa, Italy
[3] DITEN, University of Genoa, Genoa, Italy

Abstract. This paper presents an innovative prediction method for key performance indexes with multiple seasonal profiles. The proposed method, called Multiplicative Multi-Seasonal Model (MSMM) relies on a time series decomposition including multiple multiplicative seasonal profiles and a trend component. The method and its underlying model have been specifically designed to be computationally lightweight to scale to big-data scenarios envisaged in upcoming 5G-NFV environments. The MSMM performance has been evaluated on KPI traces of real operating infrastructures/services, made available by Yahoo! The obtained results outlined how the MSMM prediction method provides more accurate forest than well-known algorithm like the seasonal version of ARIMA, with much reduced computational weight.

Keywords: Predictive model · Seasonal time series · 5G · NFV

1 Introduction

In these recent years, network technologies and architectures are facing a deep revolution in order to meet tomorrow's 5G requirements, the expected number of users and of network-connected objects, as well as traffic volumes.

Classical network paradigms and protocols are rapidly proving inadequate and are being rendered obsolete by novel approaches that allow more flexible and more pervasive integration with Information Technology (IT) services. In this respect, Software Defined Networking (SDN) and Network Function Virtualization (NFV) [1] are well known to be the best candidates for achieving the suitable levels of flexibility, upgradability and integration with IT services [2].

However, this upcoming network "softwarization" process is not free of drawbacks and open issues that may even threaten its viability. For instance, the economic sustainability and scalability levels that SDN/NFV technologies can provide are causing more than a little concern in the industry and research communities [3].

Therefore, Operators need to reduce any unnecessary sources of operating expenses (OPEX), which usually correspond to more than twice the capital expenses (CAPEX) figure. As shown in Fig. 1, the only significant OPEX sources that can be reduced by technological advancement are the ones related to the energy consumption and the network management, which accounts for a figure equivalent to the entire infrastructure

© Springer International Publishing AG 2017
A. Piva et al. (Eds.): TIWDC 2017, CCIS 766, pp. 61–70, 2017.
DOI: 10.1007/978-3-319-67639-5_6

CAPEX. Thus, to reduce both these OPEX sources, it will be of paramount importance to adopt control/orchestration policies that can act in a fully autonomous fashion by allowing the dynamic optimization and consolidation of network service and infrastructure resources according to the current and the predicted incoming load.

In this perspective, the behavior of future NFV/5G networks is envisaged to be driven and influenced by a number of autonomic control elements, which might be even owned by different organizations (i.e., Infrastructure Providers, Service Providers, etc.) [7, 8]. For example, the following list summarizes some of these possible control elements:

The NFV Orchestrator (NFVO), as defined by the ETSI MANO working group [9], will be the key for allowing Service Providers autonomously configuring and optimizing network services. Each Service Provider might potentially instantiate a different NFVO per service, and enable diverse optimization mechanism/policies [10];

The Virtual Network Function (VNF) Managers (VNFM), associate to any instance of VNF composing a service. VNFM modules are meant to be provided by VNF developers, and their behavior driven by NFVO, but they can eventually contain autonomous mechanisms for VNF self-optimization/healing.

Means for data-center (i.e., NFV Infrastructure Point-of Presence – NFVI-PoP) optimization and consolidation, usually deployed by Infrastructure Providers 11. Two NFVI-PoPs may be driven by diverse optimization policies.

Means for (SDN-ready) traffic engineering/routing to control how traffic is spread and redirect trough the network interconnecting users and NFVI-PoPs.

All these elements will actuate their own control strategies obviously by collecting and suitably processing the measured values of different key performance indexes from service and/or infrastructure components.

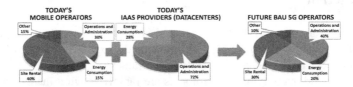

Fig. 1. Main OPEX sources related to today's Mobile Operators (Source: Yankee Group), of IaaS (Datacenter) providers (Source: IDC, Balley'12) and of future Business-as-Usual 5G Operators.

In such a context, the availability of methods/models to predict future KPI behavior in a reliable fashion will be clearly the key for increasing the control effectiveness: they can allow to pass from reactive network control loops (i.e., reconfigure the network upon an event happens) to proactive ones (i.e., tune the network before an event happens). The advantages are clearly in the possibilities of maintaining the requested performance also during "critical" situations (e.g., workload peaks, etc.).

The relevance of prediction methods/models in also well known in the context of anomaly detection, incident prediction, and infrastructure/service resource planning.

In scientific literature, many different prediction schemes have been proposed and evaluated to model Internet traffic (for example, see [12, 13], and [14]). In the last decade, well-known approaches (based on time-series auto-regression, exponential smoothing, neural networks, and wavelet among others) have been used to predict the bandwidth utilization of Internet links. Most of them have been demonstrated to represent self-similarity of network traffic in an effective way, especially by predicting typical fluctuations at diverse time scales (e.g., a day, a week, and a year – see Fig. 2), which are commonly referred as seasonalities in time series theory. In today's networks, such seasonalities often correspond to typical activity patterns of the end-user population (e.g., night and day profiles).

Anyway, the wide adoption of NFV technologies is going affect most of the assumptions and starting considerations on which existing prediction methodologies have been designed. In this respect, we can underline the following aspects:

In 5G/NFV networks, the number of KPIs to be monitored will explode and become more heterogeneous, since also typical metrics of IT resources, such as server CPU usage, will become relevant to network services' and infrastructures' operational behavior.

The monitored KPIs will probably exhibit additional seasonalities due to the presence of the aforementioned multiple control entities, migrating and scaling services or group of VNFs across multiple NFVI-PoPs.

Therefore, in the next future, KPI prediction should become extremely lightweight in order to scale towards big data analytics, and enough flexible to represent heterogeneous metrics with diverse multiple seasonalities.

Owing the considerations above, this paper introduces a novel prediction method based on a model specifically conceived to represent stationary or non-stationary time series with multiple seasonalities, and whose prediction method aims at the reducing the computational weight with respect to other state-of-the-art approaches providing similar capabilities.

The paper is organized as follows. The next section will introduce the proposed decomposition model for the KPI time series, as well as the related fitting and prediction methodologies. Performance evaluation results including a comparison with the well-known seasonal ARIMA model are in Sect. 3. The Conclusion are drawn in Sect. 4.

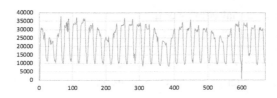

Fig. 2. Example of repetitive KPI with daily and weekly seasonalities.

2   The Multi-seasonal Multiplicative Model

As previously sketched, we represent measures of a KPI, collected at regularly spaced time intervals, as a time series y_t $t \in [0, \infty[$.

The proposed prediction method is based on a time series decomposition with multiplicative seasonality components. Time-series seasonality is well known to be multiplicative if the magnitude of the seasonal variation increases according to the trend of the time series [15]. It is additive if the seasonal slope is not dependent on the "magnitude" of the time series and, consequently, it can simply be added or subtracted from the trend level. Given the "aggregated" nature of network- and NFV-related key performance indexes, like link and RAM utilizations, multiplicative decomposition has been selected. It is worth noting that multiplicative seasonalities, even if less easy to be treated in their base theory, have been largely adopted in other sectors (e.g., in economics) [22]. Owing the above considerations, we adopt the following time series decomposition:

$$y_t = S_t(T_t + \varepsilon_t) \qquad (1)$$

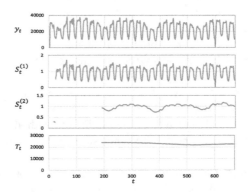

Fig. 3. Example of the proposed time series decomposition applied to the Yahoo trace real_34 (see Sect. 3), which results having two seasonalities at 24 and 168 samples, respectively.

where:

S_t represents the seasonal component;
T_t is the trend component;
ε_t is the estimation error.
S_t is specifically defined to handle multiple seasonalities, and, to this end, S_t is expressed as the product of single-seasonality profiles $S_t^{(i)}$:

$$S_t = \prod_{i=1}^{P} S_t^{(i)} \qquad (2)$$

where $P = 0, 1, \ldots$ is the number of identified seasonalities.

The i-th seasonality profile is associated to a season length equal to $\tau^{(i)}$.

2.1 Identification of Multiple Seasonalities

In order to identify how many seasonalities the time series exhibit, and to estimate their length, the procedure in 19 is used in an iterative fashion. This procedure is based on the joint analysis of peaks in the circular Auto-Correlation Function (ACF) and of the periodogram of the time series.

The procedure is initialized by using the collected samples of y_t over a training window $t \in [1, \ldots, \omega]$.

The samples y_t $\forall t \in [1, \ldots, \omega]$ are processed for detecting possible outliers (i.e., anomalous values [16, 17], and remove them. To this end, the simple procedure proposed in [18] is applied to detect potential outliers, and their values replaced with the average value of previous k and subsequent k samples.

At each iteration, the time series ACF and the related periodogram are analyzed to find the shorter-period seasonality (i.e., the first peak in both the ACF and the periodogram meeting the conditions defined in [19]). Let be $\tau^{(i)}$ the length of length of the seasonality identified at procedure step i.

The time series is smoothed by means of a low-pass Moving Average filter of length $\tau^{(i)}$ (i.e., $MA(\tau^{(i)})$) in order to remove the slope of the last identified periodicity:

$$y_t^{(i)} = MA\left(\tau^{(i)}\right)\left[y_t^{(i-1)}\right] = \frac{1}{\tau^{(i)}} \sum_{j=t-\tau^{(i)}}^{t} y_j^{(i-1)} \tag{3}$$

with $y_t^{(0)} = y_t$.

It is worth noting that the MA has been preferred to other filters (like the Exponential Weighted Moving Average – EWMA), since it allows removing selected seasonal fluctuations in a more accurate fashion.

If no seasonality is found, the algorithm is stopped. Otherwise, the smoothed time series $y_t^{(i)}$ is passed to the next iteration step for finding possible further seasonalities.

Given the iterative application of Eq. (3), it can be noted that the smoothed time series $y_t^{(i)}$ have different lengths according to the i index. In particular, $y_t^{(i)}$ will have a length of $\omega - \sum_{j=1}^{i} \tau^{(j)} + 1$.

Given that the algorithm above works over a finite window of samples, large-period seasonalities cannot be obviously detected. Therefore, we fixed the maximum seasonality periods to be detected to $\omega/3$.

2.2 Model Estimation and Fitting

The model estimation and fitting procedure is split into two simple steps. In the first one, the measured samples are used to estimate the seasonal profiles $\hat{S}_t^{(i)}$. In the second step, residual data are used to fit the trend component T_t.

As far as the first step is concerned, we estimate the seasonal profile for $\forall i \in [1, \ldots, P]$ as follows:

$$\hat{S}_t^{(i)} = \frac{1}{\zeta^{(i)}} \sum_{j=0}^{\zeta^{(i)}-1} \frac{\nabla^{j\tau^{(i)}} y_t^{(i-1)}}{\nabla^{j\tau^{(i)}} y_t^{(i)}} \tag{4}$$

where $y_t^{(i)}$ are the values obtained in Eq. 3, ∇ represents the "backshift" operators (i.e., $\nabla^n x_t = x_{t-n}$), and $\zeta^{(i)}$ is the maximum number of $\tau^{(i)}$-length seasons that present in $\nabla^{j\tau^{(i)}} y_t^{(i)}$, which can be expressed as follows:

$$\zeta^{(i)} = \frac{\tau^{(i)}}{\omega - \sum_{j=1}^{i} \tau^{(j)} + 1} \tag{5}$$

Passing to the second step, the last smoothed time series $y_t^{(P)}$, where all the seasonal patterns have been removed, is then fitted with a well-known non-seasonal Auto Regressive Integrated Moving Average (ARIMA) model 20:

$$\left(1 - \phi_1 \nabla - \ldots - \phi_p \nabla^p\right)\left(1 - \nabla\right)^d y_t^{(P)} = c + \left(1 - \theta_1 \nabla - \ldots - \theta_q \nabla^q\right)\varepsilon_t \tag{6}$$

where p the autoregressive part of the ARIMA model, d the degree of the first differencing involved, and q the order of the moving average part. The well-known Box-Jenkins procedure [20] is applied to identify the p, d, and q orders, as well as the best fitting of the parameters $\phi_1, \ldots, \phi_p$ and $\theta_1, \ldots, \theta_q$.

Figure 3 reports an example of time series decomposition over which the parameters introduced in this section are estimated and fitted.

3   Forecasting Procedure

The proposed mechanism works by updating the estimated seasonal profiles through Eq. 4 at each seasonal period length, while the ARIMA model is re-fitted every ψ samples. The seasonal profiles and the fitted ARIMA model are used to produce the forecasting values and related prediction intervals.

With the aim of reducing the computational weight of the forecasting procedure, the forecasts are not updated at any measured value collected. They are rather calculated in a "bulk" fashion at every t corresponding to an integer multiple of $\tau^{(i)}$ $\forall i \in [1, \ldots, P]$, or of ψ.

At any of these time instants, the forecasts are obtained for any future values of the time series up to the next t corresponding to an integer multiple of seasonal periods or ARIMA re-computations (i.e., from $t+1$ to $t+m$).

In other words, each prediction $\hat{y}_{t+l}$ for $\forall l \in [t+1, t+m]$ is obtained as an l-step-ahead out-of-sample forecast at time t, which, given the decomposition in Eq. 1, can be expressed as follows:

$$\hat{y}_{t+l} = \hat{T}_{t+l} \prod_{i=1}^{P} \nabla^{i\tau^{(i)} + l} \hat{S}_t^{(i)} \tag{7}$$

where $\hat{T}_{t+l}$ is the l-step-ahead forecast of the ARIMA model, which is obtained through the out-of-sample method proposed in 21.

$\hat{T}_{t+l}$ can be expressed as function of previous forecasted and measured values and residuals through the following equation:

$$\hat{T}_{t+l} = c + \phi_1 z_{t+l-1} + \ldots + \phi_p z_{t+l-p} + \ldots + \theta_1 e_{t+l-1} - \ldots - \theta_q e_{t+l-q} \qquad (8)$$

with z_i and e_i being:

$$z_i = \begin{cases} \hat{y}_i^{(P)} & \text{if } i > t \\ y_i^{(P)} & \text{if } i \leq t \end{cases} \qquad (9)$$

$$e_i = \begin{cases} 0 & \text{if } i > t \\ \varepsilon_i & \text{if } i \leq t \end{cases} \qquad (10)$$

4 Performance Evaluation

Performance evaluation has been fulfilled by using a selection of time series datasets provided by Yahoo!, and made publicly available [23]. Such datasets have been collected from Yahoo! systems and services during real operations. Each sample trace contains 8 weeks of regularly sampled KPIs (the sampling time is 1 h), and they are particularly useful for testing anomaly detection algorithms. Indeed, outliers (data point that is significantly different from the rest of the given data) in the dataset were manually labeled as anomalies by the editors. Among the various traces available, we select the ones that exhibit seasonal behaviors (usually daily or weekly seasonality or both).

In this scenario, the accuracy of the MSMM procedure has been evaluated using the forecast error measured with respect to the original datasets. The obtained errors have been compared against the ones obtained by using the classical Seasonal ARIMA (SARIMA) model.

For both the MSMM and the SARIMA procedures we used 4 weeks of the sample traces as a training window. The SARIMA forecasts are updated at each seasonal period length.

In Fig. 4, we reported the selected sample traces within the forecasts obtained with the SARIMA and the MSMM models, both implemented in Matlab. We named to the sample traces by using the file name used in the trace repository (i.e., real_3, real_13, etc.). Note that the spikes present in the traces correspond to the anomalies annotated by Yahoo! In our training procedures and in the calculation of the forecast errors we remove those anomalies according to the procedure described in Sect. 2.1.

The obtained results outline how MSMM works significantly better with respect to the SARIMA when the time series exhibits a strong multi-seasonal behavior like in the real_13, real_34 and real_39 cases. In the tested cases, the MSMM forecast error tends to be almost the half of the SARIMA ones.

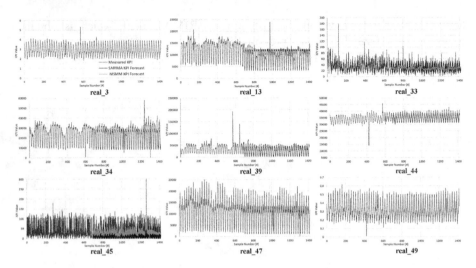

Fig. 4. Sample traces and forecasts performed with the SARIMA model (red lines) and with the MSMM procedure (blue lines). (Color figure online)

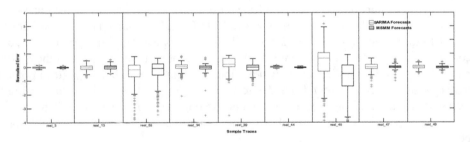

Fig. 5. Box plots of the measured normalized error of the SARIMA (blue boxes) and MSMM (black boxes) forecasts for different sample traces. (Color figure online)

Whereas in the case of time series with single seasonality, or with weak multi-seasonality (like the real_3, real_47 and real_49 traces), the error difference between the two forecast methods is reduced. This is confirmed by the box plots in Fig. 5, representing the dispersion of the normalized prediction error for both the forecast procedures.

Both the procedures completely fail to fit the real_33 and real_45 time series, since both these traces exhibit a strongly noisy behavior.

Finally, Table 1 reports the average percentage error obtained in the different tests. Note that the MSMM always provide better prediction accuracy with respect to the SARIMA model.

Table 1. Average absolute error for different sample traces.

Sample traces	MSMM avg. absolute error	SARIMA avg. absolute error
real_3	2.3%	5%
real_13	11.3%	15.7%
real_33	50%	52.3%
real_34	9.2%	13.4%
real_39	7%	19%
real_44	2.7%	4.2%
real_45	53%	55.9%
real_47	8.3%	33%
real_49	6.7%	10.4%

5 Conclusion

This paper introduced the MSMM prediction method to predict key performance indexes with multiple seasonal profiles. The method and its underlying model have been specifically designed to be computationally lightweight to scale to big-data scenarios envisaged in upcoming 5G-NFV environments. The obtained performance evaluation results have been obtained by using datasets made publicly available by Yahoo! and derived from the measurements of systems/services in operations. The achieved outlined how the MSMM prediction method provides more accurate forest than well-known algorithm like the seasonal version of ARIMA, with much reduced computational weight.

Acknowledgment. This work was supported by the INPUT (In-Network Programmability for next-generation personal cloUd service supporT) project, funded by the European Commission under the Horizon 2020 Programme (Grant no. 644672).

References

1. Chiosi, M., et al.: Network Functions Virtualization: An Introduction, Benefits, Enablers, Challenges & Call For Action, ETSI White Paper, October 2012. http://portal.etsi.org/NFV/ NFV_White_Paper.pdf
2. Matsubara, D., Egawa, T., Nishinaga, N., Kafle, V.P., Shin, M.-K., Galis, A.: Toward future networks: a viewpoint from ITU-T. IEEE Commun. Mag. **51**(3), 112–118 (2013)
3. Corcoran, P.M.: Cloud computing and consumer electronics: a perfect match or a hidden storm? IEEE Consum. Electron. Mag. **1**(2), 14–19 (2012)
4. Matsubara, D., Egawa, T., Nishinaga, N., Kafle, V.P., Shin, M.-K., Galis, A.: Toward future networks: a viewpoint from ITU-T. IEEE Commun. Mag. **51**(3), 112–118 (2013)
5. Peng, M., Li, Y., Zhao, Z., Wang, C.: System architecture and key technologies for 5G heterogeneous cloud radio access networks. IEEE Netw. **29**(2), 6–14 (2015)
6. Matias, J., Garay, J., Toledo, N., Unzilla, J., Jacob, E.: Toward an SDN-enabled NFV architecture. IEEE Commun. Mag. **53**(4), 187–193 (2015)
7. Szabo, R., Kind, M., Westphal, F.J., Woesner, H., Jocha, D., Csaszar, A.: Elastic network functions: opportunities and challenges. IEEE Netw. **29**(3), 15–21 (2015)

8. Hawilo, H., Shami, A., Mirahmadi, M., Asal, R.: NFV: state of the art, challenges, and implementation in next generation mobile networks (vEPC). IEEE Netw. **28**(6), 18–26 (2014)
9. ETSI Network Function Virtualization Management and Orchestration Working Group (NFV MANO WG). http://portal.etsi.org/tb.aspx?tbid=796&SubTB=796
10. Clayman, S., Maini, E., Galis, A., Manzalini, A., Mazzocca, N.: The dynamic placement of virtual network functions. In: Proceedings of the 2014 IEEE Network Operations and Management Symposium (NOMS), Krakow, pp. 1–9 (2014)
11. Sun, X., Ansari, N., Wang, R.: Optimizing resource utilization of a data center. IEEE Comm. Surv. Tutor. **18**(4), 2822–2846 (2016)
12. Katris, C., Daskalaki, S.: Comparing forecasting approaches for internet traffic. Expert Syst. Appl. **42**(21), 8172–8183 (2015). Elsevier, ISSN 0957-4174
13. Dalmazo, B.L., Vilela, J.P., Curado, M.: Performance analysis of network traffic predictors in the cloud. J. Netw. Syst. Manage. **25**(2), 290–320 (2017)
14. Feng, H., Shu, Y.: Study on network traffic prediction techniques. In: Proceedings of the 2005 International Conference on Wireless Communication Network and Mobile Computing, pp. 1041–1044 (2005)
15. Koehler, A.B., Snyder, R.D., Keith Ord, J.: Forecasting models and prediction intervals for the multiplicative Holt-Winters method. Int. J. Forecast. **17**(2), 269–286 (2001)
16. Fox, A.J.: Outliers in time series. J. R. Stat. Soc. Ser. B (Methodological) **34**(3), 350–363 (1972)
17. Gupta, M., Gao, J., Aggarwal, C.C., Han, J.: Outlier detection for temporal data: a survey. IEEE Trans. Knowl. Data Eng. **25**(1), 1–20 (2013)
18. Williams, A.W., Pertet, S.M., Narasimhan, P.: Tiresias: black-box failure prediction in distributed systems. In: Proceedings of the 21st International Parallel and Distributed Processing Symposium (IPDPS 2007), Long Beach, CA, USA, March 2007, pp. 1–8 (2007)
19. Vlachos, M., Yu, P., Castelli, V.: On periodicity detection and structural periodic similarity. In: Proceedings of the 5th SIAM International Conference on Data Mining (SDM 2005), Newport Beach, CA, USA, April 2005, pp. 449–460 (2005). ISBN:0898715938
20. Brockwell, P.J., Davis, R.A.: Nonstationary and seasonal time series models. In: Brockwell P.J., Davis R.A. (eds.) Introduction to Time Series and Forecasting. Springer Texts in Statistics. Springer, New York (2002). doi:10.1007/0-387-21657-X_6, ISBN 0-387-95351-5
21. Hyndman, R.J., Athanasopoulos, G.: Forecasting: Principles and Practice. OTexts Ed., Heathmont (2016). Sect. 8.8, ISBN: 978-0987507105
22. Chatfield, C., Yar, M.: Prediction intervals for multiplicative Holt-Winters. Int. J. Forecast. **7**(1), 31–37 (1991). Elsevier, ISSN 0169-2070
23. Laptev, N., Amizadeh, A., Billawala, Y.: Yahoo labs news: announcing a benchmark dataset for time series anomaly detection, March 2015. http://labs.yahoo.com/news/announcing-a-benchmark-datasetfor-time-series-anomaly-detection

Multimedia Forensics

A Copy-Move Detection Algorithm Based on Geometric Local Binary Pattern

Andrey Kuznetsov[(⊠)]

Samara National Research University, Samara, Russia
kuznetsov.a@ssau.ru

Abstract. An obvious way of digital image forgery is a copy-move attack. It is quite simple to carry out to hide important information in an image. Copy-move process contains three main steps: copy the fragment from one place of an image, transform it by some means and paste to another place of the same image. A lot of papers on development of copy-move detection algorithms exist nowadays though the achieved results are far from perfect, so they are frequently improved. In this paper, it is proposed a new copy-move detection algorithm based on geometric local binary patterns (GLBP). GLBP features are robust to contrast enhancement, additive Gaussian noise, JPEG compression, affine transform. Another advantage of these features is low computational complexity. Conducted experiments compare GLBP-based features with features based on other forms of local binary patterns. The proposed solution showed high precision and recall values during experimental research for wide ranges of transform parameters. Thus, it showed a meaningful improvement in detection accuracy.

Keywords: Forgery detection · Copy-move · Geometric local binary pattern · GLBP feature · Transform invariant

1 Introduction

Providing information to expand on some theme or to prove some facts is impossible without digital images. For this purpose, people exchange digital photos using social networks (i.e., Facebook) and image services (Instagram, Tumblr, etc.). The number of shared digital images per day for the most popular web applications is incredible: nearly 350 million images on Facebook [1] and 80 million photos in Instagram [2]. These data are not secure at all, nobody checks its originality.

Protection from digital image forgery is a challenging problem nowadays. Everyone can make changes in a digital image using modern software tools on PC or any mobile device in several minutes. But no one can predict the consequences of these changes, which can lead to concealing or modifying important image content.

One of the most frequently used digital image attack is copy-move. An image with copy-move forgery contains two or more fragments with similar content where one or more distinct fragments are copied and pasted to one or more places in the same image to hide important information. The copied regions are called duplicates. The forgery is usually harder to detect when the copied content is transformed using a pre-processing

© Springer International Publishing AG 2017
A. Piva et al. (Eds.): TIWDC 2017, CCIS 766, pp. 73–83, 2017.
DOI: 10.1007/978-3-319-67639-5_7

procedure such as contrast enhancement, noise addition, JPEG compression or affine transform (rotation and scaling) to make it fit the surrounding image area. The purpose of these modifications is to make the tampering not visible.

Two main approaches to copy-move detection are usually used. The first one concerns analysis of all host image pixels (dense-field approach), whereas the second one (keypoint-based approach) is based on keypoints analysis. A small set of pixels is selected from the host image while using the keypoint-based approach [3–5]. This approach is faster in comparison with entire image analysis. Pan et al. proposed the first keypoint-based algorithm based on Scale Invariant Feature Transform (SIFT) in 2010 [4]. It was used to extract the keypoints to guarantee robustness against affine transformations. Other local image descriptors like SURF [5] have also been considered for keypoint-based copy-move detection algorithm development. A survey provided by Christlein et al. [6] showed performance results for keypoint-based approaches. It was stated that the main problem of this approach is considerably low detection accuracy for duplicates containing smooth regions.

However, the benchmarking paper [6] also showed high performance for the dense-field approach. One of the main problems of this approach is high computational complexity due to sliding window analysis scheme. To solve it researchers use block-based analysis scheme (overlapping windows) [6–14]. The second problem, which is a background of many papers, is robustness to transformations. In the existing block-based copy-move detection algorithms Discrete Cosine Transform (DCT) [7], Principal Component Analysis (PCA) [8], Wavelet [9], SVD [10], or Histogram of Orientated Gradients (HOG) [11] are applied for features extraction to improve the robustness. Fridrich et al. [12] used quantized DCT coefficients as feature vectors. Wu et al. [13] proposed Fourier-Mellin Transform to calculate the block features resulting in scale invariance. A. Kuznetsov and V. Myasnikov [14] proposed a copy-move detection algorithm based on binary gradient contours. It showed high evaluation speed and accuracy, but no affine transform robustness was stated. Consequently, the experimental study showed that dense-field approach is more reliable than the keypoint-based approach.

The above comparison compels to focus on development an algorithm corresponding to the dense-field approach. In this paper, we propose a novel copy-move detection algorithm based on Geometric Local Binary Pattern (GLBP), proposed by S.A. Orjuela Vargas et al. [15]. It was used for texture classification and showed its robustness to different transformations. For copy-move detection purposes these features show extremely high detection accuracy for a wide range of transformations parameters. We use GLBP-based features in the following three-step copy-move detection scheme: feature extraction, feature matching and post-processing.

In Sect. 2 we briefly describe the three-step copy-move detection scheme. GLBP feature extraction process is presented in Sect. 3. In Sect. 4 we carry out a detailed investigation of the proposed algorithm robustness to contrast enhancement, JPEG compression, additive noise, affine transform. Conclusions are drawn in Sect. 5.

2   Copy-Move Detection Scheme

2.1   Feature Extraction

Let f be a host image with size $N_1 \times N_2$, $W_{k,l}$ be a processing block with size $M_1 \times M_2$. Let $t \in \mathbf{N}$ be the block $W_{k,l}$ shift. The number of blocks where features are extracted is calculated as follows:

$$L = \left(\left\lfloor \frac{N_1 - M_1}{s} \right\rfloor + 1 \right) \cdot \left(\left\lfloor \frac{N_2 - M_2}{s} \right\rfloor + 1 \right).$$

One Q-dimensional feature vector $\mathbf{h} \in \mathbf{R}^Q$ corresponds to one block $W_{k,l}$. Features are extracted using one of the algorithms [7–13] and are stored column-wise in the following matrix $\mathbf{FM}^{L \times Q} = [\mathbf{h}_0, \ldots, \mathbf{h}_{L-1}]^T$.

2.2   Feature Matching

The second step of the algorithm concerns nearest features matching. The obvious way to find the nearest neighbors is a pairwise comparison of all features, which is computationally inefficient ($O(N^2)$). To improve the speed of nearest features matching we use one of the binary search tree structures – k-d tree.

We use $\mathbf{FM}^{L \times Q}$ to generate the tree with Matlab k-d tree implementation – createns. There is used Euclidean distance as distance measure. The number of the nearest neighbors K was set to 8. Matched features indexes are stored in the matrix $\mathbf{D}^{L \times K}$, created at the end of tree constructing procedure. Its elements $d_{ij} = \arg(\mathbf{h}_{d_{ij}}), d_{ij} \in \mathbf{N}^+_{[0,L-1]}/\{i\}$ correspond to the indexes of matched features that are the nearest neighbors to $\mathbf{h}_i$.

2.3   Post-processing

The last step of the copy-move detection scheme is implemented to filter the results of features matching from false positives. During this step, we select such only features pairs $(\mathbf{h}_i, \mathbf{h}_j)$, which meet the following conditions:

1. $\forall i \in [0, L-1], j \in [0, Q-1], \|\mathbf{h}_i - \mathbf{h}_{d_{ij}}\| \leq 1$, where $\|\bullet\|$ is a Euclid norm;
2. $\forall i \in [0, L-1], j \in [0, Q-1], d(\mathbf{h}_i, \mathbf{h}_{d_{ij}}) \geq 10$, where $d(\mathbf{h}_i, \mathbf{h}_j)$ is a distance between $\mathbf{h}_i$ and $\mathbf{h}_j$.

For each pair meeting these constraints we calculate the difference between the corresponding block positions and their frequency. The most frequently occurred features are marked as copy-move in the result image.

3 Geometric Local Binary Pattern

Local Binary Pattern (LBP) [16] is a well-known and commonly used local feature for texture classification. In practice, LBP operator combines statistical and structural properties of texture analysis, and enables to construct local image descriptors. To calculate LBP code, a 3×3 window is usually used: 8 values are compared with the central pixel and a sequence of 8 bits is assigned to the center pixel (see Fig. 1).

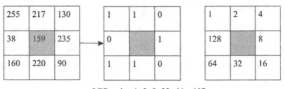

LBP code - 1+2+8+32+64 = 107

Fig. 1. LBP code calculation scheme.

It was proposed earlier [16], that such transform is robust to intensity variations, but sensitive to additive noise and cannot be applied to classify affine transformed textures. These problems make LBP useless for transformed copy-move detection. To avoid LBP usage limitations there were proposed a lot of modified patterns, like Uniform LBP [17], Robust LBP [18], Rotation Invariant Uniform LBP [19], etc.

The GLBP technique [15] used for feature extraction in this paper characterizes changes of intensities for a pixel neighborhood by evaluating neighboring points on circles with different radii around the center pixel (see Fig. 2). We take 7×7 neighborhood of a pixel and calculate intensities of points lying on three circles with radii: $r_1 = 0.7071$, $r_2 = 1.7725$, and $r_3 = 3.0536$. These points are equally spaced by an angle $2\pi/N$, $N \in \{4, 12, 20\}$. Consequently, we have 36 interpolated points, which values will be used further to compute GLBP codes.

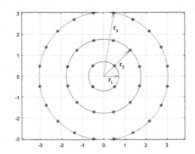

Fig. 2. 36 interpolated points for GLBP

The intensity of every interpolated point is computed through bilinear interpolation. If we consider calculating the intensity value of point $P(x,y)$ in Fig. 3, we use the following equation:

$$f_P = (1-x \quad x) \cdot \begin{pmatrix} f_{i,j} & f_{i,j+1} \\ f_{i+1,j} & f_{i+1,j+1} \end{pmatrix} \cdot \begin{pmatrix} 1-y \\ y \end{pmatrix},$$

where $x, y \in [0,1]$ are Cartesian coordinates within 2×2 neighborhood of $P(x,y)$. The coordinates (x,y) are calculated as follows:

$$x = r_i \cdot \cos((\pi + 2\pi n)/N), y = r_i \cdot \sin((\pi + 2\pi n)/N),$$

where $n \in [0, N-1]$, $i = 1...3$.

Fig. 3. Interpolation window for $P(x, y)$.

When all the locations and intensity values of the interpolated points are calculated, we proceed to GLBP code evaluation. First, the intensity values of the points are compared. The intensity value of every point is compared to the intensity value of the nearest neighbor on an inner circle. The intensity value of a point of the circle with radius r_1 is compared to the intensity value of the center pixel. Some points on the circle with radius r_3 are compared to the average of the intensity values of their two nearest neighbors. Figure 4 shows circle points comparison pattern: the arrows show points to compare.

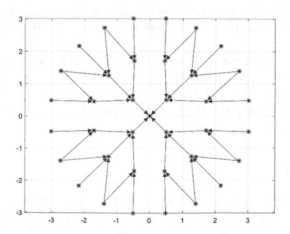

Fig. 4. Intensity values comparison pattern.

Second, we form the matrix $\mathbf{B}^{6\times6}$ that contains comparison results of intensity values. Matrix element is assigned one if the corresponding point intensity value is bigger than the intensity value to which it is compared, otherwise it is assigned zero. The bit value of comparison result is computed as follows:

$$I(P_i, P_j) = \begin{cases} 1, & f_{P_i} < f_{P_j}, \\ 0, & otherwise. \end{cases}$$

Thus, the bit matrix $\mathbf{B}^{6\times6}$ is as follows:

$$\mathbf{B} = \begin{pmatrix} B_3 & B_3 & B_3 & B_3 & B_3 & B_3 \\ B_3 & B_2 & B_2 & B_2 & B_2 & B_3 \\ B_3 & B_2 & B_1 & B_1 & B_2 & B_3 \\ B_3 & B_2 & B_1 & B_1 & B_2 & B_3 \\ B_3 & B_2 & B_2 & B_2 & B_2 & B_3 \\ B_3 & B_3 & B_3 & B_3 & B_3 & B_3 \end{pmatrix}.$$

Finally, using these bit values, we calculate 8 6-bit sequences according to the scheme on Fig. 5 and form a 8×6 bit matrix, which is called the GLBP code.

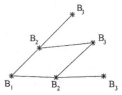

Fig. 5. Bit sequence generating scheme.

Referring to the feature extraction step of the copy-move detection algorithm (Sect. 2.1), for every block $W_{k,l}$ we have an array of $M_1 \cdot M_2$ 48-bit GLBP codes, that can be used to form a feature vector for the corresponding image location. In other words, every analyzed host image is represented by six 8bit images forming a GLBP code for every pixel.

We propose to use a histogram with 256 bins as a feature vector $\mathbf{h}_i \in \mathbf{N}^{256}, i \in [0, L-1]$ of an image block $W_{k,l}$. The histogram is generated using the following two-step procedure: divide 48-bit GLBP code into six 8bit values and calculate their frequency within the block $W_{k,l}$. This feature adds robustness to affine transform of the block.

4   Experiments

To carry out research we used a standard PC (Intel Core i5-3470 3.2 GHz, 8 GB RAM). We then selected 10 grayscale images with size 512×512 and generated forgeries using a self-developed automatic copy-move generation procedure. There were used five types of transforms to create copy-move regions: linear contrast enhancement, JPEG compression, additive noise, rotation and scale.

Four sets of test images were constructed with different copy moved region's size, 48×48, 64×64, 96×96, and 128×128. In each set, the images were forged by copying a square region at a random location and pasting it to a random non-overlapping position in the same image. There were created 250 forgeries in a set: 25 images for each of the 10 initial images (5 images for each transform type), which were further analyzed using the proposed detection algorithm.

To evaluate the performance of the proposed copy-move forgery detection method *Precision (p)* and *Recall (r)* measures were used. They are calculated using true positive (TP), false positive (FP) and false negative (FN) values:

$$p = \frac{TP}{TP + FP}, r = \frac{TP}{TP + FN}.$$

We split our experiments in a series of separate evaluations, depending on the transform used to change a duplicate. We start with contrast enhancement as the simplest one to detect. Subsequent experiments examine copy-move forgeries changed with JPEG compression, additive noise, rotation and scaling of the copied region.

Further we compare the proposed solution based on GLBP features mainly with copy-move detection algorithms based on other LBP-based features and with the leading dense-field approaches, provided in [6]. It should be mentioned that the proposed GLBP features have significantly less computational complexity than many other existing features (PCA, DCT, Zernike, etc.).

4.1 Contrast Enhancement

When the copied region is pasted to the image location that differs in neighboring contrast, one should use contrast enhancement techniques to make copy-move unable to detect by an expert. There are a lot of contrast enhancement methods: linear enhancement, histogram equalization, etc. We selected the first one to change the contrast of a duplicate, because we can modify its parameters. Linear enhancement of an image is evaluated using 2 coefficients: multiplicative (a) and additive (b). In Fig. 6

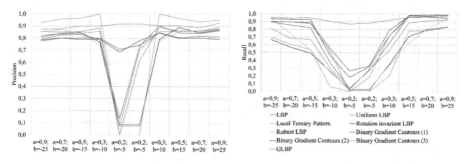

Fig. 6. Experimental results for contrast enhancement

the results for precision and recall measures are provided for different LBP-based features and the proposed GLBP-based features.

The proposed copy-move solution based on GLBP features shows high Precision and Recall values for low values of a. Most of other solutions show extremely low values of quality measures for low multiplicative parameter values.

4.2   JPEG Compression

Another popular transform for the copied region disturbance is its JPEG compression. The quality coefficient Q varies between 20 and 95 in steps of 5. For low quality factors Precision and Recall measures take high values for Binary Gradient Contours, but they are significantly higher for GLBP (see Fig. 7). Comparing with the dense-field approaches from [6] GLBP-based approach shows significantly higher Precision and Recall for all the range of Q, especially for low factor values $Q \leq 40$.

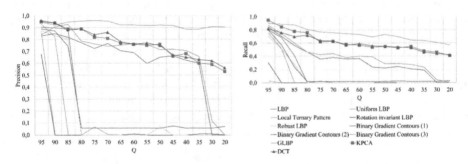

Fig. 7. Experimental results for JPEG compression.

4.3   Additive Noise

We added zero-mean Gaussian noise with standard deviation (STD) between 0.02 and 0.1, in steps of 0.02, to the pasted regions. It can be clearly seen from Fig. 8 that GLBP features show higher Precision and Recall values in comparison with other LBP-based features. If we compare the results of the proposed solution with provided in [6], our

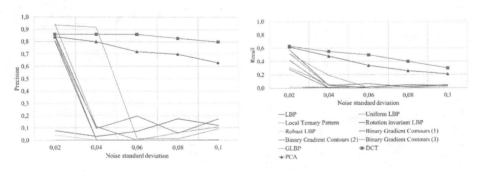

Fig. 8. Experimental results for additive noise.

method has comparable values for $STD \leq 0.04$ and obviously lower p and r values for $STD > 0.04$, because LBP-based features are not robust to noise with high STD. It ought to be noted, that using high values of noise STD lead to simple expert detection of transformed regions and can be rarely applicable.

4.4 Rotation

We rotated the copied region between $1°$ and $15°$, as is often the case in real-world image manipulations. Precision and Recall values for all the LBP-based algorithms remain relatively stable with slight increase at $15°$ for GLBP-based approach (see Fig. 9). In the interval of angle change GLBP-based approach shows similar Precision results to the leading approaches, provided in [6] (Zernike, Bravo and Luo features). Although the proposed solution showed higher Recall values in comparison with most of the dense-field approaches, provided in [6], losing only to Zernike in the defined angle range.

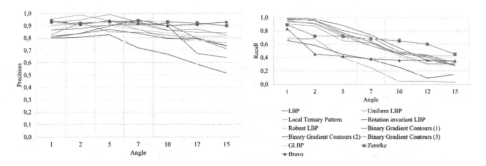

Fig. 9. Experimental results for rotation transform.

4.5 Scaling

We conducted an experiment where the inserted region was rescaled between 0.75 and 1.25 of its original size. Figure 10 shows the results of this experiment. GLBP-based approach remains stable in Precision even for high up- and down- scaling and shows

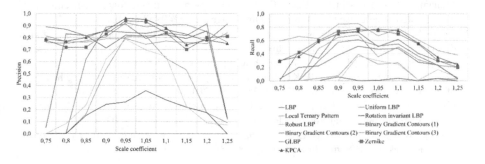

Fig. 10. Experimental results for scale transform.

considerable Recall values for all the range of scaling coefficient. As to the dense-field approaches from [6], GLBP-based solution shows comparable Precision values for the range of scale change and significantly higher Recall values for scaling more than 15%.

5 Conclusion

In this paper, we proposed a copy-move detection algorithm based on the GLBP features. The developed solution showed considerable increase in Precision and Recall values in comparison with other LBP-based features for wide ranges of transform parameters. Moreover, we compared our results with state-of-the art solutions from V. Christlein et al. survey [6]. We could gain better performance for duplicates transformed with JPEG compression, rotation and scale. Further we will carry out research in developing an algorithm using fusion of different LBP-based features to increase performance results, because some experiments showed better performance for Binary Gradient Contours features for certain transform parameters ranges.

References

1. https://www.brandwatch.com/blog/47-facebook-statistics-2016/
2. https://www.brandwatch.com/blog/37-instagram-stats-2016/
3. Bayram, S., Sencar, H.T., Memon, N.: An efficient and robust method for detecting copy-move forgery. In: Proceedings of the IEEE International Conference on Acoustics, Speech and Signal Processing, pp. 1053–1056 (2009)
4. Bravo-Solorio, S., Nandi, A.K.: Exposing postprocessed copy–paste forgeries through transform-invariant features. IEEE Trans. Inf. Forensics Secur. **7**, 1018–1028 (2012)
5. Cao, Y., Gao, T., Fan, L., Yang, Q.: A robust detection algorithm for copy-move forgery in digital images. Forensic Sci. Int. **214**, 33–43 (2012)
6. Christlein, V., Riess, C., Jordan, J., Riess, C., Angelopoulou, E.: An evaluation of popular copy-move forgery detection approaches. IEEE Trans. Inf. Forensics Secur. **7**, 1841–1854 (2012)
7. Huang, Y., Lu, W., Sun, W., Long, D.: Improved DCT-based detection of copy-move forgery in images. Forensic Sci. Int. **206**, 178–184 (2011)
8. Mahdian, B., Saic, S.: Detection of copy–move forgery using a method based on blur moment invariants. Forensic Sci. Int. **171**, 180–189 (2007)
9. Muhammad, G., Hussain, M., Bebis, G.: Passive copy move image forgery detection using undecimated dyadic wavelet transform. Digit. Investig. **9**, 49–57 (2012)
10. Kang, X., Wei, S.: Identifying tampered regions using singular value decomposition in digital image forensics. In: Proceedings of the 2008 IEEE International Conference on Computer Science and Software Engineering, pp. 926–930 (2008)
11. Lee, J.C., Chang, C.P., Chen, W.K.: Detection of copy–move image forgery using histogram of orientated gradients. Inf. Sci. **321**(C), 250–262 (2015)
12. Fridrich, J., Soukal, D., Lukáš, J.: Detection of copy-move forgery in digital images. In: Proceedings of the Digital Forensic Research Workshop. Citeseer (2003)
13. Wu, Q., Wang, S., Zhang, X.: Log-polar based scheme for revealing duplicated regions in digital images. IEEE Signal Process. Lett. **18**, 559–562 (2011)

14. Kuznetsov, A., Myasnikov, V.: A copy-move detection algorithm using binary gradient contours. In: Campilho, A., Karray, F. (eds.) ICIAR 2016. LNCS, vol. 9730, pp. 349–357. Springer, Cham (2016). doi:10.1007/978-3-319-41501-7_40

15. Orjuela Vargas, S.A., Yañez Puentes, J.P., Philips, W.: The geometric local textural patterns (GLTP). In: Brahnam, S., Jain, L., Nanni, L., Lumini, A. (eds.) Local Binary Patterns: New Variants and Applications. Studies in Computational Intelligence, vol. 506. Springer, Heidelberg (2014). doi:10.1007/978-3-642-39289-4_4

16. Wang, L., He, D.-C.: Texture classification using texture spectrum. Pattern Recogn. **23**(8), 905–910 (1990)

17. Arasteh, S., Hung, C.-C.: Color and texture image segmentation using uniform local binary patterns. Mach. Graph. Vis. **15**(3–4), 265–274 (2006)

18. Ren, J., Jiang, X., Yuan, J.: Noise-resistant local binary pattern with an embedded error-correction mechanism. IEEE Trans. Image Process. **22**(10), 4049–4060 (2013)

19. Ojala, T., Pietikinen, M., Menp, T.: Multiresolution grayscale and rotation invariant texture classification with local binary patterns. IEEE Trans. Pattern Anal. Mach. Intell. **24**(7), 971–987 (2002)

A Dataset for Forensic Analysis of Videos in the Wild

Dasara Shullani[1]([✉]), Omar Al Shaya[1,3], Massimo Iuliani[1,2], Marco Fontani[1,2], and Alessandro Piva[1,2]

[1] Department of Information Engineering, University of Florence, Florence, Italy
dasara.shullani@unifi.it
[2] FORLAB, Multimedia Forensics Laboratory, PIN Scrl, Prato, Italy
[3] Department of Electronic Media, Saudi Electronic University, Riyadh, Saudi Arabia
https://iapp.dinfo.unifi.it/

Abstract. The Multimedia Forensics community has developed a wide variety of tools for investigating the processing history of digital videos. One of the main problems, however, is the lack of benchmark datasets allowing to evaluate tools performance on a common reference. In fact, contrarily to the case of image forensics, only a few datasets exist for video forensics, that are limited in size and outdated when compared to today's real-world scenario (e.g., they contain videos at very low resolution, captured with outdated camcorders, compressed with legacy encoders, etc.). In this paper, we propose a novel dataset made of 622 native videos, most of which in FullHD resolution, captured with 35 different portable devices, belonging to 11 manufacturers and running iOS, Android and Windows Phone OS. Videos have been captured in three different scenarios (indoor, outdoor, flat-field), and with three different kinds of motion (move, still, panrot). Since videos are increasingly shared through social media platforms, we also provide the YouTube version of most videos. Finally, in order to avoid that the proposed dataset becomes outdated in a few moths, we propose a mobile application (MOSES) that allows the acquisition of video contents from recent iOS and Android devices along with their metadata. In this way, the dataset can grow in the future and remain up-to-date.

Keywords: Dataset · Video forensics · Multimedia forensics · Source identification · Social media platforms

1 Introduction

In the last decades, digital videos have become the preferred means to share information in many fields. In the wild world of web, they also invaded the social media platforms, since they allow to easily upload videos directly from portable devices. Given their digital nature, these data also convey several information related to their life cycle (e.g., source device, processing they have been subjected to), that may become relevant when videos are involved in a crime.

© Springer International Publishing AG 2017
A. Piva et al. (Eds.): TIWDC 2017, CCIS 766, pp. 84–94, 2017.
DOI: 10.1007/978-3-319-67639-5_8

During the years, Multimedia Forensics (MF) developed thus solutions for investigating visual data to determine information about their life cycle [9].

Generally, the developed techniques need to be tested on datasets freely available and shared among the community in order to properly assess their performance. From this point of view, a great effort has been made on the image side, especially to study one of the most promising image forensic task, i.e., source device identification. On the contrary, only few video datasets were provided by the forensic community and all of them are outdated. Indeed, today most videos are acquired with modern portable devices, that keep updating every year. This imposes the need of a new dataset that, besides containing an already large and heterogeneous set of videos, is designed to grow in time.

In this paper[1], we present a new video dataset comprising 35 modern smartphones/tablets belonging to 11 different brands: Apple, Asus, Huawei, Lenovo, LG electronics, Microsoft, OnePlus, Samsung, Sony, Wiko and Xiaomi. We also provide the YouTube version of most videos, so to facilitate testing forensic tools on contents that were shared through a common social media platform. Finally, we present the MOSES smartphone application, designed to allow people to contribute to the proposed dataset by uploading videos from their own device.

The remaining part of the paper is organized as follows: Sect. 2 reviews existing datasets for image and video forensics; in Sect. 3 we present the main features of the proposed video dataset; in Sect. 4 we show, as a case study, the application of the dataset to video source identification; Sect. 5 describes the MOSES application; finally, Sect. 6 draws some final remarks and concludes the paper.

2   State of the Art

In the Multimedia Forensic field a small amount of datasets were presented and used over the years, mainly focused on images. The UCID [11] dataset was one of the first to be used in this research community. It is composed of 1338 TIFF images in low resolution, namely 512×384 pixels, with the goal to evaluate image retrieval techniques.

The Dresden Image Database [5,6], published in 2010, is the most used dataset for source identification benchmarking, since it collects high resolution images (from 4352×3264 to 3072×2304 pixels) belonging to 73 devices selected from 25 camera models of diverse brands and prices. Each camera was set to acquire images at the maximum resolution possible using the highest JPEG quality; if the device allowed it, also the unprocessed image was stored. In the design of Dresden Image Database, different scenes where taken into account, such as indoor and outdoor images.

The RAw ImageS datasEt - RAISE [4] gave another important contribution to the community since it collects 8156 raw and compressed images comprising technical details and semantic content. The images were acquired with three Nikon cameras, the D40, D90 and D7000, setted to capture high resolution

---

[1] The dataset and MOSES are available online at [1].

images at 6M, 12M and 16M pixels. Then, each image was labelled with one of the following categories, depending on the depicted content: outdoor, indoor, landscape, nature, people, objects and buildings.

Other datasets were published, such as the one from the REWIND project [12] that acquired 200 uncompressed images belonging to the Nikon D60 camera, but none of them take into consideration the source identification problem.

In the video front, very few datasets are well established for forensic purposes. This is probably due to the continuous evolution of technologies, especially in the field of portable devices. In 2012, the University of Surrey created the SULFA database [10], a collection of 150 videos with low resolution, namely 320 × 240 pixels, and 10 s duration. The SULFA dataset purpose is to make it possible to test tools for the localization of cloned regions. Video contents were acquired using three camcorders: the Canon SX220, the Nikon S3000 and the Fujifilm S2800HD; then, forged videos were created using Adobe software.

The latest video dataset, to the best of our knowledge, is by Al Sanjary et al. [2], a 33 video database of 16 s downloaded from the YouTube platform. The YouTube contents were manipulated by copy-move, splicing and swapping, and compared to the unaltered downloaded version. The main issue with the Al Sanjary et al. contribution is the absence of knowledge on the devices used in the dataset and their features.

Given this scenario, we believe there is the need of a comprehensive database for video analysis that takes into account mobile devices, both smartphones and tablets, and provides videos at native resolution. Our work fills this gap producing a dataset of videos coming from 35 hand-held devices belonging to 11 manufacturers and running iOS, Android and Windows Phone OS. Each video was captured in specific scenarios, such as indoor, outdoor or flat scenes, and subsequently uploaded to the YouTube platform and downloaded at the maximum resolution available. The proposed Dataset comprises 622 native videos, most of which in FullHD resolution, and 587 videos exchanged through YouTube, resulting in a total of 1209 videos. In addition to that, we developed a mobile application (MOSES) to collect videos from iOS and Android devices, that enables the acquisition of video contents from recent device releases along with their metadata.

3   The Dataset

Our Dataset comprises 35 devices belonging to the following brands: Apple, Asus, Huawei, Lenovo, LG electronics, Microsoft, Samsung, Sony, OnePlus, Wiko, Xiaomi. These devices had installed, at the time of the acquisition, the Android operating system with version from 5.x to 7.x, or the IOS operating system with version from 7.x to 10.x, or the Windows Phone OS system. As Table 1 shows, we included devices from both high- and low-end prices, in order to provide a more heterogeneous benchmark. For each device, we collected at least 10 videos using the rear-camera at the maximum resolution possible[2], resulting in 24 devices with FullHD resolution, 9 with HD resolution and 2 with 480p resolution. Almost all acquired videos have a duration greater than 60 s, with the exception of a few videos belonging to the iPhone 5c in D5 and the Samsung Galaxy S5 in D27, that are 25-seconds long.

The video acquisition procedure was designed to capture in landscape mode, *indoor* scenarios, such as halls or rooms; *outdoor* scenarios, such as gardens or streets; and *flat* scenarios, such as blank walls or skies. Each scenario was captured with three different motion types: *still*, *move* and *pan-rot*. The *still* case features videos without any movement, apart from small shakes due to hand-acquisition. The *move* case features videos with a walking-movement, since the person that is acquiring the video is asked to walk while recording. The last case, that is the *pan-rot* movement, features a combination of pan-movement and rotation of the device, while the person stands still. Some frames of the available videos are represented in Fig. 1.

Fig. 1. Video frame samples belonging to the presented Dataset.

In a forensic perspective, it is extremely interesting to understand the processing undergone by native contents when they are exchanged through social-media platforms. Therefore, in addition to the native contents described so far, the presented Dataset includes a subset of videos passed through YouTube. To do so, we created a YouTube account and uploaded into a playlist all the collected videos for each device in the Dataset using the *Public flag*. The downloading process was carried out by the *youtube-dl*[3] command-line free software, which is able to download a whole playlist but also single videos. For each device the related playlist was downloaded by selecting the best quality possible, that is done by specifying the following parameter: *-f 137+140/bestvideo+bestaudio* in *youtube-dl*.

---

[2] Note that for Asus device D23, all videos were acquired without the highest resolution possible.

[3] youtube-dl v2017.03.10 rg3.github.io/youtube-dl/.

Table 1. Devices represented in the presented Dataset.

Manufacturer	Model	ID	Video resolution	#Videos
Apple	iPad 2	D13	1280 × 720	16
Apple	iPad mini	D20	1920 × 1080	16
Apple	iPhone 4	D9	1280 × 720	19
Apple	iPhone 4S	D2	1920 × 1080	13
Apple	iPhone 4S	D10	1920 × 1080	15
Apple	iPhone 5	D29	1920 × 1080	19
Apple	iPhone 5	D34	1920 × 1080	18
Apple	iPhone 5c	D5	1920 × 1080	19
Apple	iPhone 5c	D14	1920 × 1080	19
Apple	iPhone 5c	D18	1920 × 1080	13
Apple	iPhone 6	D6	1920 × 1080	15
Apple	iPhone 6	D15	1920 × 1080	18
Apple	iPhone 6 Plus	D19	1920 × 1080	19
Asus	Z00ED	D23*	640 × 480*	19*
Huawei	Ascend G6-U10	D33	1280 × 720	18
Huawei	Honor 5C NEM-L51	D30	1920 × 1080	19
Huawei	P8 GRA-L09	D28	1920 × 1080	19
Huawei	P9 EVA-L09	D3	1920 × 1080	19
Huawei	P9 Lite VNS-L31	D16	1920 × 1080	19
Lenovo	Lenovo P70-A	D7	1280 × 720	19
LG electronics	D290	D4	800 × 480	19
Microsoft	Lumia 640 LTE	D17	1920 × 1080	10
OnePlus	A3000	D25	1920 × 1080	19
OnePlus	A3003	D32	1920 × 1080	19
Samsung	Galaxy S III Mini GT-I8190	D26	1280 × 720	16
Samsung	Galaxy S III Mini GT-I8190N	D1	1280 × 720	16
Samsung	Galaxy S3 GT-I9300	D11	1920 × 1080	19
Samsung	Galaxy S4 Mini GT-I9195	D31	1920 × 1080	19
Samsung	Galaxy S5 SM-G900F	D27	1920 × 1080	19
Samsung	Galaxy Tab 3 GT-P5210	D8	1280 × 720	34
Samsung	Galaxy Tab A SM-T555	D35	1280 × 720	16
Samsung	Galaxy Trend Plus GT-S7580	D22	1280 × 720	16
Sony	Xperia Z1 Compact D5503	D12	1920 × 1080	19
Wiko	Ridge 4G	D21	1920 × 1080	19
Xiaomi	Redmi Note 3	D24	1920 × 1080	19

4   Case Study: Video Source Identification

In this section, we show how the proposed Dataset can be used as a benchmark for source device identification based on the camera sensor pattern noise, that is the most promising video source identification technique in the state of the art [8]. The source identification workflow is based on three steps:

- The camera fingerprint $\mathbf{K}$ is estimated from N video frames of a reference video. To do so, a denoising filter [8], is applied to each frame and the noise residuals $\mathbf{W}^{(1)}, \ldots, \mathbf{W}^{(N)}$ are obtained as the difference between each frame and its denoised version. Then the camera fingerprint estimation $\widetilde{\mathbf{K}}$ is derived by the maximum likelihood estimator [3]:

$$\widetilde{\mathbf{K}} = \frac{\sum_{i=1}^{N} \mathbf{W}^{(i)} \mathbf{I}^{(i)}}{\sum_{i=1}^{N} (\mathbf{I}^{(i)})^2}. \tag{1}$$

- given a query video, its fingerprint is estimated in the same way by the available video frames.
- The estimated reference and query pattern are compared based on the Peak to Correlation Energy (PCE) measure and a decision is taken based on a threshold [7]: if the PCE overcomes the threshold, then it is decided that the query video belongs to the reference camera.

The literature about source identification based on sensor pattern noise tells that, during reference estimation, it is better to use flat-field images/videos, so to facilitate separating the noise from the image content. Moreover, it has been demonstrated that this forensic technique remains reliable even when the query pattern is extracted from a compressed or scaled content. Interestingly, uploading and downloading a video from YouTube actually causes a (quite aggressive) re-compression. Thus, given the availability in the proposed dataset of the same video contents, both in their native and YouTube versions, we compared the video source identification performance in two cases:

1. the reference is estimated from native flat field videos and tested against generic videos;
2. the reference is estimated from native flat field video and tested against YouTube videos.

For each device, we used a video from the *flat, panrot* category to estimate the reference, while videos from all categories and motion types were used as queries. For each video, the noise pattern is estimated using the first 100 frames. We considered for each device all available matching cases (videos from the same device) and the same number of mismatching cases (videos randomly chosen from other devices).

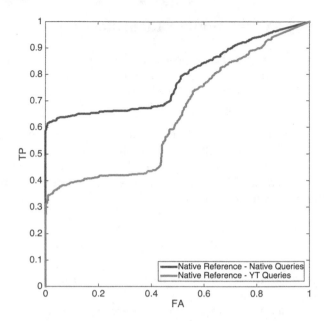

Fig. 2. (Best viewed in colors) The video source identification performance on Native and YouTube videos (in blue and red respectively) (Color figure online)

The achieved results are reported in Fig. 2 with a Receiver Operating Characteristic (ROC) curve, where true and false positive rates are compared at varying thresholds. Such results allow us to quantify the performance drop of the techniques when YouTube compression is involved in the process. Furthermore, we can clearly notice that the performance are very far from what we know from the state of the art, where this technology is known to be extremely effective, especially on native videos. We believe this is mainly due to the fact that several recent devices are equipped with in-camera digital stabilization, that impacts negatively the fingerprints alignment during the noise pattern estimation. Indeed, if we repeat the experiment excluding digitally stabilized videos as in Fig. 3, performance improve significantly both in the native and YouTube cases. The impact of digital stabilization is simply neglected in several papers, where digitally stabilized videos are just excluded, or their number in the dataset is limited so that their impact on the performance can be slightly noticed. It is then needed in the future to take into account this effect of the video acquisition process to correctly identify the video source device.

In Table 2 we briefly summarize the achieved AUC values as an overall index to measure the performance[4].

---

[4] AUC is the area under the curve. Usually its values span the [0.5, 1] interval, where 0.5 is associated to a random-guess detector, while 1 denotes a detector that behaves perfectly on the tested dataset.

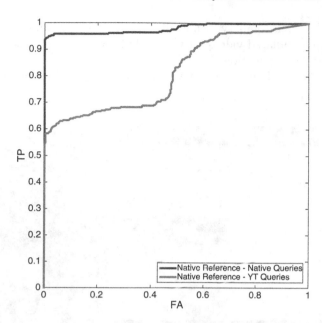

Fig. 3. (Best viewed in colors) The video source identification performance on Native and YouTube videos (in blue and red respectively), limiting the analysis to non-stabilized videos (Color figure online)

5 MOSES Mobile Application

MOSES allows everyone with a smart device, both Android- and iOS- based, to contribute to the proposed Dataset; in Fig. 4 we present some screenshots from the Android version. The end-user can record a video at default settings, under different scenarios and motions, then upload it to our servers. Each acquisition has a maximum duration of 30 s, since we have to consider the user bandwidth and storage limits, despite that, we considered it sufficient since most mobile devices record videos at a frame rate of 30 fps, resulting in the availability of video sequences composed by 900 frames. In addition, MOSES collects further information available from the camera, that are related to the source and the video file format. It is important to notice that the acquisition process is carried out by MOSES using the *native-camera application* of each device, while uploading

Table 2. Dataset paths and AUC values for video source identification test.

Reference	Test	AUC	
		All videos	Unstab. videos
Native flat-field	All natives	0.79	0.98
Native flat-field	All YouTube	0.64	0.81

videos from the device gallery is not allowed. This choice aims at preventing the upload of manipulated videos, or videos that have not been captured by the device running the application.

In Subsect. 5.1 we describe the main features of the Android implementation of MOSES.

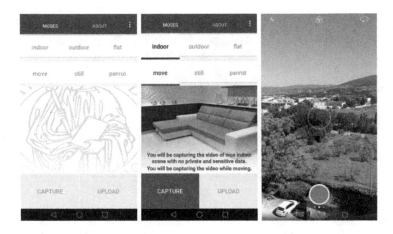

Fig. 4. The Android interface for MOSES.

5.1 Android Implementation

When MOSES starts, the user selects one of these three types of scenarios: indoor, outdoor or flat; then, he/she selects the kind of motion he/she will perform: move, still, or panrot; finally the user starts the acquisition by pressing the RECORD button. This button calls the native camera application, which can be different between distinct devices or even distinct operating systems. For some devices, you are able to change a few settings of the recording, such as the video stabilization on D16 in Table 1. After 30-seconds the recording stops and the user can choose to either cancel or upload it. If the latter is chosen, the user presses the UPLOAD button in order to send the content via FTP to our servers, without any further processing.

This application stores two files: the acquired video, and an XML file, as in Listing 1.1, which is obtained by analysing the video metadata by means of the MediaMetadataRetriever class[5] provided by Android.

The information collected from each video are related to the device itself, like the Manufacturer, obtained from android.os.Build.MANUFACTURER, the Operating System, obtained from android.os.Build.VERSION, and the Model of the device through android.os.Build.MODEL.

---

[5] https://developer.android.com/reference/android/media/MediaMetadataRetriever.
html.

Then, we recover video characteristics such as the frame rate in frame/s from the METADATA_KEY_CAPTURE_FRAMERATE field; the resolution from the height and width fields: METADATA_KEY_VIDEO_HEIGHT and METADATA_KEY_VIDEO_WIDTH. The duration in seconds of the acquired video using METADATA_KEY_DURATION and the rotation of the display during the acquisition (0-landscape or 90-portrait) from METADATA_KEY_VIDEO_ROTATION.

Moreover, we collect the acquisition timestamp and the creation timestamp: the former refers to the beginning of the recording and the latter refers to the instant in which the video is stored on the device. The date is in format yyyymmdd followed by hhmmss and is provided by the METADATA_KEY_DATE field for the creation timestamp and by the java.utils.Calendar class for the acquisition timestamp. Depending on the device availability and enabled permission, we store the device location via GPS, in Latitude and Longitude format, as provided by the LocationManager class.

Another feature of interest is the video stabilization, that is a recent improvement on handhandled devices, and it is usually software-based and provides less shaky video. It is extracted from the *Camera Characteristics* class accessing the field CONTROL_VIDEO_STABILIZATION_MODE.

In addition to the device and video main features, the user selection is also taken into account and stored in the XML file; indeed we use the <scene> and <movement> tags to specify the main characteristics of the acquired content, according to the description given in Sect. 3.

Listing 1.1. An example of XML metadata from a video acquired with MOSES in the Android version.

```xml
<track>
    ...
    <bitRate>5255207</bitRate>
    <captureTime>20170525214034</captureTime>
    ...
    <dateCreated>20170525T194047.000Z</dateCreated>
    <device>
        <brand>Lenovo</brand>
        <device>P70-A</device>
        <deviceID>865897020799766</deviceID>
        <display>P70-A_S138_151020_16G_L_ROW</display>
        <manufacturer>LENOVO</manufacturer>
        <model>Lenovo P70-A</model>
        <os>
            <name>LOLLIPOP_MR1</name>
            <release>5.1</release>
            <sdk>22</sdk>
        </os>
        <product>P70-A</product>
        <user>unknown</user>
    </device>
    <duration>5</duration>
    <frameRate>0.0</frameRate>
    ...
    <hasAudio>yes</hasAudio>
    <hasVideo>yes</hasVideo>
    <height>720</height>
    <location>43.7937419,11.2304078</location>
    <mimeType>video/mp4</mimeType>
    ...
    <resolution>921600</resolution>
    <rotation>90</rotation>
    <scene>indoor</scene>
    <movement>flat</movement>
    <timeSubdivision>00:00:05</timeSubdivision>
    <title>865897020799766201705252214034_indoor</title>
    <videoStabilizationMode>0,1</videoStabilizationMode>
    <width>1280</width>
    <year>2017</year>
</track>
```

6 Conclusions

The availability of benchmark datasets is a crucial point in every research field. In this paper, we present a digital video dataset [1] that contains 622 videos created with 35 different portable devices from 11 manufacturers. For most videos, the YouTube-shared version is also provided. We used the dataset to test the source device identification technique based on sensor pattern noise and we observed that, while performance are good as expected in the case of non-stabilized videos, they degrade significantly when stabilized videos are also considered. Thus, the dataset already poses a new challenge for the Multimedia Forensic community.

Since both devices and video encoding algorithms evolve at a fast pace, we also developed the MOSES application, that allows uploading videos from iOS and Android devices. MOSES can be used to enrich the dataset when new smartphones and tablets become available, requiring little effort from the user. By means of this first video dataset and of the MOSES app, the video forensic community will be allowed to assess the newly developed algorithms in an updated and sufficiently large video database, very near to the real application scenarios.

References

1. Dataset material (2017). https://lesc.dinfo.unifi.it/en/node/202
2. Al-Sanjary, O.I., Ahmed, A.A., Sulong, G.: Development of a video tampering dataset for forensic investigation. Forensic Sci. Int. **266**, 565–572 (2016)
3. Chen, M., Fridrich, J., Goljan, M., Lukáš, J.: Determining image origin and integrity using sensor noise. IEEE Trans. Inf. Forensics Secur. **3**(1), 74–90 (2008)
4. Dang-Nguyen, D.T., Pasquini, C., Conotter, V., Boato, G.: Raise: a raw images dataset for digital image forensics. In: Proceedings of the 6th ACM Multimedia Systems Conference (MMSys 2015), pp. 219–224. ACM, New York (2015)
5. Gloe, T., Böhme, R.: The Dresden image database for benchmarking digital image forensics. J. Digit. Forensic Pract. **3**(2–4), 150–159 (2010)
6. Gloe, T., Böhme, R.: The 'Dresden Image Database' for benchmarking digital image forensics. In: Proceedings of the 25th Symposium On Applied Computing (ACM SAC 2010), vol. 2, pp. 1585–1591 (2010)
7. Goljan, M., Fridrich, J., Filler, T.: Large scale test of sensor fingerprint camera identification. In: IS&T/SPIE Electronic Imaging, p. 72540I. International Society for Optics and Photonics (2009)
8. Lukas, J., Fridrich, J., Goljan, M.: Digital camera identification from sensor pattern noise. IEEE Trans. Inf. Forensics Secur. **1**(2), 205–214 (2006)
9. Piva, A.: An overview on image forensics. ISRN Signal Processing 2013, Article ID 496701, 22 p. (2013)
10. Qadir, G., Yahaya, S., Ho, A.T.: Surrey university library for forensic analysis (SULFA) of video content (2012)
11. Schaefer, G., Stich, M.: Ucid: an uncompressed color image database. In: Electronic Imaging 2004, pp. 472–480. International Society for Optics and Photonics (2003)
12. Vázquez-Padín, D., Pérez-González, F.: Prefilter design for forensic resampling estimation. In: 2011 IEEE International Workshop on Information Forensics and Security, pp. 1–6, November 2011

Illumination Analysis in Physics-Based Image Forensics: A Joint Discussion of Illumination Direction and Color

Christian Riess[✉]

IT Security Lab, University of Erlangen-Nuremberg, Erlangen, Germany
christian.riess@fau.de

Abstract. Illumination direction and color are two physics-based forensic cues that are based on the same underlying model. In this work, we discuss these methods in the light of their joint physical model, with a particular focus on the limitations and a qualitative study of failure cases of these methods. Our goal is to provide directions for future research to further reduce the list of constraints that these methods require in order to work. We hope that this eventually broadens the applicability of physics-based methods, and to spread their main advantage, namely their stringent models for deviations of the expected image formation.

Keywords: Blind passive image forensics · Physics-based image forensics · Illumination environments · Illumination color

1 Introduction

The goal of image forensics is to provide algorithms for determining authenticity and origin of image data [12,24,27]. With the increasing ease of creating and distributing digital imagery, attention to this field of research also increased in recent years. Within image forensics, our particular interest for this paper is in the task of detecting image manipulations. The majority of the proposed approaches to manipulation detection arguably belongs to the group of so-called statistical methods. These algorithms look for statistical deviations from an expected model that is built around e. g., compression artifacts [1,3], noise residuals [2,4,7], resampling artifacts [19,23], or copy-move forgeries [5,6]. Advantages of the statistical methods are that they can typically run offline in batch processing large amounts of images, and that they achieve excellent detection rates, particularly in scenarios where the amount of postprocessing to the imagery is limited.

Another, less popular group of methods in image forensics are the so-called physics-based approaches. Here, a model is built on a physical property of the scene [12]. Deviations from the model are assumed to be manipulations. Notable features to physics-based methods are illumination direction [15,17,22], illumination color [9,13,25], specular reflection [16,20,31], vanishing points [14], and

© Springer International Publishing AG 2017
A. Piva et al. (Eds.): TIWDC 2017, CCIS 766, pp. 95–108, 2017.
DOI: 10.1007/978-3-319-67639-5_9

shadows [18, 32]. Broadly speaking, physics-based methods are widely accepted as being less sensitive to image postprocessing like compression or downsampling. Also, the fact that the underlying models are typically drawn from physics or optics, allows in principle stronger statements on the (in-)consistency: a physics-based method typically constrains the observed interaction between scene elements or parts of scene elements. However, as a consequence, the applicability and chances for success of a physics-based method very often depends on the actual content of the scene. This dependence on scene content is oftentimes perceived as the most serious limitation of physics-based methods. The second severe limitation of many physics-based approaches is that they require user interaction to reliably work. Thus, most of the current methods can not easily be adapted to an automated batch processing pipeline.

Algorithms that exploit the interaction of illumination with the scene take a central position among physics-based methods. Our group has investigated in recent years manipulation cues from investigating illumination direction and illumination color. In this work, we provide an overview of our findings and our perspective on open issues in illumination-based forensics. By "illumination-based forensics", we denote forensic methods that operate on objects under direct illumination (as opposed to, for example, methods that explicitly make use of shadow boundaries [18]). We first introduce a general model for image formation in Sect. 2.1, and discuss this model with respect to illumination-based forensics in Sect. 2.2. The approaches to exploiting illumination environments (or direction, respectively) are presented in Sect. 3, including some notable limitations. A similar presentation is done in Sect. 4 for the forensic exploitation of illumination color. A short discussion and conclusion on the similarities and differences between both approaches is presented in Sect. 5

2 Illumination-Based Forensics

We first introduce the overall model of image formation in Sect. 2.1, and then discuss its application to image forensics in Sect. 2.2.

2.1 Image Formation

The general image formation model for a color camera is

$$i(\boldsymbol{x}, \boldsymbol{\theta}) = \int_{\Omega} \int_{\lambda} r(\boldsymbol{x}, \boldsymbol{\nu}, \lambda, \boldsymbol{\theta}) \cdot e(\boldsymbol{x}, \boldsymbol{\nu}, \lambda) \cdot c(\lambda) \, \mathrm{d}\lambda \, \mathrm{d}\boldsymbol{\nu}, \tag{1}$$

where $\boldsymbol{x}$ denotes a point in the scene and $\boldsymbol{\theta}$ subsumes geometric scene parameters, most notably the camera pose. $e(\boldsymbol{x}, \boldsymbol{\nu}, \lambda)$ denotes the intensity of incident light on $\boldsymbol{x}$ from direction $\boldsymbol{\nu}$ with wavelength λ. $r(\boldsymbol{x}, \boldsymbol{\nu}, \lambda, \boldsymbol{\theta})$ denotes the reflectance function. Finally, $c(\lambda)$ denotes the vector of camera responses for light of wavelength λ, which essentially models the red, green, and blue color filters of the camera. In the case of a grayscale camera, $c(\lambda)$ is just a one-dimensional vector containing

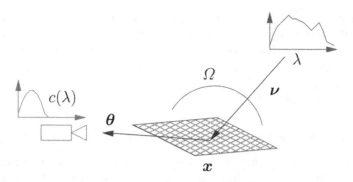

Fig. 1. Sketch for the set of angles of incident light Ω with individual directions ν, the angle of exiting light θ, and the wavelength of light λ incident on a surface location x, analogously to the image formation model of Eq. 1. (Color figure online)

a single broad color filter. The relationship of these quantities is also sketched in Fig. 1. Here, the incident spectrum of wavelengths λ is shown in magenta. The spectrum potentially varies across the hemisphere of incident angles Ω (green), where ν (blue) denotes one specific direction of incidence of light onto a surface location x. The reflectance function at x is evaluation with respect to the direction of exitance θ (red). The contribution of each color to the respective color channel is determined by the color filters $c(\lambda)$ (cyan). Note that this model only covers photometric effects, but does not include any non-linearities. For image forensics, the probably most important non-linear contributions are the camera's gamma function and JPEG compression. We omitted these effects from Eq. 1 because these effects are introduced by the digital signal processor, i.e., after the physical image formation.

The image formation model in Eq. 1 is rather general. Specializations can be done by specifying the reflectance function $r(x, \nu, \lambda, \theta)$. For example, the widely known Lambertian reflectance model can be expressed as

$$r_{\text{Lambert}}(x, \nu, \lambda, \theta) = \rho(x, \lambda) \cdot \max\left(\frac{n(x) \circ \nu}{\|n(x)\|\|\nu\|}, 0\right), \qquad (2)$$

where $\rho(x, \lambda)$ denotes the albedo for wavelength λ at position x, and $n(x)$ denotes the surface normal at point x and $\circ$ denotes the scalar product. This reflectance model is also referred to as "purely diffuse" reflectance, since the reflected intensity only depends on the angle between incident light and surface normal, but not on the position of the viewer. Another alternative is the dichromatic reflectance model by Shafer [28]. Here, the reflectance term splits into a diffuse and a specular portion,

$$r_{\text{Dichrom}}(x, \nu, \lambda, \theta) = \alpha r_{\text{Lambert}}(x, \nu, \lambda, \theta) + (1 - \alpha) r_{\text{spec}}(x, \nu, \lambda, \theta), \qquad (3)$$

where the weighting term α depends on the surface material at x. The characteristic of the specular component r_{spec} is that it is zero everywhere except of the specific constellation where angle of incidence $\boldsymbol{\nu}$, surface normal $\boldsymbol{n}(\boldsymbol{x})$ and the vector of the viewing direction $\boldsymbol{\theta}$ are coplanar, and the angles $(\boldsymbol{\nu}, \boldsymbol{n}(\boldsymbol{x}))$ and $(\boldsymbol{n}(\boldsymbol{x}), \boldsymbol{\theta})$ are identical. For color research, one additional, common assumption for the dichromatic reflectance model is the so-called neutral interface reflectance assumption. It states that the observed color in a pure specularity is identical to the color of the light source.

2.2 Forensic Applications of the Image Formation Model

The key assumption of illumination-based forensics is that with an appropriate choice of the reflectance function $r(\boldsymbol{x}, \boldsymbol{\nu}, \lambda, \boldsymbol{\theta})$, and sufficient information about the environment (e.g., about number and positions of light sources, or object surface normals), it is possible to explain the observed pixels with the model. In particular, this also allows to compare two objects with respect to the quality of the model fit. Thus, if an image is manipulated, e. g., by splicing it from two sources, it may be the case that one object matches the model while the other one does not. Such a disagreement between objects within the same image is then taken as an indicator for manipulation.

In practice, existing methods estimate the model parameters from each object (as if the object would be an original, and belong to that scene). In a second step, model parameters between objects are compared, and outliers are marked as manipulated. In the context of Eq. 1, any of the explicitly or implicitly given model parameters can be used for detecting inconsistencies. For example, methods that are based on the illumination direction estimate the surface normal $\boldsymbol{n}(\boldsymbol{x})$ to compute the intensity distribution of the lighting environment $e(\boldsymbol{x}, \boldsymbol{\nu}, \lambda)$, integrated over all λ in the visible range and all $\boldsymbol{x}$ in a sufficiently local neighborhood. Methods based on the illumination color are in a less apparent way linked to Eq. 1, but they basically exploit small variations in the surface normals $\boldsymbol{n}(\boldsymbol{x})$ to estimate $e(\boldsymbol{x}, \boldsymbol{\nu}, \lambda) \cdot c(\lambda)$, integrated over all $\boldsymbol{\nu}$, and all $\boldsymbol{x}$ in a sufficiently local neighborhood.

3 Illumination Direction

The key ideas for examining illumination direction were presented by Johnson and Farid [15] and Kee and Farid [17]. Both works propose ways to estimate the distribution of incident light $e(\boldsymbol{x}, \boldsymbol{\nu}, \lambda)$ using estimates of the surface normals $\boldsymbol{n}(\boldsymbol{x})$. At object contours, the z-component of surface normals is 0, i. e., the normals are located in the image plane. Johnson and Farid propose to estimate the orientation of these normals from orientation of the contour. Assuming furthermore Lambertian reflectance on a monochromatic image, and user-selected directly illuminated (non-shadowed) contours along the same surface material, the estimation of $e(\boldsymbol{x}, \boldsymbol{\nu}, \lambda)$ can be written as a least squares fit of the observed contour intensities to a spherical harmonics model [15].

Specifically, the estimation problem can be written as

$$Ah = i, \tag{4}$$

where $i = (i(\boldsymbol{x}_1), \ldots, i(\boldsymbol{x}_N))^{\mathrm{T}}$ denotes the N-element vector of observed (gray-level) intensities along the contour, and $A \in \mathbb{R}^{n \times 5}$ denotes a matrix of spherical harmonics bases that are evaluated for the surface normals $(n(\boldsymbol{x}_1), \ldots, n(\boldsymbol{x}_N))$ associated with each of the N contour points. The unknown vector $\boldsymbol{h} \in \mathbb{R}^{5 \times 1}$ consists of the five coefficients that parameterize a second-order 2-D spherical harmonics model. For increased robustness, this linear system of equations is solved using a Tikhonov regularizer [15].

The same idea is used in the work by Kee and Farid [17], with the main exception that an *a priori* known object class — faces — is used to estimate the surface normals. Due to major progress in recent years in fitting a 3-D face model to a 2-D face image, it became possible to obtain 3-D surface normals for all face pixels instead of only the 2-D contour normals. This allows to estimate 3-D lighting environments, with essentially the same fitting approach as above. The main difference is that a second-order 3-D model consists of nine coefficients instead of five.

There are two immediate advantages from the availability of 3-D normals. First, since all face pixels can be used instead of only a few contour pixels, the numerical estimation of the lighting environment becomes much more robust. Second, the 3-D model allows to not only distinguish 2-D projections of light sources onto the image plane, but their location in 3-D space. Both factors together make the 3-D approach more accurate than the 2-D approach, at the expense of being only applicable to scenes with at least two faces.

3.1 Addressing the Constraints: Surface Albedo, Automation and Shape-from-Shading

With the outlined basic idea published, a number of follow-up works aim at reducing the constraints that are imposed on the methods. For example, for numerical stability of the 2-D contour-based approach, it is necessary to collect occluding contours from an angular range of about 120° or more. The brightness information along the contours must be obtained from materials with the same object color (albedo). In our work, we found that this requirement of constant albedo is one of the big obstacles for using the method in practice. When selecting in an image contours along two objects for comparison, we regularly were unable to find admissible, monochromatic occluding contours across the required angular range. Thus, we proposed to include a multiplicative factor to the estimated coefficients that neutralizes surface colors [26]. A similar idea has been proposed by Peng et al. for the 3-D approach, namely to obtain a texture estimate together with the face fit that is used to normalize the intensity distribution [22]. Furthermore, since face detection is a well-examined computer vision task, the same group also proposed a slight extension of the original method that automatically finds faces and fits a face model to it [21]. Another severe restriction of the 3-D method is that it can only detect manipulations that involve faces. This has been addressed by Fan et al. by experimenting with shape from shading on more general objects [11]. Nevertheless, this additional flexibility

Fig. 2. Examples for different surface materials and textures. Top left: synthetic materials like outdoor clothing typically violate the Lambertian reflectance model. Top right: unstructured materials like hair are very prone to mislead the estimation, and hence need to be segmented out beforehand. Bottom row: texture like on the jeans or the makeup is oftentimes barely separable from intensity gradients that arise from varying illumination.

naturally comes at the expense of a somewhat reduced model accuracy, which, by extension, reduces the ability of the method to detect manipulations.

3.2   Unsolved Challenges in Lighting Environments for Forensics

We noticed in our experiments with 2-D and 3-D estimators for lighting environments, that there also exists a number of "hidden" constraints. These constraints can be readily derived from the underlying model, but we find them to be somewhat less obvious. We group these constraints into surface materials/texture, geometry, and scene layout.

Surface Material and Texture: Many artificial materials exhibit unusual reflectance behavior, that greatly differs from the assumed Lambertian reflectance model. An example case is shown in Fig. 2 in the top left. While casual clothing is oftentimes approximated as Lambertian, this does not hold for synthetic outdoor clothing like the shown ski suit. Also, hair (Fig. 2, top right) and smooth textures on the surface (Fig. 2, bottom row) are cases where material and illumination information are easily confused, leading to failure cases. An approach to mitigate these issues in an automated manner might be to use specialized detectors for the most common cases. For example, the color gradients

Fig. 3. Examples for object geometries that do not permit a reliable 3-D estimation of the direction of the incident illuminant. The reason is that these objects do not exhibit normals in all directions, but only along a lower-dimensional manifold. In the left and middle image, the columns and the hangar roof spread out the surface normals along a 2-D plane. In the right image, the flat building facade confines all surface normals to be parallel. As a result, the observations are severely undersampled and can not be used for a stand-alone estimation of the illuminant direction.

on the jeans in Fig. 2 on the bottom left is actually a colored gradient, and could probably as such be filtered out.

Geometry: Scene geometry can cause subtle, yet significant errors in the estimation of the illuminant direction. One requirement of the method is that a sufficient variety of surface normals is observed. However, many man-made structures exhibit surfaces that reside on a lower-dimensional manifold, and hence can not provide a sufficient variety of surface normals. Example images are shown in Fig. 3. On the left, the surface normals on the columns all reside on a plane that perpendicularly intersects the columns. As a consequence, a 3-D lighting estimator that solely relies on these normals is unable to distinguish different elevation angles of the illuminant. An almost identical examples is shown in the middle image for the cylindrical hangar roof. A third example, where all surface normals are even parallel, is the building facade shown in the right image. It is important to note, and to communicate to users of lighting-environment methods that in such cases the scene geometry inherently limits the applicability of the method, even if the normals on these problematic surfaces are admissible with respect to the other required constraints.

Scene Layout: Upon closer examination, it turns out that a surprising number of scene layouts, i. e., constellations of objects, cameras, and light sources, create very challenging cases for the use of methods based on the direction of the illumination. The canonical best case for the analysis of 2-D lighting environments are light sources that are located between camera and object. Since the 2-D approach is only able to distinguish the projection of the lighting environment onto the image plane, analysis becomes in principle easier if the light sources are located closer to the object than to the camera. A good case in terms of lighting positioning for the 2-D estimator is shown in Fig. 4 in the top left. Three other typical cases are shown in the remaining pictures from Fig. 4. In the top right, the light is mainly coming from the front. This is a case where the 2-D estimator

Fig. 4. Examples for scene geometry and lighting. Top left: with a single dominant light source between camera and object, in a lateral position, this is a case where the 2-D lighting estimator is expected to perform very reliably. Top right: light sources located more in front of the object are challenging for the 2-D estimator, but can be estimated with the 3-D lighting estimator. Bottom left: the light source is located behind the object, which is modelled by neither of the two estimators. Bottom right: another failure case for both estimators is the absence of a direct light source, e. g., in a shadow region.

becomes less accurate. However, the 3-D estimator can operate on images of this type. In the bottom left, the light source is located behind the person, which is not modelled by the methods and hence is a situation where the method can not be used. Similarly in the bottom right, where there is apparently no directional light, but only ambient illumination.

Not shown in this image, but in Fig. 6, are two cases where the scene consists of more than a single light source. This is no problem if the mixture of light sources is identical on the compared objects or persons. However, the problem becomes ill-posed in the case of multiple inhomogeneous light sources, which makes the two lighting environments incomparable [22].

4   Illumination Color

A second approach to use Eq. 1 for the detection image manipulations is to solve for the spectral distribution of the light source $e(\boldsymbol{x}, \boldsymbol{\nu}, \lambda) \cdot c(\lambda)$. Gholap and Bora proposed to examine objects that can be assumed to follow the dichromatic reflectance model, and to use the intersection point of so-called "dichromatic lines" to detect image manipulations [13]: if each of the three objects is illuminated by the same light source, the three dichromatic lines are expected to intersect in one point.

In our work, we followed a slightly different approach. We propose to subdivide the image into small regions, and to estimate the color of the illuminant locally for each region [25]. In computer vision, estimating the color of the illuminant is typically a preparatory step to white balancing (the field of research is called "color constancy"). However, in a forensic context, we assume that the image is manipulated if these local estimates differ too much. The color constancy estimators with the lowest error rates are statistical, and many of these are based on machine learning. Such estimators are not optimal from a theoretical perspective: if a statistical estimator is applied locally to an image region, the area may just not contain sufficiently diverse pixel information in order to allow a low-error estimate. Second, the statistical estimators typically lack a theoretical model for their success cases and failure cases. In that sense, an illuminant color framework containing statistical estimators is not entirely physics-based anymore. To mitigate these issues, we preferably work with physics-based illuminant color estimator by Tan et al. that assumes the dichromatic reflectance model [29]. This estimator requires surface patches that exhibit some variation in the surface normals. However, the requirements are much milder than for the set of surface normals that are needed for estimating an illumination environment. However, the method additionally requires that some of the pixels exhibit partially specular reflectance. It turns out that this requirement is a major source of error in many practical scenarios, particularly for pixel regions in the background. However, in our previous work, we paired the physics-based estimator with a statistical estimator, with the goal to backup the physics-based estimator in such cases [9].

An interesting idea for the purpose of source camera identification has been proposed by Deng et al., by assuming that repeated white balancing with the camera's internal white balancing algorithm is an idempotent operation [10]. This allows to find a camera-model specific white balancing algorithm for a given input image.

4.1   Addressing the Constraints: Surface Albedo and Learned Decision Boundaries

In our experiments, it turned out that a direct, agnostic comparison of locally estimated illuminant colors is oftentimes a too weak decision criterion. The estimation of an illuminant color is an underconstrained problem, and as such must rely on constraints to be solvable. Estimations on local image patches, as proposed for the purpose of image forensics, by tendency further increases the error rates. We observed that particularly the object color influences the direction of the illuminant estimate. As a consequence, we propose a method that operates on areas where we can assume to observe roughly the same underlying material, namely on faces [9]. The idea is to relate illuminant estimates from similar

Fig. 5. Example face shots exhibiting small specularities. Physics-based illuminant estimators oftentimes benefit from specular areas. Instead of estimating these regions directly, it may be beneficial to heuristically search for objects like faces, expecting that nose, cheeks or forehead exhibit slight specularities.

underlying objects to be able to set up a tighter decision boundary. In this work, the decision is learned from a rather sophisticated feature map, which unfortunately leaves the physics-based grounds of the method. Nevertheless, this closes the gap towards a more reliable detection method based on illuminant color.

4.2   Unsolved Challenges in Color Constancy for Forensics

Although the underlying ideas for using illuminant color in image forensics have already been presented a while ago, there are — particularly on the theoretical side — a number of unsolved questions with respect to the realization of an end-to-end physics-based pipeline. Thus, the purpose of this section is to provide a brief introduction into what we belief are the major open issues that need to be addressed.

Dependence on Specularities: Most physics-based illuminant color estimators expect at least partially specular pixels to perform their estimation. Conversely, if a region contains only purely diffuse pixels, it is most likely that a specularity-based estimator will fail. However, specularity segmentation is in general similarly hard as the color constancy problem itself. Nevertheless, it may be an option to use prior information from another channel to constrain the domain of where specularities are more likely to be found. For example, oftentimes exhibit faces a slight specular spots at the tip of the nose. Example pictures are shown in Fig. 5. In such a case, it may suffice to find faces and search within the face for specularities instead of blindly segmenting the whole image for specularities.

Physics-based Decisions: One major missing link for a fully, end-to-end physics-based method that exploits the illuminant color is a physically motivated, yet reliable, metric to distinguish consistent areas from inconsistent areas. Several results have been reported for statistical decision functions that build on top of the illuminant color estimators [8,9,30]. Therefore, it might be a good approach

Fig. 6. Examples for multiple illuminants. Indoor scenes with windows are common multi-illuminant cases. Another case (not shown here) are pictures taken with a flash light.

to search for general, ideally analytical, rules for distinguishing consistent from inconsistent illuminations.

Scene Layout: Analogously to the analysis of illumination environments, scene layout, and particularly local illuminants have great impact on the success of the illuminant estimators. For example, a considerable number of indoor scenes are multi-illuminant scenes, with sunlight from a window, another electric light, and maybe even additional secondary light sources, e. g., from electronic devices, or interreflections from furniture or walls. Two examples for such cases are shown in Fig. 6. Another common source for two illuminants are photographs that are taken with flash light that also include some background illumination. Resolving cases with multiple different, inhomogeneous illuminants can lead to very difficult situations, since the task of comparing illumination environments is not well-defined anymore: a difference in illuminant colors can either be due to a spliced manipulation, or due to the fact that there are two different light sources in the scene. It turns out that this problem is exactly analogous to multiple light sources for estimating illuminant environments at the end of Sect. 3.2.

5   Discussion and Conclusion

We provide an overview of physics-based methods that analyze illumination environments and illumination color for the purpose of exposing image manipulations. Physics-based methods share the advantage that they are based on rigorous models, but they suffer from their relatively strict assumptions on the content of the scene. This inherently limits their applicability, particularly in an automated batch-processing scenario.

In our review, we show that both families of physics-based methods are based on essentially the same models for image formation, but both families focus on different quantities in the model. For estimating illumination environments, the surface normals of an object are required. For estimating the illuminant color, it is required that an object exhibits a certain variation in the surface normals, but less than for illumination environments. Additionally, for an end-to-end physics-based model, it is required that some pixels exhibit partially specular reflectance to estimate the illuminant color. Thus, both families of methods have similar, yet somewhat different requirements on the object areas they operate on.

As a consequence, estimators for illumination environments have stricter requirements on a sufficiently diverse geometric structure of the object. For example, all normal vectors of a column reside in a plane, and hence the estimated illuminant environment is also confined to that plane. Conversely, estimators for the illuminant color only require a small variation of the surface normal. However, physics-based estimators typically require at least partially specular pixels, which are oftentimes only very sparsely contained in a scene, and may be difficult to segment automatically. We also provide several other pointers to ongoing challenges with both estimators.

Since both methods are based from the same underlying formulation, it may be interesting to further explore the consequences of this joint lineage. For example, it appears to be interesting to search for a confidence measure that is derived from the methods' dependence on the underlying geometry. It may also be interesting to further, more rigorously investigate in which cases each of the two approaches can succeed, and to quantify their overlap in applicability to forensic examination of images.

Acknowledgements. This material is based on research sponsored by the Air Force Research Laboratory and the Defense Advanced Research Projects Agency under agreement number FA8750-16-2-0204. The U.S. Government is authorized to reproduce and distribute reprints for Governmental purposes notwithstanding any copyright notation thereon.

The views and conclusions contained herein are those of the authors and should not be interpreted as necessarily representing the official policies or endorsements, either expressed or implied, of the Air Force Research Laboratory and the Defense Advanced Research Projects Agency or the U.S. Government.

References

1. Barni, M., Chen, Z., Tondi, B.: Adversary-aware, data-driven detection of double JPEG compression: how to make counter-forensics harder. In: IEEE International Workshop on Information Forensics and Security, December 2016
2. Bayar, B., Stamm, M.C.: A deep learning approach to universal image manipulation detection using a new convolutional layer. In: ACM Workshop on Information Hiding and Multimedia Security, pp. 5–10, June 2016
3. Bianchi, T., Piva, A., Perez-Gonzalez, F.: Near optimal detection of quantized signals and application to JPEG forensics. In: IEEE International Workshop on Information Forensics and Security, pp. 168–173, November 2013
4. Chen, M., Fridrich, J., Goljan, M., Lukás, J.: Determining image origin and integrity using sensor noise. IEEE Trans. Inf. Forensics Secur. 3(1), 74–90 (2008)
5. Christlein, V., Riess, C., Jordan, J., Riess, C., Angelopoulou, E.: An evaluation of popular copy-move forgery detection approaches. IEEE Trans. Inf. Forensics Secur. 7(6), 1841–1854 (2012)

6. Cozzolino, D., Poggi, G., Verdoliva, L.: Efficient dense-field copy-move forgery detection. IEEE Trans. Inf. Forensics Secur. **10**(11), 2284–2297 (2015)
7. Cozzolino, D., Poggi, G., Verdoliva, L.: Splicebuster: a new blind image splicing detector. In: IEEE International Workshop on Information Forensics and Security, pp. 1–6 (2015)
8. de Carvalho, T.J., Faria, F.A., Pedrini, H., Torres, R.S., Rocha, A.: Illuminant-based transformed spaces for image forensics. IEEE Trans. Inf. Forensics Secur. **11**(4), 720–733 (2015)
9. de Carvalho, T.J., Riess, C., Angelopoulou, E., Pedrini, H., Rocha, A.: Exposing digital image forgeries by illumination color classification. IEEE Trans. Inf. Forensics Secur. **8**(7), 1182–1194 (2013)
10. Deng, Z., Gijsenij, A., Zhang, J.: Source camera identification using auto-white balance approximation. In: Proceedings of the 13th IEEE International Conference on Computer Vision (ICCV 2011), Barcelona, Spain, pp. 57–64, November 2011
11. Fan, W., Wang, K., Cayre, F., Xiong, Z.: 3D lighting-based image forgery detection using shape-from-shading. In: Proceedings of the 20th European Signal Processing Conference (EUSIPCO-2012), Bucarest, Romania, pp. 1777–1781, August 2012
12. Farid, H.: Photo Forensics. MIT Press, Cambridge (2016)
13. Gholap, S., Bora, P.K.: Illuminant colour based image forensics. In: IEEE Region 10 Conference TENCON (TENCON 2008), Hyderabad, India, November 2008
14. Iuliani, M., Fanfani, M., Colombo, C., Piva, A.: Reliability assessment of principal point estimates for forensic applications. J. Vis. Commun. Image Representation **42**(1), 65–77 (2017)
15. Johnson, M., Farid, H.: Exposing digital forgeries in complex lighting environments. IEEE Trans. Inf. Forensics Secu. **2**(3), 450–461 (2007)
16. Johnson, M.K., Farid, H.: Detecting photographic composites of people. In: Shi, Y.Q., Kim, H.-J., Katzenbeisser, S. (eds.) IWDW 2007. LNCS, vol. 5041, pp. 19–33. Springer, Heidelberg (2008). doi:10.1007/978-3-540-92238-4_3
17. Kee, E., Farid, H.: Exposing digital forgeries from 3-D lighting environments. In: Proceedings of the 2nd IEEE International Workshop on Information Forensics and Security (WIFS 2010), Seattle, WA, USA, December 2010
18. Kee, E., O'Brien, J.F., Farid, H.: Exposing photo manipulation from shading and shadows. ACM Trans. Graph. **33**(5), 165:1–165:21 (2014)
19. Kirchner, M.: Linear row and column predictors for the analysis of resized images. In: ACM SIGMM Multimedia & Security Workshop, pp. 13–18, September 2010
20. O'Brien, J.F., Farid, H.: Exposing photo manipulation with inconsistent reflections. ACM Trans. Graph. **31**(1), 1–11 (2012)
21. Peng, B., Wang, W., Dong, J., Tan, T.: Automatic detection of 3-D lighting inconsistencies via a facial landmark based morphable model. In: IEEE International Conference on Image Processing, pp. 3932–3936 (2016)
22. Peng, B., Wang, W., Dong, J., Tan, T.: Optimized 3D lighting environment estimation for image forgery detection. IEEE Trans. Inf. Forensics Secur. **12**(2), 479–494 (2017)
23. Popescu, A.C., Farid, H.: Exposing digital forgeries by detecting traces of resampling. Signal Process. **53**(2), 758–767 (2005)
24. Redi, J., Taktak, W., Dugelay, J.-L.: Digital image forensics: a booklet for beginners. Multimed. Tools Appl. **51**(1), 133–162 (2011)
25. Riess, C., Angelopoulou, E.: Scene illumination as an indicator of image manipulation. In: Böhme, R., Fong, P.W.L., Safavi-Naini, R. (eds.) IH 2010. LNCS, vol. 6387, pp. 66–80. Springer, Heidelberg (2010). doi:10.1007/978-3-642-16435-4_6

26. Riess, C., Unberath, M., Naderi, F., Pfaller, S., Stamminger, M., Angelopoulou, E.: Handling multiple materials for exposure of digital forgeries using 2-D lighting environments. Multimed. Tools Appl. **76**(4), 4747–4764 (2016)
27. Sencar, H.T., Memon, N. (eds.): Digital Image Forensics: There is More to a Picture than Meets the Eye. Springer, New York (2013). doi:10.1007/978-1-4614-0757-7
28. Shafer, S.A.: Using color to separate reflection components. J. Color Res. Appl. **10**(4), 210–218 (1985)
29. Tan, R., Nishino, K., Ikeuchi, K.: Color constancy through inverse-intensity chromaticity space. J. Optical Soc. Am. A **21**(3), 321–334 (2004)
30. Wu, X., Fang, Z.: Image splicing detection using illuminant color inconsistency. In: Proceedings of the 3rd IEEE International Conference on Multimedia Information Networking and Security (MINES 2011), Shanghai, China, pp. 600–603, November 2011
31. Yu, H., Ng, T.-T., Sun, Q.: Recaptured photo detection using specularity distribution. In: Proceedings of the 15th IEEE International Conference on Image Processing (ICIP 2008), San Diego, CA, USA, pp. 3140–3143, October 2008
32. Zhang, W., Cao, X., Zhang, J., Zhu, J., Wang, P.: Detecting photographic composites using shadows. In: Proceedings of the IEEE International Conference on Multimedia and Expo (ICME 2009), Cancun, Mexico, pp. 1042–1045, June 2009

Random Matrix Theory for Modeling the Eigenvalue Distribution of Images Under Upscaling

David Vázquez-Padín[✉], Fernando Pérez-González,
and Pedro Comesaña-Alfaro

Signal Theory and Communications Department,
University of Vigo, Vigo, Spain
{dvazquez,fperez,pcomesan}@gts.uvigo.es

Abstract. The stochastic representation of digital images through a
two-dimensional autoregressive (2D-AR) model offers a proper way to
approximate the empirical distribution of the eigenvalues coming from
genuine images. By considering this model, we apply random matrix theory to analytically derive the asymptotic eigenvalue distribution of causal
2D-AR random fields that have undergone an upscaling operation with
a particular interpolation kernel. This eigenvalue characterization is useful in developing new forensic techniques for image resampling detection
since we can use theoretical bounds to drive the decision of detectors
based on subspace decomposition. Moreover, experimental results with
real images show that the obtained asymptotic limits turn out to be
excellent approximations, even when working with images of small size.

Keywords: Image forensics · Marčenko-Pastur law · Random matrix
theory · Resampling detection · Two-dimensional autoregressive model

1 Introduction

In multimedia forensics, the detection of resampling traces in a digital signal is an
important step towards determining whether its content has been manipulated.
For example, the presence of resampling artifacts in a specific region of a digital
image is indicative of the application of a geometric transformation in that part
of the captured scene. This is due to the fact that any spatial transformation
requires the calculation of new samples through the interpolation of existing ones,
which unavoidably leaves characteristic dependencies among adjacent samples.

Since by exposing this characteristic footprint the presence of forgeries can be
eventually revealed, the forensic analysis of resampled signals has been largely
investigated during last years. Although many different directions have been
explored [4,5,7,10], most of the available techniques share a common processing
structure: first, a residue signal (where resampling artifacts are observable) is
extracted from the image under investigation; then, given the periodic nature
of the residue signal in case of resampling, a frequency analysis is carried out

© Springer International Publishing AG 2017
A. Piva et al. (Eds.): TIWDC 2017, CCIS 766, pp. 109–124, 2017.
DOI: 10.1007/978-3-319-67639-5_10

to unveil the presence of resampling traces. Very recently, however, we have proposed in [13,15] a different way of analyzing resampled images under an upscaling scenario, i.e., by approaching image resampling detection as a subspace decomposition problem. In these works we have shown that an upscaled image can be seen as a low-dimensional signal surrounded by a high-dimensional noise, which through a Singular Value Decomposition (SVD) as in [13] or a precise eigenvalue characterization as in [15] can be used to expose the implicit signal-plus-noise structure from upscaled images that is not present in genuine ones.

In this paper, we complement the work in [15] by detailing the analytical derivation of the asymptotic eigenvalue distribution of causal 2D-AR random fields (used as an underlying model for genuine images) in an upscaling scenario. To characterize the behavior of the eigenvalues, we resort to Random Matrix Theory (RMT) and by using one of its fundamental results, i.e., the Marčenko-Pastur law [8], we propose theoretical bounds to drive the decision of the resampling detector designed in [15]. Even though the analytically obtained decision threshold is only applicable to images without demosaicing traces, we believe that avoiding the use of a training set to establish an empirical threshold is an advantage over state-of-the-art techniques. Finally, since the robustness of the resampling detector depends on the relation between the variance of the signal and that of the background noise, we analyze the performance limits of the proposed approach from a theoretical perspective using the 2D-AR model.

The structure of the paper is as follows. In Sect. 2, we first introduce the notation used throughout the paper, then we describe the resampling process together with the subspace decomposition approach, and finally we present the 2D-AR model adopted for representing genuine images. The eigenvalue characterization of genuine and upscaled images is carried out in Sect. 3, while the experimental validation with real images is performed in Sect. 4. Conclusions are finally drawn in Sect. 5.

2   Preliminaries

Prior to the formulation of the resampling procedure and the formalization of the model adopted for natural images, we briefly describe the notation used throughout the paper. Matrices will be denoted by capital bold letters. Given an arbitrary square matrix $\mathbf{A}$ of size $N \times N$, we will frequently work with a rectangular submatrix $\mathbf{A}_K$ of size $N \times K$ and aspect ratio $\beta \triangleq \frac{K}{N}$, which is constructed by extracting $K \leq N$ consecutive columns from $\mathbf{A}$. The sample autocorrelation matrix of $\mathbf{A}_K$ is $K^{-1}\mathbf{A}_K\mathbf{A}_K^T$, but we will mostly work with the renormalized sample autocorrelation $\mathbf{\Sigma}_{A_K} \triangleq N^{-1}\mathbf{A}_K\mathbf{A}_K^T$. By convention, we assume that the eigenvalues of a given matrix are sorted in descending order. Table 1 summarizes the notation used for representing different attributes of an arbitrary $N \times N$ matrix $\mathbf{A}$.

Table 1. Summary of notation

Symbol	Meaning
$A_{i,j}$	(i,j)-th element of matrix $\mathbf{A}$, with $i,j \in \{0,\ldots,N-1\}$
σ_A^2	Variance of the entries of $\mathbf{A}$
$\mathbf{A}_K$	$N \times K$ submatrix with K consecutive columns from $\mathbf{A}$
β	Aspect ratio of an $N \times K$ matrix, i.e., $\beta = \frac{K}{N}$
$\boldsymbol{\Sigma}_{A_K}$	Renormalized sample autocorrelation matrix of $\mathbf{A}_K$
$\lambda_i\left(\boldsymbol{\Sigma}_{A_K}\right)$	i-th eigenvalue of $\boldsymbol{\Sigma}_{A_K}$, with $i = 1,\ldots,N$
$\lambda_-\left(\boldsymbol{\Sigma}_{A_K}\right)$	Smallest eigenvalue of $\boldsymbol{\Sigma}_{A_K}$
$\lambda_+\left(\boldsymbol{\Sigma}_{A_K}\right)$	Largest eigenvalue of $\boldsymbol{\Sigma}_{A_K}$
$f_{\boldsymbol{\Sigma}_{A_K}}(\lambda)$	Probability density function of the eigenvalues of $\boldsymbol{\Sigma}_{A_K}$

2.1 Resampling Process Description

Let us assume that the input to the resampling operation is a digital image with a single color channel (hereinafter, indistinctly called genuine or natural image) that does not contain traces from any preceding demosaicing process and has negligible quantization noise. Representing the referred input image as a matrix $\mathbf{X}$, we consider that the resampling operation scales the two dimensions of $\mathbf{X}$ in a uniform way and by means of a resampling factor $\xi > 1$, which is defined as $\xi \triangleq \frac{L}{M}$ with L and M coprime natural numbers. The pixel values in the new resampled grid are calculated by linearly combining a finite set of neighboring samples from the input matrix $\mathbf{X}$ with a two-dimensional (2D) interpolation kernel that is symmetric and separable (i.e., the kernel can be expressed as the outer product of two vectors). Consequently, each (i,j)-th pixel value $Y_{i,j}$ from an upscaled image $\mathbf{Y}$ can be computed as

$$Y_{i,j} = \sum_{u,v \in \mathbb{Z}} h\left(i\tfrac{M}{L} + \phi - u\right) h\left(j\tfrac{M}{L} + \phi - v\right) X_{u,v}, \tag{1}$$

where $X_{u,v}$ denotes the (u,v)-th element of the genuine image $\mathbf{X}$, ϕ is a shift between the original and the resampled grid,[1] and $h(\cdot)$ is the one-dimensional (1D) impulse response of the interpolation kernel, whose width is $k_w \in 2\mathbb{Z}^+$, i.e., k_w is a positive even number.

Our analysis will be carried out over a block $\mathbf{Y}$ of size $N \times N$ extracted from the upscaled version by ξ of a rectangular $U \times V$ genuine image $\mathbf{X}$, i.e., with $N \leq \xi \cdot \min(U,V)$. Assuming that both matrices $\mathbf{X}$ and $\mathbf{Y}$ are aligned with respect to their upper-left corner and also that N is a multiple of L, the $N \times N$ block $\mathbf{Y}$ can be expressed using (1) in matrix form:

$$\mathbf{Y} = \mathbf{H}\hat{\mathbf{X}}\mathbf{H}^T, \tag{2}$$

---

[1] The value of ϕ is generally taken as $\phi = \frac{1}{2}\left(\frac{M}{L} + 1\right)$, as in `imresize` from MATLAB.

where the entries of $\mathbf{H}$ are given by

$$H_{i,j} = h\left(i\frac{M}{L} + \varphi - j\right), \tag{3}$$

with $\varphi \triangleq \phi + k_w/2 - 1$, such that $\hat{\mathbf{X}}$ only contains the first $R \times R$ pixels from $\mathbf{X}$ that are used in the calculation of $\mathbf{Y}$ with $R \triangleq N\frac{M}{L} + k_w$, i.e., $\hat{X}_{u,v} = X_{u,v}$, for $u, v = 0, \ldots, R - 1$. Provided that N is larger than R, we will assume that the $N \times R$ interpolation matrix $\mathbf{H}$ is full column rank (i.e., $\text{rank}(\mathbf{H}) = R$), which is true for all kernels considered in this paper. However, the reader is referred to [6] to check the conditions that $\mathbf{H}$ must satisfy to have full column rank.

After the calculation of all the resampled pixels from the upscaled image, a quantization is generally applied as a last step to fit the original precision of the input image $\mathbf{X}$. We assume that a uniform scalar quantizer with step size Δ is used. Denoting the resulting quantized image by a matrix $\mathbf{Z}$, we can model it as

$$\mathbf{Z} = \mathbf{Y} + \mathbf{W}, \tag{4}$$

where we opt for an additive white noise model, such that the entries of the quantization noise matrix $\mathbf{W}$ are i.i.d. $\mathcal{U}\left[-\frac{\Delta}{2}, \frac{\Delta}{2}\right)$ with zero mean and variance $\sigma_W^2 = \frac{\Delta^2}{12}$. This model is suitable in practice as long as the probability density function (pdf) of the genuine image is smooth and its variance is much larger than the variance of the quantization noise, but it will not be valid for modeling flat regions, which might appear in practice due to undesired artifacts such as saturation. In Sect. 4 we will see how to deal with these special cases.

2.2   Subspace Decomposition to Expose Resampling Traces

As noted above, it was first observed in [13] that an upscaled and later quantized image presents a particular signal-plus-noise structure that does not show up in natural images. This comes from the fact that when a genuine image $\mathbf{X}$ is upscaled by ξ, the rank of $\mathbf{Y}$ in (2) is at most equal to the rank of the interpolation matrix $\mathbf{H}$ (i.e., $\text{rank}(\mathbf{Y}) \leq \text{rank}(\mathbf{H}) = R$ with $R \approx N/\xi$), which implies that any N-dimensional column/row from $\mathbf{Y}$ will lie in an R-dimensional subspace. On the other hand, the noise $\mathbf{W}$ in (4) is expected to span the full space. Therefore, from the eigendecomposition of the sample autocorrelation matrix of $\mathbf{Z}$, we count on finding R leading eigenvalues corresponding to the signal subspace, while the remaining ones will correspond to the background noise. This makes possible the detection of resampling traces using any subspace decomposition approach.

In this work, we draw on the most-celebrated result from RMT, i.e., Marčenko-Pastur Law (MPL) [8], whose main characteristic states that for a given random matrix $\mathbf{A}_K$ with i.i.d. entries and aspect ratio β, the eigenvalues of Σ_{A_K} tend to cluster around the variance σ_A^2 as β converges to zero. Respectively, we are interested in checking whether this property also applies when a submatrix $\mathbf{Z}_K$ with small β is extracted from $\mathbf{Z}$ in (4), so that on the one hand the signal eigenvalues cluster around σ_Z^2, while the noise eigenvalues do so around σ_W^2. The eigenvalue characterization carried out in Sect. 3 will theoretically support these findings.

2.3 Causal 2D-AR Random Fields for Modeling Genuine Images

Based on our previous analysis in [14], we consider a causal two-dimensional autoregressive model with a single correlation coefficient ρ as the stochastic representation for natural images without traces of demosaicing, so denoting by $\mathbf{X}$ the generated 2D-AR random field of size $N \times N$, it can be expressed as

$$\mathbf{X} = \mathbf{U}\mathbf{S}\mathbf{U}^T, \tag{5}$$

where $\mathbf{S}$ is an $(N + Q - 1) \times (N + Q - 1)$ random matrix whose i.i.d. entries follow a zero-mean normal distribution with variance σ_S^2, and $\mathbf{U}$ is a Toeplitz matrix of size $N \times (N + Q - 1)$, with Q denoting the length of the truncated infinite impulse response of the AR model. Hence, matrix $\mathbf{U}$ is fully described as $U_{i,j} = u_Q[j - i]$, where sequence $u_Q[n] \triangleq \rho^{Q-1-n}$, for $n = 0, \ldots, Q - 1$, and is zero elsewhere, i.e.,

$$U_{i,j} = \begin{cases} \rho^{Q-1-(j-i)}, & \text{if } (j - i) = 0, \ldots, Q - 1 \\ 0, & \text{otherwise} \end{cases},$$

where the value of Q is generally taken as $Q > N$ to minimize modeling errors due to truncation. The practical suitability of this model is also reported in [14].

2.4 Interpolation Kernels

Even though the upcoming eigenvalue characterization can be applied to any linear and separable interpolation kernel, we will provide examples with the most commonly available kernels, namely: Linear, Catmull-Rom, B-spline, and Lanczos, to highlight the different behavior among them and specific properties of each other. Table 2 collects their 1D impulse response and their width.

Table 2. Impulse response and width of several interpolation kernels.

Kernel Type	Impulse Response
Linear $(k_w = 2)$	$h(t) = \begin{cases} 1 - \lvert t \rvert, & \text{if } \lvert t \rvert \leq \frac{k_w}{2} \\ 0, & \text{otherwise} \end{cases}$
Catmull-Rom $(k_w = 4)$	$h(t) = \begin{cases} \frac{3}{2}\lvert t \rvert^3 - \frac{5}{2}\lvert t \rvert^2 + 1, & \text{if } \lvert t \rvert \leq \frac{k_w}{4} \\ -\frac{1}{2}\lvert t \rvert^3 + \frac{5}{2}\lvert t \rvert^2 - 4\lvert t \rvert + 2, & \text{if } \frac{k_w}{4} < \lvert t \rvert \leq \frac{k_w}{2} \\ 0, & \text{otherwise} \end{cases}$
B-spline $(k_w = 4)$	$h(t) = \begin{cases} \frac{1}{2}\lvert t \rvert^3 - \lvert t \rvert^2 + \frac{2}{3}, & \text{if } \lvert t \rvert \leq \frac{k_w}{4} \\ -\frac{1}{6}\lvert t \rvert^3 + \lvert t \rvert^2 - 2\lvert t \rvert + \frac{4}{3}, & \text{if } \frac{k_w}{4} < \lvert t \rvert \leq \frac{k_w}{2} \\ 0, & \text{otherwise} \end{cases}$
Lanczos $(k_w = 6)$	$h(t) = \begin{cases} \text{sinc}(t)\text{sinc}\left(\frac{t}{3}\right), & \text{if } \lvert t \rvert < \frac{k_w}{2} \\ 0, & \text{otherwise} \end{cases}$

3   Eigenvalue Characterization

In this section, we formally characterize the statistical distribution of the sample eigenvalues coming from genuine images (modeled as causal 2D-AR random fields) and their upscaled versions (before and after quantization). As noted above, we base our analysis on well-known results from RMT that allow us to model the asymptotic behavior of the eigenvalues through deterministic functions. Table 3 lists some of the solved problems in RMT that relate to our case.

The first work in Table 3 corresponds to the contribution by Marčenko-Pastur that provides a closed-form expression for the eigenvalue distribution of random matrices with i.i.d. entries. Although this result cannot be applied to filtered white noise processes as the one that emerges from the 2D-AR model, it can actually be used to represent the eigenvalues coming from the matrix $\mathbf{W}$ with i.i.d. quantization noise in (4). On the other hand, the study of the sample eigenvalues of filtered processes has been tackled in the last two works of Table 3, where the considered random matrices have independent columns, but an arbitrary dependence within each column. In both cases, no closed-form solution is obtained, but the eigenvalues are characterized indirectly through the Stieltjes transform, whose inversion formula uniquely determines their pdf.

Table 3. Solved RMT problems.

Type of matrix	Eigenvalue characterization from RMT
Random matrix (i.i.d. entries)	Marčenko-Pastur law [8] (closed-form expression)
Random matrix (i.i.d. stationary time series in columns)	Bai and Zhou [1] (through Stieltjes transform)
Random matrix (a linear process in each column)	Pfaffel and Schlemm [9] (through Stieltjes transform)

Unfortunately, given the form of our random matrix $\mathbf{X}$ in (5) and its upscaled version $\mathbf{Y}$ in (2), where both matrices present dependencies among rows and columns, neither of these results can be applied directly to our case. Therefore, we also opt for characterizing the pdf of the sample eigenvalues indirectly through the Stieltjes transform. To that end, we resort to a procedure proposed by Tulino and Verdú in [12, Theorem 2.43] that addresses the calculation of the so-called η-transform [12, Sect. 2.2.2] of an unnormalized sample autocorrelation matrix $\mathbf{B}\mathbf{B}^T$, where $\mathbf{B}$ has the form $\mathbf{B} = \mathbf{C}\mathbf{S}\mathbf{A}$, which coincides with the matrix form of $\mathbf{X}$ and $\mathbf{Y}$. Similarly, matrix $\mathbf{S}$ has i.i.d. entries, and matrices $\mathbf{C}$ and $\mathbf{A}$ induce the linear dependencies. Once the η-transform is obtained, the relationship in [12, Eq. (2.48)] allows us to retrieve the corresponding Stieltjes transform, whose inversion formula in [12, Eq. (2.45)] finally provides the pdf of the sample eigenvalues.

Algorithm 1 summarizes the above steps to obtain the asymptotic pdf of the eigenvalues of $\boldsymbol{\Sigma}_{B_K} = N^{-1}\mathbf{B}_K\mathbf{B}_K^T$ when considering an arbitrary submatrix

---

Algorithm 1. Main steps to obtain the asymptotic eigenvalue pdf of $\boldsymbol{\Sigma}_{B_K}$

1. Compute the η-transform (see [14, Appendix A]: $\eta_{\boldsymbol{\Sigma}_{B_K}}(\gamma)$
2. Retrieve the Stieltjes transform through: $\eta_{\boldsymbol{\Sigma}_{B_K}}(\gamma) = \dfrac{\mathcal{S}_{\boldsymbol{\Sigma}_{B_K}}(-\frac{1}{\gamma})}{\gamma}$
3. Apply the inversion formula: $f_{\boldsymbol{\Sigma}_{B_K}}(\lambda) = \lim_{\nu \to 0^+} \frac{1}{\pi}\mathrm{Im}\left[\mathcal{S}_{\boldsymbol{\Sigma}_{B_K}}(\lambda + j\nu)\right]$

$\mathbf{B}_K$ of size $N \times K$, which is made up of $K \leq N$ consecutive columns from an $N \times N$ matrix $\mathbf{B}$. Accordingly, in the following subsections, we particularize the calculation of the asymptotic eigenvalue distribution for genuine images in Sect. 3.1, and for unquantized upscaled images in Sect. 3.2. Finally, pairing these results with the characterization of the quantization noise through the MPL, we describe in Sect. 3.3 the gap that emerges in images that have been upscaled and later quantized.

For the sake of simplicity, and without loss of generality, in Sects. 3.1 and 3.2 we assume that the entries of $\mathbf{S}$ are i.i.d. with variance $\sigma_S^2 = 1$ as in [12]. More generally, in Sect. 3.3, we assume an arbitrary variance σ_S^2 to further evaluate the effect of the signal-to-quantization-noise ratio. Notice that the eigenvalue distribution for $\sigma_S^2 \neq 1$ is directly obtained by multiplying by σ_S^2 the eigenvalues for $\sigma_S^2 = 1$.

3.1 Eigenvalue Distribution for Genuine Images

Given the 2D-AR causal model for genuine images in (5), here we analyze the eigenvalues of $\boldsymbol{\Sigma}_{X_K}$ when $\mathbf{X}_K$ is constructed by taking K consecutive columns from the $N \times N$ random field $\mathbf{X}$ (without loss of generality, we will assume that we retain the *first* K columns), such that

$$\mathbf{X}_K = \mathbf{U}_N \mathbf{S} \mathbf{U}_K^T, \tag{6}$$

where $\mathbf{U}_K$ is obtained from $\mathbf{U}$ by keeping the first K rows, and $\mathbf{U}_N = \mathbf{U}$ is so written to stress the fact that it has N rows. In (6) $\mathbf{S}$ is an $(N+Q-1)\times(N+Q-1)$ random matrix with i.i.d. $\mathcal{N}(0,1)$ entries.

For the calculation of the η-transform of $\boldsymbol{\Sigma}_{X_K}$ according to [12, Theorem 2.43], we first need to derive the asymptotic spectra of the matrices that induce the linear dependencies, i.e., $\mathbf{D} = \mathbf{U}_N \mathbf{U}_N^T$ and $\mathbf{T} = \mathbf{U}_K^T \mathbf{U}_K$. It is easy to show that both matrices are full-rank and, for a sufficiently large value of K and N, have identical asymptotic spectra. Therefore, we focus on obtaining the asymptotic spectrum of $\mathbf{D}$, which can be seen as an unnormalized version of the autocorrelation matrix of $\mathbf{U}_N$, itself described by $u_Q[n]$ (see Sect. 2.3).

If we assume that $Q \geq N$, we can straightforwardly show that $\mathbf{D}$ is a symmetric Toeplitz matrix, whose (i,j)-th element is given by $(1-\rho^{2(Q-|i-j|)})\cdot\rho^{|i-j|}/(1-\rho^2)$. If we let $Q \to \infty$, this simplifies to $D_{i,j} = \rho^{|i-j|}/(1 - \rho^2)$. Now, in order to calculate the asymptotic eigenvalue spectrum of $\mathbf{D}$, we can invoke Szegö's fundamental theorem of eigenvalue distribution [3], which establishes that for a

Toeplitz symmetric matrix $\mathbf{D}$ defined by sequence $d[n]$ (i.e., $d[|i - j|] \triangleq D_{i,j}$), where $d[n]$ is absolutely summable,[2] its asymptotic eigenvalue spectrum tends to the Fourier transform of $d[n]$, i.e., $d(\omega)$. Therefore, when $N \to \infty$, the eigenvalues of $\mathbf{D}$ and (by extension) $\mathbf{T}$ will asymptotically converge to

$$d(\omega) = \frac{1}{1 + \rho^2 - 2\rho \cos(\omega)}, \quad \omega \in [0, 2\pi). \tag{7}$$

The η-transform of $\boldsymbol{\Sigma}_{X_K}$ depends on two independent random variables $\mathfrak{D}$ and $\mathfrak{T}$ which are distributed as the asymptotic spectra of $\mathbf{D}$ and $\mathbf{T}$. Both random variables can be seen as the result of applying the transformation $d(\omega)$ in (7) to a random variable $\Omega \sim \mathcal{U}[0, 2\pi)$, such that $\mathfrak{D} = d(\Omega)$ and $\mathfrak{T} = d(\Omega)$. Therefore, as described in [14, Appendix A], once $d(\omega)$ is available, the η-transform of $\boldsymbol{\Sigma}_{X_K}$ can be numerically calculated. However, for completing the pdf of the eigenvalues of $\boldsymbol{\Sigma}_{X_K}$ we need to calculate its asymptotic fraction of zero eigenvalues (in the sequel, AFZE), which is

$$1 - \min \left\{ \beta P(\mathfrak{T} \neq 0), P(\mathfrak{D} \neq 0) \right\}. \tag{8}$$

Given that $\mathbf{D}$ and $\mathbf{T}$ have full rank and their asymptotic spectra through (7) satisfy $d(\omega) > 0$, we know that $P(\mathfrak{T} \neq 0) = P(\mathfrak{D} \neq 0) = 1$. Therefore, since $\beta \leq 1$, the AFZE of $\boldsymbol{\Sigma}_{X_K}$ equals $(1 - \beta)$. So finally, applying steps 2 and 3 from Algorithm 1, we obtain the asymptotic pdf of the eigenvalues of $\boldsymbol{\Sigma}_{X_K}$, i.e.,

$$f_{\boldsymbol{\Sigma}_{X_K}}(\lambda) = (1 - \beta)\delta(\lambda) + \lim_{\nu \to 0^+} \frac{1}{\pi} \text{Im} \left[\mathcal{S}_{\boldsymbol{\Sigma}_{X_K}}(\lambda + j\nu) \right],$$

where $\delta(\cdot)$ denotes the Dirac delta function.

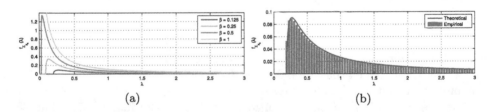

(a)   (b)

Fig. 1. Partial representation of the analytically derived pdf of the eigenvalues of $\boldsymbol{\Sigma}_{X_K}$, i.e., $f_{\boldsymbol{\Sigma}_{X_K}}(\lambda)$, for different values of β and $\rho = 0.97$ in (a). Graphical comparison in (b) of the theoretical result for $\beta = 0.125$ and the histogram corresponding to 50,000 realizations ($N = 1024$). The mass points at $\lambda = 0$ (present for $\beta < 1$) are not shown.

Figure 1(a) depicts the derived pdf $f_{\boldsymbol{\Sigma}_{X_K}}(\lambda)$ for different values of β (fixing $\rho = 0.97$) and quite remarkably, as predicted by MPL for random matrices with

---

[2] There is an additional technical condition that applies in the cases considered in this paper, namely, that the set $\{\omega : d(\omega) = x\}$ has measure zero for all $x \in \mathbb{R}$.

i.i.d. entries, we find that the lower the value of β, the more the eigenvalues of Σ_{X_K} get squeezed towards the variance of $\mathbf{X}$. This generalization of the MPL to stochastic representations of genuine images is key for our purposes. Furthermore, in Fig. 1(b), we can see that the conformity between the empirical pdf for finite matrices ($N = 1024$) and its asymptotic version is nearly perfect.

3.2   Eigenvalue Distribution for (Unquantized) Upscaled Images

In this case, we are interested in computing the eigenvalue distribution of Σ_{Y_K}, where $\mathbf{Y}_K$ is a submatrix of size $N \times K$ that is extracted from an upscaled image $\mathbf{Y}$. Modeling $\hat{\mathbf{X}}$ in (2) as in (5), we can write

$$\mathbf{Y}_K = \mathbf{H}_N \mathbf{U} \mathbf{S} \mathbf{U}^T \mathbf{H}_K^T,$$

where $\mathbf{U}$ is now a Toeplitz matrix of size $R \times (R + Q - 1)$ described by sequence $u_Q[n]$. In the above equation, matrices $\mathbf{H}_N$ and $\mathbf{H}_K$ are constructed as in (3), with respective sizes $N \times R$ and $K \times R$, containing both shifted copies of the L different polyphase components of $h(iM/L + \varphi)$, $i \in \mathbb{Z}$. Notice that (3) is such that the first row in $\mathbf{H}_N$ (or $\mathbf{H}_K$) corresponds to the zeroth polyphase component; however, as we will see, this arbitrary assignment has no effect on our analytical derivations.

As in the previous section, in order to compute the η-transform of Σ_{Y_K}, we need to characterize the asymptotic spectra of matrices $\mathbf{D} = \mathbf{C}\mathbf{C}^T = \mathbf{H}_N \mathbf{U} \mathbf{U}^T \mathbf{H}_N^T$ and $\mathbf{T} = \mathbf{A}\mathbf{A}^T = \mathbf{U}^T \mathbf{H}_K^T \mathbf{H}_K \mathbf{U}$. For convenience, we start focusing on the nonzero eigenvalues of $\mathbf{D} = \mathbf{C}\mathbf{C}^T$, which are the same as those of matrix $\mathbf{D}' \triangleq \mathbf{C}^T \mathbf{C}$. Let us consider its inner matrix $\mathbf{R} \triangleq \mathbf{H}_N^T \mathbf{H}_N$, with entries given by

$$R_{i,j} = \sum_{l=0}^{R-1} h\left(l\tfrac{M}{L} + \varphi - i\right) h\left(l\tfrac{M}{L} + \varphi - j\right). \tag{9}$$

Although this matrix is not Toeplitz, it can be seen to contain in its rows the different components of a polyphase decomposition of the kernel autocorrelation function. Since these rows are roughly similar, it makes sense to convert $\mathbf{R}$ into Toeplitz by averaging those components. Let $\bar{\mathbf{R}}$ be such matrix, with

$$\begin{aligned}
\bar{R}_{i,j} &= \frac{1}{M} \sum_{k=0}^{M-1} \sum_{l=0}^{R-1} h\left(l\tfrac{M}{L} + \tfrac{k}{L} + \varphi - i\right) h\left(l\tfrac{M}{L} + \tfrac{k}{L} + \varphi - j\right) \\
&= \frac{1}{M} \sum_{k=0}^{R \cdot M-1} h\left(\tfrac{k}{L} + \varphi - i\right) h\left(\tfrac{k}{L} + \varphi - j\right), \tag{10}
\end{aligned}$$

which, as it can be readily checked is symmetric Toeplitz, so $\bar{R}_{i,j}$ only depends on $|i - j|$. Then, $\bar{\mathbf{R}}$ is completely characterized by the sequence $r_{hh}[|i - j|] \triangleq \bar{R}_{i,j}$. Now, since $\mathbf{U}$ is also Toeplitz, by expressing products of Toeplitz matrices as convolutions of their corresponding representative sequences, it is possible to see that $\mathbf{D}' = \mathbf{U}^T \mathbf{H}_N^T \mathbf{H}_N \mathbf{U}$ is described by sequence $u_Q[n] * r_{hh}[n] * u_Q[-n]$.

This sequence is absolutely summable even for $Q \to \infty$ and $\mathbf{D}'$ is symmetric Toeplitz; therefore, we can resort again to Szegö's theorem [3] to approximate the asymptotic eigenvalue distribution of $\mathbf{D}'$ when both $Q, N \to \infty$, as follows

$$d'(\omega) = \left(\frac{1}{1 + \rho^2 - 2\rho\cos(\omega)} \right) \sum_{n=-(k_w-1)}^{k_w-1} r_{hh}[n]\cos(n\omega), \tag{11}$$

where $\omega \in [0, 2\pi)$. This discussion extends to the nonzero eigenvalues of $\mathbf{T}$, which can also be approximated by $d'(\omega)$.

A crucial difference with respect to the case of genuine images (Sect. 3.1) is that now both $\mathbf{D}$ and $\mathbf{T}$ will have null eigenvalues, given that matrices $\mathbf{H}_N$ and $\mathbf{H}_K$ do not have full rank. Actually, the ranks of both matrices depend on the applied resampling factor ξ, and it is easy to check that $\lim_{N\to\infty} \text{rank}(\mathbf{H}_N)/N \to \xi^{-1}$, and $\lim_{K\to\infty} \text{rank}(\mathbf{H}_K)/K \to \xi^{-1}$. From the rank properties for real matrices, we have that $\text{rank}(\mathbf{D}) = \text{rank}(\mathbf{C}) = \text{rank}(\mathbf{H}_N)$ because $\mathbf{U}$ has full rank, so $\text{rank}(\mathbf{D})/N \to \xi^{-1}$ and, by extension, $\text{rank}(\mathbf{T})/K \to \xi^{-1}$. We can conclude that the AFZE of $\mathbf{D}$ and $\mathbf{T}$ is given by $(1 - \xi^{-1})$.

Figure 2 depicts the eigenvalues of matrix $\mathbf{D}$ for different values of ξ and for the interpolation kernels in Table 2, and the approximation in (11). Although the derived approximation is generally accurate, we observe that for certain pairs of ξ and kernel, it is not able to follow the existing discontinuities. The most evident examples show up with the Linear kernel for $\xi = \frac{4}{3}$ and $\xi = \frac{8}{5}$. This difference comes from approximating $\mathbf{R}$ by $\tilde{\mathbf{R}}$. However, since the range of the eigenvalues is well matched and their evolution is tracked up to a good degree, we adopt this approximation.

From the plots in Fig. 2, it is interesting to observe that the largest eigenvalues of the four kernels converge to the same value, while the smallest ones differ noticeably. Although for Catmull-Rom and Lanczos kernels the smallest eigenvalues are almost identical, the Linear kernel provides smaller eigenvalues as ξ gets closer to 1, and the B-spline kernel produces the smallest eigenvalues at almost one order of magnitude below.

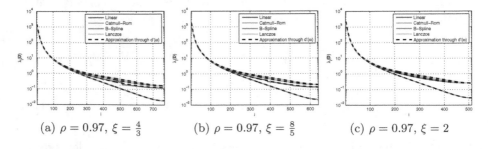

(a) $\rho = 0.97$, $\xi = \frac{4}{3}$ (b) $\rho = 0.97$, $\xi = \frac{8}{5}$ (c) $\rho = 0.97$, $\xi = 2$

Fig. 2. Evolution of the nonzero eigenvalues of $\mathbf{D}$ for different values of ξ and the interpolation kernels in Table 2. *Solid lines* represent the ordered eigenvalues $\lambda_i(\mathbf{D})$, while *dashed lines* correspond to the approximation $d'(\omega)$ in (11) sorted in descending order, with $\omega = 2\pi \frac{i-1}{N\xi^{-1}}$, $i \in \{1, \dots, N\xi^{-1}\}$, $(N = 1024)$.

The procedure to compute the η-transform of $\boldsymbol{\Sigma}_{Y_K}$ is exactly the same as the one followed with genuine images by taking $d'(\omega)$ as $d(\omega)$ in [14, Appendix]. However, note that when computing E_1 and E_2 as in [14, Eq. 11] and $\eta_{\boldsymbol{\Sigma}_{Y_K}}$ as in [14, Eq. 12], we must take into account that now the random variable Ω is of mixed type with a probability mass at $\omega = 0$ of size $(1 - \xi^{-1})$, and a continuous pdf $f_\Omega(\omega) = (2\pi\xi)^{-1}$ in $(0, 2\pi)$, i.e., the pdf of a uniform random variable, but scaled by ξ^{-1} so that the total probability adds up to 1.

Once the η-transform has been computed, we have to determine the AFZE of $\boldsymbol{\Sigma}_{Y_K}$, which is given by (8). In this case, we know that $P(\mathfrak{T} \neq 0) = P(\mathfrak{D} \neq 0) = \xi^{-1}$ and so the AFZE equals $(1 - \beta\xi^{-1})$ for $\beta \leq 1$. Finally, applying steps 2 and 3 from Algorithm 1, we have

$$f_{\boldsymbol{\Sigma}_{Y_K}}(\lambda) = \left(1 - \beta\xi^{-1}\right)\delta(\lambda) + \lim_{\nu \to 0^+} \frac{1}{\pi}\text{Im}\left[\mathcal{S}_{\boldsymbol{\Sigma}_{Y_K}}(\lambda + j\nu)\right].$$

The upper panels of Fig. 3 show the derived pdf $f_{\boldsymbol{\Sigma}_{Y_K}}(\lambda)$ for different interpolation kernels and values of β, whereas the lower ones compare the theoretical pdf against its empirical version under a fixed setting with $N = 1024$. Clearly, the theoretical model fits very well the empirical eigenvalue distribution and, in view of the shape of the pdfs, there is no doubt that the eigenvalues of $\boldsymbol{\Sigma}_{Y_K}$ are compacted in the same way as those from $\boldsymbol{\Sigma}_{X_K}$, which confirms that the squeezing effect of the eigenvalues as β decreases is also valid for upscaled images. This feature will be decisive for distinguishing the signal subspace from the background noise. Moreover, the influence of each particular interpolation kernel on the distribution of the eigenvalues of $\boldsymbol{\Sigma}_{Y_K}$ for a fixed β can be appreciated in the lower pannels of Fig. 3. Consistent with the conclusions drawn from Fig. 2, the B-spline kernel concentrates the smallest eigenvalues towards zero. As we will see in Sect. 4, the distinct behavior among these kernels will result in different performance when conducting resampling detection.

3.3 Eigenvalue Distribution for Upscaled and Quantized Images

Adopting the $N \times N$ matrix $\mathbf{Z}$ in (4) as the model for upscaled and later quantized images, here we analyze the eigenvalues of $\boldsymbol{\Sigma}_{Z_K}$, where $\mathbf{Z}_K$ is an $N \times K$ submatrix extracted from $\mathbf{Z}$. In particular, drawing on the previous eigenvalue characterization of $\boldsymbol{\Sigma}_{Y_K}$ and using the MPL for modeling the eigenvalues coming from the quantization noise matrix $\mathbf{W}$, we delve into the characteristics of the signal-plus-noise structure of $\mathbf{Z}$ already discussed in Sect. 2.2.

From the preceding analysis in Sect. 3.2 we know that for a sufficiently large value of K, the submatrix $\mathbf{Y}_K$ has rank P strictly smaller than K (i.e., rank$(\mathbf{Y}_K)/K \to \xi^{-1}$). Therefore, in $\boldsymbol{\Sigma}_{Z_K}$, there are P leading eigenvalues corresponding to the signal subspace and $K - P$ corresponding to the background noise (the remaining $N - K$ are zero). To model this transition between the signal subspace and the noise space, we center our attention on the eigenvalues $\lambda_i(\boldsymbol{\Sigma}_{Z_K})$ located on each side of the boundary. Then, we derive a lower bound for the last eigenvalue coming from the signal subspace, i.e., $\lambda_P(\boldsymbol{\Sigma}_{Z_K})$,

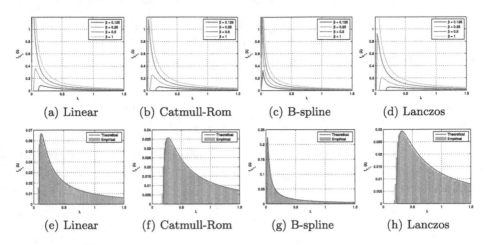

Fig. 3. Partial representation of the analytically derived pdf $f_{\boldsymbol{\Sigma}_{Y_K}}(\lambda)$ for different interpolation kernels and values of β in the *upper panels* ($\xi = 1.5$, $\rho = 0.97$). Graphical comparison in the *lower panels* of the theoretical pdf and the histogram from 50,000 realizations ($N = 1024$, $\beta = 0.125$, $\xi = 2$, $\rho = 0.97$). All mass points are omitted.

and an upper bound for the first eigenvalue belonging to the noise space, i.e., $\lambda_{P+1}(\boldsymbol{\Sigma}_{Z_K})$. As fully reported in [14,15], these two bounds can be obtained by resorting to Weyl's inequality applied to the singular values [11, Exercise 1.3.22], so that the following lower bound applies for $\lambda_P(\boldsymbol{\Sigma}_{Z_K})$:

$$\lambda_P(\boldsymbol{\Sigma}_{Z_K}) \geq \lambda_P(\boldsymbol{\Sigma}_{Y_K}) - \lambda_1(\boldsymbol{\Sigma}_{W_K}) \geq \sigma_S^2 \lambda_-(\boldsymbol{\Sigma}_{Y_K}) - \lambda_+(\boldsymbol{\Sigma}_{W_K}), \qquad (12)$$

where $\lambda_+(\boldsymbol{\Sigma}_{W_K})$ denotes the largest eigenvalue of $\boldsymbol{\Sigma}_{W_K}$ given by MPL and $\lambda_-(\boldsymbol{\Sigma}_{Y_K})$ represents the smallest nonzero eigenvalue of $\boldsymbol{\Sigma}_{Y_K}$. Remember that $\lambda_-(\boldsymbol{\Sigma}_{Y_K})$ can be obtained through the calculation of $f_{\boldsymbol{\Sigma}_{Y_K}}(\lambda)$ as in Sect. 3.2, albeit now it appears scaled by σ_S^2 because the derived pdf $f_{\boldsymbol{\Sigma}_{Y_K}}(\lambda)$ assumes $\sigma_S^2 = 1$. On the other hand, the upper bound for $\lambda_{P+1}(\boldsymbol{\Sigma}_{Z_K})$ is given by

$$\lambda_{P+1}(\boldsymbol{\Sigma}_{Z_K}) \leq \lambda_1(\boldsymbol{\Sigma}_{W_K}) \leq \lambda_+(\boldsymbol{\Sigma}_{W_K}) \rightarrow \sigma_W^2(1 + \sqrt{\beta})^2. \qquad (13)$$

Finally, combining (12) and (13) we can characterize the asymptotic gap that marks the transition between the signal subspace and the noise as

$$\frac{\lambda_P(\boldsymbol{\Sigma}_{Z_K})}{\lambda_{P+1}(\boldsymbol{\Sigma}_{Z_K})} \geq \frac{\sigma_S^2 \lambda_-(\boldsymbol{\Sigma}_{Y_K}) - \lambda_+(\boldsymbol{\Sigma}_{W_K})}{\lambda_+(\boldsymbol{\Sigma}_{W_K})} \rightarrow \left(\frac{\sigma_S^2}{\sigma_W^2}\right) \frac{\lambda_-(\boldsymbol{\Sigma}_{Y_K})}{(1 + \sqrt{\beta})^2} - 1. \qquad (14)$$

From (14), it is clear that the magnitude of the gap will monotonically increase with the signal-to-noise ratio $\left(\frac{\sigma_S^2}{\sigma_W^2}\right)$. In addition, it will also increase as $\beta \rightarrow 0$, since $\lambda_-(\boldsymbol{\Sigma}_{Y_K})$ and $(1 + \sqrt{\beta})^2$ respectively increases and decreases as $\beta \rightarrow 0$. However, as reported in [14], the gap will become smaller as both the resampling factor ξ and the correlation coefficient ρ approach 1.

Regarding the impact of the interpolation kernel, since the magnitude of the gap is directly proportional to $\lambda_-(\Sigma_{Y_K})$, we can conclude that the smallest gap will take place with the B-spline kernel since it contributes with the smallest magnitude of $\lambda_-(\Sigma_{Y_K})$ (see Fig. 3(e–h)). Conversely, the Lanczos kernel will produce the largest gap together with the Catmull-Rom, whereas the Linear kernel will be halfway between Catmull-Rom and B-spline.

4   Experimental Results

Exploiting the above eigenvalue characterization, we have proposed in [15] a resampling detector whose test statistic κ (cf. [15, Eq. 11]) is used to determine whether an observed matrix $\mathbf{Z}$ comes from a genuine image (i.e., hypothesis $\mathcal{H}_0$), or from an upscaled and quantized image (i.e., hypothesis $\mathcal{H}_1$). The experimental validation of the proposed detector proved its practical applicability, but here we are more interested in evaluating its performance from a theoretical perspective.

As an example, given that we know through (14) that the magnitude of the gap between the signal subspace and the noise depends on the signal-to-noise ratio $\left(\frac{\sigma_S^2}{\sigma_W^2}\right)$, we can evaluate the detector performance as a function of this quantity using synthetic 2D-AR random fields. The obtained results of Area Under the Curve (AUC) corresponding to the Receiver Operating Characteristic (ROC) of the detector are shown in Fig. 4(a) for different values of $\left(\frac{\sigma_S^2}{\sigma_W^2}\right)$ and ξ (using the Linear kernel and performing 1000 realizations). As expected, the larger the signal-to-noise-ratio, the better the detection performance. Notice also that the convergence to perfect detection is faster for larger resampling factors.

On the other hand, it is interesting to note that we can determine a theoretical threshold to drive the decision of our detector. This comes from the analysis performed in Sect. 3: first, we know that under $\mathcal{H}_0$ the last nonzero eigenvalue of Σ_{Z_K}, i.e., $\lambda_K(\Sigma_{Z_K})$, is lower bounded by $\sigma_S^2 \lambda_-(\Sigma_{X_K})$; then, from (13) we know that the upper bound for $\lambda_K(\Sigma_{Z_K})$ under $\mathcal{H}_1$ is given by MPL at $\sigma_W^2(1+\sqrt{\beta})^2$; so, provided that $\sigma_S^2 \gg \sigma_W^2$ (which is typically the case for real images), the condition $\sigma_S^2 \lambda_-(\Sigma_{X_K}) > \sigma_W^2(1+\sqrt{\beta})^2$ will be generally satisfied (recall that $\lambda_-(\Sigma_{X_K})$ increases as $\beta \to 0$). As a conclusion, assuming that this condition is commonly satisfied in most practical cases, the proposed detector can operate with a fixed threshold at $\sigma_W^2(1+\sqrt{\beta})^2$.

The soundness of this limit with real images is verified by testing a total of 1317 uncompressed images from the Dresden Image Database [2] (only raw images from different Nikon cameras are selected). To avoid the presence of demosaicing traces, the genuine images are constructed by getting access to the output of the camera sensor using the tool dcraw and picking always the same green pixel position from each 2×2 Bayer pattern. For performing each full-frame resampling operation we employ the tool convert from ImageMagick's software. As interpolation kernels, we use those described in Table 2. We constrain the set of resampling factors to the interval [1.05, 2] uniformly sampled with step 0.05.

Figure 4(b) shows part of the histogram of $\lambda_K(\Sigma_{Z_K})$ under each hypothesis after processing the central 128×128 block from each genuine and upscaled

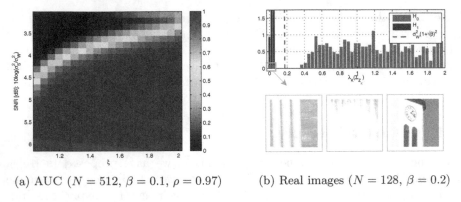

(a) AUC ($N = 512$, $\beta = 0.1$, $\rho = 0.97$)   (b) Real images ($N = 128$, $\beta = 0.2$)

Fig. 4. Evaluation of the detector performance in terms of AUC for different values of $\left(\frac{\sigma_S^2}{\sigma_W^2}\right)$ and ξ in (a). In (b), histogram of the values of $\lambda_K(\boldsymbol{\Sigma}_{Z_K})$ when considering real images (*top*) and examples of genuine blocks with linear dependencies (*bottom*). (Color figure online)

image by $\xi \in [1.05, 2]$ with the Linear interpolation kernel. As can be observed, the discussed threshold almost perfectly separates both hypotheses, excepting the highlighted cases that correspond to genuine image blocks which present linear dependencies in their content (e.g., flat regions). This is the reason why the test statistic κ defined in [15, Eq. 11] must consider different blocks and identify rank-deficient matrices to circumvent these special cases and also their upscaled versions (which do not follow the model in Sect. 2.1). Hence, when using the test statistic κ with non-demosaiced images, we can configure the detector to work with the above threshold so that it labels an observed image block $\mathbf{Z}$ as upscaled whenever $\kappa < \sigma_W^2(1 + \sqrt{\beta})^2$, and genuine otherwise.

To confirm the good behavior of our detector using this predefined threshold, we conduct the same experiments over all the interpolation kernels, but now processing smaller blocks of size 32×32, so as to test our detector in realistic conditions where the tampered regions might be small. The performance of the proposed detector is measured in terms of AUC and detection rate at a fixed False Alarm Rate (FAR). For comparison, we consider our previous work in [13] based on subspace decomposition, namely the "SVD-based" detector, and also the state-of-the-art "LP-based" detector proposed in [5] (where LP stands for Linear Predictor). We configure our detector to work with submatrices of small aspect ratio $\beta = 0.2812$ (i.e., $K = 9$, $N = 32$), because it makes the separation between the smallest eigenvalue under each hypothesis more evident. For [13] we take $\xi_{\min} = 1.05$ and for [5] we fix a neighborhood of 3 rows/columns.

The AUC for each combination of ξ and interpolation kernel is obtained by applying the three detectors on both the genuine and the correspondingly upscaled images. Given that our detector works with a predefined threshold, we can avoid the use of a training set for computing the detection rates. However, for deriving the empirical thresholds for the other two methods, the database is

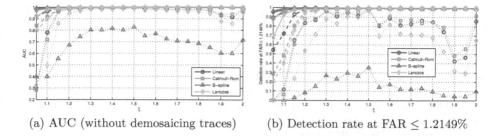

(a) AUC (without demosaicing traces)   (b) Detection rate at FAR $\leq$ 1.2149%

Fig. 5. Evaluation of our detector (*solid lines*) against the SVD-based [13] (*dashed lines*) and the LP-based [5] (*dotted lines*) for image blocks of size 32×32.

randomly split in two disjoint sets, where 1/3 of the images are used for training and the remaining ones for testing. The FAR obtained with the application of our method is fixed as a reference for comparing the detection rates of the three detectors. This means that for the detectors in [5,13], the training set is used to empirically determine the thresholds that give the same FAR. Finally, using the obtained thresholds, these detectors are applied on the test set of upscaled images to compute the detection rates.

Figure 5(a) shows the obtained AUC for each detector. As expected from the analysis in Fig. 4(a), the detection performance of our method improves as the resampling factor increases and, in coherence with the statistical distribution of the eigenvalues shown in Fig. 3, the best results are achieved for the interpolation kernels B-spline and Linear since their smallest eigenvalues converge faster to zero than for Catmull-Rom and Lanczos. This improves the separability between upscaled and genuine images and, interestingly, the performance of the SVD-based detector, which also exploits the idea behind the subspace decomposition, resembles that of our method, still showing worse results. The LP-based detector is outperformed by the other two because the spectral density estimator used in [5] becomes inaccurate when dealing with small block sizes.

Figure 5(b) depicts the detection rates at FAR $\leq$ 1.2149%. Remember that this value of FAR, which turns out to be appealing in practice, results from the application of our detector using the predefined threshold over the genuine images. In all cases, our method always achieves the best detection performance. Furthermore, the results obtained in the range $1.05 \leq \xi \leq 1.2$ are clearly superior to those of the other methods, which is also of interest in practical scenarios, since credible forgeries are typically performed using slight transformations.

5   Conclusions

The eigenvalue characterization of genuine and resampled images has been addressed in this paper using a causal 2D-AR model and drawing on valuable results from RMT. The remarkable agreement between the theoretical distributions and their empirical versions made possible the translation of theoretical bounds to practical solutions for resampling detection. Further research should focus on introducing a suitable model for the demosaicing process, so as to generalize all these theoretical findings to more realistic scenarios.

Acknowledgments. This work is funded by the Agencia Estatal de Investigación (Spain) and the European Regional Development Fund (ERDF) under project WINTER (TEC2016-76409-C2-2-R), and by the Xunta de Galicia and the ERDF under projects Agrupación Estratéxica Consolidada de Galicia accreditation 2016–2019 and Red Temática RedTEIC 2017–2018.

References

1. Bai, Z., Zhou, W.: Large sample covariance matrices without independence structures in columns. Statistica Sinica **18**(2), 425–442 (2008)
2. Gloe, T., Böhme, R.: The Dresden image database for benchmarking digital image forensics. In: ACM SAC, pp. 1584–1590, March 2010
3. Grenander, U., Szegö, G.: Toeplitz Forms and Their Applications. University of California Press, Berkeley (1958)
4. Kirchner, M.: Fast and reliable resampling detection by spectral analysis of fixed linear predictor residue. In: ACM MM&Sec, pp. 11–20, September 2008
5. Kirchner, M.: Linear row and column predictors for the analysis of resized images. In: ACM MM&Sec, pp. 13–18, September 2010
6. Li, Y., Ding, Z.: Blind channel identification based on second order cyclostationary statistics. In: IEEE ICASSP. pp. 81–84, April 1993
7. Mahdian, B., Saic, S.: Blind authentication using periodic properties of interpolation. IEEE Trans. Inf. Forensics Secur. **3**(3), 529–538 (2008)
8. Marčenko, V.A., Pastur, L.A.: Distribution of eigenvalues for some sets of random matrices. Math. USSR Sb. **1**(4), 457–483 (1967)
9. Pfaffel, O., Schlemm, E.: Eigenvalue distribution of large sample covariance matrices of linear processes. Prob. Math. Stat. **31**(2), 313–329 (2011)
10. Popescu, A.C., Farid, H.: Exposing digital forgeries by detecting traces of resampling. IEEE Trans. Signal Process. **53**(2), 758–767 (2005)
11. Tao, T.: Topics in Random Matrix Theory. American Mathematical Society, Providence (2012)
12. Tulino, A.M., Verdú, S.: Random matrix theory and wireless communications. Found. Trends Commun. Inf. Theor. **1**(1), 1–182 (2004)
13. Vázquez-Padín, D., Comesaña, P., Pérez-González, F.: An SVD approach to forensic image resampling detection. In: EUSIPCO, pp. 2067–2071, September 2015
14. Vázquez-Padín, D., Pérez-González, F., Comesaña Alfaro, P.: Derivation of the asymptotic eigenvalue distribution for causal 2D-AR models under upscaling. arXiv:1704.05773 [cs.CR], April 2017
15. Vázquez-Padín, D., Pérez-González, F., Comesaña Alfaro, P.: A random matrix approach to the forensic analysis of upscaled images. IEEE Trans. Inf. Forensics Secur. **12**(9), 2115–2130 (2017)

Security Protocols

A Security Evaluation of FIDO's UAF Protocol in Mobile and Embedded Devices

Christoforos Panos[1], Stefanos Malliaros[2], Christoforos Ntantogian[2],
Angeliki Panou[2], and Christos Xenakis[2(✉)]

[1] Department of Informatics and Telecommunications,
University of Athens, Athens, Greece
cpanos@di.uoa.gr
[2] Department of Digital Systems, University of Piraeus, Pireas, Greece
{stefmal,dadoyan,apanou,xenakis}@unipi.gr

Abstract. The FIDO (Fast Identity Online) Universal Authentication Framework is a new authentication mechanism that replaces passwords, simplifying the process of user authentication. To this end, FIDO transfers user verification tasks from the authentication server to the user's personal device. Therefore, the overall assurance level of user authentication is highly dependent on the security and integrity of the user's device involved. This paper analyses the functionality of FIDO's UAF protocol and identifies a list of critical vulnerabilities that may compromise the authenticity, privacy, availability, and integrity of the UAF protocol, allowing an attacker to launch a number of attacks, such as, capturing the data exchanged between a user and an online service, impersonating a user at any UAF compatible online service, impersonating online services to the user, and presenting fake information to the user's screen during a transaction.

Keywords: Authentication · FIDO · Security analysis · Trusted computing · TPM · Remote attestation · TrustZone · Mobile and embedded devices

1 Introduction

The most traditional form of authentication, i.e., one-factor, password-based authentication, has become a deficient and inconvenient solution for the modern-day user, who must keep track and maintain an ever-growing list of login credentials and passwords. In 2014, an average user had 25 accounts and performed logins 8 times a day, using 6.5 passwords [1]. Even more importantly, password-based authentication is becoming less secure. Users typically rely on low entropy passwords so that they are easy to remember. Furthermore, recent password breaches resulted in large password lists (55000 accounts from Twitter [2], 450000 accounts from Yahoo [3], and 6.5 million from LinkedIn [4]), which, in conjunction with today's abundant computing power, made password cracking a viable attack vector. The FIDO (Fast Identity Online) Alliance [5], a new industry working group, has been founded to define an open, interoperable set of authentication mechanisms that reduces the reliance on passwords and addresses the limitations and vulnerabilities of existing authentication schemes.

© Springer International Publishing AG 2017
A. Piva et al. (Eds.): TIWDC 2017, CCIS 766, pp. 127–142, 2017.
DOI: 10.1007/978-3-319-67639-5_11

The FIDO set of specifications supports multifactor authentication (MFA) and public key cryptography. Two protocols are being developed, namely the universal second factor authentication (U2F) [6] and the universal authentication framework (UAF) [7]. Both protocols may either work in conjunction, or independently. The U2F protocol augments the security of existing password authentication mechanisms by adding a second factor to user login, and, therefore, does not alleviate the use of passwords. A user logs on using a username and a password, while the protocol prompts the user to present a second factor device for authentication. The UAF protocol, on the other hand, offers password-less authentication.

The operation of the UAF protocol involves the communication of two computing entities, one maintained by the service provider that requires a user's authentication and one controlled by the user that must be authenticated. The service provider is referred as the relying party and is typically composed of a web server and a UAF server. The web server provides a front-end interface to the users, while the UAF server is responsible for communicating UAF protocol messages to a user's device. On the client side, the users' computing entity consists of one or more UAF authenticators, the UAF client and user agent software. The UAF authenticator is an entity connected or integrated within user devices responsible for (i) user authentication and (ii) the generation and association of key pairs with relying parties. The UAF client constitutes the user-side endpoint of the UAF protocol (typically a browser plugin) and its main responsibility is the interaction and coordination of UAF protocol operations with the UAF authenticators on one end and the relying party on the other end. Finally, the user agent software is the software used by the end user (such as a browser or an application).

During the UAF protocol's operation, a user initially registers his/her device to a relying party, using one or more local authentication mechanisms such as a biometric scan, based on the authenticator policy imposed by the relying party. At this stage, the following operations take place: (i) the relaying party utilizes an attestation mechanism to validate the legitimacy of the UAF authenticator(s) hosted by the user's device, and (ii), the UAF authenticator(s), associate the biometric scan with a newly generated key pair, retain the private key, and register the device to the relying party using the public key. Once registered, the user simply repeats the local authentication action whenever it is required to be authenticated to the service. The device's UAF authenticator verifies the user based on the authentication action, while the relying party verifies the device by transmitting a challenge, which is signed by the previously generated private key. Therefore, the overall assurance level of user authentication is highly dependent on the security and integrity of the user's device involved.

The UAF protocol provides several important advantages over traditional authentication mechanisms: it offers strong authentication (due to its reliance on public key cryptography); it simplifies the registration and authentication procedure; it alleviates the need for maintaining passwords, dealing with complex password rules, or going through password recovery procedures; and it strengthens user privacy, since all identifying information is stored locally, at the user's device. However, the operation of UAF relies on one fundamental assumption: the entities responsible for most of UAF's critical functionality, namely the UAF authenticator and the UAF client, are trusted and cannot be tampered by a malicious attacker. If either of these entities is compromised, then, an attacker would be able to launch a number of critical attacks, such as, capture the data exchanged between a user and an online service, impersonate a user at any UAF compatible online service, impersonate online services to the user, present fake information to the user's screen during a transaction, access private keys used for authentication, to name a few, essentially compromising the authenticity, privacy, availability, and integrity of the UAF protocol.

In this paper, we perform an informal security analysis in which we identify several attack vectors that can be set to compromise the legitimate operation of the UAF protocol, including the ability of an attacker to: (i) gain unprivileged access to the cryptographic material stored within the UAF authenticator, and (ii) highjack either the UAF authenticator or the UAF client. Our analysis concentrates on the client-side UAF protocol functionality, which includes the most critical protocol entities, namely, the storage location for the authentication keys and the entities performing the authentication operation (i.e., the UAF authenticators and the UAF client). These entities typically operate in a consumer platform such as a mobile device, which is susceptible to a variety of attacks such as malware and viruses, its users deploy unsupervised software, and the deployed operating systems may be susceptible to several vulnerabilities. On the other hand, the server-side entities of the UAF protocol (i.e., the relying party) rely on widely adopted functionality typically associated with web servers (such as the use of TLS cryptographic protocols). Furthermore, we investigate and identify how an attacker can circumvent the security measures provided by the UAF protocol. Finally, we provide a threat analysis and investigate the impairment that may be caused by an attacker in the event of a successful exploitation of the UAF protocol. Overall the contributions of this paper are the following:

- We define and comprehensively analyze the client-side operation of the UAF protocol, including any associated security measures proposed by the UAF protocol specifications.
- We perform, to the best of our knowledge, the first undisclosed security analysis of the UAF protocol. Based on this analysis, we identify several critical attack vectors that can be exploited by a malicious entity in order to compromise the authenticity, privacy, availability, and integrity provided by the UAF protocol.
- Our analysis also reveals vulnerabilities in the security measures employed by the UAF protocol, as well as to entities outside the scope of the UAF protocol, which, can be exploited to circumvent the security measures, or, target the legitimate operation of the UAF protocol.
- Based on our security analysis, we identify and categorize the critical assets related to the UAF protocols' secure operation.
- We perform a threat analysis in which we investigate and identify several critical attacks that can be deployed by a malicious entity exploiting the attack vectors identified in our security evaluation, including user and relaying party impersonation, phishing, and the disclosure of encrypted data.

The rest of this paper is organized as follows. In Sect. 2 we analyze the functionality of the UAF protocol, outline the entities involved in the process of user registration and authentication, present the security measures proposed by the UAF specifications and evaluate existing literature related to the evaluation of FIDO's security features and functionality. In Sect. 3, we perform a security analysis of the

UAF protocol, in which we identify several vulnerabilities and limitations that may be exploited by an attacker in order to circumvent any security measures and compromise the legitimate operation of the UAF protocol. Furthermore, we perform a threat analysis, with the goal of identifying the critical assets of the UAF protocol as well as the threats resulting from the attacks identified in the security evaluation. Finally, Sect. 4 contains the conclusions.

2   Background

In this section, we first provide an overview of the UAF protocol's functionality. This overview covers the most critical aspects of the protocol's operations, including the process of registering and authenticating a user to a relying party. A more detailed analysis of the UAF protocol exists in [7]. Furthermore, in Sect. 2.2, we survey any literature associated with the security evaluation of the UAF protocol. We outline the security measures proposed by the FIDO Alliance, analyze several entities associated with the security of the UAF protocol, and identify any associated vulnerabilities and limitations.

2.1   UAF Protocol Operations

The UAF protocol (see Fig. 1) encompasses three major operations, namely, registration, authentication, and deregistration. During the registration operation, the UAF protocol allows a user to register to a relying party using one or more UAF authenticators. Once registration is complete, the user can then invoke the authentication operation, in which the relying party prompts for a user authentication using the UAF

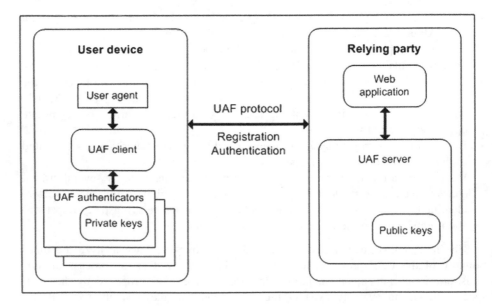

Fig. 1. The UAF protocol

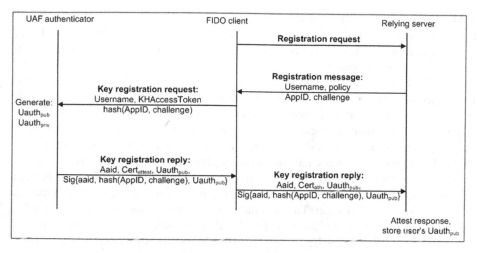

Fig. 2. The UAF registration operation

authenticator previously used during the registration operation. Finally, in the dereg-istration operation, the relying party can trigger the deletion of the authentication key material and remove the user from its list of authenticated users.

2.1.1 The UAF Registration Operation

The registration operation is initiated when a user requests a registration to a relying party, either through a compatible application or through a browser. The relying party replies to the registration request by transmitting a registration message with the fol-lowing parameters: the AppID, the authenticator policy, the server generated challenge, and the username to the UAF client residing in the user's device (illustrated in Fig. 2). The AppID parameter is used by the UAF client to determine if the calling application (or website) is authorized to use the UAF protocol and it is associated with a key pair by the UAF authenticator (during key generation), so that access to the generated key pair is limited to its respective application. The authenticator policy lists the type of UAF authenticators required by the relying party, while the server generated challenge is a random nonce value used to protect against replay attacks. Finally, the username parameter is used by the UAF authenticator to distinguish key pairs that belong to the same application (or website), but to different users.

Once the UAF client receives the registration message from the relying party, it first identifies the calling app (or website) and then determines (based on the AppID parameter) whether the associated application is trusted and allowed to proceed with a registration request. To accomplish this, the UAF client queries the relying party for the trusted facet list (i.e., a list of all the approved entities related to the calling app) and, based on this list, decides whether registration will proceed or not. For example, if the registration request was initiated by an application, then the trusted facet list will contain a signature of the calling application that the UAF client can use to verify the app. If, on the other hand, the registration was initiated by a website, then the trusted facet list will contain all the associated and approved domain names. Subsequently, the

UAF client will check the authenticator policy parameter and generate a key registration request to the set of UAF authenticator(s) mandatory by the policy. If the required UAF authenticators are not present in the user's device, then the registration operation will be canceled.

The UAF client communicates with the UAF authenticator(s) using the authenticator specific module (ASM), a software associated with a UAF authenticator that provides a uniform interface between the hardware and the UAF client software. At this stage, the UAF client performs the following operations: it first calls the UAF authenticator in order to compute the final challenge parameter (FCP), which is a hash of the AppID and the server challenge. Then, it generates the KHAccessToken, which is an access control mechanism for protecting an authenticator's UAF credentials from unauthorized use. It is created by ASM by mixing various sources of information together. Typically, KHAccessToken contains the following four data items: AppID, PersonaID, ASMToken and CallerID. The AppID is provided by the relying party and it is contained within every UAF message. The PersonaID is obtained by ASM from the operating system, and, typically, a different PersonaID is assigned to every user account. The ASMToken is a random generated secret which is maintained and protected by ASM. In a typical implementation ASM will randomly generate an ASMToken when it is first executed and will store this secret until it is uninstalled. CallerID is the calling UAF client's platform assigned ID. Once the FCP and the KHAccessToken are computed, the UAF client will send the key registration request to the UAF authenticator including the FCP, the KHAccessToken, and the username parameter.

Following the reception of a key registration request by a UAF authenticator, the later will first prompt the user for authentication, and, then, generate a new key pair (Uauth.pub, Uauth.priv), store it on its secure storage, and associate it with the received username and KHAccessToken. Subsequently, the UAF authenticator will create the key registration data (KRD) object containing the FCP, the newly generated user public key (Uauth.pub), and the authenticator's attestation ID (AAID), which is a unique identifier assigned to a model, class or batch of UAF authenticators, and it is used by the relying party to identify a UAF authenticator and attest its legitimacy. Once the KRD is generated, the UAF authenticator will sign it using its attestation private key and return to the UAF client a key registration reply (which the later forwards to the relying party) that encompasses: the signed KRD, the AAID, Uauth.pub, and its attestation certificate (Certattest). Upon the reception of the key registration reply by the relying party, the later cryptographically verifies the KRD object, uses the AAID to identify if the UAF authenticator is a legitimate authenticator with a valid (i.e., unrevoked) attestation certificate, and, finally, stores the Uauth.pub key in a database for the purposes of user authentication in any subsequent authentication requests.

2.1.2   The UAF Authentication Operation

The authentication operation (illustrated in Fig. 3) is initiated when a user requests a service that requires authentication to a relying party, either through a compatible application or through a browser (in a similar fashion with the registration operation outlined above). The relying party replies to the authentication request by transmitting an authentication message with the following parameters: the AppID, the authenticator policy, and a server generated challenge, to the UAF client residing in the user's

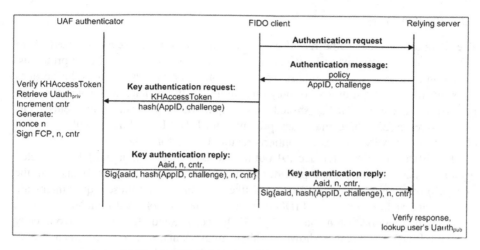

Fig. 3. The UAF authentication operation

device. The UAF client receiving the authentication request, first identifies the calling app (or website) and then determines (based on the AppID parameter) whether the associated application is trusted and allowed to proceed with the authentication request. Subsequently, the UAF client checks the authenticator policy parameter and sends a key authentication request to the set of UAF authenticator(s) mandatory by the policy. If the required UAF authenticators are not present in the user's device, then the authentication operation will be canceled. Using ASM, the UAF client performs the following operations: it first calls the UAF authenticator in order to compute the FCP, which is a hash of the AppID and the server challenge. Then, it retrieves the KHAccessToken, and finally, sends the key authentication request to the UAF authenticator (s) including the FCP and the KHAccessToken.

Following the reception of a key authentication request by a UAF authenticator, the later will first check if the UAF client is authorized to request an authentication for that particular user key, based on KHAccessToken. If the UAF client is authorized, then the UAF authenticator will prompt the user for authentication, and, then, retrieve the associated Uauth.priv from its secure key storage. Subsequently, the UAF authenticator will create the SignedData object containing the FCP, a newly generated nonce, and a Sign Counter (cntr). The cntr variable is a monotonically increasing counter, incremented on every sign request performed by the UAF authenticator for a particular user key pair. This value is then used by the relaying party to detect cloned authenticators. Once the SignedData object is generated, the UAF authenticator will sign it using the Uauth.priv key and return to the UAF client a key authentication reply (which the later forwards to the relying party) that encompasses: the signed object SignedData, the FCP, the nonce n, and the counter cntr. Finally, upon the reception of the key authentication reply by the relying party, the later first retrieves Uauth.pub from its database, cryptographically verifies the signedData object, and stores the value of the cntr counter. If the verification of the SignedData object succeeds, then the user is successfully authenticated.

2.2   Related Work

The literature includes some recent work that elaborates on the security of FIDO. In [22], the authors pinpoint and evaluate a set of trust requirements of FIDO protocols. Based on their analysis, the authors reach the conclusion that the FIDO solution does not solve the trust requirements of previous online identity management solutions (e.g., passwords) and instead it has shifted these requirements to other components in its architecture. In [23], three attacks are presented for FIDO UAF, but the authors do not elaborate extensively on the assumptions required to perform these attacks.

The FIDO security reference [9] outlines a list of assets that must be protected against malicious behavior and provides a limited set of security requirements with the goal of protecting these assets. We would like to point out that these requirements are optional and vendors receiving FIDO certification are not obliged to implement them. A variety of vendors such as Samsung, LG, Qualcomm, and Huawei [8] have already received FIDO certification, however, their implementations are proprietary, and, therefore, not open to 3rd party evaluation. Per FIDO specifications, the critical assets of the UAF protocol are the private key of the authentication key pair, the private key of the UAF authenticator attestation key pair, and the UAF authenticator attestation authority private key [7]. Furthermore, the UAF protocol specifications incorporate the following (optional) security requirements: the authentication keys must be securely stored within a UAF authenticator and thus protected against any misuse, users must authenticate themselves to the UAF authenticator before the authentication keys are accessed, the UAF authenticators may support authenticator attestation using a shared attestation certificate, and a UAF authenticator may implement a secure display mechanism (also referred as transaction confirmation mechanism), which can be used by the UAF client for displaying transaction data to the user. Therefore, the UAF specifications do not incorporate any mechanisms that safeguard the cryptographic material stored in the UAF authenticators, or protect against attacks that may target the UAF client. Instead, the responsibility for the design and implementation of any security measures that protect these critical entities is passed on to the vendors.

One solution to address the security requirements of the UAF specifications and provide a secure operational environment for the UAF authenticators, is the incorporation of trusted computing platform technologies [10]. The trusted computing platform constitutes specialized hardware that provides a variety of services, such as secure input/output, device authentication, integrity measurement, sealed storage, remote attestation, cryptographic acceleration, protected execution, root of trust, and digital rights management. Two prevalent platforms for trusted computing currently exist [10], the Trusted Platform Module (TPM) [11], which is based on the specifications created by the Trusted Computing Group, and the TrustZone (TZ) platform [12], created by the ARM corporation. The TPM is a co-processor, which provides basic cryptographic capabilities like random number generation, hashing, protected storage of sensitive data (e.g. secret keys), asymmetric encryption, as well as generation of signatures. The TPM platform presents some significant limitations [10]: (i) the need for a separate module increases the cost of a device; (ii) it cannot be deployed on legacy devices; (iii) it does not protect against runtime attacks; (iv) it relies on the assumption that a TPM cannot be tampered; (v) the physical size and energy consumption requirements make it an unsuitable solution for mobile and embedded devices; (vi) in case of a TPM compromise, the hardware module must be physically replaced; and (vii) the supported cryptographic algorithms have been found to pose security concerns (i.e., SHA-1), and are not well suited for resource restricted devices (i.e., RSA).

The TrustZone platform, is part of ARM's processor cores and system on chip (SoC) reference architecture. The associated hardware is part of the SoC silicon, and thus, it does not require any additional hardware. The primary objective of TrustZone is to establish a hardware-enforced security environment providing code isolation, that is, a clear separation between trusted software, which is granted access to sensitive data like secret keys, and other parts of the embedded software. To achieve this, the TrustZone platform provides two virtual processing cores with different privileges and a strictly controlled communication interface, enabling the creation of two distinct execution environments, encapsulated by hardware. Nevertheless, to the best of our knowledge, Samsung is the only certified vendor that implements a UAF authenticator using the TrustZone platform [13]. Furthermore, this approach only protects the UAF authenticator, while the UAF client is still susceptible to a variety of attacks (analyzed in detail in Sect. 3.2). Finally, extensive literature has shown that the TrustZone platform itself is not immune to weakness and vulnerabilities [14, 15, 18, 19].

3   UAF Security Analysis

In the following section, we provide an informal security analysis in which we manually identify several attack vectors that can beset to compromise the legitimate operation of the UAF protocol, including the ability of an attacker to: (i) gain unprivileged access to the cryptographic material stored within the UAF authenticator, and (ii) highjack either the UAF authenticator or the UAF client. Furthermore, we investigate and identify how an attacker can circumvent the security measures provided by the UAF protocol, including the authenticator attestation mechanism, the transaction confirmation mechanism, the trusted facet list, and the sign counter. Finally, we provide a threat analysis and investigate the impairment that may be caused by an attacker in the event of a successful exploitation of the UAF protocol.

3.1   UAF Protocol Vulnerabilities and Limitations

As we previously analyzed in Sect. 2.1, two UAF protocol entities, namely the UAF authenticator and the UAF client, reside at the client's device. These entities are responsible for most of UAF's critical functionality, including the authentication of users, the creation and maintenance of the cryptographic material used for either the attestation of the UAF authenticator or the authentication to a relying party, the presentation of UAF related information to the user, and the initiation and management of both the registration and authentication procedures. Therefore. if either of these entities is compromised, an attacker would be able to launch several critical attacks, compromising the authenticity, privacy, availability, and integrity of the UAF protocol. Subsequently, in Sects. 3.1.1 and 3.1.2, we identify several vulnerabilities present in the specifications of the UAF authenticator and the UAF client, respectively.

3.1.1   UAF Authenticator Vulnerabilities

The first and most apparent attack vector of the UAF protocol is the authentication keys. Therefore, an attacker may attempt to (directly or indirectly) gain unprivileged access to these keys. As we previously mentioned in Sect. 2.1.1, the responsibility of storing the authentication keys lies with the UAF authenticator and based on the UAF protocol security requirements, the UAF authenticator utilises some form of secure/privileged storage. However, it has been shown in the literature that such types of key storage solutions can still be compromised [16]. As we mentioned in Sect. 2.2, UAF authenticators typically rely on trusted computing platforms for the storage of cryptographic material. Cooijmans et al. [15] have shown that on several widely adopted trusted computing platforms, an attacker with privileged rights can gain the ability of using encrypted credentials by moving them to a different directory, which designates a malicious application as the owner of the credentials. Finally, an attacker may also attempt to indirectly gain access to the authentication keys, by fully compromising the UAF authenticator(s). Based on the literature, an attacker can gain full access to a trusted computing platform by performing an integrated circuit attack (i.e., ICA) [14]. One limitation of this attack is the requirement to have physical access to the user's device. However, once the attack is performed, the attacker can then create a cloned UAF authenticator, alleviating any further need for the original user's device.

When utilizing a cloned UAF authenticator, an attacker must then evade the security mechanisms of the UAF protocol, implemented on the purpose of identifying such malicious behavior. Recall from Sect. 2.1 that the UAF protocol incorporates two security mechanisms that safeguard the operation of the UAF authenticator: (i) an attestation mechanism, in which the UAF authenticator must prove its legitimacy by providing an attestation signature during the registration process and (ii) a sign counter (cntr) mechanism, which is a monotonically increasing counter, incremented on every sign request performed by the UAF authenticator for a particular user key pair and used by the relaying party to detect cloned UAF authenticators.

Regarding the attestation mechanism, we have identified three approaches that can be used by an attacker to circumvent detection. In the first method, an attacker may utilize the extracted attestation key from the compromised UAF authenticator and perform registration requests to relying parties, impersonating the legitimate user. Since the attestation keys for each UAF authenticator are not unique (i.e., a group of UAF authenticators share the same attestation key pair), the malicious behavior cannot be easily detected by the relying party. If, however, the attestation keys are revoked by the device's vendor, then there is a risk of detection by the relying party. A second method that can be used by an attacker when employing a cloned authenticator is to avoid the attestation mechanism all together. This can be achieved by exploiting a limitation in the attestation process. Recall from Sect. 2.1 that the attestation process takes place only during the registration operation. Therefore, an attacker may allow the legitimate UAF authenticator to perform the registration process, and, subsequently, without the users' knowledge, use the cloned authenticator to authenticate itself to the relying party, masquerading as the legitimate user. Finally, an attacker may use the cloned UAF authenticator temporarily to collect personal information related to the legitimate user, and, then, register at other relying parties using a different, non-cloned UAF authenticator. Subsequently, since the attestation procedure takes place at a non-cloned authenticator, there is no risk of revocation, while the attacker retains the ability to impersonate the legitimate user to any relying party.

On the other hand, the second security measure proposed by the UAF specifications (i.e., sign counter), can be circumvented by an attacker, if the later actively attempts to perform an authentication operation immediately after the completion of cloning a UAF authenticator. Recall from Sect. 2.1 that during the authentication operation, a relying party will assume a UAF authenticator is legitimate if the sign counter encapsulated in the key authentication reply is equal to the sign counter maintained by the relying party incremented by one. Therefore, a race condition evolves between the legitimate and the cloned UAF authenticator, since only the UAF authenticator that manages to perform an authentication request first, will be considered legitimate by the relying party (while the second authenticator will attempt to authenticate using an older value of the sign counter). Thus, an attacker can circumvent this security measure by performing an authentication request to the relying party as soon as the UAF authenticator is cloned, maximizing his chances of winning the race condition.

3.1.2 UAF Client Vulnerabilities

The second critical entity of the UAF protocol that resides at a user's device is the UAF client. Recall from Sect. 2 that the UAF client acts as an intermediator between the relying party on one hand and the UAF authenticator on the other and it is responsible for most of UAF's protocol operations, short of generating the encryption keys or performing cryptographic operations. Furthermore, the UAF client is implemented entirely in software, making it an ideal candidate for software attacks. Even more importantly, the UAF protocol does not incorporate any security measures that safeguard the UAF client from attacks or verifies that a user's device operates a legitimate version of the client. The UAF protocol specifications propose the execution of the UAF client in a "privileged" environment, however, since the client is typically embedded within a browser either fully or as a plug-in, it is de-facto implemented as a normal application.

The simplest method of delivering a malicious UAF client to a user's device is by deceiving the user to install the application voluntarily. Common delivery methods include attachments in e-mails or browsing a malicious website that installs software after the user clicks on a pop-up. Other methods of compromising a UAF client is through malicious software residing at the user's device (such as a virus, worm. trojan, or root kit) or by exploiting an operating system vulnerability. The latter, enables the execution of a plethora of attacks such as spoofing of inter-process communication, privilege escalation, return-oriented programming, or code injection attacks. For example, in a variety of sources such as [17, 20, 21], the authors demonstrate methodologies for accomplishing privilege escalation in the android operating system, one of the most widely used platforms, which includes a variety of privilege protection mechanisms, such as application specific sandboxing and Mandatory Access Control (MAC) policies. Furthermore, in the most recent versions of android, privilege escalation is typically achieved using system less root [20], which is the process of gaining escalated privileges without any modification to the system partition, thus evading detection by any security mechanisms that validate an operation system through a checksum of its system partition (i.e., a common security mechanism used by most of the trusted computing platforms).

3.2   Threat Analysis

In the following section, we provide a threat analysis based on the vulnerabilities identified in Sect. 3.1. First, we outline the assets that reside at the client side, which are critical for the legitimate operation of the UAF protocol. In this list, we also include assets that are not part of the UAF protocol, such as, the underlying operating system and the utilization of a trusted computing platform, since (as we have shown in Sect. 3.1), they are detrimental to the security of the UAF protocol. We then investigate the consequences that may be caused in the event of a successful exploitation of the vulnerabilities identified in Sect. 3.1. Table 1 provides a summary of the critical assets related to the UAF protocols' secure operation, the threats identified in the threat analysis, and, the consequences induced by the threats, if the later are carried out successfully by an attacker.

Table 1. Threats related to the UAF protocol and their associated consequences

Asset	Threat	Consequences
Attestation private key	Attacker gains access to the attestation keys	Impersonate user, create a clone authenticator
Authentication private key	Attacker gains access to the authentication keys	Impersonate user, capture user data
UAF authenticator	User installs a malicious authenticator	Impersonate user, capture user data, register the user to a fraudulent replaying party
TrustZone, UAF authenticator	Attacker compromises the trusted computing platform	Create cloned authenticator, impersonate user, compromise the UAF authenticator
UAF client, UAF authenticator, TrustZone	Attacker gains physical access to a user's device	Create cloned authenticator, impersonate user, compromise the UAF authenticator, install malicious UAF client
UAF authenticator	Attacker employs a cloned authenticator	Impersonate user, capture user data, register the user to a fraudulent relaying party
UAF client	User installs a malicious client	Register to a fraudulent relaying party, phishing – lead to malicious websites, downgrade authentication policy, capture user data, circumvent transaction confirmation security mechanism, allow malicious apps to register/impersonate the user
Operating system	Attacker can execute privileged code at the user's device	Compromise the UAF client

3.2.1 Critical Assets Related to the UAF Protocols' Secure Operation

As we mentioned in Sect. 2.2, the UAF specifications [9] provide a limited list of assets that must be protected in an implementation of the UAF protocol. These assets include the private key of the authentication key pair, the private key of the UAF authenticator attestation key pair, and the UAF authenticator attestation authority private key. However, as we have seen in Sect. 3.1, an attacker may also target several other assets that are either part of the UAF protocol, or they are integral in its secure operation. In particular, an attacker may either target the UAF authenticator(s) or the UAF client that are present in a legitimate users' device. Furthermore, an attacker may indirectly compromise the secure operation of the UAF protocol by exploiting existing vulnerabilities (i) at the underlying operating system in which the UAF protocol is executed, or (ii) at the trusted computing platform (typically the TrustZone platform), used for the hardware-assisted protection of the encryption keys and the operation of the UAF authenticator(s).

3.2.2 Threat Evaluation

Based on the security analysis in Sect. 3.1, the private keys stored in the UAF authenticator, namely the attestation private key and the authentication private keys pose a critical attack vector of the UAF protocol. Recall from Sect. 2.2 that these keys are used by the UAF authenticator to sign registration and authentication replies, respectively. On the other hand, the relying party uses these signed replies to authenticate the UAF authenticator and verify its legitimacy. Therefore, if an attacker compromises the attestation private key, he would then be capable of impersonating the legitimate user by registering to other relying parties on the users' behalf, without the latter's consent (including fraudulent relaying parties). In order to have access to the authentication keys associated with the malicious registrations and to avoid detection by the user, the attacker will have to import the attestation private key to a cloned and silent authenticator, i.e., an authenticator that appears to have been manufactured by the same vendor as the legitimate one and does not prompt the user for any action during the registration and authentication operations of the UAF protocol. On the other hand, if the attacker compromises one or more authentication private keys, he would then be capable of impersonating the legitimate user by authenticating as the user to relying parties. The attacker is limited, however, to relying parties that the legitimate user has already registered. Nevertheless, once authenticated, the attacker can then collect personal data related to the legitimate user and stored at the relying party, as well as perform transactions with the relaying party without the users' consent.

An attacker may also attempt to indirectly gain access to the attestation and authentication keys, by fully compromising the UAF authenticator(s) residing at the device of a legitimate user. This can be accomplished in the following ways: the user unwillingly installs a malicious authenticator to his/her device, the attacker compromises the UAF authenticator by targeting the UAF authenticators' underlying trusted computing platform, and, the attacker gains physical access to the device and either installs a malicious authenticator, or tampers with the legitimate UAF authenticator(s) installed on the device. As a result, any subsequent registration and authentication requests will be captured by the malicious authenticator, enabling the attacker to impersonate the legitimate user, collect personal data, and perform transactions on the users' behalf, similarly to the cloned authenticator threat we analyzed previously. Furthermore, the attacker can also extract the attestation and authentication keys, in order to create a cloned authenticator that resides outside the device of the user.

The UAF client signifies another critical attack vector identified in the security evaluation. An attacker may attempt to compromise the UAF client by exploiting one or more of the following vulnerabilities: gaining physical access to the user's device and manually installing a malicious client, deceiving the user to install the malicious client voluntarily, using other malicious software residing at the user's device (such as a virus, worm. trojan, or root kit) in order to install the malicious client, or by exploiting an operating system vulnerability. Having successfully compromised the UAF client, an attacker is then capable of launching several additional attacks against the UAF protocol, such as: allowing itself or other malicious applications to perform registration/authentication operations without the user's consent, enforce the use of the weakest/less secure UAF authenticator during a legitimate registration process, direct a user to a fake or malicious relying party, and defeat the user consent, transaction confirmation, and trusted facet list security measures of the UAF protocol. Recalling from Sect. 2.1.1, during the registration operation, the UAF client is responsible for initiating registration requests, determining if applications (or websites) are authorized to use the UAF protocol, present a UI to the user, and directing the relying party challenge to the UAF authenticator based on the authenticator policy transmitted by the relying party (i.e., based on the trusted facet list). Since the UAF client is the only entity responsible for assessing the trusted facet list, it can allow the registration operation for any website, or from any application, regardless of what is enforced by the trusted facet list security measure. Therefore, the user may unwillingly be redirected to a malicious relying party masqueraded as a legitimate one, so that personal/valuable information can be phished by an attacker. Furthermore, as we mentioned previously, it is the UAF client's responsibility for presenting a UI to the user, and, therefore, even if the user's device incorporates a transaction confirmation security mechanism, the confirmation will always be true, since the mechanism validates if the information provided to the user is tampered/modified/spoofed after leaving the UAF client, and not if the later modified the displayed content. Finally, a malicious UAF client may forward a relying party challenge to the weakest UAF authenticator (preferably one with a low entropy secret). Subsequently, during authentication, the attacker could attempt to discover the secret and access the user's account without the legitimate users' consent.

4   Conclusions

The UAF protocol provides several important advantages over traditional authentication mechanisms, such as strong authentication and a simplified registration and authentication procedure. However, the UAF protocol also transfers user authentication operations from the server-side to the client-side. Therefore, the critical functionality of the UAF protocol typically operates in a consumer platform such as a mobile device, which is susceptible to a variety of attacks such as malware and viruses, its users deploy unsupervised software, and the deployed operating systems may be susceptible to several vulnerabilities. In this paper, we have provided a comprehensive security analysis of the UAF protocol and have identified several vulnerabilities that may be exploited by an attacker in order to compromise the authenticity, privacy, availability, and integrity of the UAF protocol. More specifically, we have investigated methods of attacking the two entities of the UAF protocol residing at a user's device, namely, the UAF authenticator and the UAF client, including the ability of an attacker to gain unprivileged access to the cryptographic material stored within the UAF authenticator and highjack either the of these two entities. Furthermore, we have investigated and identified how an attacker can circumvent the security measures provided by the UAF protocol, including the authenticator attestation mechanism, the transaction confirmation mechanism, the trusted facet list, and the sign counter. Finally, we provided a threat analysis in which we analyze the impairment that may be caused by an attacker in the event of a successful exploitation of the UAF protocol. Based on our threat analysis, by exploiting the identified vulnerabilities, an attacker would be able to capture the data exchanged between a user and an online service, impersonate a user at any UAF compatible online service, impersonate online services to the user, perform transactions on the users' behalf without the latter's consent, present fake information to the user's screen during a transaction, re-direct the user to a fraudulent relying party during registration, force the use of a weak or malicious UAF authenticator, allow malicious applications to register to a legitimate relying party, and access private keys used for authentication of a user.

Acknowledgments. This research has been funded by the European Commission in part of the ReCRED project (Horizon H2020 Framework Programme of the European Union under GA number 653417).

References

1. Das, A., et al.: The tangled web of password reuse. In: NDSS, vol. 14 (2014)
2. 55K Twitter Passwords Leaked. http://www.newser.com/story/145750/55k-twitter-passwords-leaked.html
3. Yahoo Hacked: 450,000 passwords posted online. http://www.cnn.com/2012/07/12/tech/web/yahoo-users-hacked
4. 6.46 million LinkedIn passwords leaked online. http://www.zdnet.com/blog/btl/6-46-million-linkedin-passwords-leaked-online/79290
5. FIDO Alliance: Fido security reference. http://www.fidoalliance.org/specifications
6. Srinivas, S., et al.: Universal 2nd factor (U2F) overview. FIDO Alliance Proposed Standard, pp. 1–5 (2015)
7. FIDO Alliance: FIDO UAF Protocol Specification v1.1: FIDO Alliance Proposed Standard (2016)
8. FIDO Alliance: FIDO Certified Products. https://fidoalliance.org/certification/fido-certified-products/. Accessed 5 June 2017
9. FIDO Alliance: Fido security reference (2014). www.fidoalliance.org/specifications
10. Panos, C., et al.: A specification-based intrusion detection engine for infrastructure-less networks. Comput. Commun. **54**, 67–83 (2014)
11. Trusted Computing Platform Alliance: TCPA main specification v. 1.2. http://www.trustedcomputing.org

12. Winter, J.: Trusted computing building blocks for embedded linux-based ARM trustzone platforms. In: Proceedings of the 3rd ACM Workshop on Scalable Trusted Computing. ACM (2008)
13. Common Criteria for Information Technology Security Evaluation. SAMSUNG SDS FIDO Server Solution V1.1 Certification Report (2016)
14. Helfmeier, C., Nedospasov, D., Tarnovsky, C., Krissler, J.S., Boit, C., Seifert, J.-P.: Breaking and entering through the silicon. In: Computer and Communications Security (CCS), pp. 733–744 (2013)
15. Cooijmans, T., de Ruiter, J., Poll, E.: Analysis of secure key storage solutions on Android. In: Proceedings of the 4th ACM Workshop on Security and Privacy in Smartphones & Mobile Devices. ACM (2014)
16. Cooijmans, T., et al.: Secure key storage and secure computation in Android. Master's thesis, Radboud University Nijmegen (2014)
17. Davi, L., Dmitrienko, A., Sadeghi, A.-R., Winandy, M.: Privilege escalation attacks on Android. In: Burmester, M., Tsudik, G., Magliveras, S., Ilić, I. (eds.) ISC 2010. LNCS, vol. 6531, pp. 346–360. Springer, Heidelberg (2011). doi:10.1007/978-3-642-18178-8_30
18. Shen, D.: Exploiting Trustzone on Android. In: Black Hat USA (2015)
19. Rosenberg, D.: Qsee trustzone kernel integer over flow vulnerability. In: Black Hat Conference (2014)
20. Abhishek, P.C.: Student research abstract: analysing the vulnerability exploitation in Android with the device-mapper-verity (dm-verity) (2017)
21. Does, T., Maarse, M.: Subverting Android 6.0 fingerprint authentication (2016)
22. Loutfi, I., Jøsang, A.: FIDO trust requirements. In: Buchegger, S., Dam, M. (eds.) NordSec 2015. LNCS, vol. 9417, pp. 139–155. Springer, Cham (2015). doi:10.1007/978-3-319-26502-5_10
23. Hu, K., Zhang, Z.: Security analysis of an attractive online authentication standard: FIDO UAF protocol. IEEE China Commun. 13(12), 189–198 (2016)

Delay Tolerant Revocation Scheme for Delay Tolerant VANETs (DTRvS)

Chibueze P. Anyigor Ogah[✉], Haitham Cruickshank, Philip M. Asuquo, Ao Lei, and Zhili Sun

5G Innovation Centre (5GIC), Institute for Communication Systems, University of Surrey, PATS Driveway, Guildford, Surrey GU2 7XS, UK
{c.anyigorogah,h.cruickshank,p.asuquo,a.lei,z.sun}@surrey.ac.uk

Abstract. This article discusses an effective revocation scheme for disconnected Delay Tolerant Vehicular Ad hoc Networks (VANETs). Malicious vehicles can exhibit various misbehaviour such as dropping packets due to selfish reasons. Selfishness can be due to the need to conserve limited resources such as energy and bandwidth. This forces vehicles to either drop all or some of the packets they receive. This is particularly obtainable in multi-hop forwarding networks where packets are routed from one vehicle to another towards their destination. When some packets are dropped, the usefulness of the system is not fully realised since it affects the quality of information available to vehicles for making driving decisions such as road manoeuvres. Additionally, packet dropping can degrade the routing efficiency of the system. In extreme cases of misbehaviour, it is important to stop such vehicles from further participation in network communication. One way of achieving this is through revocation. However, it is important to establish mechanisms for identifying such vehicles before blacklisting them for revocation. Our objective here is to address the question of how much we can use a trust-based scheme where vehicles cannot always be expected to follow normal protocols for revocation. Revocation or suspension of misbehaving vehicles is essential to avoid havoc and possible economic damage.

Keywords: Revocation · Malicious vehicles · VANETs · Vehicular Delay Tolerant Networks · VDTN

1 Introduction

Many years of advances in wireless network technology have ushered in a variety of application domains of Vehicular Ad hoc Networks (VANETs) resulting in disruptive changes to the way vehicles interact. Examples of the applications of VANET technology include Intelligent Transport Systems (ITSs), Connected Autonomous Vehicles (CAVs), Internet of Things (IoT), Internet of Vehicles (IoVs), Vehicular Delay Tolerant Networks (VDTNs), and Delay Tolerant Networks (DTNs). Specific application domains such as ITSs, IoVs, and CAVs have

© Springer International Publishing AG 2017
A. Piva et al. (Eds.): TIWDC 2017, CCIS 766, pp. 143–164, 2017.
DOI: 10.1007/978-3-319-67639-5_12

attracted a great deal of attention in recent years both in the academia and industries. The key feature of these technologies is that vehicles fitted with multiple sensors collect various forms of data including the location information of drivers. The information collected can be analysed and exchanged among vehicles for various purposes including road safety, efficient traffic management and driver/user convenience. In the near future, it is expected that millions of vehicles will be connected through a complex network infrastructure to form IoVs using various technologies, both in industrial and domestic contexts. VANETs for ITS are characterised by dynamic mobility patterns, infrequent connectivity, and frequent topology changes in addition to the somewhat hostile environments in which wireless networks are deployed.

Despite the benefits of vehicular communication, the open nature of wireless communication makes them vulnerable to a variety of security threats. For instance, a malicious vehicle can engage in packet dropping attacks in order to deny other vehicles access to safety information in multi-hop networks. Such malicious vehicles can also lie about their location information in order to deceive other vehicles. In emergency situations, accurate location information is needed to correctly direct rescue workers and the police for timely and efficient victim evacuation.

In this paper, we consider a disconnected network architecture based on the IEEE 802.11p framework which is representative of ITS in its early stage of deployment when the network lack end-to-end connectivity similar to DTNs and VDTNs. When vehicles misbehave and fail to follow normal network protocol, it is necessary to revoke their right to the use of network resources. We discuss a scheme that addresses the revocation of vehicles that disrupt network activity through malicious behaviour. The challenge of vehicle revocation in an intermittently connected VANET for ITS infrastructure is explored. Our proposed revocation scheme involves a misbehaviour detection system based on trust and opinion aggregation from vehicle encounters. A vehicle's opinion about the behaviour of another is used to decide on the revocation of privileges. The trust-based scheme identifies a vehicle's malicious activity using a pre-defined metric namely message delivery and drop probability. Our findings from the trust-based misbehaviour detection scheme are used to implement our proposed Delay-Tolerant Revocation Scheme (DTRvS). A detailed description of our revocation mechanism is given including an evaluation and analysis of our results. We also discuss the attitude of malicious vehicles towards misbehaviour reporting and CRL distribution. We devise a credit-based scheme aimed at coercing selfish vehicles to report misbehaviour and distribute CRL messages in an efficient manner. We also provide a security and efficiency analysis of our scheme. Finally, we provide a summary of findings and discuss the economics of revocation and its implications on network security.

The rest of this paper is organized as follows. We describe the motivation for our scheme in Sect. 2. In Sect. 3, we provide a description of our model with attributes of the attacker. The details of our scheme is presented in Sect. 4. In Sect. 5, we discuss our experiments and performance evaluation of our system. Finally, we conclude the paper in Sect. 6.

2   Motivation for DTRvS

A major issue in vehicular networks is ensuring entity- and data-oriented trust. Entity-oriented trust involves the assurance that vehicles partaking in network communication are trustworthy enough to follow the strict security protocols of the system to deliver safety messages securely and efficiently [3]. Data-oriented trust on the other hand focuses on the trustworthiness of the messages exchanged between different network entities. Vehicles in a VANET can misbehave in a variety of ways including dropping of messages and falsification of location information. Alteration and delay of messages by relay vehicles can lead to serious consequences. It is important to ensure that location messages exchanged between vehicles are not dropped, altered or delayed en-route to their destinations. In the next section, we highlight the draw-backs of existing schemes and justification for our proposed DTRvS.

Although authentication mechanisms ensure the authenticity of vehicles joining and using the network, even genuinely authenticated vehicles can misbehave and inject fake messages into the network [7,8]. Hence, data trust becomes even as important as entity-oriented trust. A key requirement is to ensure the Basic Safety Messages (BSMs) are unaltered and reliable enough for making driving decisions [9]. However, during the course of the operation of the network, due to selfish or other malicious intentions, some vehicles may deviate from normal protocol operation and misbehave in order to mislead other vehicles and put them at risk [8,10]. Vehicle misbehaviour can be broadly classified into deliberate or non-deliberate misbehaviour. Deliberate misbehaviour means intentional misbehaviour in which a vehicle chooses to announce fake location messages, while non-deliberate misbehaviour can be due to a faulty component or software malfunction in say, the OBU or other sensor components.

Irrespective of the reason, there is a need to isolate such vehicles from participating in network communication. In [9], the authors point out that authentication alone cannot solve the trust issue in VANETs since it does not address the quality of messages exchanged. Furthermore, the operating environment of ITS especially in its early stages of deployment where the network exhibits intermittent connectivity similar to DTNs and VDTNs poses major challenges in detecting malicious behaviour, and more so in eliminating malicious vehicles from network communication. In the next sections, we describe some preliminaries necessary to understand our DTRvS proposal.

The key contributions we made in this article are as follows:

- First, we formulate a distributed trust-based scheme to identify malicious activity and its impact on network performance. Our scheme is delay/disruption-tolerant and scalable even under high vehicle density and mobility.
- We propose DTRvS for distributing CRLs in an efficient and scalable manner. This means that our proposed scheme is tailored to be aware of the network operating environment and is able to distribute CRLs in an efficient manner while relying on a few stationary RSUs.

- We propose a scheme tailored to incentivize vehicles into reporting misbehaviour in order to improve the revocation process.

3   Model Description

The network model considered assumes a distributed hierarchical architecture based on the European Telecommunications Standards Institute (ETSI) and Institute of Electrical and Electronics Engineers (IEEE) recommendations with multiple Trusted Key Managers (TKMs) and Certificate Authorities (CAs). The initial registration involves attribute verification, issuance of certificates and keys for signing messages as well as establishment of methods for trust, misbehaviour detection & verification, and vehicle revocation. The TKMs are responsible for the generation and dissemination of CRLs. They maintain a dictionary of attack and misbehaviour types which is also installed on each vehicle's OBU and the RSUs.

Each vehicle also develops an opinion of other vehicles it interacts with. The opinion is used to build the trust vehicles have on each other after an interaction in the form of opinion scores. Vehicle encounters with each other can be a direct or indirect (see Fig. 1). The diagram show how trust is established between three vehicles V_i, V_j and V_k through direct and indirect relationships. The details of the misbehaviour detection scheme is described later in Sect. 4.3.

In addition to extending the telecommunication infrastructure, the key function of the RSUs serve as the verifiers of misbehaviour reports from vehicles. The RSUs are deployed in a distributed manner and directly report to the TKMs via a reliable secure wired communication channel that issues the final revocation order. They can also play a role in the incentive scheme for rewarding malicious reporters. They are assumed to be reliable and can store messages in a DTN fashion to be offloaded to the next available carrier vehicle in a multi-hop fashion [11].

3.1   Attacker Model

We mentioned two types of malicious vehicles earlier on - those deliberately malicious and those with malfunctioning components. We make no distinctions between the two for reasons of safety in the sense that each type of malicious behaviour poses a risk to the operation of the network. Our model closely follows that defined in [12] where malicious attackers drop packets. However, our scheme can be tweaked to support a variety of other attack types. Specifically, we consider a network where a reasonable percentage of the vehicles say 10–50% are malicious. Note that the TKM may define different attack types on initialization and bootstraps the attack dictionary on each vehicle's OBU. Subsequently, new attack types can be added to the attack dictionary as new malicious behaviour definitions emerge.

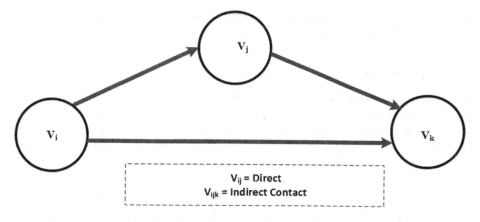

Fig. 1. Establishing trust relationship between vehicles

4   Details of the Proposed DTRvS Scheme

In this section, we provide preliminary discussions to set the stage towards a clearer understanding of our DTRvS scheme. Then we provide a general overview and the details of the individual components that form the foundation for our proposed revocation scheme. We also describe the CRL forwarding strategy based on delay tolerant routing as the basis for efficient vehicle revocation.

The delay-sensitive operating environment of IC-VANETs calls for novel techniques in the design of certificate revocation and distribution that are efficient in terms of latency (and delay tolerant) in order to avert crisis and economic loss [13] early enough after malicious vehicles are identified. An understanding of the constant connect-and-disconnect pattern is important in order to address the CRL distribution problem. In the past, the following methods have been adopted to distribute CRLs viz: request-response, publish-subscribe, blacklist broadcast, whitelist broadcast, and publish with proxy subscribe [13]. The IETF94 DTN Working Group recommends the publish with proxy subscribe technique together with δ-CRLs for classical DTNs [13,14] where a dedicated Certificate Revocation Manager (CRM) handles the revocation operation. Our scheme seeks to answer the question of how to ensure efficient revocation in IC-VANETs in a delay tolerant and distributed manner. Having identified misbehaving nodes as mentioned above, we employ a stripped down version of the conventional X.509 CRL certificate in the form of δ-CRLs in line with the IETF Working Group recommendation [13,15]. Instead of the usual headers that add too much overhead, the key fields in our scheme include the serial number, revocation reason, in addition to the pseudonym with which the event was signed. A typical X.509 CRL is made up of about 39 bytes in addition to a fixed 400 bytes. We adopt the scheme in [15] which is compliant with the X.509 data structure with a total of 38 bytes (a 6 bytes serial number, a 12 bytes revocation reason number and a 20 bytes pseudonym of the identity of the vehicle) with no additional fixed fields compared to the standard X.509 CRL. This makes the CRL of a smaller size compared to the standard X.509 CRL.

4.1   Bilinear Pairing

Our scheme is based on the assumption of bilinear pairing, on which the secure initialization is also based [16,17]. Let $\mathbb{G}$ be a cyclic additive group and $\mathbb{G}_T$ be a cyclic multiplicative group; both $\mathbb{G}$ and $\mathbb{G}_T$ are of the same prime order q i.e., $|\mathbb{G}| = |\mathbb{G}_T| = q$. The TKM selects P as the generator of $\mathbb{G}$. We also assume that $\hat{e}: \mathbb{G} \times \mathbb{G} \to \mathbb{G}_T$ is a bilinear mapping with the following attributes:

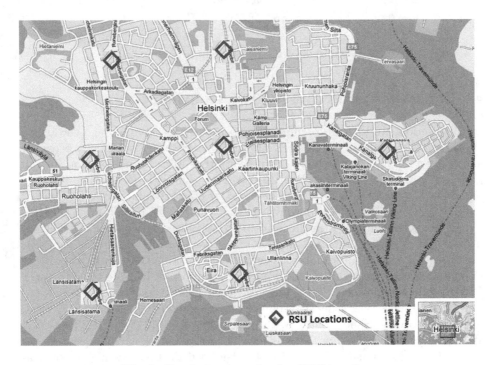

Fig. 2. Simulation area showing RSU locations

- *Bilinear*: $\hat{e}(aP,\, bQ) = \hat{e}(P,Q)^{ab}$ for all $P,Q \in \mathbb{G}$ and $a, b \in_R \mathbb{Z}_q$.
- *Non-degenerate*: $\hat{e}(P,Q) \neq 1_{\mathbb{G}_T}$.
- *Symmetric*: $\hat{e}(P,Q) = \hat{e}(Q,P)$ for all $P,Q \in \mathbb{G}$.
- *Admissible*: The bilinear map $\hat{e}$ is efficiently computable, i.e., there is an efficient algorithm to compute $\hat{e}P_x, Q_y$ for any $P_x, Q_y \in \mathbb{G}$.

According to [18], such an admissible bilinear map e can be implemented using Tate [16] and Weil's [17] pairing based on elliptic curve techniques. Usually, the security of the proposed scheme will depend on the ability of the attacker to solve the hard computational problem as follows:

– *Elliptic Curve Discrete Logarithm Problem (ECDLP)*: given a point P of order q on an elliptic curve and a point Q on the same curve, then the ECDLP problem can be used to determine the integer l, $0 \leq l \leq q - 1$ such that $Q = lP$.

4.2   Trust-Based Misbehaviour Detection and Revocation

In this section, we describe the phases of our trust-based misbehaviour detection and revocation scheme. These include the misbehaviour detection and analysis phase, misbehaviour reporting and verification phase, and credit-based reporting scheme and certificate revocation phases. The certification revocation phase involves certificate revocation and CRL dissemination.

4.3   Misbehaviour Detection and Analysis Phase

In the misbehaviour detection phase, our proposed scheme aims to study the impact of packet dropping attacks on routed BSM messages by malicious vehicles. This ensures that malicious vehicles are detected early enough and barred from participating in network communication through revocation [19]. The misbehaviour detection scheme is based on a trust- and reputation-based system which not only addresses the message quality problem but also helps to check the behaviour of individual vehicles themselves. Many reputation-based schemes have been proposed in the past with one basic goal - to gauge the health of the network, detecting and reporting the misbehaviour of vehicles sending messages [1, 10, 20].

We adopt similar trust models as in [6, 12, 20, 21]. We highlight the need to clearly identify false alarms which can be in the form of false positives and true negatives. False alarms can be due to collusion attacks by vehicles to discredit well behaved vehicles. In our scheme, there is the challenge of incident reporting due to the disconnected and dynamic nature of the network. To address this, we use the technique of additive reporting based on the majority opinion of reporting vehicles which is derived from the Dempster-Shafer Theory (DST) [22]. This is based on the principle that, during the course of communication, vehicles exchange opinions regarding their belief in the accuracy of the information they receive and the behaviour of the vehicles they come into contact and exchange messages with. Similar to [9, 20], each vehicle's OBU runs a trust module. During each contact opportunity between two vehicles, say V_i and V_j, each vehicle records its encounter, denoted by the vector, E_k^{ij} of the other as expressed in 1 below.

$$E_k^{ij} = \{e_1, e_2, e_3, ..., e_n\} \tag{1}$$

where each encounter $e_i \in E_k^{ij}$ represents a particular instance or attribute of V_j's behaviour such as packet dropping, message delay, timely message forwarding, accurate or inaccurate location reporting. Additionally, we highlight that each element of the encounter record may be accorded different weights depending on the importance the receiver/observer vehicle attaches to it. Let the weight factor be ω, then 1 can be re-written as

$$E_k^{ij} = \omega\{e_1, e_2, e_3, ..., e_n\} \tag{2}$$

where $\sum_{i=0}^{n} \omega = 1$.

Components of the Reputation System. After an encounter, a vehicle say V_i, records its trust rating or evaluation of the behaviour which is the sum of its observation $\sum T_{ij}$, about vehicle V_j behaviour. Our reputation system can be modelled using the probability of binary events which owes its origin to beta probability density function. The beta probability density function is a proven and valid mathematical foundation for obtaining and combining reputation or opinion ratings from multiple sources. Such systems owe their origin to the field of e-commerce systems and applications as analysed in literature on probability theory such as in [23]. The beta probability density function, $F(p|\alpha, \beta)$ can be represented with indices of two parameters α and β, which can be expressed using the gamma function Γ as shown in 3 below.

$$F(p|(\alpha, \beta) = \frac{\Gamma(\alpha + \beta)}{\Gamma(\alpha)\Gamma(\beta)} p^{\alpha-1}(1 - p)^{\beta-1} \tag{3}$$

where $0 \leqslant p \leqslant 1, \alpha > 0, \beta > 0$, and Γ is the gamma function. According to Josang [23], $p \neq 0$ if $\alpha < 1$, and $p \neq 1$ if $\beta < 1$. Hence, the probability expectation value, E_x of the beta probability density function becomes

$$E_x(p) = \frac{\alpha}{(\alpha + \beta)} \tag{4}$$

Specifically, if a vehicle keeps an encounter record as either accurate, C_R or inaccurate I_S, for instance, and if out of E number of encounters, where C_R occurs R times and I_S occurs S times, then the probability density function of C_R in future observations or encounters can be expressed as a function of its previous observed values as in 5.

$$\alpha = R + 1 \quad \text{and} \quad \beta = S + 1 \tag{5}$$

where $R, S \geq 0$. For instance, assuming a vehicle records E encounters classified under two possible outcomes $\{C_R, I_S\}$ where C_R occurs 8 times while I_S occurs 2 times, we can express the beta function as $F(p|9, 3)$. This means that the probability of expectation value of C_R is given by $E_{x(p)} = 0.9$. From the foregoing, we can define the reputation function based on Josang's [23] equation as in Definition 1 below.

Definition 1 (Vehicles' Reputation Function): Let $R_{V_j}^{V_i}$ and $S_{V_j}^{V_i}$ denote the total number of accurate and inaccurate records about vehicle V_j as observed by another vehicle V_i, then the function $f(p|R_{V_j}^{V_i}; S_{V_j}^{V_i})$ can be defined as in 6 below.

$$f(p|R_{V_j}^{V_i}, S_{V_j}^{V_i}) = \frac{\Gamma(R_{V_j}^{V_i} + S_{V_j}^{V_i} + 2)}{\Gamma(R_{V_j}^{V_i} + 1)\Gamma(S_{V_j}^{V_i} + 1)} p^{R_{V_j}^{V_i}}(1 - p)^{S_{V_j}^{V_i}} \tag{6}$$

where $0 \leqslant p \leqslant 1, 0 \leqslant R_{V_j}^{V_i}, 0 \leqslant R_{V_j}^{V_i}$. The function $f(p{-}R_{V_j}^{V_i}, S_{V_j}^{V_i})$ can be taken to be the reputation function of V_j as observed by V_i which we simply write as $f(p{-}_{V_j}^{V_i})$. By comparing 4 to 5, we can re-write the probability of expectation as

$$E_x(f(p|R_{V_j}^{V_i}, S_{V_j}^{V_i})) = \frac{R_{V_j}^{V_i}+1}{R_{V_j}^{V_i}+S_{V_j}^{V_i}+2} \tag{7}$$

Vehicle Reputation Rating. According to Josang [23], the reputation function suits mathematical manipulation, but is not ideal for communicating reputation to human users. Hence, the use of probability of expectation value is more ideal since humans are more familiar with the concept of probability using numbers as estimates. It is then more appropriate to use the reputation rating which can be evaluated in the range of $[0, 1]$, where a neutral rating can be chosen arbitrarily depending on system requirements e.g. 0.5 for a neutral rating. A practical use of the neutral rating is during the initial registration of vehicles where a vehicle is assigned an average rating to ensure that its is able to establish initial communication with new contacts. Note that a vehicle's reputation can increase or degrade over time depending on its behaviour.

Definition 2 (Reputation Rating): Let $R_{V_j}^{V_i}$ and $S_{V_j}^{V_i}$ denote the total amount of accurate and inaccurate records about vehicle V_j as observed by another vehicle V_i; then the function $T_{ij}(R_{V_j}^{V_i}, S_{V_j}^{V_i})$ defined by

$$T_{ij}\left(R_{V_j}^{V_i}, S_{V_j}^{V_i}\right) = \left(E_x(f(p|R_{V_j}^{V_i}, S_{V_j}^{V_i})) - 0.5\right).2 = \frac{R_{V_j}^{V_i} - S_{V_j}^{V_i}}{R_{V_j}^{V_i} + S_{V_j}^{V_i} + 2} \tag{8}$$

is the estimate of the trust rating, T_{ij} of V_j by V_i. We write this simply as $T_{ij}(_{V_j}^{V_i})$. Generally, the reputation rating can be used to express the extent of trust that can be held for a particular vehicle after the observation period. In particular, in our scheme, it expresses the behaviour of a target vehicle and can be used by vehicles and RSUs to advise the TKM regarding vehicle toward revocation. Here, $R_{V_j}^{V_i}$ represents the record about V_j in support of good behaviour, while $S_{V_j}^{V_i}$ represents the record about V_j in support of bad behaviour.

Combining Multiple Reputation Reports. It is possible to combine reputation rating from multiple observers or multiple records from the same observer over time in order to effectively and convincingly evaluate a target vehicle. This can be done by combining all the accurate and inaccurate encounter reports comprising $\sum C_R$ and $\sum I_S$. The reputation of a vehicle V_j recorded by two observers V_i and V_k can be respectively expressed as $f(p|R_{V_j}^{V_i}, S_{V_j}^{V_i})$ and $f(p|R_{V_j}^{V_k}, S_{V_j}^{V_k})$, or as $f(_{V_j}^{V_i})$ and $f(_{V_j}^{V_k})$ for short. The idea is explored in detail in Definition 3 below.

Definition 3 (Reputation Combination): Let $f(p|R_{V_j}^{V_i}, S_{V_j}^{V_i})$ and $f(p|R_{V_j}^{V_k}, S_{V_j}^{V_k})$ be reputation functions about Vj as recorded by V_i and V_k. The reputation function $f(p|R_{V_j}^{V_{ik}}, S_{V_j}^{V_{ik}})$ is defined by 9. Note that the combined reputation report can be extended to as many vehicles or encounter records as possible up to N number of vehicles.

$$R_{V_j}^{V_{ik}} = R_{V_j}^{V_i} + R_{V_j}^{V_k} \tag{9}$$

and 10

$$S_{V_j}^{V_{ik}} = S_{V_j}^{V_i} + S_{V_j}^{V_k} \tag{10}$$

are Vj's combined reputation function recorded by V_i and V_k. In more formal terms, we can use the $\oplus$ operator to represent the combination operation. Thus we can re-write 9 and 10 as

$$f(p|R_{V_j}^{V_{ik}}, \frac{V_{ik}}{V_j}) = f(p|R_{V_j}^{V_i}, S_{V_j}^{V_i}) \oplus f(p|R_{V_j}^{V_k}, S_{V_j}^{V_k}) \tag{11}$$

or simply as

$$f_{V_j}^{V_{ik}} = f_{V_j}^{V_i} \oplus f_{V_j}^{V_k} \tag{12}$$

The combination is commutative and associative under the $\oplus$ operation. This means that the order of the functions is of no relevance. Our scheme does not allow the same reputation function to be counted twice. We avoid this by counting reputation reports based on time of the report. Due to the disconnectedness of the network, we highlight the need to take into consideration the ageing of a vehicles reputation over time. The ageing of the reputation depends on the frequency of the contact between vehicles, hence, more frequent contact implies more reliable reputation rating.

4.4   Misbehaviour Reporting and Verification Phase

In this phase of the scheme, vehicles submit opinions based on their evaluations in the detection phase to RSUs mentioned in Sect. 4.3 above in an opportunistic manner using an opportunistic routing protocol such as the Spray and Wait protocol described in [5]. A key objective of this phase is to ensure the detection of false positives and true negatives due to collusion attacks where malicious vehicles collude to report an overwhelming negative opinion about a non-malicious vehicle for instance. We also highlight the possibility of vehicle selfishness where vehicles collude to protect their interest groups and not report incidences of misbehaviour. To encourage vehicles to report misbehaviour, it is easy to incorporate an incentive scheme into the protocol to reward well behaved vehicles such as the scheme in [4].

4.5   Stimulating Misbehaviour Reporting

We design an incentive scheme that stimulates vehicles to report malicious behaviour. To that end, we formulate the following in order to calculate the incentive for reporting malicious behaviour. The incentive scheme is key to the efficiency of our system and is meant to persuade more vehicles to report misbehaviour. Recall that vehicles are meant to report their evaluations periodically to the TKM via RSUs. When a vehicle suspects misbehaviour, it sends a message in which it sets a misbehaviour flag containing its pseudonym identity and that of the reported vehicle. A vehicle V_i's report can be of the form

$$V_i \Rightarrow RSU\{msg, PseuID, T, Sign, Type, eInvoice\}P_i \qquad (13)$$

where *eInvoice* is an invoice with which V_i can redeem a credit, *msg* is the message, *PseuID* is the pseudonym identity, *Sign*, *Type* is the type of misbehaviour, and P_i is the public key of V_i. How can the credit be used by the vehicle? The credit can be used to redeem charging points such as in the case of electric vehicles given vouchers which can be used to recharge their batteries. To encourage more cooperation, vehicles can be compensated based on the number of accurate misbehaviour reports submitted to the TKM.

4.6   Certificate Revocation and CRL Dissemination Phase

Vehicle revocation involves techniques through which a convicted malicious vehicle's privileges and right of access to network resources is terminated or suspended. The authors in [24,25] have shown that incorrect location information from even as little as 10% of the vehicles in the network can impact on safety message delivery rate drastically.

We mentioned two main situations where vehicle revocation is required. First, when a malicious vehicle deliberately sends modified or manipulated messages. Secondly, a vehicle that send invalid messages due to a malfunctioning OBU device, a technical problem in its components or a software bug. Irrespective of the primary cause, such malicious vehicles must be ex-communicated from the network at the earliest possible time. In addition to efficient revocation in terms of timeliness, revocation cost such as bandwidth costs and scalability, it is vital that the privacy of revoked vehicles is not jeopardized.

Some factors considered in this scheme which affect revocation in VANETs include the delay involved in reporting and verifying maliciousness as well as the delay incurred in distributing the revocation information (CRL). These delays especially that incurred is distributing CRLs results in a vulnerability window for other well-behaved vehicles that may not be informed of the malicious tendencies or actions of such ill-behaved vehicles [26]. The vulnerability window creates a time delay so that well-behaved vehicles fail to receive CRL updates early enough to prevent them from being corrupted by malicious vehicles. Ultimately, the vulnerability window needs to be as small as possible to avoid irrecoverable damage. In disconnected VANETs, these delays are increased due to the opportunist nature of contacts between vehicles and RSUs. Hence, we take the vulnerability window into consideration in the design of our scheme and simulation studies. This also informed our choice of opportunistic routing protocols throughout our experiments, and RSUs for improved coverage.

After the misbehaviour detection phase, the essence of CRL distribution is to ensure that messages signed by vehicles with revoked certificates are disregarded by honest recipient vehicles. For this, there are two options we can adopt. First, we can send CRLs to misbehaving vehicles to self-revoke themselves and stop signing messages. We can also flood CRLs messages to all vehicles within the network. However, flooding has been found to be bandwidth intensive especially in a constrained network. Secondly, we can inform well behaved vehicles of the identities of malicious vehicles and stop them from processing messages received from them. We adopt this option in our implementation since it helps reduce the vulnerability window. Our scheme is based on a distributed and hierarchical system where the revocation responsibility is split between the TKMs and RSUs [27] i.e. the TKMs issue revocation orders while the RSUs distribute the CRLs. In our scheme, we aim to send the CRLs to healthy non-malicious vehicles first. This way, the vulnerability window is reduced and the potential damages due to erroneous messages contained beforehand. The X.509 standard [28] (RFC 5280 p69) also defines several states in which a certificate can be in including the *hold* or *revoked* state. A certificate in the revoked state is also considered irreversibly revoked. The hold state is flagged against a certificate when it is established that such a certificate has been improperly issued by a fake TKM, or the private-key has been compromised. Unlike the revoked state, the hold state of a certificate is considered reversible, and shows that a certificate is temporarily invalid. A vehicle certificate can be flagged off into the hold state for reasons such as if the vehicle holding it is uncertain if the private key it received is lost or stolen. Once it is established that the key has not been tampered with during the period of the hold state, the status can then be reversed. This results in the TKM removing the certificate from the CRLs in the future. Other reasons why a certificate may be revoked or held is due to validity versus expiry issues. However, it is noteworthy that a certificate may be expired, yet still valid. This implies that all expired certificates should be flagged as invalid. Hence, a more robust scheme such as the trust scheme described above is needed to avoid errors that can arise in verifying misbehaviour reports and ensure proper key management.

4.7   Issues with CRL Distribution: Incentive Scheme for Misbehaviour Reporting

We have discussed the reluctance of selfish vehicles to report misbehaviour. In the same manner, some vehicles also inhibit the distribution of CRLs messages where some vehicles can delay or drop CRL messages from reaching their destinations. The intermittent nature of connections in IC-VANETs presents a new set of challenges for the revocation system. We highlight that though it is not possible for malicious vehicles to cause harm during the brief moments of disconnection since they cannot send messages, their certificates should still be revoked as soon as possible. A lot of work abounds regarding revocation mechanisms. While previous work assumed reliable connectivity [29], the closest to our scheme is the work in [1] where the authors used a scheme where there is no PKI, such a system makes misbehaviour more difficult to detect.

CRL Distribution Using History of Encounters. We have discussed the reluctance of selfish vehicles to report misbehaviour. In the same manner, some vehicles also inhibit the distribution of CRLs messages where some vehicles can delay or drop CRL messages from reaching their destinations. The intermittent nature of connections in IC-VANETs presents a new set of challenges for the revocation system in terms of delivering CRLs in a timely manner. While previous work assumed reliable connectivity [29], the closest to our scheme is the work in [1], the authors used a scheme where there is no PKI, such a system makes misbehaviour more difficult to detect. To improve the efficiency of CRL delivery, we employed the technique of encounter based routing of CRL messages. The basic idea behind the scheme is that vehicles will most likely pass messages to regularly encountered contacts than those they do not encounter frequently. Similar encounter-based routing have been used in [30].

5   Performance Analysis and Evaluation

In this section, we describe our simulation set-up and evaluate our results. We show the feasibility of our scheme and compare our results against previous schemes.

5.1   Simulation Setup

Our simulation involves vehicles and RSUs deployed in downtown Helsinki, Finland measuring 4500×3400 m^2. The vehicles move with a variable speed of 25–30 km^{-h} while the RSUs are positioned at selected locations around the simulation area. Generally, we maintain a similar set of settings for all the experiments (see Table 1). For example, all simulations use map-based mobility model. However, we have mentioned a set of simulation parameters specific to each experiment corresponding to each results analysed in the sections that follow.

5.2   Analysis of Results

In this section, we validate the impact on the delivery of safety messages under varying degrees of maliciousness in the network. We then present a detailed account of the performance of our proposed revocation scheme. Our evaluation metrics include the message delivery ratio and delivery probability under the influence of malicious vehicles. Finally, we explain the relationship between the performance metrics and the efficiency of our protocol.

Table 1. Simulation parameters

Parameter	Description
Duration	6 h
Number of vehicles; RSUs; buffer size	50, 100, 150, 200, 250 vehicles; 7 RSUs; 20 MB
Speed limit	25–30 km/h
Transmission coverage	RSUs: 200 m; Vehicles 150 m
Mobility model	Shortest path map based movement
Packet size	5M–10M
Message generation interval	25 s–35 s

Impact of Malicious Vehicles on BSM Message Delivery. In Fig. 3, we show the impact of malicious behaviour on BSM message delivery under a varying number of malicious vehicle populations. This performance is demonstrated using two popular opportunistic routing protocols namely Spray & Wait and PRoPHET. Our choice of Spray & Wait is due to the fact that it is a multi-copy routing protocol. In contrast to PRoPHET which is a single-copy protocol, Spray & Wait ensures there are multiple copies of the messages in the network. The importance of a multi-copy routing protocol is buttressed by the nature of the network that lacks consistent connectivity. Hence, multiple copies ensures redundancy in message delivery.

In this experiment, the delivered messages as a metric reflects the number of safety messages judged to be possibly 100% unaltered and successfully received by destination vehicles. The presented results highlight the difference in performance between our two selected routing protocols - a multi-copy Spray & Wait and a single-copy PRoPHET routing protocols. We observe a 90% delivery probability with Spray & Wait when no malicious vehicles were introduced into the network, gradually dropping to about 45% when 50% of the vehicles became malicious. We can attribute the performance of the almost flat curve for the performance of PRoPHET routing to the single copy protocol. We highlight that PROPHET exhibits an intelligent routing scheme where vehicles that make frequent contacts are more likely to exchange messages than infrequent contact vehicles. This means that a vehicles that are prone to drop messages are unlikely candidates in subsequent meetings.

Impact of Malicious Vehicles on Message Delivery Probability. In Fig. 4, we show the impact of malicious vehicles on BSM message delivery probability. The message delivery probability reflects the ratio of the total number of messages delivered to the total number of messages initially created for delivery. As a preliminary, the impact of malicious vehicle on the delivery probability is vital to the design of the revocation scheme in terms of the CRL delivery

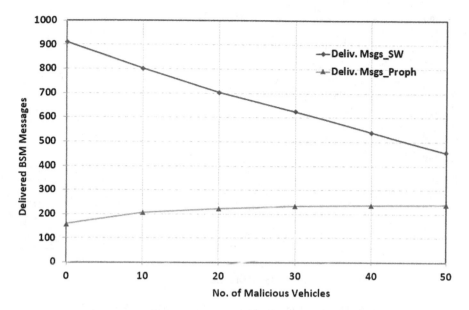

Fig. 3. Delivered messages vs. number of malicious vehicles

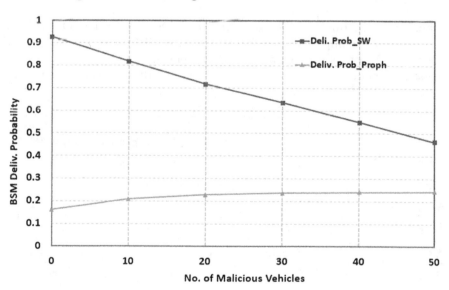

Fig. 4. Delivery probability vs. number of malicious vehicles

probability. The progression of the delivery probability supports the behaviour in Fig. 3. Here, we observe an almost equivalent decrease in the delivery probability values for both Spray & Wait and PRoPHET routing protocols.

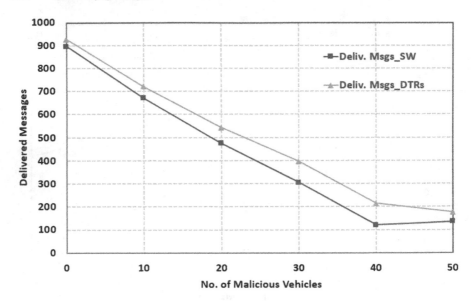

Fig. 5. Delivered messages vs. no. of malicious Vehicles

Impact of Malicious Vehicles on Message Delivery with DTRvS. In Fig. 5, we show the impact of malicious vehicles on CRL message delivery with and without DTRvS which follows after the scheme in [1]. It reflects the number of messages accurately delivered to their destination. In our scheme, we leverage

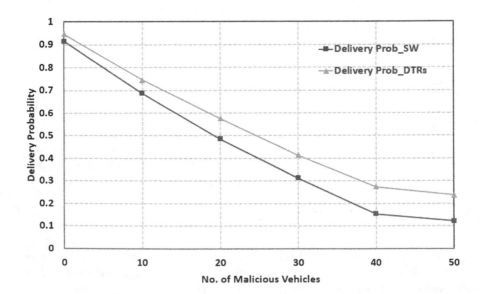

Fig. 6. CRL delivery probability vs. number of malicious vehicles

the available RSUs to deliver CRLs to non-malicious malicious vehicles. The objective is to deliver messages as quickly as possible. That way, messages from malicious vehicles are rejected by healthy vehicles early enough to avoid damage.

CRL Delivery Probability Vs. Number of Malicious Vehicles with DTRvS. In Fig. 6, we present the performance of our proposed scheme with respect to CRL delivery probability. The significance of the results here suggests the feasibility that our proposed scheme is able to coerce more vehicles to honest vehicles to relay CRL messages as highlighted by the gradual but slight decrease in the delivery probability corresponding to malicious densities from 0 to 50%. The peak was at 91% and 93%, and 12% and 22% for Spray & Wait and DTRvS when zero and 50% malicious vehicles were introduced into the network respectively. From the trend in Fig. 6 it is expected that increase in the malicious tendency above 50% will result in further degradation in the delivery probability.

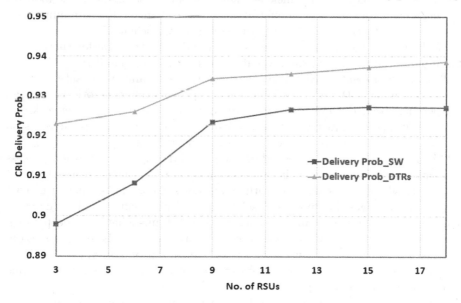

Fig. 7. Delivered CRL messages vs. number of RSUs

CRL Delivery Probability vs. Number of Deployed RSUs with DTRvS. The objective in this experiment is to ascertain the impact of using RSUs as relay stations to deliver CRL messages using our proposed scheme. Note that we assumed a disconnected network where the infrastructure cannot support end-to-end communication as in VDTNs. We also assumed that 50% of the vehicles in this experiment exhibit malicious tendencies. Hence, we isolate them and send CRL messages to the 50% healthy vehicles. Our routing protocol of choice is Spray & Wait since it provides some redundant packets in the network to ensure a best effort delivery. We deployed 3 to 18 RSUs in this experiment

with increments of three (i.e. 3, 6, 9, 12, 15, 18). The results of our experiment
are shown in Fig. 7. As expected, we observe that the chance of CRL delivery
is increasingly improved with the increase in the number of RSUs. However, we
record about 5% improvement when DTRvS is used as against the use of native
Spray & Wait for routing. Another factor shown in Fig. 6 is in line with the
IETF proposal and supported by [31,32] where multiple copies of the CRL are
circulated within the network as against single-copy routing. We expect that
multiple copies will result in more vehicles getting a copy of the CRL, hence
higher delivery probability for more copies propagated as well as higher number
of messages delivered.

5.3   Efficiency and Robustness Analysis

In Table 2, we compare our scheme to other revocation schemes proposed in
literature for robustness and efficiency. Our comparison is based on the mode of
key distribution, format and amount of messages exchanged, the communication
overhead, the attacker model and trust establishment scheme.

Both the schemes in [33,34] use a centralised infrastructure for the revocation administration. In [2], the revocation scheme is distributed but relies on a
Key Generation Centre (KGC) for the bootstrapping and initialisation of the
network. Similar to the schemes in [2], our proposed scheme is both distributed
and decentralised. However due to the disconnected nature of the network and
its inherent lack of infrastructure at the early stages of deployment, it relies on
the RSUs to efficiently distribute the revocation messages.

The number of messages needed or exchanged during the revocation process
is critical to the efficiency of the revocation system. Too many messages leads
to high signalling overhead. While other schemes such as [33,34] incur the least
amount of messages, our proposed scheme drastically reduces this. The overhead incurred include exchanges needed to establish misbehaviour and perform
revocation, especially, only one instant of revocation message is sent per session.
In other to ensure its effectiveness, our base routing protocol, Spray and Wait
ensures redundancy by sending several copies of the same message at a time
using the same infrastructure.

Our proposed scheme is based on the distribution of CRLs in a similar manner
to other compared schemes in Table 2. However, the misbehaviour detection
established helps us to identify well-behaved vehicles and directly send messages
to them instructing to reject messages from malicious vehicles. This way, we
achieve efficient management of bandwidth and reduce the overhead and delay
drastically compared to other schemes.

We highlight that most of the compared schemes are not clear on the means
of identifying misbehaving vehicles and are based on assumptions. Among the
compared schemes, closest to ours is the scheme in [2], we use a trust-based misbehaviour detection scheme where vehicles derive opinions of each other during
exchange of messages. The opinion reports are then verified by the CA before
revocation is initiated. This feature is not present in the scheme proposed in [1]
and leaves the system open to abuse by the vehicles due the absence of a central

Table 2. Comparison of revocation schemes

Scheme	Raya et al. [33]	Lin et al. [34]	Djamaludin [1]	Hoeper [2]	DTRvS
Key distribution	CA	CA	LFC	IBC	RSUs
Infrastructure	Central	Central	Distr	Distr	Distr
Message format	CRL	△CRL	△CRL	△CRL	△CRL
Adversary model	Weak	Weak	Strong	Strong	Strong
No. of messages	N	N	O(edges)	O(edges)	N
Revocation type	Vehicle + key	Vehicle + key	Key only	Vehicle	Vehicle
Delay tolerance	No	No	Yes	No	Yes
Trust-based	No	No	No	No	Yes

authority. A major shortcoming of using a CA for key revocation is scalability, because CRLs can grow very large in size for large domains and networks even with compression.

While misbehaviour should be detected early enough, the cost and logistics involved in spreading the revocation information to avoid further damage are critical factors to consider in the design of revocation systems. It is necessary to understand the economics of its implementation with regard to infrastructural needs especially in challenged networks. The strength of our scheme is in its delay tolerance to withstand the lack of end-to-end connectivity in the network. However, we expect it to perform even better in a network with full infrastructure support. Since the RSUs are involved in the misbehaviour detection phase, they can be configured to intelligently select well-behaved vehicles to send revocation messages to. That way we are able to achieve revocation without relying on the CA as in other schemes.

6   Conclusion

In this article, we highlighted the consequences of vehicles misbehaviour in VANETs and the need for a revocation solution that is effective in delay tolerant conditions. We also described the challenges in detecting misbehaviour in intermittently connected network environments such as DTNs and VDTNs which are the closest characterisations of the early stages of ITS deployment such as in rural areas. It described trust-based schemes as a means of detecting misbehaviour. Our scheme introduces a delay-tolerant revocation scheme aimed at evicting malicious vehicles. We demonstrated the effectiveness of our scheme through simulations. Our scheme owes its effectiveness to the introduced incentive scheme that encourages vehicles to report misbehaviour.

Acknowledgement. The funding for this work is from the Overseas Scholarship Scheme (OSS) of the Petroleum Technology Development Fund (PTDF) of the Federal Government of Nigeria with support from the PETRAS Project (in conjunction with

IoTUK) and the Institute for Communication Systems, home of The 5G Innovation Center (5GIC), University of Surrey, Guildford, United Kingdom.

References

1. Djamaludin, C.I., Foo, E., Camtepe, S., Corke, P.: Revocation and update of trust in autonomous delay tolerant networks. J. Comput. Secur. **60**, 15–36 (2016). ISSN 0167-4048
2. Hoeper, K., Gong, G.: Monitoring-based key revocation schemes for mobile ad hoc networks: design and security analysis (2009)
3. Zhang, J.: A survey on trust management for VANETs. In: Proceedings of the 2011 IEEE International Conference on Advanced Information Networking and Applications (AINA 2011), pp. 105–112. IEEE Computer Society, Washington, DC (2011). ISBN 978-0-7695-4337-6
4. Rongxing, L., Xiaodong, L., Haojin, Z., Xuemin, S., Preiss, B.: Pi: a practical incentive protocol for delay tolerant networks. IEEE Trans. Wirel. Commun. **9**(4), 1483–1493 (2010). ISSN 1536-1276
5. Spyropoulos, T., Psounis, K., Raghavendra, C.S.: Spray and wait: an efficient routing scheme for intermittently connected mobile networks. In: Proceedings of the 2005 ACM SIGCOMM Workshop on Delay-Tolerant Networking, pp. 252–259. ACM, New York (2005). ISBN 1-59593-026-4
6. Hasan, O., Brunie, L., Bertino, E., Shang, N.: A decentralized privacy preserving reputation protocol for the malicious adversarial mode. IEEE Trans. Inf. Forensics Secur. **8**(8), 949–962 (2013). ISSN 1556-6013
7. Ruj, S., Cavenaghi, M.A., Huang, Z., Nayak, A., Stojmenovic, I.: On data-centric misbehavior detection in VANETs. In: Vehicular Technology Conference (VTC Fall), pp. 1–5. IEEE (2001). ISSN 1090-3038
8. Golle, P., Greene, D., Staddon, J.: Detecting and Correcting Malicious Data in VANETs. In: Proceedings of the 1st ACM International Workshop on Vehicular Ad Hoc Networks (VANET 2004), pp. 29–37. ACM, New York (2004). ISBN 1-58113-922-5
9. Dotzer, F., Fischer, L., Magiera, P.: VARS: a vehicle ad-hoc network reputation system. In: Sixth IEEE International Symposium on a World of Wireless Mobile and Multimedia Networks (WoWMoM 2005), pp. 454–456 (2005)
10. Raya, M., Papadimitratos, P., Aad, I., Jungels, D., Hubaux, J.-P.: Eviction of misbehaving and faulty nodes in vehicular networks. IEEE J. Sel. Areas Commun. **25**(8), 1557–1568 (2007). ISSN 0733-8716
11. Isento, J.N.G., Rodrigues, J., Dias, J., Paula, M.C.G., Vinel, A.: Vehicular delay-tolerant networks: a novel solution for vehicular communications. IEEE Intell. Transp. Syst. Mag. **5**(4), 10–19 (2013). ISSN 1939-1390
12. Timpner, J., Schrmann, D., Wolf, L.: Trustworthy parking communities: helping your neighbor to find a space. IEEE Trans. Dependable Secur. Comput. **13**(1), 120–132 (2016). ISSN 1545-5971
13. Viswanathan, K., Templin, F.: (Internet-Draft) Architecture for a Delay-and-Disruption Tolerant Public-Key Distribution Network (PKDN). Internet Engineering Task Force (2016)
14. Cao, Y., Wang, N., Kamel, G.: A publish/subscribe communication framework for managing electric vehicle charging. In: 2014 International Conference on Connected Vehicles and Expo (ICCVE), pp. 318–324 (2014). ISSN 2378-1289

15. Bhutta, M.N.M., Cruickshank, H., Sun, Z.: Public-key infrastructure validation and revocation mechanism suitable for delay/disruption tolerant networks. In: IET Information Security (IET) (2016)
16. Galbraith, S.D., Harrison, K., Soldera, D.: Implementing the tate pairing. In: Fieker, C., Kohel, D.R. (eds.) ANTS 2002. LNCS, vol. 2369, pp. 324–337. Springer, Heidelberg (2002). doi:10.1007/3-540-45455-1_26
17. Boneh, D., Franklin, M.: Identity-based encryption from the weil pairing. In: Kilian, J. (ed.) CRYPTO 2001. LNCS, vol. 2139, pp. 213–229. Springer, Heidelberg (2001). doi:10.1007/3-540-44647-8_13
18. Wasef, A., Shen, X.: EDR: efficient decentralized revocation protocol for vehicular ad hoc networks. IEEE Trans. Veh. Technol. 58(9), 5214–5224 (2009). ISSN 0018-9545
19. Naor, M., Nissim, K.: Certificate revocation and certificate update. IEEE J. Sel. Areas Commun. 18(18), 561–570 (2000). ISSN 0733-8716
20. Li, W., Song, H.: ART: an attack-resistant trust management scheme for securing vehicular ad hoc networks. IEEE Trans. Intell. Transp. Syst. 17(4), 960 969 (2016). ISSN 1524-9050
21. Li, Z., Chigan, C.T.: On joint privacy and reputation assurance for vehicular ad hoc networks. IEEE Trans. Mob. Comput. 13(10), 2334–2344 (2014). ISSN 1536-1233
22. Shafer, G.: Dempster-Shafer theory. In: Encyclopedia of Artificial Intelligence, pp. 330–331. Wiley, Hoboken (1992)
23. Josang, A., Ismail, R.: The beta reputation system. In: Proceedings of the 15th Bled Conference on Electronic Commerce, p. 41 (2002)
24. Tim, I., Elmar, S.: Greedy routing in highway scenarios: the impact of position faking nodes. In: Proceedings of Workshop on Intelligent Transportation (WIT) (2006)
25. Kim, Y., Lee, J.-J., Helmy, A.: Impact of location inconsistencies on geographic routing in wireless networks. In: Proceedings of the 6th ACM International Workshop on Modelling Analysis and Simulation of Wireless and Mobile Systems, San Diego, pp. 124–127. ACM, New York (2003). ISBN 1-58113-766-4
26. Kherani, A., Rao, A.: Performance of node-eviction schemes in vehicular networks. IEEE Trans. Veh. Technol. 59(2), 550–558 (2010). ISSN 0018-9545
27. Petit, J., Schaub, F., Feiri, M., Kargl, F.: Pseudonym schemes in vehicular networks: a survey. IEEE Commun. Surv. Tutor. 17(1), 228–255 (2015). ISSN 1553-877X
28. Housley, R., Polk, W., Ford, W., Solo, D.: Internet X.509 public key infrastructure certificate and certificate revocation list (CRL) profile. In: IETF, Network Working Group (2002)
29. Laberteaux, K.P., Haas, J.J., Hu, Y.-C.: Security certificate revocation list distribution for VANET. In: Proceedings of the Fifth ACM International Workshop on VehiculAr Inter-NETworking, San Francisco, pp. 88–89. ACM, New York (2008). ISBN 978-1-60558-191-0
30. Nelson, S.C., Bakht, M., Kravets, R.: Encounter-based routing in DTNs. In: IEEE INFOCOM, pp. 846–854 (2009)
31. Spyropoulos, T., Psounis, K., Raghavendra, C.S.: Efficient routing in intermittently connected mobile networks: the multiple-copy case. IEEE/ACM Trans. Netw. 16(1), 77–90 (2008). ISSN 1063-6692
32. Spyropoulos, T., Psounis, K., Raghavendra, C.S.: Single-copy routing in intermittently connected mobile networks. In: 2004 First Annual IEEE Communications Society Conference on Sensor and Ad Hoc Communications and Networks. IEEE SECON 2004, pp. 235–244 (2004)

33. Raya, M., Jungels, D., Papadimitratos, P., Aad, I., Hubaux, J.-P.: Certificate revocation in vehicular networks. In: Laboratory for Computer Communications and Applications (LCA) School of Computer and Communication Sciences, EPFL, Switzerland (2006)
34. Xiaodong, L., Rongxing, L., Chenxi, Z., Haojin, Z., Pin-Han, H., Xuemin, S.: Security in vehicular ad hoc networks. IEEE Commun. Mag. **46**(4), 88–95 (2008). ISSN 0163-6804

Impact of Spreading Factor Imperfect Orthogonality in LoRa Communications

Daniele Croce[1,2(✉)], Michele Gucciardo[1], Ilenia Tinnirello[1],
Domenico Garlisi[1,2], and Stefano Mangione[1]

[1] DEIM, Università di Palermo, viale delle scienze ed. 9, 90128 Palermo, Italy
{daniele.croce,michele.gucciardo,ilenia.tinnirello,
domenico.garlisi,stefano.mangione}@unipa.it
[2] CNIT Consortium, Viale G.P. Usberti, 181/A, 43124 Parma, Italy

Abstract. In this paper we study the impact of imperfect-orthogonality in LoRa spreading factors (SFs) in simulation and real-world experiments. First, we analyze LoRa modulation numerically and show that collisions between packets of different SFs can indeed cause packet loss if the interference power received is strong enough. Second, we validate such findings using commercial devices, confirming our numerical results. Third, we modified and extended LoRaSim, an open-source LoRa simulator, to measure the impact of inter-SF collisions and fading (which was not taken into account previously in the simulator). Our results show that non-orthogonality of the SFs can deteriorate significantly the performance especially of higher SFs (10 to 12) and that fading has virtually no impact when multiple gateways are available in space diversity.

1 Introduction

In recent years, we have assisted to an impressive proliferation of wireless technologies and mobile-generated traffic, which is now the highest portion of the total internet traffic and will continue to grow with the emergence of Internet-of-Things (IoT) applications [1]. Such a proliferation has been characterized by an high-density deployment of base stations (based on heterogeneous technologies, such as 4G cellular base stations and WiFi Access Points), as well as by high-density wireless devices, not limited to traditional user terminals. Indeed, with the advent of IoT applications, many smart objects, such as domestic appliances, cameras, monitoring sensors, etc., are equipped with a wireless technology. Understanding how wireless networks would respond to the increasing capacity demand is therefore of crucial importance. However, high-density deployments of wireless networks are difficult to study in real testbeds or installations, especially when we can expect that hundreds or even thousands of mobile devices (not limited to traditional user terminals, but including smart objects and sensors) are simultaneously active in the same environment.

This work has been partially supported by EU funded research project symbIoTe, H2020-ICT-2015 grant agreement number 688156.

© Springer International Publishing AG 2017
A. Piva et al. (Eds.): TIWDC 2017, CCIS 766, pp. 165–179, 2017.
DOI: 10.1007/978-3-319-67639-5_13

In this paper we consider the emerging LoRa technology, which represents a critical example of wireless technology working with high-density devices. Indeed, LoRa technology has been conceived for Low Power Wide Area Networks (LPWAN), characterized by low data rate requirements per single device, large cells and heterogeneous application domains, which may lead to extremely high numbers of devices coexisting in the same cell. For this reason, LoRa provides different possibilities to orthogonalize transmissions as much as possible – Carrier Frequency (CF), Spreading Factor (SF), Bandwidth (BW), Coding Rate (CR) – and provide simultaneous collision free communications. However, despite the robustness of the LoRa PHY [2] patented by Semtech, in WAN scenarios where multiple gateways can be installed, the scalability of this technology is still under investigation [3]. Current studies are mostly based on simulation results [4] and assume that the utilization of multiple transmission channels and spreading factors lead to a system that can be considered as the simple superposition of independent (single channel, single spreading factor) sub-systems. This is actually a strong simplification, especially because the spreading factors adopted by LoRa are pseudo-orthogonal [5] and therefore, in near-far conditions, collisions can prevent the correct reception of the overlapping transmissions using different spreading factors.

For characterizing these phenomena, in this paper (i) we analyze LoRa chirp modulation both numerically and experimentally, showing that collisions between packets of different SFs can indeed cause packet loss if the interference received is strong enough; (ii) we quantify the power threshold for which such loss occurs, for all combinations of SFs; (iii) we modified and extended LoRaSim [6], an open-source LoRa simulator presented in [3], to measure the impact of both inter-SF collisions and fading (which was also not taken into account in previous works). First, we analyzed numerically LoRa modulation (based on chirp spread spectrum) and LoRa access mechanism (based on aloha and duty cycle enforcement), including simple models for traffic sources and physical channels, and we developed a software receiver, able to process a signal trace received by a well known USRP software-defined-radio (SDR) platform. Second, we designed and implemented a traffic generator for LoRa-based networks (to be run on a second USRP platform) to generate, in a controlled and repeatable manner, a *combined* radio signal given by the super-position of multiple LoRa signals, generated by different devices operating in the same cell, as they would be seen by a LoRa gateway when colliding. We use these first two elements to prove that if a collision occurs between packets of different SF, both packets are correctly received only when the difference in received power is below a certain threshold (which we quantify for each combination of SFs), otherwise only the packet with highest RSSI is correctly received. Third, to measure the impact caused by this non-orthogonality, we modified and extended the LoRaSim simulator to include such phenomena and model log-normal fading.

Our experimental results show that non-orthogonality of the SFs can deteriorate significantly the performance of LoRa communications, especially of higher SFs (10 to 12) where packets last longer and are thus more vulnerable to collisions. With multiple neighboring cells, this phenomenon is further exacerbated and, in some scenarios, high SFs can experience severe losses. In the same scenarios, when considering the SFs perfectly orthogonal, the capacity is significantly overestimated, as the measured losses are almost halved. Finally, we demonstrate that in multi-gateway or multi-cell topologies fading has virtually no impact on performance, because antenna diversity gives more chances to receive the same packet on different gateways.

2   Related Work

Since LoRa is quite a recent technology, relatively few works have already been published on its performance. Specifically, [7] focus on LoRa applications and PHY, while in [8] some test-bed and simulation results are presented but with a low number of devices. In [9] authors model LoRaWAN performance analytically in a scenario with high number of devices and propose solutions to improve its performance.

Most of the current studies are based on simulation results. Authors in [3] implemented and used the LoRaSim simulator [6] to investigate the capacity limits of LoRa networks. They showed that a typical deployment can support only 120 nodes per 3.8 ha, although performance can be improved with multiple gateways. The paper in [5] compared the performance of LoRa and ultra narrowband (Sigfox-like) networks, showing that ultra narrowband has a larger coverage but LoRa networks are less sensitive to interference. Finally, authors in [10] presented details on the patented LoRa PHY and introduced *gr-lora*, an open source SDR-based implementation of LoRa PHY.

All of these works, however, assume that the SFs adopted by LoRa are perfectly orthogonal, thus simplifying the analysis and consequently the network capacity. Instead, in this paper we show that, due to the imperfect orthogonality of the SFs, inter-SF collisions can prevent the correct reception of the transmissions with serious impact on LoRa performances. To the best of our knowledge, we are the first to demonstrate and quantify this performance degradation.

3   LoRaWAN Networks and Protocols

In this section we briefly describe the LoRaWAN network architecture and MAC/PHY protocols, in order to present the main features that affect the network capacity. LoRaWAN is a protocol specification built on top of the LoRa PHY technology, a PHY layer patented by Semtech that works on ISM bands (namely, at 868 MHz with 3 default channels in Europe) with a limited duty cycle allowed to each device [11]. The typical LoRaWAN network consists of end-devices (sensors or actuators), multiple gateways which forward packets coming from the wireless medium to a backhaul interface, and a logically centralized server which analyzes information collected by all the devices and optimizes the network configuration.

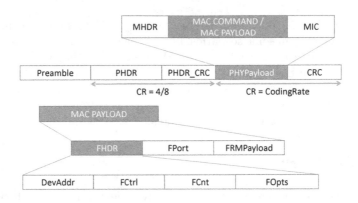

Fig. 1. LoRa frame structure.

Differently from traditional cellular networks, end-devices are not associated to a particular gateway to have access to the network. Gateways serve simply as link layer relayers and forward all the packets received from end-devices to the network server, by adding information regarding the reception quality. Thus, in general, the same packet can be forwarded by multiple gateways and the central server is responsible of detecting duplicate packets and choosing the appropriate gateway for transmitting downlink packets (if any).

Gateways are usually equipped with multiple transceivers for receiving simultaneously on multiple (configurable) frequency channels, while end devices can dynamically select one transmission channel, among a set of available ones, at each transmission attempt. Some channels are reserved for data transmission, one channel is reserved for gateway's responses, while some other channels are usually served for control information and in particular for transmitting network joining requests from end devices.

LoRaWAN provides an open source MAC layer that is based on a simple Aloha protocol, in order to minimize the complexity and the energy consumption of the devices. End devices do not perform carrier sense; moreover, they listen to the medium for receiving packets only in special time windows after uplink transmissions (class A devices), or at regular time intervals (class B devices). Only class C devices have continuously active receivers. Frames can be acknowledged or not. In the acknowledged mode, the modulation format can be automatically adapted as function of the number of retransmissions (for increasing or decreasing robustness).

Figure 1 summarizes the structure of a LoRaWAN frame. The frame starts with a preamble, which is used for synchronization and for defining the modulation format (specifically, the spreading factor used for modulating the frame, as clarified in the following sub-section). The preamble is followed by a PHY Header and a Header CRC, whose total length is 20 bits encoded with the most reliable code rate of 4/8. The PHY header contains information such as payload length and whether the optional payload CRC is included or not in the frame. The MAC header is one byte only; it defines the protocol version and message type,

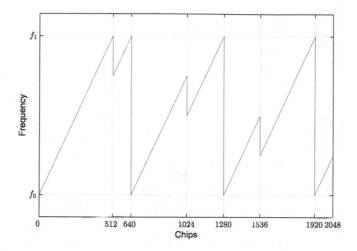

Fig. 2. Modulating signal with $SF = 9$ for one basic upchirp and three symbols: 128, 256 and 384.

i.e., whether it is a data or a management frame, whether it is transmitted in uplink or downlink, whether it shall be acknowledged. Finally, the Frame header contains network-level information, such as the device address (composed of a network identifier and device-specific identifier given upon association), network control information about the configuration of the uplink data rate parameters, a sequence number, and frame optional data for commands. A port number is used for distinguishing flows between gateways and end devices, including flows containing MAC commands for the configuration of devices.

3.1   LoRa Modulation

LoRa modulation is derived from *Chirp Spread Spectrum (CSS)*, which makes use of *chirp signals*, i.e. frequency-modulated signals obtained when the modulating signal varies linearly in the range $[f_0, f_1]$ (upchirp) or $[f_1, f_0]$ (downchirp) in a symbol time T. Binary modulations, mapping 0/1 information bits in upchirps/downchirps, have been demonstrated to be very robust against in-band or out-band interference [2]. LoRa employs a M-ary modulation scheme based on chirps, in which symbols are obtained by considering different circular shifts of the basic upchirp signal. The temporal shifts, characterizing each symbol, are slotted into multiples of time $T_{chip} = 1/BW$, called chip, being $BW = f_1 - f_0$ the bandwidth of the signal. It results that the modulating signal for a generic n-th LoRa symbol can be expressed as:

$$f(t) = \begin{cases} f_1 - n \cdot k \cdot T_{chip} + k \cdot t & \text{for } 0 \leqslant t \leqslant n \cdot T_{chip} \\ f_0 + k \cdot t & \text{for } n \cdot T_{chip} < t \leqslant T \end{cases}$$

where $k = (f_1 - f_0)/T$ is the slope of the frequency variations. The total number of symbols (coding SF information bits) is chosen equal to 2^{SF}, where SF is

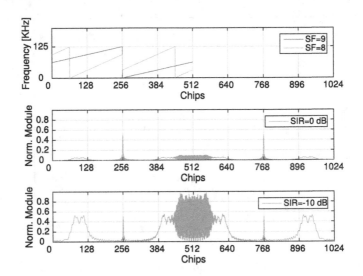

Fig. 3. An example of combined signal, obtained by the sum of two modulated chirps with $SF = 9$ (blue line) and $SF = 8$ (red line), and correlation results with the basic upchirp with $SF = 9$. (Color figure online)

called spreading factor. The symbol duration T required for representing any possible shift is $2^{SF} \cdot T_{chip} = 2^{SF}/BW$. It follows that, for a fixed bandwidth, the symbol period increases with SF, enlarging the temporal occupancy of the signal. Figure 2 shows the modulating signal used for a basic upchirp and three examples of circular shifts obtained for $SF = 9$: the symbol time is $512\, T_{chip}$, while the three exemplary shifts code the symbols 128, 256 and 384.

The preamble of any LoRa frame is obtained by sending a sequence of at least ten upchirps, followed by two downchirps. Payload data are then sent by using the M-ary modulation symbols. LoRa provides three BW settings (125, 250 or 500 KHz) and seven different SF values (from 6 to 12). In general, a larger bandwidth translates in a data rate increase and a receiver sensitivity deterioration. Conversely, higher spreading factors can be used for improving the link robustness at the cost of a lower data rate.

An interesting feature of LoRa modulation is the pseudo-orthogonality of signals modulated under different spreading factors. This feature can be exploited for enabling multiple concurrent transmissions that can be easily separated by the receiver thanks to the fact that the cross-energy between two signals, say $s_1(t)$ and $s_2(t)$, modulated with different spreading factors is almost zero regardless of the starting of the symbol times:

$$E_{s_1,s_2}(\tau) = \int_0^T s_1(t) \cdot s_2(t-\tau)^* dt \simeq 0$$

where T is the symbol period of the signal with the highest spreading factor. An example of signal separation is illustrated in Fig. 3, where one signal modulated with $SF = 9$, representing symbol 256 (blue line), is overlapped to two symbols modulated with $SF = 8$ (red line). For sake of presentation, in the figure, the symbol times of the two signals start at the same time. For receiving the signal modulated with $SF = 9$ it is enough to correlate the overlapped signal with the relevant $SF = 9$ upchirp signal. The middle plot of the figure shows the correlation results (i.e. the variation of the cross-energy between the overlapped signal and the upchirp signal at different temporal shifts). The figure clearly highlights two peaks when the upchirp signal is shifted of 256 and $256 + 2^9$ chip times T_{chip}: indeed, in these positions the similarity of the sum signal with the basic upchirp at $SF = 9$ is high because the upchirp overlaps with one of the two piecewise chirps of the symbol modulated with $SF = 9$. Conversely, in the other positions, the correlation is almost zero as the symbol modulated with $SF = 8$ and the upchirp are almost orthogonal to the basic upchirp.

Note that the separation mechanism works as long as the amplitudes of the overlapping signals are comparable or belong to a given range. The bottom plot of Fig. 3 shows the correlation results when the signal modulated with $SF = 8$ has an amplitude 20 times higher than the amplitude of the symbol at $SF = 9$. In this case, correlation peaks due to cross-energy can occur in positions different from the symbol time (e.g. around $512\ T_{chip}$) and demodulation errors can occur.

4   Analysis of LoRa Collisions

Goal of this section is quantifying how the power ratio between a reference signal and an overlapping interfering signal can affect the demodulation results, even when the interfering signal is transmitted with a spreading factor different from the desired signal one. To this purpose, we consider both simulation results, based on a MATLAB implementation of a multi-channel LoRa demodulator, and experimental results, based on a commercial LoRa receiver and a USRP used as an artificial synthesizer of LoRa overlapped signals.

4.1   MATLAB Simulation Results

We implemented a LoRa demodulator in MATLAB based on the parallel correlation of the received signal with a bank of upchirp signals modulated with different spreading factors (from $SF = 7$ to $SF = 12$). For identifying the transmission symbol, we observed that for circular shifts lower then an half of the symbol period (i.e. for the first half of all the possible symbols), the first correlation peak has a smaller amplitude than the second one. This is due to the fact that the first piecewise chirp overlaps with the reference upchirp for a lower duration that the second one. On the contrary, for symbols shifted of more than $T/2$, the first peak has a bigger amplitude than the second one. We exploited this property for implementing a decision logic based on the identification of the highest correlation peak. In brief, the MATLAB demodulator works as follows: (i) cross-correlating the received signal and the reference upchirp at the selected

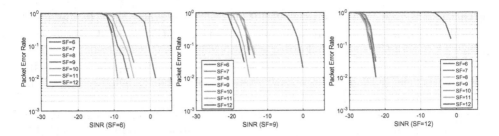

Fig. 4. PER of three different spreading factors in function of the SIR.

spreading factor; (ii) looking for two (related) correlation peaks within the symbol periods, whose distance is T; (iii) choosing the highest peak for quantifying the symbol shift.

We also implemented another demodulation solution, proposed in [12,13], which works by multiplying the received signal with the basic downchirp signal in order to obtain two piecewise signals at a fixed frequency f_i and $f_i + BW$ (whose value f_i is proportional to the circular shift of the symbol), by downsampling the resulting signal with a sampling rate equal to the bandwidth of the signal for creating an alias of the signal $f_i + BW$ at frequency f_i and by finally performing an FFT on the signal for identifying f_i.

We performed a number of simulations for testing the MATLAB implementations of LoRa demodulator in case of reception of two overlapping signals modulated with different spreading factors. Our goal is identifying a Signal to Interference Ratio (SIR) threshold under which the correct demodulation of the desired signal is affected by errors. In each simulation run, we created an overlapped signal by summing one random symbol modulated with a reference spreading factor SF_{ref} with a number of random interfering symbols modulated with a different spreading factor SF_{int}. For each run we can distinguish two cases: if $SF_{ref} > SF_{int}$ then the reference symbol is combined with more than one interfering symbol (e.g. for $SF_{ref} = 12$ and $SF_{int} = 10$, the number of interfering symbols N overlapping with the reference signal is equal to 4). Conversely, if $SF_{ref} < SF_{int}$, the same interfering symbol is overlapped to multiple symbols of the reference signal. The amplitude A_{int} of the interferer signal is set to one, whereas the amplitude A_{ref} of the reference is multiplied with a tunable value leading to different SIR values:

$$A_{int} = \sqrt{10^{-SIR/10} \cdot A_{ref}}$$

The resulting combined signal has been then processed by the MATLAB demodulators, in absence of noise on the channel and assuming perfect synchronization of the symbols. The results achieved with the two implementations (correlation- and FFT-based) are comparable both in terms of symbol demodulation performance and complexity. In the following, we only show results for the correlation-based demodulator.

Table 1. SIR thresholds of correct demodulation for the different SFs in Matlab simulations.

SF_{ref} \ SF_{int}	6	7	8	9	10	11	12
6	0	-4.5	-6	-7.5	-9	-9	-10.5
7	-6	0	-7.5	-9	-9	-12	-12
8	-10.5	-10.5	0	-9	-12	-12	-15
9	-13.5	-13.5	-13.5	0	-13.5	-15	-15
10	-16.5	-16.5	-16.5	-16.5	0	-15	-18
11	-19.5	-19.5	-19.5	-19.5	-19.5	0	-18
12	-22.5	-22.5	-22.5	-22.5	-22.5	-22.5	0

A Packet Error Rate (PER) statistic has been generated comparing the demodulated symbols with the modulated ones. For each simulation run, we randomly generated 100 packets of 10 Bytes each with SF_{ref} against a correspondingly number of symbols with SF_{int} (increased or decreased by appropriate powers of 2 to cover the SF_{ref} symbol length), and varied the SIR values from -30 dB to $+6$ dB with steps of 1.5 dB. Figure 4 shows the results of these simulations for three different SF_{ref} values as an example. The curves in the figures represents the error probability for one selected SF_{ref} against all the possible SF_{int} obtained with our MATLAB demodulator. Similar results have been obtained with the other implementation. From the figure, it can be easily recognized that for each SF_{ref} it exists a minimum SIR threshold below which the success probability starts degrading (high PER). Furthermore, the smaller the interfering spreading factor, the higher the SIR must be to have an acceptable PER.

Table 1 summarizes the SIR thresholds considering a PER of 1%. In the table, we also consider the case when the interfering signal has the same spreading factor of the reference signal. As also documented in the Semtech specifications, LoRa modulations achieves very high probability of capture effects even with low SIR values (approximately 0 dB for the different spreading factors in our simulations, versus 6 dB specified in [14]). In other words, it is very likely that in case of collisions between two signals modulated with the same spreading factor, the strongest signal can be correctly demodulated.

4.2   USRP Experiments

For validating the thresholds found with the Matlab simulator, we performed a number of experiments on real LoRa links in case of continuous collisions of the packets. To this purpose we used a Semtech SX1272 transceiver, controlled by an Arduino Yun, for sending packets (with a 19 byte payload) modulated with all the possible spreading factors and a USRP B210 for recording the traces. After this preliminary phase, we manipulated the traces extracting exactly one packet

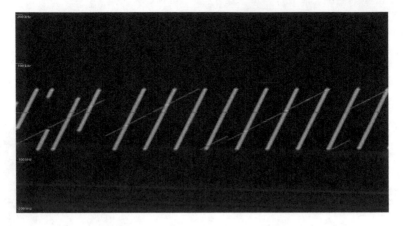

Fig. 5. An example of collision between $SF_{ref} = 12$ (the darker chirps) and $SF_{int} = 10$ (the brighter chirps) with $SIR = -4\,\mathrm{dB}$.

for each SF_{ref} and adding a variable silence period to it as inter-packet delay. This operation gave us the necessary flexibility for combining traces at different spreading factors through Gnuradio and send them over the air via the USRP. Using two file source blocks, we loaded continuously one trace at SF_{ref} and one trace at SF_{int}. The delay between packets at different spreading factors was set in order to achieve the condition of continuous collision. Figure 5 shows an example of overlapping symbols modulated with $SF_{ref} = 12$, $SF_{int} = 10$ and with a $SIR = -4\,\mathrm{dB}$. We then: (i) modified the amplitude of the interferer packets according to the desired SIR level through a multiplier block; (ii) summed the two traces with a sum block; (iii) sent the combined signal over the air through an USRP block. Then, the combined signal sent by the USRP was received by the SX1272 transceiver which logged, through an Arduino LoRa library, the packets received correctly. Finally the packet success probability was calculated. The results of the experiments are summarized in Table 2, for the same subset of reference and interfering spreading factors presented in the previous subsection. Comparing this table with Table 1, it can be observed that the thresholds for correct demodulation are higher with the real transceiver.

5 Simulation-Based Capacity Results

To measure the impact caused by the non-orthogonal SFs, we modified and extended the LoRaSim simulator [6] to include such phenomena. LoRaSim is a Python-based discrete event simulator implemented with SimPy [15] by the authors of [3] (which we warmly thank for publishing the source code). It allows nodes to be placed in a 2-dimensional space with up to 24 LoRa gateways which act as sinks for the data retrieval (uplink communication only). The parameters that can be defined are: Transmit Power (TP), Carrier Frequency (CF), Spreading Factor (SF), Bandwidth (BW) and Coding Rate (CR). The node's

Table 2. SIR thresholds of correct demodulation for different SFs with SX1272 transceiver.

SF_{ref} \ SF_{int}	7	8	9	10	11	12
7	na	na	na	na	na	na
8	-6	na	na	na	na	na
9	-7	-7	na	na	na	na
10	-9	-9	-9	na	na	na
11	-13	-13	-13	-13	na	na
12	-16	-16	-16	-16	-16	na

behaviour is described by the average packet transmission rate λ and packet payload B (with fixed preamble of 8 symbols). Finally, the gateways can receive multiple signals with different SF and BW combinations.

We modified LoRaSim so that if a collision occurs between packets of different SF, both packets are correctly received only when the difference in received power is below a certain threshold (in the experiments we set a conservative threshold of 6 dB for all collisions), otherwise only the packet with highest RSSI is received and the other discarded[1]. We also extended the simulator to account for log-normal fading which was not implemented yet. As we will show, fading has very limited impact on LoRa communications when packets can be received by several gateways, while it can affect the reception of the packets when there is only one gateway in visibility. Unless differently noted, the transmission parameters used by the nodes are the following: TP = 14 dBm, CF = 868 MHz, BW = 500 kHz, CR = 4/5 and B = 20 Bytes.

For comparison purposes, we use the same metric used in [3] to evaluate the performance of LoRa networks, namely the Data Extraction Rate (DER), defined as the quota of packets correctly received by at least one gateway over a period of time. Indeed, in LoRa deployments all messages are received by the backend system, independently of the final destination of the packet, i.e. each transmitted message should be received by at least one base station. Thus, the achievable DER depends on the position, number and behaviour of LoRa nodes and gateways, and its values vary between 0 and 1, with 1 representing an optimal LoRa deployment.

5.1 Single Cell

The first set of experiments aims to asses the impact of the non-orthogonality of LoRa's SFs. To this purpose, Fig. 6 shows the DER for 1000 nodes in a single isolated cell, with 1, 4 and 16 gateways respectively. The 7 SFs are uniformly assigned to the nodes (i.e. each SF is assigned to 1000/7 nodes), although for

---

[1] We omit the case of collisions between packets of different BW for the sake of simplicity.

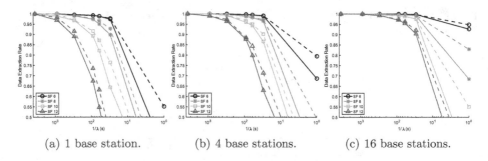

Fig. 6. Capacity of a single LoRa cell with one or more gateways.

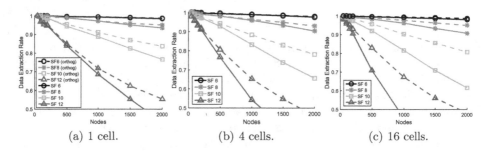

Fig. 7. LoRa performance in a single isolated cell and with multiple adjacent cells (one gateway per cell).

easiness of presentation in the figure we show only a subset of the SFs, namely nodes using SFs 6, 8, 10 and 12. Finally, the dashed lines correspond to the results obtained by considering the SFs as perfectly orthogonal.

From the figure, it is clear that the impact of non orthogonality is limited when the traffic rate of the nodes is low (higher values of $1/\lambda$). However, the performance deteriorates quickly as collisions appear, especially for high SF (10–12) where packets last longer and are thus more vulnerable. As demonstrated in [3], when there are more gateways the capacity increases thanks to antenna diversity, mitigating the impact of collisions both between packets with same SF or different SFs. However, this comes at the cost of installing several base stations to cover the same area, which might not always be economically feasible.

5.2   Multiple Cells

A second set of experiments aims to assess the impact of non-orthogonal SFs in presence of multiple adjacent LoRa cells. Figure 7 shows the performance of LoRa in a single isolated cell and in a grid composed of 4 and 16 adjacent cells – one gateway per cell. In these experiments we set the nodes rate to a fixed $\lambda = 1/90(s^{-1})$ and increase the number of nodes in each cell, up to 2000 nodes per cell. Again, the dashed lines correspond to the results obtained by considering the SFs as perfectly orthogonal, while the solid lines represents the performance

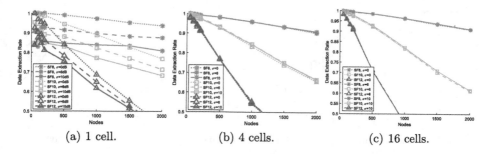

(a) 1 cell.   (b) 4 cells.   (c) 16 cells.

Fig. 8. Performance in presence of log-normal fading for a single isolated cell and with multiple adjacent cells (one gateway per cell).

taking into account inter-SF collisions. Figure 7 shows that such collisions deeply affect the performance of the highest SFs, especially when the number of adjacent cells increases. For example, with 16 cells, SF 12 experiences 30% of DER loss already with 500 nodes, while if we consider the SFs as orthogonal, the DER loss is almost halved.

5.3   Impact of Fading

Up to now, in the simulations we considered only collisions between nodes, ignoring the impact of fading. We thus extended the LoRaSim simulator to include such phenomena, with a log-normal model of increasing $\sigma = 0, 6, 10$ dB. Figure 8 shows the performance of LoRa with the joint effect of inter-SF collisions and fading, again in a single and multi-cell topology with 4 and 16 adjacent cells respectively. Interestingly, while fading has a certain impact on the single cell scenario, with multiple cells fading has virtually no impact on performance. This is due to antenna diversity which gives more chances to receive the same packet on different gateways, compensating the probability of being lost on one link because of fading.

5.4   Network Planning Hints

The above results are particularly important for network operators to correctly plan the parameters of their LoRa networks. In particular, our results suggest that increasing the SF might not always be a good solution to improve performance in presence of congestion or to compensate fading channels. Indeed, despite being more robust to noise, our results show that higher SFs are more vulnerable to inter-SF collisions and that fading becomes negligible in presence of multiple base stations. Instead, it could be more effective to use a low SF in order to lower the chances of packet collisions.

As a rule of thumb, since the length of each chirp doubles every time the SF increases, it could be sufficient to half the number of nodes in the next higher SF, so to balance the doubled time-on-air of the corresponding packets. In Fig. 9

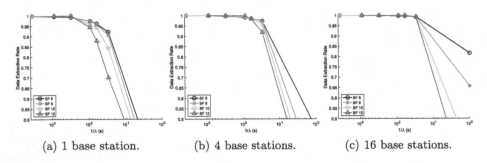

(a) 1 base station.   (b) 4 base stations.   (c) 16 base stations.

Fig. 9. Capacity of a single LoRa cell with one or more gateways, nodes distributed according to spreading factors.

we run the same experiments of the ones in Fig. 6, although distributing the SF proportionally as we just explained. The figure shows that the performance is now similar for all SFs, with slightly reduced capacity for the nodes with lower SFs (SF 6 supports now 2^7 times more nodes than SF 12) but a much higher capacity for the higher SFs.

Finally, it should be noted that in real deployments network planning is more complex because performance is affected by the transmit power of the nodes and on the distance from the gateway (respectively, uniform and random in our experiments).

6   Conclusion

In this paper we have shown that, because of imperfect orthogonality between different spreading factors, a LoRa network cell cannot be studied as a simple super-position of independent networks working on independent channels. Although parallel reception of multiple overlapping frames is generally possible, when the power of the interfering signal significantly overcomes the reference signal, the correct demodulation of the reference signal can be prevented. This can happen in typical near-far conditions, when the interfering signal is much closer to the gateway than the reference signal, or when multiple interfering signals are simultaneously active. Deploying multiple gateways can mitigate the capacity loss due to this phenomena, because each gateway experiences a different SIR value. Moreover, it also mitigates the probability of bad channel conditions for the reference signal due to fading.

Implications of imperfect orthogonality between different spreading factors for network planning are still under investigation. For example, allocating higher spreading factors, characterized by lower receiver sensitivities, to far users could not necessarily improve their link capacity in case of congested networks. Indeed, higher spreading factors could be more prone to collisions due to longer transmission times.

References

1. Worldwide connected devices forecast. www.statista.com
2. Semtech: LoRa Modulation Basics. AN1200.22, Revision 2, May 2015. www.semtech.com
3. Bor, M.C., Roedig, U., Voigt, T., Alonso, J.M.: Do LoRa low-power wide-area networks scale? In: Proceedings of MSWiM 2016, pp. 59–67 (2016)
4. Reynders, B., Pollin, S.: Chirp spread spectrum as a modulation technique for long range communication. In: SCVT 2016, Mons, pp. 1–5 (2016)
5. Reynders, B., Meert, W., Pollin, S.: Range and coexistence analysis of long range unlicensed communication. In: ICT 2016, Thessaloniki, pp. 1–6 (2016)
6. http://www.lancaster.ac.uk/scc/sites/lora/
7. Vangelista, L., Zanella, A., Zorzi, M.: Long-range IoT technologies: the dawn of LoRa™. In: Atanasovski, V., Leon-Garcia, A. (eds.) FABULOUS 2015. LNICSSITE, vol. 159, pp. 51–58. Springer, Cham (2015). doi:10.1007/978-3-319-27072-2_7
8. Augustin, A., Yi, J., Clausen, T., Townsley, W.: A study of LoRa: long range & low power networks for the Internet of Things. Senors 16(9), 1466 (2016)
9. Bankov, D., Khorov, E., Lyakhov, A.: On the limits of LoRaWAN channel access. In: 2016 International Conference on Engineering and Telecommunication (EnT), Moscow, pp. 10–14 (2016)
10. Knight, M., Seeber, B.: Decoding LoRa: realizing a modern LPWAN with SDR. In: Proceedings of the GNU Radio Conference, [S.l.], v. 1, n. 1, September 2016
11. Sornin, N., Luis, M., Eirich, T., Kramp, T., Hersent, O.: Lorawan specification v1.0, Technical report, LoRa Alliance, Technical report (2015)
12. Bernard, O., Seller, A., Sornin, N.: Low power long range transmitter. European Patent Application EP 2763321 A1 by Semtech Corporation (2014)
13. Goursaud, C., Gorce, J.M.: Dedicated networks for IoT: PHY/MAC state of the art and challenges. In: EAI Endorsed Transactions on Internet of Things (2015)
14. Semtech Corporation: LoRa SX1272/73 transceiver datasheet (2015)
15. SimPy event discrete simulation for Python. https://simpy.readthedocs.io

Software Defined Networks

A Network-Assisted Platform
for Multipoint Remote Learning

Alfio Lombardo, Corrado Rametta[✉], and Christian Grasso

DIEEI, University of Catania, Catania, Italy
{alfio.lombardo, corrado.rametta,
christian.grasso}@dieei.unict.it

Abstract. In the last few years, Software Defined Networks (SDN) and Network Functions Virtualization (NFV) have been introduced in the telecommunications world as a new way to design, deploy and manage networking services. Working together, they are able to consolidate and deliver networking components using standard IT virtualization technologies making, in such a way, Telco infrastructures more flexible and adaptive in respect to the needs of both end-users, Telco operators and service providers.

In this context, this paper presents a softwarized architecture for a multipoint remote learning service, allowing network and application functions deployment simplification and management cost reduction. In such a way, the proposed architecture enables even small/medium learning service providers to organize tele-teaching courses without the need of adopting a dedicated and expensive data delivery infrastructure. Unlike an over-the-top approach, in-network platform implementation provides flexibility and allows users, that is, students and teachers, to meet in virtual classrooms wherever they are, automatically arranging and adapting multipoint communications links at run-time according to the time-variant conditions of the underlying network and the overlay user behavior.

Keywords: SDN · NFV · Network orchestration · Multipoint communication · Remote learning

1 Introduction

The new paradigms of Software Defined Networks (SDN) [1, 2] and Network Functions Virtualization (NFV) [3, 4] have recently redefined the vision of the communications networking, providing network managers with a complete and programmatic control of a dynamic view of the network. The power of SDN is based on its characteristic of decoupling control and data planes, moving the network intelligence to a centralized controller. On the other hand, the emerging technology of NFV introduces an important change in the network service provisioning approach, leveraging standard IT virtualization technology to consolidate many network equipment facilities onto standard servers that could be located in data centers, network nodes or even in the end user premises [5, 6]. Therefore, with the NFV paradigm, network functions become software applications that can easily be migrated according to specific policies aimed at

© Springer International Publishing AG 2017
A. Piva et al. (Eds.): TIWDC 2017, CCIS 766, pp. 183–196, 2017.
DOI: 10.1007/978-3-319-67639-5_14

optimizing energy efficiency, costs and performance. The combined application of both SDN and NFV is strongly stimulating the interest of service providers and network operators to make the innovation cycles of networks and services faster and easier, reducing both OPEX (OPerating EXpenditure) and CAPEX (CAPital EXpenditure), thanks to the enormous possibilities of making operation processes (e.g. configuration of network devices) automatic, and network functions and services more flexible and cheaper.

One step ahead has been done by the INPUT project [7] that, starting from the fact that Telco Operators are making big investments to migrate towards a "softwarized" network based on the joint SDN/NFV paradigm, so transforming their network in a large distributed data center, they can extend their gain, initially thought in terms of CAPEX and OPEX, to receive additional economic benefits by also providing application-layer services, like the ones today provided by over-the-top service providers.

One of the most appealing services that can benefit by the application of these technologies is remote learning. The most common deployment of this kind of service is with a number of physical classrooms, remotely dislocated, that are connected to the classroom where the teacher is present through a videoconference system.

Instead, a more dynamic approach that allows both teachers and students to be everywhere in the world, requires a more flexible remote-learning platform that allows self-configuration according to the current number and the Internet access points of its users, the relevant traffic, and the levels of quality of service (QoS) and quality of experience (QoE) required by them.

A first attempt of a virtual class implementation was based on multicast IP [8–10], which is realized inside the underlying network with a routing protocol that allows a source to send IP packets to a "group" so that the IP packets can reach all the members of that group without multiple "unicast routing". Unfortunately, since the number of user groups that are concurrently active in the specific case of remote learning can be large, and each of them is composed by a relatively small number of users, multicast IP control complexity associated with group set-up and maintenance, together with problems of security holes in the systems where multicast is deployed [11], have constituted an obstacle in wide deployments of this approach [12, 13]. A solution aimed at alleviating the work of the underlying network in realizing multipoint content distribution trees to support virtual classroom setup was proposed in [14] with a hybrid unicast/multicast approach based on the deployment of an over-the-top network of gateways implemented by using Click modular routers [15, 16], connected to each other with unicast overlay links, and each behaving as the root of a local multicast tree.

Another technique, aimed at solving setup and management issues of the previous solutions is the dynamic deployment of overlay networks based on multicast peer-to-peer (P2P) [17–19], but it can present instabilities due to peer volatility [20] and free-riding [21].

With all this in mind, the approach considered in this paper, which does not suffer of all the above problems, is based on the possibility that the remote-learning telecommunication infrastructure is provided by the Telco Operator thanks to its distributed data center realized leveraging on the SDN/NFV paradigm. In this way, the platform elements are characterized by fast and simplified deployment with a consequent reduction of management costs [22] and power consumption [23–25] achieved by avoiding use of specific hardware devices. The target is to enable medium/small learning service providers to setup lecture courses without the need of adopting a dedicated and expensive data delivery infrastructure and/or subscribing expensive contracts with Telco Operators.

More in detail, Sect. 2 will give a brief description of the proposed architecture. In Sect. 3, we provide a detailed description of the main elements of the proposed remote learning platform, i.e. the platform orchestrator and the remote-learning delivery tree. Section 4 will propose three typical use cases related to the use of the platform. Finally, in Sect. 5 some conclusions and future works will be illustrated.

2 Architecture Overview

The platform we propose in this paper leverages on the *NFV-on-the-edge* paradigm to realize a P2P multipoint remote-learning service. Its architecture is shown in Fig. 1. It is characterized by five main elements:

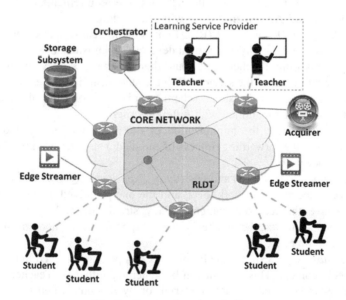

Fig. 1. Remote learning platform

(1) *Learning Service Providers*: with this term we refer to Universities, schools, or even small training organization that do not have the economic capacity - or it is out of their core business scope - to deploy their own learning service delivery network. Their goal is to create virtual classrooms where a *Teacher* meets some *Students* to provide them with a remote learning service constituted by a multipoint audio/video channel and sharing of some stored educational material for off-line additional learning. The platform provides to learning service providers

the possibility of scheduling lecture events, whose list will be made available to the Students.

(2) *Students*: they are the end-users of the system; they connect to the Telco Operator network and require the remote learning service to receive multimedia streaming sent by the Teachers though the platform. As it will be clarified in the next section, Students will be able to perform some actions such as *Select Teacher*, *Select Recorded Lecture*, *Playout or Record Live Lecture*, and *View Recorded Lecture*.

(3) *Teacher*: he is the producer of multimedia streams that the platform has to forward to the Students. The platform should provide to each Teacher the possibility of connecting wherever he is to transmit video to all the Students that are registered to his lectures.

(4) *Orchestrator*: it runs on a dedicated server and communicates with all the platform nodes through the Telco IP network. Its goal is to allocate, migrate and terminate VMs running platform functions (at both the network- and the application-levels), and to control the traffic paths according to the run-time evolution of the network. More specifically, it is in charge of managing and orchestrating the whole platform, the service chains and the traffic paths according to the amount of traffic crossing the network, the requirements of the Telco and the Service Level Agreement (SLA) with the customers.

(5) *Remote-Learning Delivery Tree* (RLDT): it is the logical structure, made up of the network nodes and the physical virtual devices, which is responsible for receiving media streams from Teachers, and route them in the 'best way' to the Students, that are the end-users of the service. With the statement 'in the best way' we mean optimal according to a decisional scheme implemented by the platform Orchestrator, that could be identified with different criteria:

   a. *Consolidation*, i.e. the minimization of the number of nodes and resources involved in the forwarding process of the media streams from the Teachers to their Students;
   b. *Quality of Service* (*QoS*) and *Quality of Experience* (*QoE*), i.e. the end-to-end performance at the network level, and the one perceived by end users willing to receive the required contents. They strictly depend on the number of intermediate nodes, the number of virtual functions each node must process at the same time, etc.

(6) *Storage Subsystem* (SS): it is the framework component involved in the storage of multimedia content. This content can be generated either by Teachers to provide Students with some educational material, or by Students when they require the recording of a lecture. If more than one Student requests recording of the same lecture, only one file is saved on the SS system.

3   Main Platform Elements in Detail

In this section, we present a detailed description of the above-mentioned elements of the platform. Platform Orchestrator, Remote-Learning Delivery Tree (RLDT) and Storage Subsystem (SS) are the main components inside the platform, whereas Students and

Teachers are the final users of the platform, the first receivers of multimedia contents, the latter having the possibility to offer contents without the need of a dedicated and expensive delivery network. Orchestrator, RLDT and SS are virtual or physical elements running inside the Telco Operator network to provide a service to its customers, i.e. any learning service provider willing to provide multimedia educational services without expensive infrastructures.

3.1   Platform Orchestration

The platform Orchestrator is the main element of the whole platform. As shown in Fig. 2, it is logically composed of four sub-blocks, that is, the *front-end* and the *back-end*, the *Content Remote-Learning Delivery Tree Topology* and the *Table of Recordings*.

The *front-end* process is a high-level management application, independent of the SDN-NFV underlying architecture, which manages:

- Authentication, authorization and accounting (AAA) of each client accessing the platform;
- Each request coming from clients (Teachers and Students);
- The data storage process;
- Communications exchange with the back-end services and with the Storage Subsystem.

The main purpose of the *back-end* process is the translation of the high-level rules received by the Orchestration Engine, which are framework-independent, into operative rules dependent on the adopted framework for what concerns the software defined networking, the virtualization of the network and application services.

Both the *Remote-Learning Delivery Tree Topology* and the *Table of Recordings* are data sets allowing the Orchestrator to retrieve information regarding respectively the platform topology, in terms of Acquirer and Edge Streamer nodes, and the entire list of recorded contents, sortable by the ID of Students that requested the content.

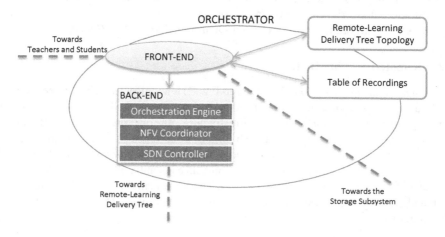

Fig. 2. Block diagram of the platform orchestrator

As regards the main functionalities carried out by the back-end, they could be summarized as follows:

a. *Software Defined Network (SDN) Controller*: it is the core application of the connection infrastructure underlying a softwarized network; it acts as a sort of operating system for the network, sending rules to the nodes about port forwarding, and choosing optimal paths for application data delivery;
b. *Network Function Virtualization (NFV) Coordinator*: it refers to the capability of managing the lifecycle of virtual machines running streaming, forwarding and/or storage functionalities inside the Telco Operator network. It is based on the information coming from both the Orchestration Engine and the SDN Controller. The NFV Coordinator is in charge of creating, migrating and destroying VMs, communicating with the virtual machine hypervisor residing on each TPE/TPC (Telco Provider Edge/Telco Provider Core) node, and sending it the instructions regarding the execution of the VMs, in terms of amount of CPU, network bandwidth and storage to be allocated;
c. *Orchestration Engine*: it is the component that gathers information about the network. This information include network topology, number of connected Teachers (video senders) and Students (video receivers), required contents, availability of network devices implementing NFV, etc. According to the MANO specifications [26], it implements policies and algorithms to decide how to manage the resources of the network devices. The implemented policies can refer to a wide range of aspects: energy consumption, end-to-end delay between source and destination of a data flow, number of hops of the path, overall number of virtual machines active at the same time, quality of service, Service Level Agreement (SLA) with customers, etc.

As far as the SDN Controller is concerned, it exposes a northbound API to the applications, in order to both enable them to request and manipulate services provided by the network, and allow the network to expose its state back to the applications. In this respect, applications could request resource reservation in an integrated manner, according to the requirements (in terms of time, latency and bandwidth) needed to perform certain tasks, or to implement migration between different hosting servers. The Orchestration network-status awareness for applications is necessary to provide a reliable service according to the expected Quality of Experience (QoE).

3.2   Remote-Learning Delivery Tree

The *Remote-Learning Delivery Tree* (refer to Fig. 3) is a logical forwarding tree based on physical and virtual machines instantiated within the physical SDN-NFV nodes of the core/edge Telco Operator network infrastructure. In our proposal of softwarized remote-learning platform, we distinguish among three types of nodes: acquirers, core nodes and edge streamers. Acquirers and edge streamers are *Virtual Network/Application Functions* running on virtual machines dynamically instantiated by the Orchestrator at the edge of the Telco Operator network [27]. These elements respectively represent the root and the leaves of the logical remote-learning delivery trees managed by the Orchestrator.

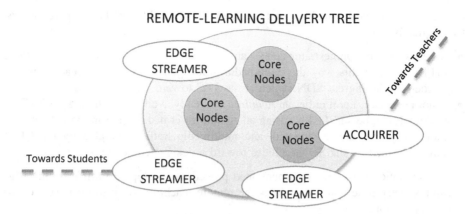

Fig. 3. Block diagram of the remote-learning delivery tree

The root of the logical tree is represented by the *Acquirer node*, i.e. a Layer-7 VM that interfaces with one or more *Teachers* to receive the live streams, the schedule and the description of transmitted events from them. The *Acquirer node* is also the first element of the forwarding chain from the *Teacher* to the *Students*. In fact, it routes data streams according to the management rules received by the *Orchestrator*. The Acquirer can contain a sub-chain of virtual network and application functions to manage the incoming flows, for example to control both their transmission rate [28] and encoding rate [29, 30], or to encrypt them [31, 32].

The core of the RLDT is represented by the *SDN/NFV Nodes* that are created/destroyed (if virtualized) and managed by the *Orchestrator* according to the number of end users (teachers and students) connected to the platform. In such a way, the platform is characterized by an adaptive topology that changes on the base of the number of connected clients and their positions at the edge of the Telco network. Nodes of the core RLDT operate up to the Layer-3, and can be realized by using SDN-compliant hardware or physical/virtual general-purpose machines interfacing in both cases with the *back-end process* of the *Orchestrator* for what concerns the management of their forwarding rules.

Finally, the *Edge Streamers* are devices located at the edge of the Telco Operator network. Their task is to manage the communication between the platform and the *Student Applications*, transmitting the data stream, making – if necessary – the transcoding to adapt the content format to the end-user device capabilities, and other addition tasks related to the data and control planes. Under this perspective and for the sake of clarity we consider *Acquirer* and *Edge Streamers* as *Virtual Service Applications* because they operate over the Layer-3 and up to Layer-7. Meanwhile the core of the RLDT is composed by *Software Defined Network nodes*, i.e. virtual or physical devices operating up to Layer-3 and responsible for forwarding media traffic through the distribution network according to the SDN paradigm.

More in detail, when a Teacher wants to give a lecture, he joins the network by using his application. Once authenticated and authorized by the network, the Orchestrator evaluates the network topology and the current availability of the Acquirer nodes. Consequently:

- if necessary, the Orchestrator creates an *Acquirer* node at the Telco Provider Edge (TPE) node; in this way the multimedia traffic generated by the Teacher is forwarded by the ingress SDN switch at the TPE toward the new Acquirer;
- if not necessary, i.e. if either an *Acquirer* is already available at the ingress TPE, or QoS/QoE can be satisfied by using an Acquirer yet instantiated in the network, no more Acquirers are instantiated, and multimedia traffic generated by the CP is directly routed by the SDN facilities toward a designated acquirer.

Let us notice that the above-mentioned procedure is adopted to manage the edge streamers every time that a user joins the remote teaching platform by means of his client application.

In the light of what has been discussed so far, the RLDT elements interface with the back-end process at the Orchestrator side for two reasons: management of the software-defined platform and management of the virtualized elements.

3.3 Storage Subsystem

The detailed architecture and the description of the Storage Subsystem (SS) are out of scope of this paper, and they will be considered in a future work. For the sake of clarity, here we will refer to the SS as a logical subsystem having the objective of saving educational material provided by the Teacher, and live lecturers when at least one Student requires this action.

3.4 Students and Teachers

Both Students and Teachers are the end users of the remote-learning delivery platform. Students subscribe a service with their Learning Service Providers, and obtain by the Telco Operator a client software (i.e. Mobile App, Web Portal or similar), thanks to which it is possible to receive multimedia content provided by Teachers. Teachers, on the other hand, obtain a client software to give lecturers and publish education material on the Storage Subsystem. Based on the number of users connected and requiring contents, the Telco operator, by using a softwarized approach, sets up and manages the number of nodes and the amount of resources involved in the service.

4 Proof of Concept: Three Typical Use Cases

In this section, we provide a description of three common use cases concerning the use of a remote-learning platform like the one proposed in this paper. The basic functionalities and services that a platform should provide to end users are the playout of a live streaming event related to a Teacher lecture, the recording of a Teacher lecture, and the playout of a previously recorded lecture. These cases will be described in the following.

4.1   Live Lecture Playout

The basic function that a remote-learning delivery platform must provide is the playout of a live lecture. Once a Student connects to the platform by using his own App, he authenticates to the network and then he is able to view the list of all the Learning Service Providers registered to the platform. For each Learning Service Provider, it will be possible to consult the list of running and incoming live lectures. From the GUI of the mobile App or through a web portal, a Student selects a lecture and chooses the *play_content* option. We can follow the message exchange described in Fig. 4 to clarify what happens before and during the live streaming phase:

1. the Student client application communicates the *lecture ID* of the required Teacher to the *front-end process* of the Orchestrator;
2. the *front-end process* consults the remote-learning delivery tree topology with the aim of identifying the edge streamer and the intermediate nodes involved in the delivery procedure; according to the implemented policies (out of scope of this paper) the orchestration engine:
   a. creates/destroys edge streamers and
   b. sets the forwarding rules of the involved nodes.
3. virtual function management actions and forwarding rules are sent to the back-end process that translates them according to the RLDN network architectural choices, i.e. taking into account the virtual machine hypervisor and the SDN approach (for example OpenFlow compliant);
4. the *back-end* process sends management rules to the *Remote-Learning Delivery Tree* and, more in detail, to the physical and virtual devices involved in the streaming procedure from the acquirer to the edge streamer connected to the Student client;

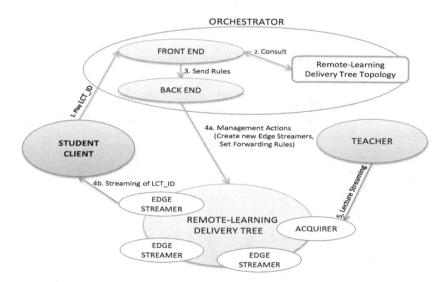

Fig. 4. Play of a live streaming content

5. once the RLDT has been instantiated, the Student will be able to receive the required stream from the selected Teacher.

4.2 Recording of a Live Lecture

A Student, by accessing the Lecture Schedule through his mobile app, is able to select a Lecture event and choose the *record_event* option (see Fig. 5) by sending the related message to the *front-end process*. The latter consults the *recording table* to check if a recording request has been yet received for the same event; if this is the case, the *front-end process* only updates the database inserting the Student among users who have registered the lecture; on the contrary, if this is the first recording request for the selected event:

(a) the *front-end process* sends the recording command to the *back-end process*;
(b) the latter communicates with the *Acquirer* inserting the *Storage Subsystem* among the recipients of the data flow;
(c) the *front-end process* notifies the *Storage Subsystem* about the incoming stream to be recorded (i.e. communicating that it will receive a data stream on a given port corresponding to the related content).

The Teacher, through its client application, sends the data flow to the Acquirer that, on one side forwards it through the RLDT towards all the Students willing to watch the live lecture, and on the other side sends the data stream to the Storage Subsystem to realize the recording procedure.

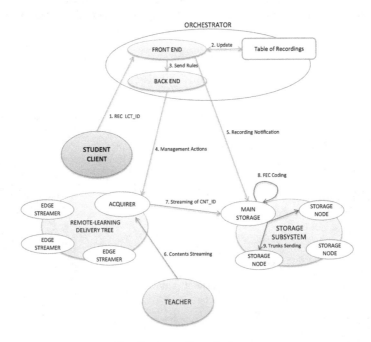

Fig. 5. Recording of a lecture

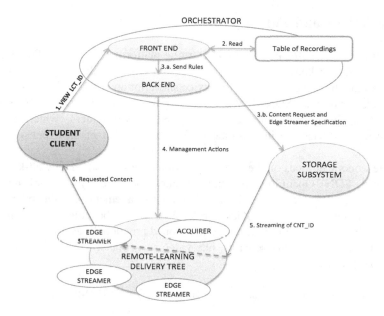

Fig. 6. Playout of a recorded lecture

4.3   Playout of a Recorded Lecture

Each Student is able to playout the recorded lectures by using his mobile App. More in detail, as shown in Fig. 6, the Student client application is connected to the *front-end process* running at the *Orchestration node* where all the information about the saved lectures are registered in a local database. Among the available contents, the Student selects the ID he is interested to, and chooses the *view_recorded_lecture* option. Then:

1. the Student *Client App* connects to the *Front-end process;*
2. the *front-end process* accesses the Student's *Table of Recordings;*
3. the *front-end process* discovers the *Edge Streamer node* the client is connected to, and the storage node closer to this edge streamer node, then it sends:
   a. the management rules to the *back-end process*, i.e. it updates – if necessary – the forwarding rules and creates an Edge Streamer;
   b. the lecture request message to the SS, indicating the destination edge streamer and the source storage node in case there are multiple copies of the same content;
4. the *back-end process* translates the management rules according to the adopted SDN-NFV framework;
5. the SS begins the transmission to the designated *Edge Streamer* that forwards the data stream to the destination node.

5 Conclusions and Future Works

This paper presents a softwarized remote-learning platform designed to allow Learning Service Providers to benefit of a cheap, smart and easily deployable delivery infrastructure, without the need of expensive service subscription with a Telco Operator. The basic idea is to apply an SDN-NFV approach to allow a Telco Operator to provide a smart and flexible architecture to Learning Service Providers, which can offer remote-learning services to its customers without the need of an expensive ad-hoc infrastructure.

Future works will focus on the deployment of a prototype based on well-known and consolidated SDN OpenFlow-compliant framework, such as OpenDaylight or OpenContrail for what concerns the networking management. On the other side, a virtualization framework (OpenStack, or VmWare) will be chosen to manage the virtual machines implementing the above-mentioned functionalities. The same platform will be extended to different use cases, like video surveillance [33–35] and interactive video games [36, 37].

Acknowledgements. This work was partially supported by the EU INPUT project.

References

1. White paper on Software-Defined Networking: The New Norm for Networks. https://www.opennetworking.org/
2. Kreutz, D., Ramos, F.M.V., Verissimo, P.E., Rothenberg, C.E., Azodolmolky, S., Uhlig, S.: Software-defined networking: a comprehensive survey. Proc. IEEE **103**(1), 14–76 (2015)
3. White paper on Network Functions Virtualisation. http://portal.etsi.org/NFV/NFV_White_Paper.pdf
4. Network Functions Virtualisation – White Paper #3, Network Operator Perspectives on Industry Progress. https://portal.etsi.org/Portals/0/TBpages/NFV/Docs/NFV_White_Paper3.pdf
5. Faraci, G., Schembra, G.: An analytical model to design and manage a green SDN/NFV CPE node. IEEE Trans. Netw. Serv. Manage. **12**(3), 435–450 (2015)
6. Lombardo, A., Manzalini, A., Schembra, G., Faraci, G., Rametta, C., Riccobene, V.: An open framework to enable NetFATE (Network Functions at the edge). In: Proceedings of 1st IEEE Conference on Network Softwarization (NetSoft), 13–17 April 2015 (2015)
7. H2020 INPUT Project. http://www.input-project.eu/
8. Huang, X.B., Wei, J.P., Lu, W.Y., Fan, Y.M., Tan, Z.Q.: A peer-to-peer hybrid multicast infrastructure for remote learning. In: 2008 ISECS, Guangzhou, pp. 270–275 (2005)
9. Wang, K., Agarwal, A.: Multicast traffic merging in DiffServ-supported MPLS networks. In: CCECE 2003, vol. 2, pp. 905–910 (2003)
10. Subekti, L.B., et al.: Design of virtual ClassBox system for supporting distance learning. In: 2012 7th International Conference on Telecommunication Systems, Services, and Applications (TSSA), Bali (2012)
11. Diot, C., Levine, B.N., Lyles, B., Kassem, H., Balensiefen, D.: Deployment issues for the IP multicast service and architecture. IEEE Netw. **14**(1), 78–88 (2000)
12. Perlman, R., et al.: Simple multicast: a design for simple, low-overhead multicast. IETF draft, draft-perlman-simple-multicast-03.txt, October 1999

13. Holbrook, H., Cain, B.: Source specific multicast. IETF draft, draftholbrook-ssm-00.txt, March 2000
14. Maraviglia, G., et al.: Synchronous multipoint e-learning realized on an intelligent software-router platform over unicast networks: design and performance issues. In: Proceedings of ETFA 2007, Patras, Greece, 25–28 September 2007 (2007)
15. Morris, R., Kohler, E., Jannotti, J., Kaashoek, M.F.: The click modular router. In: Proceedings of the 17th ACM Symposium on Operating Systems Principles (SOSP 1999), pp. 217–231, Kiawah Island, South Carolina, December 1999
16. Calarco, G., Raffaelli, C., Schembra, G., Tusa, G.: Comparative analysis of SMP click scheduling techniques. In: Proceedings of QoSIP 2005, Catania (Italy), 2–4 February 2005, pp. 379–389 (2005)
17. Padmanabhan, V.N., Wang, H.J., Chou, P.A.: Resilient peer-to-peer streaming. In: 11th IEEE International Conference on Network Protocols, Proceedings, pp. 16–27 (2003)
18. Tran, D.A., Hua, K.A., Do, T.T.: A peer-to-peer architecture for media streaming. IEEE J. Sel. Areas Commun. 22(1), 121–133 (2004)
19. Busà, A.G., Lombardo, A., Barbera, M., Schembra, G.: CLAPS: a cross-layer analysis platform for P2P video streaming. In: Proceedings of IEEE ICC 2007, GLASGOW, Scotland (UK), 24–28 June 2007 (2007)
20. Almeida, E.C.D., Sunyé, G., Traon, Y.L., Valduriez, P.: A framework for testing peer-to-peer systems. In: 2008 19th International Symposium on Software Reliability Engineering (ISSRE), Seattle, WA (2008)
21. Barbera, M., Lombardo, A., Schembra, G., Tribastone, M.: A markov model of a freerider in a bittorrent P2P network. In: Proceedings of IEEE Globecom 2005, St. Louis, MO, USA, 28 November – 2 December 2005, pp. 985–989 (2005)
22. Li, Y., Chen, M.: Software-defined network function virtualization: a survey. IEEE Access 3, 2542–2553 (2015)
23. Jamieson, P., Luk, W., Wilton, S.J.E., Constantinides, G.A.: An energy and power consumption analysis of FPGA routing architectures. In: 2009 International Conference on Field-Programmable Technology, Sydney, NSW, pp. 324–327 (2009)
24. Lombardo, A., et al.: Measuring and modeling energy consumption to design a green NetFPGA giga-router. In: Proceedings of IEEE Globecom 2012, Anaheim, California, USA, 3–7 December 2012 (2012)
25. Bolla, R., Bruschi, R., Ranieri, A.: Performance and power consumption modeling for green COTS software router. In: 2009 First International Communication Systems and Networks and Workshops, Bangalore (2009)
26. ETSI NFV GS, Network Function Virtualization (NFV) Management and Orchestration, NFV-MAN 001 v0.8.1, November 2014
27. Faraci, G., et al.: A processor-sharing scheduling strategy for NFV nodes. J. Electr. Comput. Eng. Special Issue Des. High Throughput Cost Efficient Data Center Netw., Article ID 3583962 (2016)
28. Lombardo, A., Barbera, M., Panarello, C., Schembra, G.: Active window management: an efficient gateway mechanism for TCP traffic control. In: Proceedings of IEEE ICC 2007, GLASGOW, Scotland (UK), 24–28 June 2007 (2007)
29. Galluccio, L., et al.: An analytical framework for the design of intelligent algorithms for adaptive-rate MPEG video encoding in next generation time-varying wireless networks. IEEE J. Sel. Areas Commun. 23(2), 369–384 (2005)
30. Lombardo, A., Schembra, G.: Performance evaluation of an adaptive-rate MPEG encoder matching IntServ traffic constraints. IEEE Trans. Netw. 11(1), 47–65 (2003)

31. Dumbere, D.M., Janwe, N.J.: Video encryption using AES algorithm. In: Second International Conference on Current Trends in Engineering and Technology (ICCTET 2014), Coimbatore (2014)
32. Li, M., Yang, C., Tian, J.: Video selective encryption based on hadoop platform. In: 2015 IEEE International Conference on Computational Intelligence & Communication Technology, Ghaziabad, pp. 208–212 (2015)
33. Lombardo, A., et al.: Multipath routing and rate-controlled video encoding in wireless video surveillance networks. Multimed. Syst. **14**(3), 155–165 (2008)
34. Fu, X., Guo, B.I.: Framework for distributed video surveillance in heterogeneous environment. In: 2008 International Conference on Intelligent Information Hiding and Multimedia Signal Processing, Harbin, pp. 826–829 (2008)
35. Detmold, H., van den Hengel, A., Dick, A., Falkner, K., Munro, D.S., Morrison, R.: Middleware for distributed video surveillance. IEEE Distrib. Syst. Online **9**(2), 1 (2008)
36. Jin, H., Yao, H., Liao, X., Yang, S., Liu, W., Jia, Y.: PKTown: a peer-to-peer middleware to support multiplayer online games. In: MUE 2007, Seoul, pp. 54–59 (2007)
37. Amiri, M., Al Osman, H., Shirmohammadi, S., Abdallah, M.: SDN-based game-aware network management for cloud gaming. In: 2015 International Workshop on Network and Systems Support for Games (NetGames), Zagreb, pp. 1–6 (2015)

A De-verticalizing Middleware for IoT Systems Based on Information Centric Networking Design

Giuseppe Piro[1,3]([✉]), Giuseppe Ribezzo[1,3], Luigi Alfredo Grieco[1,3],
and Nicola Blefari-Melazzi[2,3]

[1] Department of Electrical and Information Engineering (DEI),
Politecnico di Bari, Bari, Italy
{giuseppe.piro,giuseppe.ribezzo,alfredo.grieco}@poliba.it
[2] Department of Electronic Engineering,
University of Rome "Tor Vergata", Rome, Italy
blefari@uniroma2.it
[3] CNIT, Consorzio Nazionale Interuniversitario per le Telecomunicazioni,
Parma, Italy

Abstract. The Internet of Things is rapidly diffusing and many stand-alone platforms have been deployed in different domains. Since these solutions are still isolated, the definition of a globally unified platform embracing different and heterogeneous Internet of Things systems is gaining momentum. In the Internet Research Task Force context, the Information-Centric Networking Research Group envisages the possibility to reach this challenging goal by properly leveraging the communication primitives of the Information-Centric Networking paradigm. In line with this vision, this contribution proposes a concrete solution that offers: name-based communication scheme, flexible data delivery, support for heterogeneous network infrastructures, platform interoperability, and technology-independent implementation of high-level applications. Moreover, a proof-of-concept implementation is presented for further describing the main functionalities of the designed approach and demonstrating its correct execution in a real environment.

Keywords: ICN-IoT · Internames · Middleware · Experimental testbed

1 Introduction

Today, the Internet of Things (IoT) still appears as a *fragmented ecosystem* composed of many vertical solutions, where objects are generally connected to a local environment, use heterogeneous communication technologies, and leverage proprietary software components and data representation formats. This aspect strongly hinders large-scale Machine-to-Machine (M2M) deployments [1]. However, to face such a technological barrier, research community and standardization bodies are formulating novel de-verticalized platforms able to unify heterogeneous vertical silos [2]. But, grounded on a host-driven Internet model,

© Springer International Publishing AG 2017
A. Piva et al. (Eds.): TIWDC 2017, CCIS 766, pp. 197–211, 2017.
DOI: 10.1007/978-3-319-67639-5_15

they may leverage significant limitations in terms of interoperability, mobility, multicast communications, and security.

M2M applications are inherently information-centric: a user is usually interested into a content generated within a specific environment, without needing to know the exact reference to the set of smart objects able to provide the asked information. In this perspective, the Information-Centric Networking paradigm [3], formulated to answer to Future Internet requirements, can natively enable large-scale M2M services as a communication bus, while overcoming the drawbacks of the conventional host-driven Internet model by means of a fast, reliable, effective, scalable, and secure contents dissemination, while increasing the resilience of information and communication technology services with respect to user mobility and system failures [4,5]. The adoption of ICN within a single (and isolated) IoT domain was already investigated in several works (see for instance [4–12]. Preliminary solutions targeting the realization of a unified IoT ecosystem interconnecting vertical solutions across multiple and heterogeneous organizations and domains were discussed in [13–15]. Furthermore, such an idea was recently supported by standardization activities. In fact, the Information-Centric Networking Research Group (ICNRG), chartered in the Internet Research Task Force (IRTF) context, started working on a unified *ICN-IoT middleware*, by specifying its requirements and functionalities [16,17]. But, at the time of this writing and for the best of authors knowledge, concrete definition of its functionalities and real implementations are not yet available.

To bridge this gap, a de-verticalizing middleware for IoT systems based on the ICN communication paradigm is presented herein. More specifically, this work presents a three-folded contribution:

- First, baseline guidelines and functionalities already presented in [16,17] are carefully taken into account for designing a complete ICN-based middleware, which supports platform interoperability, technology-independent implementation of high-level applications, and flexible data delivery. With the conceived middleware, high-level applications may retrieve resources exposed by heterogeneous IoT platforms through a standardized set of APIs. Moreover, both request-response and publish-subscribe communication models are supported. Therefore, data consumers are only in charge to declare the list of names associated to the contents of their interest. Then, the middleware translates such high-level requests into specific networking operations and concrete protocol messages, which depend on the underlying communication technology.
- Second, to better enable name-based communication scheme also in heterogeneous network infrastructures, the interaction among entities of the middleware distributed across communicating peers are interconnected through a ICN communication bus, which evolves from Internames [18]. Internames was recently devised as a new ICN implementation that substitutes the baseline ICN host-to-name principle with a name-to-name principle, thus allowing name-based data dissemination also in heterogeneous network architectures. In its preliminary formulation, Internames only supported request-response communication schemes. In this contribution, instead, Internames is further

improved with additional features enabling the publish-subscribe communication scheme, while effectively exposing a flexible interface with the ICN-based middleware.

- Third, to showcase the viability of conceived architecture, a preliminary proof-of-concept implementation is developed. Without loss of generality, it considers a heterogeneous network architecture made up by two different realms (e.g., ICN and IP), connected to each other through a border router. An IoT domain based on the oneM2M [19] exposes its resources through a gateway, attached to the IP realm. Moreover, a data consumer interested to data generated in the IoT domain is attached to the ICN realm. Thus, the testbed aims at demonstrating that a data consumer is able to retrieve contents of its interest by using communication primitives made available by the developed middleware, without taking care of the underlaying communication technology, the protocol architecture deployed in the IoT domain, and the heterogeneous nature of the network. By generalizing, a consumer may use the developed middleware for reaching heterogeneous resources exposed by vertical IoT domains, thus overcoming the technological barrier that characterize current solutions.

The rest of this paper is organized as follows: the state of the art is discussed in Sect. 2. The designed solution and preliminary proof-of-concept implementation are presented in Sects. 3 and 4, respectively. Finally Sect. 5 draws the conclusions and provides some hints on future activities.

2   State of the Art

2.1   Internet-Based Middleware Architectures for the IoT

A Machine-to-Machine (M2M) service involves a message exchange between at least two communicating peers: data producer (i.e., who exposes a resource) and data consumer (i.e., who is interested in that resource). In the case these entities use different communication technologies, their interaction could be adversely affected by many concerns at the system or hardware levels. Middlewares generally provide a solid answer to fragmentation issues affecting current IoT platforms [2]. Available solutions include event-based middlewares (like those developed in GREEN, RUNES, and PRISMA projects) and service-oriented middlewares (like SenseWrap, CHOReOS, and oneM2M). Unfortunately, these solutions are strongly grounded on a host-driven Internet model. Thus, they exhibit many issues in terms of scalable content distribution, mobility, security and trust, resilience of ICT services to system failures, and content availability, while experiencing a limited interoperability and a not scalable deployment at large scale. Indeed, a change of perspective is highly required for reinventing M2M communication techniques on top of new networking principles.

2.2 Information-Centric Networking and Internames

Recently, the Information-Centric Networking (ICN) emerged as a new communication paradigm leveraging flexible and efficient mechanisms for content disseminations [3]. Differently from the conventional host-centric communication model (i.e., the one at the basis of the current Internet architecture), ICN focuses on the content rather than on who is providing the content, and targets receiver-driven communications, based on content names, name-based routing, and self-certifying packets. Specifically, a data consumer expresses an interest for a content. Then, the ICN architecture takes care of routing-by-name the content request towards the best source (that could be the data producer, a replica server, or an in-network cache) and sends back to the user the related data. The ICN concept is at the basis of many concrete network architectures, which include data-oriented network architecture (DONA), Network of Information (NetInf), publish/subscribe Internet technology (PURSUIT), scalable and adaptive Internet solutions (SAIL), CONVERGENCE, Named-Data Networking (NDN), MobilityFirst, COntent Mediator architecture for content-aware nETworks (COMET) and GreenICN [3]. Even if they differently address some key aspects (including naming schema and security, routing strategies, cache management), most of these architectures offer the following advantages: efficient content-routing, in-network caching, simplified handling of mobile and multicast communication, simplified support for time/space-decoupled communications, simplified support for peer-to-peer communications, content-oriented security model, content-oriented access control, content-oriented quality of service differentiation, creation and dissemination of contents in a modular and personalized way [3].

ICN architectures are generally deployed as overlay networks (i.e., built on top of the current Internet architecture) or ad-hoc systems (i.e., isolated network realms that can be connected to the current Internet by means of a gateway node). Therefore, the Future Internet is expected to be heterogeneous: various network realms, based on different communication protocols, can be interconnected each other.

The possibility to handle name-based communications also in such kind of heterogeneous scenarios is given by Internames [18]. It is a novel network architecture that evolves from the baseline ICN host-to-name principle to a name-to-name principle, in which names can identify not only contents, but also source/destination entities and services [18]. In its preliminary definition, Internames only offers request-response communication scheme and integrates three main logical nodes: Object Resolution Service (ORS) and Name Resolution Service (NRS), and Named Router (NR). ORS offers search engine functionalities and maps a list of meta-data to a set of names formatted according to the structure envisaged for the conceived solution[1]. NRS handles routing operations

---

[1] Note that these functionalities are very similar to those already provided by Google (or any other search engine) in today's Internet. Therefore, no further implementation details will be investigated in this paper.

within the heterogeneous network infrastructure. By knowing the physical location of IoT resources, it finds the best routing path through which forwarding the requests generated by data consumers. NRS is contacted by the data consumer or by other routers along the path every time a request should be sent towards a new network realm. This routing functionality receives in input the name of the content to be retrieved and returns in output the next hop of the path and the related network protocol to use. Finally, NR provides an interface among heterogeneous realms, thus implementing protocol mapping functionalities (simply namely *tunnel* service).

2.3 ICN for the IoT

The adoption of ICN within a single (and isolated) IoT domain was already investigated in several works, like [4–12]. Unfortunately, all of these contributions do not address the aim of realizing a unified IoT ecosystem interconnecting vertical solutions across multiple and heterogeneous organizations and domains.

Nevertheless, it is very important to remark, instead, that name-based communications can more easily enable large-scale M2M services. Preliminary contributions in this direction are discussed in the literature. First of all, the performance gain (expressed in terms of latencies, bandwidth consumptions, and communication scalability) offered by ICN in a smart grid environment is investigated in [13]. The work [14] focuses on oneM2M and proposes to adopt ICN principles for increasing scalability, robustness, and flexibility by means of distributed service discovery, point-to-point subscription and data exchange, and monitoring of the Quality of Service with dynamic and name-based routing paths. The adoption of ICN primitives in oneM2M is also explored in [4]. In this case, a scenario where a number of resources are made available by constrained devices and exposed through a gateway node is taken into account. Then, ICN communication primitives are implemented for easing the data retrieving process within the constrained IoT domain and the gateway implements the mapping between oneM2M resources to ICN names and the translation of oneM2M messages to ICN packets. Finally, the work in [15] presented a high-level design of an ICN-based middleware architecture enabling advanced IoT applications in the mobile cloud computing context, while ensuring good performance gains in terms of bandwidth and energy requirements.

2.4 ICN-IoT: A Promising Solution Emerging from IETF
Standardization Activities

To further support research contributions described in the previous Section, the IRTF ICNRG working group is targeting the designing of an unified IoT platform based on ICN principles, namely ICN-IoT [16,17]. Specifically, ICN-IoT identifies contents and devices through unique names, that do not contain any explicit reference to the data producer. System interoperability can be reached by defining a unified name space. When a data consumer would like to retrieve a given content, it issues a request to the ICN-IoT middleware, specifying only the corresponding name. Then, the middleware will implement all the required networking functionalities (name resolution, discovery, delivering, etc.) to retrieve the requested content. By leveraging in-network storage/caching and multicast functionalities, natively offered by ICN, ICN-IoT may speed up data delivery, reduce the overall traffic volume, and save the amount of requests processed by (constrained) IoT devices. Data exchange is based on the receiver-oriented communication scheme. Accordingly the middleware can realize a seamless support for the mobility, delay tolerant communications, and reliable content delivery over unreliable links.

Note that at the time of this writing, the ICN-IoT vision has not been translated yet to practical implementations. To bridge this gap and by leveraging on design principles already investigated in the IRTF ICNRG working group, our contribution intends to provide a significant step forward by formulating the key functionalities of a middleware architecture for an unified IoT ecosystem and developing a proof-of-concept implementation working in real experiments.

3   The Proposed Architecture

The reference scenario addressed in this work is depicted in Fig. 1. It integrates: vertical IoT domains implementing standalone solutions and exposing their resources through gateway devices; data consumers willing to retrieve contents from different IoT domains; a heterogeneous network architecture; border routers connecting network realms; and many logical nodes distributed in each network realms for offering search engines, message routing, and rendezvous functionalities. In addition, the conceived IoT platform leverages a distributed middleware layer and adopts an extended version of the Internames communication bus. In particular, the middleware and Internames are jointly used to enable the following main features: (i) name-based communication scheme, (ii) flexible data delivery, (iii) support for a heterogeneous network infrastructure, (iv) platform interoperability, and (v) technology-independent implementation of high-level communication tasks.

3.1   Name-Based Communication Scheme

According to [18], names can identify not only contents, but also source/destination entities and services. To support data exchange and service provisioning in the reference heterogeneous network, a realm-based name structure is adopted:

$$n2n://[\text{realm ID}]/\textbf{ICN} - \textbf{IoT}/[\text{service}]/<>*,$$

where [realm ID] is the network realm where the content is available, ICN-IoT represents the key word identifying the developed platform, [service] is the type of service associated with the content (including networking functionalities and M2M applications), $<> *$ is the rest of the name that stores all the other details associated to a given data. The namespace is application-oriented: an example

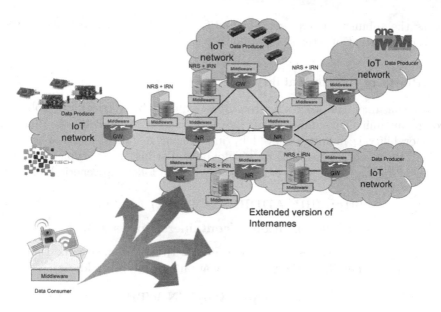

Fig. 1. Big picture of the designed platform, deployed on a reference scenario.

is provided in Sect. 3.3, which simplifies the comprehension of the discussed concepts.

3.2 Flexible Data Delivery and Support for a Heterogeneous Network Infrastructure

To guarantee a flexible data delivery, the middleware exposes a set of APIs supporting both *request-response* and *publish-subscribe* communication models. With the request-response scheme, data are retrieved synchronously: every time the data consumer would fetch that content, it has to send a request towards the data producer, which will immediately provide the corresponding answer. The publish-subscribe communication model, instead, exploits an asynchronous data delivery process. In this case, in fact, the data consumer issues a subscription request for a given content of interest. Then, every time a new content is generated, the data producer is in charge of delivering that data to all subscribed data consumers.

The data exchange is orchestrated trough logical nodes, distributed among realms (i.e., each realm has a reference instance of the logical node; all the logical nodes share information about content names, the realm where IoT systems are attached to, subscription requests, and so on). They are: Object Resolution Service (ORS), Name Resolution Service (NRS), and Internames Rendezvous Node (IRN). Note that ORS and NRS maintain the same functionalities as in Internames [18]. In addition, IRN is introduced in this work to manage publish-subscribe functionalities, track the set of contents available in M2M platform, process the submission requests, and notify subscribed data consumers every time a new content of interest is available.

3.3 Platform Interoperability

A data consumer can access to resources exposed by vertical IoT solutions through an unified communication interface (i.e., the middleware). Platform interoperability is mainly achieved by introducing a unified name space that maps all the resources available in IoT domains. For instance, a typical resource in a oneM2M implementation is identified with the following generic URI:

http://[IP ADDRESS]:[PORT] /om2m/

[gscl]/[applications]/[containers]/[instance].

In our platform, the resource is identified with a simplified name that does not contain any details on the physical location (e.g., the IP address):

n2n://[realm ID]/ICN-IoT/

[gscl]/[applications]/[containers]/[instance].

Therefore, all the nodes in the unified IoT platform (that are data consumers, routers, ORS, IRN, NRS, and gateway devices) always identify the resource by using the latter name, i.e., the one expressed in the generic form *n2n://[realm ID]/ICN-IoT/[service]/<> *. Then, the gateway device is in charge of implementing a kind of translation between the requests coming from the unified IoT platform and the set of messages available in the vertical IoT solution it exposes.

3.4 Technology-Independent Implementation of High-Level Communication Tasks

The designed middleware is depicted in Fig. 2. It integrates three main modules: the *API manager* that offers the set of APIs to the application, the *networking manager* that implements atomic networking operations, and the *technology manager* that hosts technology-dependent instances able to process messages coming from the network realm (IP or ICN). In summary, the high level application interacts with the API manager and it may use APIs for initiating some operations belonging to request-response or publish-subscribe communication schemes. Each API triggers the execution of one or more atomic networking operations, handled by the networking manager. The commands generated by the networking manager are finally managed by the technology manager that translate them to concrete messages encoded according to the protocol adopted by the underlying communication technology. Finally, messages processed by

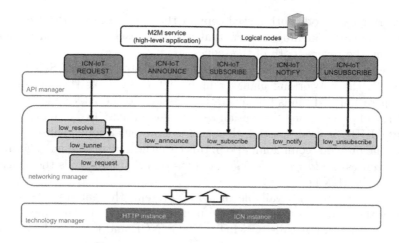

Fig. 2. A sketch of the implemented middleware.

the technology manager are delivered to the application or to the networking manager, as detailed below.

APIs fully hide the details of the underlaying communication technology and allow developers to implement their applications without knowing the exact set of operations executed by both network and technology managers. They are: **ICN-IoT REQUEST, ICN-IoT ANNOUNCE, ICN-IoT NOTIFY, ICN-IoT SUBSCRIBE**, and **ICN-IoT UNSUBSCRIBE**. The first one is used to retrieve a content through the request-response communication scheme. The others, instead, support publish-subscribe procedures. All of them, however, take as a parameter the name of the content to request, announce, notify, or for which making or cancelling a subscription.

A given content can be directly retrieved by using ICN-IoT REQUEST. The networking manager processes the high-level command as follows. If the node is directly connected to the realm specified in the name and the realm is based on the ICN protocol, the networking manager executes the *low_request* atomic networking operation and immediately sends the request by using ICN primitives; If the node is directly connected to the realm specified in the name and the realm is based on the IP protocol, the networking manager contacts the NRS node for getting the IP address of the gateway that exposes that resource (this task is performed by *low_resolve*); then it executes the *low_request* atomic networking operation for sending the request by using IP primitives; If the node is not connected to the realm specified in the name, it is necessary to establish a multi-hop routing path across heterogeneous domains; to this end, the networking manager contacts the NRS node for getting routing information (this task is performed by *low_resolve*); then, *low_tunnel* is executed for delivering the request towards the next hop (a border router) identified by the NRS; the process is iterated until reaching the realm that hosts the data consumer. At the end, a node that is in posses of the considered data (i.e., the data producer or an intermediary node with a seed copy of the data) receives the request and generates the corresponding answer, that will feed back to the data consumer, by following the reverse path of the request.

A data consumer can make a subscription by using ICN-IoT SUBSCRIBE. Accordingly, the networking manager immediately executes the *low_subscribe* atomic operation and sends the generated message to the IRN node. Then, the IRN node will process the subscription request and update its database. ICN-IoT UNSUBSCRIBE is used, instead, to cancel the aforementioned subscription. In line with the previous command, also in this case the networking manager immediately executes the *low_unsubscribe* atomic operation and sends the generated message to the IRN node.

When a new data is available in a IoT system, the gateway device communicates this event to the rest of the platform, by issuing an announcement message. To this end, it calls ICN-IoT ANNOUNCE and triggers the execution of the *low_announce* atomic operation. The message is sent to the IRN node, that consequently starts the notification process, by calling ICN-IoT NOTIFY (first) and executing *low_notify* (then). Finally, as soon as a data consumer receives a notification, it will use the request-response scheme detailed before to fetch the content for which it made a subscription.

4   Preliminary Proof-of-Concept Implementation

A preliminary proof-of-concept is implemented in java. The resulting testbed also integrates data captured by real sensors and it is available at

$$\text{http://telematics.poliba.it/icn-iot}$$

for a live demonstration. From one side, it clarifies networking operations handled during the communication processes orchestrated by the designed middleware. From another side, it aims at demonstrating that the data consumer application is able to retrieve values collected by the sensing resource available within a remote IoT domain by only using the communication functionalities made available by the developed middleware, while completely ignoring all the details about the underlaying technologies, the heterogeneous nature of the network, and the specific protocol architecture implemented in the IoT domain.

The developed network architecture is composed by two network realms (see Fig. 3): *net_IP* based on the IP protocol and *net_NDN* based on the Named Data Networking (NDN) protocol. Note that NDN represents a concrete implementation of ICN, where the communication is receiver-driven: contents are sent only in response to the respective requests, in a one-to-one relation; only two types of messages are admitted, that are *INTEREST* and *DATA*; an user may ask for a content by issuing an *INTEREST* message, routed towards the nodes in posses of the required information; then, these nodes are triggered to reply with a corresponding *DATA* message [20]. The two realms are connected through a border router, that also hosts NRS and IRN nodes. The router is identified with the name *Router_ID* and implements protocol mapping functionalities, i.e., the *tunnel* service, as illustrated in [18]. An IoT system, based on oM2M (e.g., the well-known implementation of the oneM2M specification [21]), exposes resources through a gateway device directly connected to the NDN realm. The IoT domain is deployed with OpenMote platforms[2] and each constrained device hosts four types of sensors measuring temperature, relative humidity, ambient light, and acceleration. The data consumer is attached to the IP realm.

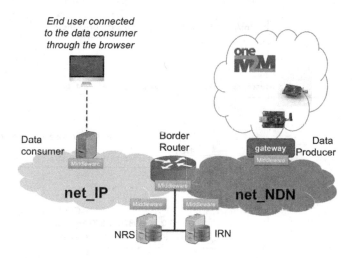

Fig. 3. Big picture of the developed testbed.

4.1   Testbed at Work

The set of operations executed during the testbed configuration and data retrieving process are summarized in Fig. 4. They include:

1. The border router initiates the $/ICN - IoT/tunnel/$ service. It is attached to both IP and NDN realms. The technology manager of the designed middleware hosts a HTTP server (IP address set to 10.0.0.1, port 8080) for the IP realm and a NDN instance for the NDN realm. The NDN instance registers the prefix $/ICN - IoT/tunnel/Router\_ID/$ in the NDN realm, thus being able to receive any request belonging to the *tunnel* service (i.e., inter-realm routing).

2. NRS initiates the $/ICN - IoT/resolve/$ service. It is attached to both IP and NDN realms. The technology manager of the designed middleware hosts a HTTP server (IP address set to 10.0.0.1, port 5353) for the IP realm and a NDN instance for the NDN realm. The NDN instance registers the prefix $/ICN - IoT/resolve/$ in the NDN realm, thus being able to receive any request belonging to the *resolve* service.

3. IRN initiates both $/ICN - IoT/subscribe$ and $/ICN - IoT/announce/$ services. It is attached to both IP and NDN realms. The technology manager of the designed middleware hosts a HTTP server (IP address set to 10.0.0.1, port

---

[2] http://www.openmote.com.

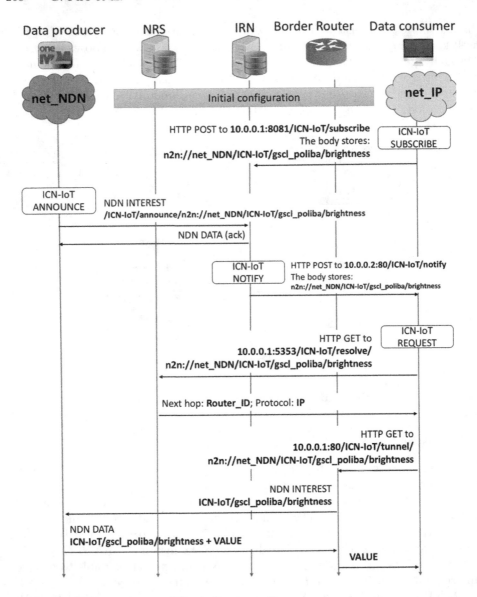

Fig. 4. Sequence diagram.

8081) for the IP realm and a NDN instance of the NDN realm. The NDN instance registers the prefixes $/ICN - IoT/subscribe/$ and $/ICN - IoT/announce/$ in the NDN realm, thus being able to receive any request belonging to the *subscribe* and *announce* services.

4. The data consumer calls ICN-IoT SUBSCRIBE to issue a subscription request for the considered content. The middleware executes the *low_subscribe* atomic operation and sends a HTTP POST message to the IRN, whose body stores the name of the content of its interest.

5. The ambient light sensor is stimulated for capturing a variation of the brightness. The gateway devices recognizes the resource update according to the oM2M architecture and calls ICN-IoT ANNOUNCE to communicate the event to the rest of the platform. Therefore, the networking manager executes the *low_announce* and sends a NDN INTEREST to the reference IRN node. After having updated the database, the IRN node answers with a NDN DATA packet of confirmation.

6. IRN calls ICN-IoT NOTIFY and notifies the data consumer by sending a HTTP POST message, whose body stores the name of the updated content.

7. The data consumer requests the data through ICN-IoT REQUEST. First, the middleware executes the *low_resolve* atomic operation for contacting the NRS node and getting routing information. NRS answers with the next hop (i.e., the border router) and the communication protocol to use (i.e., IP).

8. The middleware instance of the data consumer executes the *low_tunnel* atomic operation and sends a HTTP GET packet to the border router, asking for the content of interest.

9. The router processes the message and realizes that the requested data is available in the NDN realm to which it is directly connected. Therefore, it forwards the request to the data consumer by using a NDN INTEREST packet (the message is generated by the *low_request* atomic operation).

10. The network gateway generates the corresponding request, that will be forwarded back to the data consumer.

To conclude, Fig. 5 shows how the end user is able to collect data generated in the IoT platform. The goal of the experimental testbed is indeed reached.

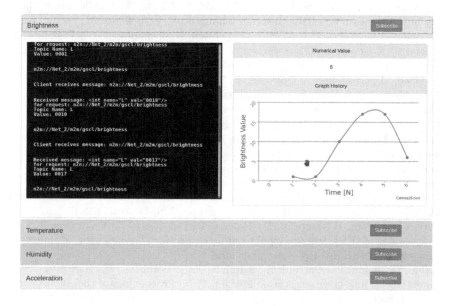

Fig. 5. Screenshot of the data consumer application.

5   Conclusions and Future Works

This paper presents a unified IoT platform based on Information-Centric communication primitives and explains its main functionalities through the analysis of a proof-of-concept implementation. In line with recent design criteria emerged in the context of the IETF ICNRG working group, the designed (and developed) platform enables interoperability among vertical IoT solutions that expose heterogeneous resources across the boundaries of organizations and domains, while offering flexible name-based communication schemes and ensuring a fully technology-independent implementation of high-level applications. For what concerns future works, the developed platform will be extended with security functionalities and additional key features able to support the mobility of both data consumers and data producers.

Acknowledgment. This work was framed in the context of the project BonVoyage, which received funding from the European Union's Horizon 2020 research and innovation programme under grant agreement No 635867. The authors would like to acknowledge Giovanna Capurso for the work done on the graphical interface. The outcomes of this work are also exploited in the Galileo cooperation program "A de-verticalized machine-to-machine platform for smart building applications" (Project n.: G15_12).

References

1. Vermesan, O., Friess, P.: Internet of Things-From Research and Innovation to Market Deployment. River Publishers, Alborg (2014)
2. Razzaque, M.A., Milojevic-Jevric, M., Palade, A., Clarke, S.: Middleware for internet of things: a survey. IEEE Internet Things J. **3**(1), 70–95 (2016)
3. Xylomenos, G., Ververidis, C., Siris, V., Fotiou, N., Tsilopoulos, C., Vasilakos, X., Katsaros, K., Polyzos, G.: A survey of information-centric networking research. IIEEE Commun. Surv. Tutor. **16**(2), 1024–1049 (2014)
4. Amadeo, M., Campolo, C., Quevedo, J., Corujo, D., Molinaro, A., Iera, A., Aguiar, R.L., Vasilakos, A.V.: Information-centric networking for the internet of things: challenges and opportunities. IEEE Netw. **30**(2), 92–100 (2016)
5. Chen, J., Li, S., Yu, H., Zhang, Y., Raychaudhuri, D., Ravindran, R., Gao, H., Dong, L., Wang, G., Liu, H.: Exploiting ICN for realizing service-oriented communication in IOT. IEEE Commun. Magaz. **54**(12), 24–30 (2016)
6. Quevedo, J., Corujo, D., Aguiar, R.: A case for ICN usage in IoT environments. In: Proceedings of IEEE Global Communications Conference, pp. 2770–2775 (2014)
7. Hail, M.A., Fischer, S.: IoT for AAL: an architecture via information-centric networking. In: Proceedings of IEEE Globecom, pp. 1–6, December 2015
8. Fotiou, N., Islam, H., Lagutin, D., Hakala, T., Polyzos, G.C.: Coap over ICN. In: Proceedings of IEEE International Conference on New Technologies, Mobility and Security (NTMS), pp. 1–4, November 2016
9. Hahm, O., Adjih, C., Baccelli, E., Schmidt, T.C., Wählisch, M.: ICN over TSCH: potentials for link-layer adaptation in the IoT. In: Proceedings of the ACM Conference on Information-Centric Networking, New York, NY, USA, pp. 195–196 (2016)

10. Lenord Melvix, J.S.M., Lokesh, V., Polyzos, G.C.: Energy efficient context based forwarding strategy in named data networking of things. In: Proceedings of ACM Conference on Information-Centric Networking, ser. ACM-ICN 2016, New York, NY, USA, 2016, pp. 249–254 (2016)
11. Enguehard, M., Droms, R., Rossi, D.: SLICT: secure localized information centric things. In: Proceedings of ACM Conference on Information-Centric Networking, pp. 255–260 (2016)
12. Shang, W., Bannis, A., Liang, T., Wang, Z., Yu, Y., Afanasyev, A., Thompson, J., Burke, J., Zhang, B., Zhang, L.: Named data networking of things. In: Proceedings of IEEE International Conference on Internet-of-Things Design and Implementation (IoTDI), pp. 117–128, April 2016
13. Katsaros, K.V., Chai, W.K., Wang, N., Pavlou, G., Bontius, H., Paolone, M.: Information-centric networking for machine-to-machine data delivery: a case study in smart grid applications. IEEE Netw. **28**(3), 58–64 (2014)
14. Grieco, L.A., Alaya, M.B., Monteil, T., Drira, K.: Architecting information centric ETSI-M2M systems. In: IEEE International Conference on Pervasive Computing and Communications Workshops (PERCOM), pp. 211–214, March 2014
15. Piro, G., Amadeo, M., Boggia, G., Campolo, C., Grieco, L.A., Molinaro, A., Ruggeri, G.: Gazing into the crystal ball: when the future internet meets the mobile clouds. IEEE Trans. Cloud Comput. **PP**(99), 1 (2016)
16. Zhang, Y., Raychadhuri, D., Grieco, L.A., Sabrina, S., Liu, H., Wang, G.: ICN based Architecture for IoT, IRTF Internet Draft, draft-zhang-icn-iot-architecture-01. IRTF, Internet Draft (2016)
17. Zhang, Y., Raychadhuri, D., Grieco, L.A., Baccelli, E., Burke, J., Ravindran, R., Wang, G., Lindren, A., Ahlgren, B., Schelen, O.: Design Considerations for Applying ICN to IoT, IRTF Internet Draft, draft-zhang-icnrg-icniot-00. IRTF, Internet Draft (2017)
18. Blefari Melazzi, N., Detti, A., Arumaithurai, M., Ramakrishnan, K.: Internames: a name-to-name principle for the future internet. In: 10th International Conference on Heterogeneous Networking for Quiteuality, Reliability, Security and Robustness (QShine), pp. 146–151, August 2014
19. Swetina, J., Lu, G., Jacobs, P., Ennesser, F., Song, J.: Toward a standardized common M2M service layer platform: introduction to oneM2M. IEEE Wirel. Commun. **21**(3), 20–26 (2014)
20. Zhang, L., Afanasyev, A., Burke, J., Jacobson, V., Claffy, K., Crowley, P., Papadopoulos, C., Wang, L., Zhang, B.: Named data networking. In: ACM SIG-COMM Computer Communication Review (CCR), July 2014
21. Alaya, M.B., Banouar, Y., Monteil, T., Chassot, C., Drira, K.: OM2M: extensible ETSI-compliant M2M service platform with self-configuration capability. Procedia Comput. Sci. **32**, 1079–1086 (2014)

Technologies for IoT

Measuring Spectrum Similarity in Distributed Radio Monitoring Systems

Roberto Calvo-Palomino[1,2](✉), Domenico Giustiniano[1](✉),
and Vincent Lenders[3](✉)

[1] IMDEA Networks Institute, Madrid, Spain
[2] Universidad Carlos III of Madrid, Madrid, Spain
{roberto.calvo,domenico.giustiniano}@imdea.org
[3] Armasuisse, Thun, Switzerland
vincent.lenders@armasuisse.ch

Abstract. The idea of distributed spectrum monitoring with RF front-ends of a few dollars is gaining attention to capture the real-time usage of the wireless spectrum at large geographical scale. Yet the limited hardware of these nodes hinders some of the applications that could be envisioned. In this work, we exploit the fact that, because of its affordable cost, massive deployments of spectrum sensors could be foreseen in the early future, where the radio signal of one wireless transmitter is received by multiple spectrum sensors in range and connected over the public Internet. We envision that nodes in this scenario may collaboratively take decisions about which portion of the spectrum to monitor or not. A key problem for collaborative decision is to identify the conditions where the nodes receive the same spectrum data. We take an initial step in this direction, presenting a collaborative system architecture, and investigating the challenges to correlate pre-processed data in the backend, with key insights in the trade-offs in the system design in terms of network bandwidth and type of over-the-air radio signals. Our results suggest that it is feasible to determinate in the backend if two sensors are reading the same analog/digital signal in the same frequency, only sampling during 200 ms and sending just 1 KB of data per sensor to the backend.

1 Introduction

Networked and distributed infrastructure using spectrum analyzers connected over the public Internet are emerging as an attractive alternative to traditional methods to monitor the spectrum usage based on expensive and specialized hardware of governmental agencies [1–3]. More recently, commoditized low-cost RF front-end are allowing to trade-off radio devices with high sensitivity, low-sweeping time and small frequency offset with low-cost spectrum monitoring hardware and software-defined signal processing in order to build a pervasive and affordable solution [4–7]. The main advantage of low-end distributed solutions is that they may allow to create a wide-scale and real-time spectrum monitoring system. A common assumption of most of concepts proposed in the literature

© Springer International Publishing AG 2017
A. Piva et al. (Eds.): TIWDC 2017, CCIS 766, pp. 215–229, 2017.
DOI: 10.1007/978-3-319-67639-5_16

is that they consider the different spectrum sensors as separate entities, each responsible to monitor the spectrum in a given area and with fully autonomous decisions [8].

However, in a crowded deployment, sensors may partially sense the same spectrum. We then envision a collaborative environment where a large number of sensing nodes work together in a coordinated manner. Only recently, some work has shown that collaboration among sensors is possible, and transmitting I/Q samples to the backend, data can be decoded in the backend with a distributed time-division scheduler [9]. The envisioned application in [9] requires a high network bandwidth load per device (in the order of a few or tens of Mb/s, depending on the number of sensors in range). Complementary to that work, we consider the goal of identify spectrum sensor nodes in coverage of the same transmitter. This problem requires to find a solution that (i) takes fast decisions, so that nodes may quickly verify if they are in range of the same transmitter, and (ii) needs low network bandwidth to minimize the load on the network. Applications of this knowledge could be several. For instance, collaboration to reach a common goal has the potential to reduce the time to monitor the spectrum using low-cost hardware. This could alleviate a main problem of current low-cost spectrum sensors deployments, that require between 40 and 70 s to sweep a spectrum of 1.7 GHz of bandwidth [7]. As a result of the frequency-dependent propagation characteristics, two nodes measuring the same or similar spectrum could then make a joint decision to avoid to both listening to the same portion of the spectrum, and instead spend more time on frequencies with little similarity with other nodes. Another exemplary application is the one of a sensor that finds out an anomaly in the signal. Here the node may ask the help of other sensors to confirm this anomaly.

In this work, we demonstrate and implement a system architecture able to collect the sensor's spectrum data and determine the similarity of the radio signal received at nearby locations by different sensing nodes. Our work provides the following key contributions:

- We overcome the limitation of CPU resources of embedded nodes, which dramatically reduce the time that a node can dedicate to gather spectrum samples, by proposing a synchronous sampling process in the sensors to determine the precise moment in time where multiple sensors can read the spectrum at the same time.
- We reduce the bandwidth used per each sensor by operating in the Fast Fourier Transform (FFT) domain and averaging the magnitude FFT on the sensors in order to send the minimum amount data needed to detect similarity to the backend.
- We evaluate and demonstrate a procedure to compute the spectrum correlation of the signals read by sensors, and apply it to analog and digital channels with spectrum resolution of 9.3 kHz.

We demonstrate that our system can reliably correlate real data spectrum (analog and digital signals) collected by different sensors sampling during 200 ms and sending only 1 KB of data per sensor to the backend.

The remainder of this paper is organized as follows. In Sect. 2 we present the sensor platform. We then present the main research challenges in Sect. 3 and the system methodology for distributed spectrum correlation in Sect. 4. The evaluation of the proposed concepts is the focus of Sect. 5. We then present related work in Sect. 6 and finally draw the conclusion in Sect. 7.

2   Platform for Collaborative Spectrum Sensing

This section describes the main concepts that feature our low-cost spectrum sensing platform for distributed and collaborative spectrum data collection. A high-level representation of the system is shown in Fig. 1.

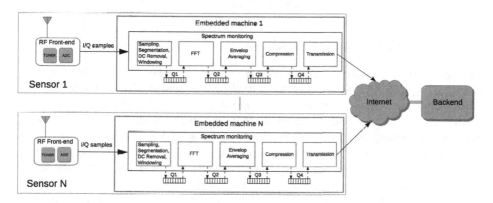

Fig. 1. High level architecture of each spectrum sensing node and overview of the overall system.

2.1   RF Data Acquisition

Our architecture supports any RF front-end as long as it reports the raw I/Q samples over USB interface. To sample the spectrum, we rely on low-cost RTL-SDR USB dongles as RF interfaces, that support continuous tuning range between 24 MHz and 1766 MHz [7]. In this work we use the recent RTL-SDR *'Silver v3'*[1] device (shown in Fig. 2(b)) that has a nominal maximum frequency error of 1 part-per-million (PPM) and a temperature compensated crystal oscillator (TCXO). The TCXO allows to keep stable the frequency offset even with changing temperature environments. We use the C library *librtlsdr* from the OsmocomSDR project[2] to acquire the digital samples. To manage the spectrum samples, we rely on low-cost embedded machines. Figure 2(a) shows the RaspberryPi (RPi), that provides one CPU and GPU core[3]. For network connectivity, we rely on the on-board Ethernet.

---

[1] http://www.rtl-sdr.com/buy-rtl-sdr-dvb-t-dongles/.
[2] http://osmocom.org.
[3] In details, the RPi is model 3, with 1.2 GHz 64-bit quad-core and 1 GB of RAM.

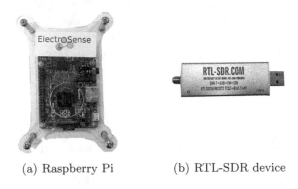

(a) Raspberry Pi   (b) RTL-SDR device

Fig. 2. Hardware used.

2.2   Software-Defined Radio Sensor

The spectrum monitoring module of our sensors accesses the RF front-end to retrieve I/Q samples and sends magnitude FFT samples to the backend. It implements in software the necessary signal processing mechanisms for spectrum analysis such as sampling, segmentation, windowing, DC removal, FFT, envelope detection, etc. in different software threads. A preliminary design and implementation of our sensor was presented in [7]. The FFT is computed in the GPU, since it is more efficient than the CPU for parallel signal processing[4].

The different threads are connected through queues, so that processing steps get decoupled from one another and in order to increase the efficiency in processing (e.g. blocks can be configured to process the queuing system's items at different granularities, i.e. one by one or in batches of several items). In order to prioritize the samples' reading over other threads, the main signal processing tasks of our architecture (Sampling, FFT, Envelope Detection, Compression and Transmission) are scheduled using default scheduler of Linux systems (Completely Fair Scheduler, CFS) with FIFO policy, which ensures that these tasks have a high priority in the system in terms of execution with respect to any other tasks in the system.

Each node of our system is able to compute magnitude FFT samples over a signal bandwidth of 2 MHz. (The node collects 2.4 MHz of spectrum, but we remove the edge of the spectrum where we observe that the frequency response is not flat.) Data are sensed, analyzed and compressed without any losses, with a default spectral resolution of 9.3 kHz. In the default configuration, an averaging factor of five is used in the data (i.e. 5 FFT blocks are used for averaging). In this configuration, uploading compressed data streams require a rate of 750 Kb/s when continuously monitoring a fixed band of 2 MHz. As a result of the time spent to switch frequency, the uplink rates is reduced to 120 kb/s when the sensor is instructed by the backend to hop across the full wideband spectrum of

---

[4] For instance, we have experimentally measured that batches of 100 FFTs of 256 samples/bins each are computed in ≈10 us using the GPU of the RPi, almost four time less that using the CPU.

1742 MHz. The code implemented in the sensors is available as open source on github[5].

2.3 Backend

The backend is a server or set of servers with sufficient large storage and computation capabilities. Its main responsibility is to control the sensors and store, process and decode data received from the sensors, and perform data post-processing.

3   Challenges

Measuring the similarity between data spectra collected by independent sensors at different locations and connected to a backend over the Internet could allow us to explore intelligent collaborative decisions. For instance, the entire spectrum could be monitored faster. In another application, sensors may collaborate to detect anomalies if they learn that they are in range of the same transmitter in that specific frequency band. Also, sensors may decide to monitor a bandwidth larger than the one of the single sensor (with each node sampling on a 2 MHz band only partially overlapped with other sensors in range) and then jointly reconstruct the spectrum more efficiently in the backend.

In order to realize this vision, there are three fundamental challenges that need to be addressed with low-cost spectrum sensors:

- **Challenge 1: Time Synchronization.** Each node reads spectrum data, performs some pre-processing and sends it to the backend for post-processing. As nodes heavily relies on software-defined radios, delays are possible in the pre-processing in the sensors, which would adversely affect any attempt to compare data from different sensors. Therefore, it is essential to have synchronized information in time.
- **Challenge 2: Rapid decision making.** The system should take quick decisions about if a set of spectrum sensors can work collaboratively to achieve a common goal. The amount of analyzed data plays an important role to converge to a decision in the shortest possible time.
- **Challenge 3: Network bandwidth used.** The sensors send spectrum data to the backend where a decision is taken in order to allow the collaborative approach. The more data sent, the better the performance in the backend. Yet the greater is the bandwidth used. The system should find the right trade-off to provide enough context information to detect similarity in the spectrum using the minimum network bandwidth.

---

[5] It can be downloaded at https://github.com/electrosense/es-sensor.

4   Measuring Spectrum Similarity

In this section, we describe the methodology proposed to address the challenges presented in Sect. 3. The methodology is composed by three main concepts.

First, the sensors have a coarse synchronization in time using Network Time Protocol (NTP). The sensors can then read spectrum data with synchronization with millisecond precision over the public Internet, and better that one millisecond precision in local area networks (as measured in ad-hoc experiments). In our architecture, each sensor synchronizes its internal clock with NTP server every 60 s. A finer synchronization could be achieved using the time reference provided by an additional GPSDO module, as supposed by previous work in this area [9]. Yet, this may not be available in all the spectrum sensors, as they are run by users of the community, with they own hardware.

Second, each spectrum sensor activates the sampling thread for a fixed period, and then executes the other threads. This period is the same for each sensor. The total time to execute the entire set of operations should be such that the embedded machine can send spectrum data with the minimum delay (i.e. there are no other tasks pending).

Finally, in order to reduce the network bandwidth used, some operations need to be computed on the sensors as described in Sect. 2. Sensors should decide the parameters such as averaging over larger set of FFT blocks, if the bandwidth should be reduced further. This however comes at the cost of additional delay in the decision making. In the following section we describe this problem in details.

4.1   Spectrum Correlation

We perform signal correlation analysis in the backend to understand the similarity in the spectrum data collected by different sensors. Figure 3 shows the overview of the architecture that is responsible to compute the spectrum similarity (it is presented for two sensors, but it could be generalized to any number of sensors). First, the same center frequency and *sampling_time* is set in both sensors. During this sampling time the sensors continuously read the spectrum. After that, the raw data spectrum is split in N segments of *duty_cycle* long each one. For every segment, the FFT is computed according to the *fft_size* (which defines the number of bins). Each *fft_block* has the spectrum information of 2.0 MHz bandwidth channel. Therefore, the FFT blocks contain frequency information that is averaged using *avg_factor* blocks to produce M averaging blocks. These averaging blocks are sent to the backend for every sensor involved in the similarity spectrum evaluation. Tuning the different values of the system (*sampling_time*, *fft_size* and *avg_factor*) the amount of data sent to the backend (bandwidth used) can be modulated depending of the needs.

The backend computes the Pearson correlation coefficient using the averaged FFT blocks received from every sensor. The correlation is computed for every pair of averaged FFT blocks coming for different sensors. Then, the average is computed using the correlation output for every averaging block. The system

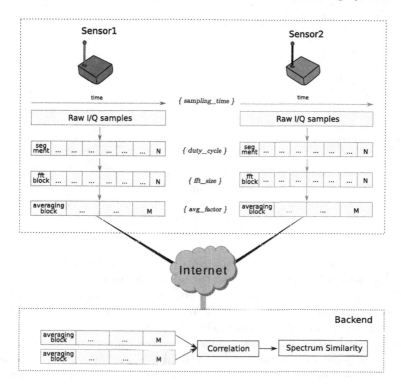

Fig. 3. Technique for computing spectrum similarity between two sensors.

evaluates this value to determine if the sensors are reading similar spectrum and if it is possible to enable the collaborative approach between them.

5   Evaluation

This section presents the experimental evaluation of our architecture. The aim is to determine the minimum network bandwidth and time needed to achieve a good signal correlation for analog and digital signals. For analog signals we choose FM and for digital signals we use Long-Term Evolution (LTE). The FM radio in Spain occupies the range from 87.5 MHz to 108 MHz. Each FM radio channel uses 200 kHz of bandwidth to transmit the signal. For LTE, we monitor three channels of 10 MHz bandwidth that are available in Spain at center frequencies equal to 796, 806 and 816 MHz.

Sampling Process' Synchronization. The synchronization between sensors is an important issue to achieve a good correlation between the signals. In our experiment, the sensors use Ethernet connection through Internet to synchronize their internal clock through NTP. This technology provides us an accuracy of 0.1 ms in a local network scenario and around a millisecond over Internet. The backend is responsible to define the precise moment when the sensors start to

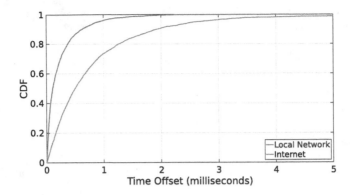

Fig. 4. Time offset between sensors in LAN and Internet.

sample at the same time. This operation provides a coarse synchronization due to the delays added by the network and the operative system. Figure 4 shows the time offset between sensors when they are in the same local network (LAN) or connected through Internet. The 90% of the time the sensors have a time offset lower than 2 ms when they are connected through Internet. In our solution we are interested to enable the collaboration among sensors connected through Internet (no just in the same local network). This provides a lower bound for the amount of data to be transmitted from the sensors for spectrum similarity analysis.

Spectrum Correlation. The spectrum correlation value is the metric used to determinate if the sensors are receiving a similar signal in the same frequency at the same time. The data provided by each sensor covers 2.0 MHz of bandwidth. The spectrum resolution in this bandwidth is determined by the *fft_size* used. We run experiments with *fft_size* = *256*, which implies that each *fft_block* of 2.0 MHz contains 214 frequency bins. We also set duty_cycle equal to 2 ms. Figure 5(a) shows the correlation between the analog signal acquired by two sensors that are 3 m away. In the case that the sensors are set to the same frequency band ($f_c = 101$ MHz) the correlation value reaches 0.7 for average factors higher than 10. Note that with a avg_factor of 10, the average is computed every 20 ms. The correlation keeps stable and close to 0 in the case that two sensors are set to a different frequency bands. Therefore, we can reliably detect that the sensors are not reading in the same frequency band. Figure 5(b) shows how we reach a good correlation value between digital signals if the sensors are configured with averaging factor from 20 on-wards. Again the correlation over digital signals when two sensors are set to a different frequencies is stable and close to −0.3.

Impact of Spectrum Resolution. The FFT resolution is an important parameter to set in our system because it will decide, first, the computational cost on the sensor in order to compute the FFT and then the average of the FFT bins, and second the bandwidth used in order to transfer the FFT bins from the sensors to the backend. We would like to reach the maximum correlation value with the minimum data sent to the backend. Figure 6 shows that there is not so

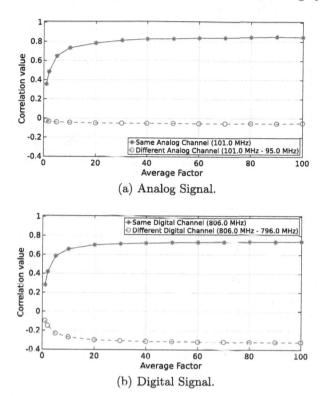

(a) Analog Signal.

(b) Digital Signal.

Fig. 5. Analog and digital signal correlation between sensors with different averaging (fft_size = 256 and duty_cycle = 2 ms.)

much difference among using different FFT values (256 up to 2048) in order to reach a good correlation value. However, using digital signals, we can see how the lower is the fft_size the better is the correlation value. For digital signals that change faster that analog ones and contain more information seems to be a good option to use low values of fft_size to reach the maximum correlation between signals. In addition, larger fft_size tend to be affected by larger noise, which can negatively affect the correlation. Both analog and digital signals can be correlated using low values of fft_size (256), which also minimizes the bandwidth used by the sensors to perform the correlation on the backend.

Distance between the Sensors. The distance between the sensors is an important factor that can affect the spectrum correlation among sensors. If the sensors are located far from each other, the channel path loss can severely affect any collaborative strategy. This phenomenon is frequency dependent, since the path loss model decays with $20 \log_{10} f_c$, where f_c indicates the carrier frequency. Therefore higher density is expected at higher frequency to harness the spectrum correlation.

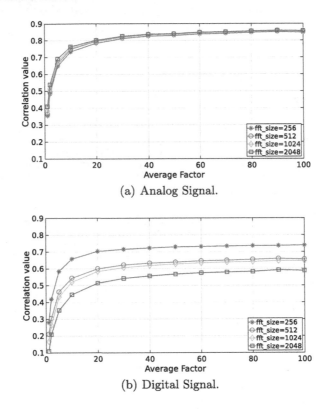

(a) Analog Signal.

(b) Digital Signal.

Fig. 6. Analog and digital signal correlation (same frequency band) between sensors with different *fft_size* (duty_cycle = 2 ms.)

In this experiment we locate several sensors at indoor environment with different distances between each other. The distances between sensors are 3, 15, 25 and 50 m respectively. We remark that the tests are conducted in indoor environment. Figure 7(a) shows the signal correlation of the sensors located at different distances and scanning an analog signal. Up to 15 m the correlation value is close to 0.8 and with distances between 25 and 50 m the correlation is around 0.6. Figure 7(b) shows the same scenario but using digital signals. The correlation for distances up to 15 m reports a value above 0.6 but for longer distances the correlation decrease dramatically. These results suggest that for analog signals the sensors could work collaboratively together for maximum distances of 50 m and for digital signals the limit is around 15–20 m.

Minimum bandwidth required. The goal of this experiment is to provide an answer to the following question: what is the minimum sampling time and the minimum data sent to the backend in order to measure the similarity in the spectrum? In a distributed approach, like the one studied in this work, it is required to make decisions in the shortest possible time and with the minimum

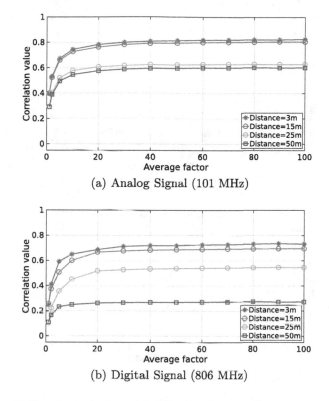

(a) Analog Signal (101 MHz)

(b) Digital Signal (806 MHz)

Fig. 7. Signal correlation with different distances between sensors

amount of data. Therefore, it is important to evaluate the convergence time to decide if the sensors are getting similar spectrum or not, and the minimum data sent over Internet to perform the correlation in the backend.

In order to detect when the system converges, we define the *cumulative correlation (CC) metric* as the average of the last K observations of correlation values. Figure 8 shows the CC metric over time for analog and digital signals. We can observe that after 0.2 s we reach a stable correlation value that allows us to distinguish if the sensors are reading a similar spectrum or not. Figure 9 shows the data sent to the backend over time for different fft_size configurations. As we determined in the previous experiment, the best configuration of fft_size to perform the correlation in the backend is 256. In addition to that, we have already found that after 0.2 s the correlation gets stable. From Fig. 9, we can then conclude that every sensor needs to send only 1 KB to the backend in order to get a reliable decision about the spectrum similarity.

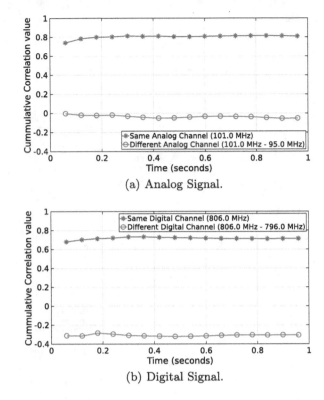

(a) Analog Signal.

(b) Digital Signal.

Fig. 8. Convergence of signal correlation using fft_size = 256, avg_factor = 30 and duty_cycle = 2 ms.

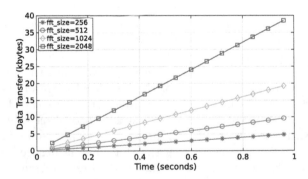

Fig. 9. Data transferred to the server for a duty_cycle = 2 ms and avg_factor = 30.

6   Related Work

Monitoring large spectra is more challenging that conventional approach that sense narrowband frequency spectrum [10–12]. Large corporation have shown interest in the topic of large-scale spectrum sensing. Google has lunched the

Spectrum Database [13], a joint initiative between Google, industry and regulators to make more spectrum available by using a database to enable dynamic spectrum sharing in TV white spaces. They provide an access to the data to query white space availability based on time and location. Microsoft Spectrum Observatory [1] is a platform with cost of approximately 5000 dollars that is currently operating in a few locations worldwide. Using data collected with the Spectrum Observatory, [14] proposed a system that identifies transmitters from raw spectrum measurements without prior knowledge of transmitter signatures. It harnesses the observation that wireless signal fading follows a Rayleigh distribution and applies a novel machine learning algorithm and experimentally identifies transmitters robustly. SpecNet [3] is a platform developed by Microsoft Research that allows researches to conduct spectrum measurements studies remotely in real-time for opportunistic spectrum access.

In their recent work, [8] described the implementation and evaluation of a real-time, centralized spectrum monitoring and alert system. These controllers rely on real-time awareness of spectrum activity. However, the analysis is conducted using binary vectors, by comparing each power value in the received power vector to a user-defined threshold. Cooperative sensing has been introduced in [15], and it describes a scenario with sensing nodes that distributively monitor a frequency spectrum. In [16], they proposed to use a cooperative environment to distinguish between an unused band and deep fade due to shadowing or fading effects. The works above did not complement the proposed simulation environment with a system-level design and implementation. [17,18] employ correlation techniques in different environments, but the study is based on simulations only. No system architecture problems were studied in these work for their actual implementation.

SpecInsight was introduced in [19] and is a system for acquiring 4 GHz of spectrum in real-time using USRP radios with tens of MHz in 7 locations in the US. SpecInsight applies a multi-armed bandit game to the problem of selecting the frequency bands to monitor. Because of the high-end platform used in the work, there are little opportunities for pervasive deployments. In the context of low-cost spectrum sensing systems, [6,7] use Raspberry Pi embedded hardware and DVB-T receivers with only 2 MHz of band to monitor 1.7 GHz of spectrum with software defined radio capabilities and implement low-complexity algorithms for distributed spectrum sensing. In addition, [7] proposed different frequency hopping strategies to overcome the hardware limitations of low-cost radios and incorporates different analysis and error/noise correction techniques for flexible and configurable remote wide-spectrum monitoring. In [4], the authors performed an initial feasibility study to verify the efficiency of using RTL-SDR USB dongles connected to laptop or smartphone devices to build a low-cost commoditized spectrum analysis system.

7 Conclusion

We have addressed the compute in the backend the similarity in the spectrum of data collected by low-cost sensors in range of the same transmitter. We have proposed various methods to achieve reliable correlation in presence of noisy data both for analog and digital signals. We have proved that our architecture provides good spectrum correlation for sensors in radio range. We have then studied problems such as how the spectrum correlation varies with the distance between sensors. Our system can reliably correlate the spectrum of analog and digital signals of different sensors using data collected during 200 ms and sending only 1 KB of data per sensor to the backend. Our results are promising and can allow intelligent collaborative decisions among sensors in different locations, even when there is only a coarse information of the physical location of the sensors.

Limitations of the Current Approach and Directions of Research

In this work we have shown the feasibility of correlating the spectrum data received by independent sensors. In particular, the study has considered both analog and digital signals, yet with unique transmitter sources (cell tower of FM radio and LTE signal). More in general, medium access protocols and topological issues may require more signal processing and intelligent logic. In particular, multiple transmitters, all of them placed in different locations, may share the same spectrum, yet being in range of the same spectrum sensor. The spectrum sensor could declare high spectrum similarity or not depending on (a) the medium access protocol (which transmitter is using the spectrum at a given moment in time) and (b) its relative position with respect to the sensors. Possible directions of research to solve this problem are to identify the transmitter, e.g. detecting a specific signature, its signal strength, or even estimating both spectrum similarity and the position of the transmitter. Conclusions could then be drawn about the probability of spectrum similarity based on the spectrum activity of each transmitter.

Acknowledgments. This work has been funded in part by the TIGRE5-CM program (S2013/ICE-2919). We thank the anonymous reviewers for their valuable comments and suggestions.

References

1. Microsoft spectrum observatory. http://observatory.microsoftspectrum.com/
2. Naganawa, J., Kim, H., Saruwatari, S., Onaga, H., Morikawa, H.: Distributed spectrum sensing utilizing heterogeneous wireless devices and measurement equipment. In: 2011 IEEE Symposium on New Frontiers in Dynamic Spectrum Access Networks (DySPAN), pp. 173–184, May 2011
3. Iyer, A., Chintalapudi, K.K., Navda, V., Ramjee, R., Padmanabhan, V., Murthy, C.: Specnet: spectrum sensing sans frontiéres. In: 8th USENIX Symposium on Networked Systems Design and Implementation (NSDI). USENIX, March 2011
4. Nika, A., Zhang, Z., Zhou, X., Zhao, B.Y., Zheng, H.: Towards commoditized real-time spectrum monitoring. In: Proceedings of the 1st ACM Workshop on Hot Topics in Wireless, ser. HotWireless 2014, pp. 25–30. ACM, New York (2014)

5. Arcia-Moret, A., Pietrosemoli, E., Zennaro, M.: WhispPi: white space monitoring with Raspberry Pi. In: Global Information Infrastructure Symposium (GIIS 2013) (2013)
6. Grnroos, S., Nybom, K., Bjrkqvist, J., Hallio, J., Auranen, J., Ekman, R.: Distributed spectrum sensing using low cost hardware. J. Signal Process. Syst. Signal Image Video Technol. 113 (2015)
7. Pfammatter, D., Giustiniano, D., Lenders, V.: A software-defined sensor architecture for large-scale wideband spectrum monitoring. In: Proceedings of the 14th International Symposium on Information Processing in Sensor Networks, ser. IPSN 2015, Seattle, WA, USA, pp. 71–82 (2015)
8. Souryal, M., Ranganathan, M., Mink, J., Ouni, N.E.: Real-time centralized spectrum monitoring: feasibility, architecture, and latency. In: 2015 IEEE Symposium on Dynamic Spectrum Access Networks (DySPAN), September 2015
9. Calvo-Palomino, R., Giustiniano, D., Lenders, V.: Electrosense: crowdsourcing spectrum monitoring. In: 2017 IEEE International Conference on Computer Communications (Infocom), May 2017
10. Akyildiz, I.F., Lee, W.-Y., Vuran, M.C., Mohanty, S.: Next generation/dynamic spectrum access/cognitive radio wireless networks: a survey. Comput. Netw. **50**(13), 2127–2159 (2006)
11. Axell, E., Leus, G., Larsson, E., Poor, H.: Spectrum sensing for cognitive radio : state-of-the-art and recent advances. IEEE Signal Process. Magaz. **29**(3), 101–116 (2012)
12. Quan, Z.Q.Z., Cui, S.C.S., Sayed, A.H., Poor, H.: Wideband spectrum sensing in cognitive radio networks. In: 2008 IEEE International Conference on Communications (2008)
13. Google spectrum database. https://www.google.com/get/spectrumdatabase/
14. Zheleva, M., Chandra, R., Chowdhery, A., Kapoor, A., Garnett, P.: Txminer: identifying transmitters in real-world spectrum measurements. In: 2015 IEEE Symposium on Dynamic Spectrum Access Networks (DySPAN), September 2015
15. Mishra, S., Sahai, A., Brodersen, R.: Cooperative sensing among cognitive radios. In: 2006 IEEE International Conference on Communications, pp. 1658–1663 (2006)
16. Ghasemi, A., Sousa, E.S.: Collaborative spectrum sensing for opportunistic access in fading environments. In: 2005 1st IEEE International Symposium on New Frontiers in Dynamic Spectrum Access Networks (DySPAN 2005), pp. 131–136 (2005)
17. Cacciapuoti, A.S., Akyildiz, I.F., Paura, L.: Correlation-aware user selection for cooperative spectrum sensing in cognitive radio ad hoc networks. IEEE J. Sel. Areas Commun. **30**(2), 297–306 (2012)
18. Sampietro, M., Accomoando, G., Fasoli, L.G., Ferrari, G., Gatti, E.C.: High sensitivity noise measurement with a correlation spectrum analyzer. IEEE Trans. Instrum. Measurement **49**(4), 1–3 (2000)
19. Shi, L., Bahl, P., Katabi, D.: Beyond sensing: multi-GHZ realtime spectrum analytics. In: 12th USENIX Symposium on Networked Systems Design and Implementation (NSDI 2015). USENIX Association, Oakland (2015)

Green and Heuristics-Based Consolidation Scheme for Data Center Cloud Applications

Alessandro Carrega[1][(✉)] and Matteo Repetto[2]

[1] DITEN – University of Genoa, Genoa, Italy
alessandro.carrega@unige.it
[2] CNIT – Research Unit of Genoa, Genoa, Italy
matteo.repetto@cnit.it

Abstract. The consolidation of resources is one of the most efficient strategies to reduce the power consumption in data centers. Various algorithms have been proposed in order to reduce the total number of required servers and network devices. The practice developed in response to the problem of server *sprawl*, a situation in which multiple, under-utilized servers (and/or network devices) take up more space and consume more resources than can be justified by their workload; with the effect to power off unused equipment. Generally, consolidation mechanisms consider different parameters related to the services neglecting the specific function of the Virtual Machines (VMs) in the application framework (e.g., core component, backup replica, member of a set of workers for load balancing).

In this work, we developed a new consolidation algorithm that takes into account the particular function of each VM with the aim to apply power saving mechanisms without compromising the desired service level. The results of the simulations show that it is possible to obtain significant values of energy saving. In particular, we show, with different heuristics, the optimal trade-off between service level and power efficiency achieved by the proposed model.

Keywords: Green · Energy-aware · Consolidation · Virtual machines · Cloud applications · Optimization · Heuristics

1 Introduction

The linear relationship between the power consumption and the current workload is the ideal objective to obtain an energy-efficient data centers. This goal can be realized with energy saving mechanisms, as, for example, frequency/voltage scaling, and *sleep* states [1].

The most efficient mechanism to reduce the power consumption is called *Sleeping*[1] [1]. [3] is the first work that introduced the concept of *resource consolidation* in order to maximize the effectiveness of this mechanism. In more

---

[1] Sleeping (i.e., ACPI S3 state [2]) consists of very low energy consumption states for electronic devices, where most functions are disabled but the system can resume to full operation in a very short time (typically under a few hundred milliseconds).

© Springer International Publishing AG 2017
A. Piva et al. (Eds.): TIWDC 2017, CCIS 766, pp. 230–250, 2017.
DOI: 10.1007/978-3-319-67639-5_17

details, it is possible to sleep a significant amount of idle infrastructures (servers and network machines) grouping applications together on the smallest number of servers.

The first proposed strategies for consolidation only take into account the energy consumed by servers. These strategies model the power consumption of servers according to their current processing load (mainly in terms of CPU usage). Successive more advanced algorithms have been proposed considering network equipment as well as Heating, Ventilation and Air Conditioning (HVAC) systems [1]. In these cases, they also take into consideration the additional energy consumption generated by network traffic and the heat removal for various configurations of active servers in the particular data center installation. The central issue remains the need to migrate the applications between different servers, with interruptions of service time for short periods of time, that could be not acceptable for mission-critical applications [4,5].

To reduce the power consumption without performance degradation, consolidation algorithms consider additional parameters as Quality of Service (QoS) metrics, Service Level Agreement (SLA), and network traffic patterns. Nevertheless, larger energy saving could be achieved by also taking into account the particular role of single Virtual Machines (VMs) into a complex service framework. In more details, this work is focused on elastic cloud applications [6], realized with different software components running in separate VMs. In this context, the workload variations make complex to find a right trade-off between performance, operational costs, and power consumption [7]. Indeed, for different reasons like backup, resilience, or performance (e.g., to serve sudden increases in requests), the service provider would need to run several idle replicas. However, this scheme would lead to inefficiency for infrastructure owners and higher operational costs for service providers, because of the VMs running idle most of the time.

In this work, we introduce a system model for energy efficiency management of cloud applications in data centers, which take into account both servers and network equipment. The main novelty of this mechanism is the specific classification of VMs into different groups, based on their particular role in the service framework they are part of. With such idea, the proposed algorithm enables infrastructure providers to selectively use aggressive energy saving mechanisms for servers that only run idle VMs, bringing them back to full operation in a matter of few hundred milliseconds (compared to a few minutes for typical VM provisioning). This opportunity allows achieving a better trade-off between energy efficiency and service level in real environments. We argue that the classification of VMs required by our algorithm could be easily inferred by specific information embedded by service developers into software templates, meta-models, and annotations, which are becoming common development paradigms for cloud applications [8–11].

The paper is organized as follows. Initially, Sect. 2 reviews related work. Section 3 describes our system model, while Sect. 4 describes the consolidation algorithm. Section 5 shows results from our simulations. Finally, Sect. 6 gives our conclusions and plans for future work.

2   Related Work

Resource *consolidation* is one of the most effective ways to save energy in data centers. It implies gathering VMs on the minimum number of servers needed to fulfill their requirements (CPU, RAM, I/O bandwidth), in order to shut down the remaining infrastructure. The infrastructure under consideration always includes physical servers, and sometimes also encompasses network and HVAC equipment.

The consolidation problem has often been modeled as a modified *bin packing* problem, seeking the optimal operating point between energy and performance [12]. However, VM placement is not exactly equivalent to a three-dimensional (CPU, RAM, I/O) bin packing problem, and some anomalies could arise from this approach and similar ones in the literature [13]. Given the NP-completeness of the problem, most authors end up proposing heuristics to find a sub-optimal solution in acceptable time [12–15].

Several researchers have tackled the trade-off between traffic routing and power consumption in data center networks. Heller et al. [16] model the consolidation of network flows as a Multi-Commodity Flow Problem (MCFP) and a greedy bin packing. In other cases, VMs are explicitly placed to minimize the network power consumption. Shirayanagi et al. [17] target fault-tolerance and take into consideration placement of backup VMs. Wang et al. [18] cluster VMs according to their traffic patterns, and then place them on different racks with a classical k-cut algorithm; finally, the minimal number of network switches to carry the total traffic is computed, assuming a balancing algorithm is used (VLB/ECHP). The complexity and the large state of such systems are major computational problems; to this aim, hierarchical approaches have been proposed by Zhang et al. [19].

The problem of consolidation has also been modeled by jointly considering the power consumption of servers and network equipment. Kliazovich et al. [7] define a composite metric based on a hierarchical model that accounts for the power consumption of servers and network equipment, which is used to find the best balance between server utilization and queue size. Fang et al. [20] decompose the problem into three parts: (i) *traffic-aware grouping*, modeled as a Balanced Minimum k-cut Problem, (ii) *distance-aware VM-group to server-rack mapping*, modeled as a Quadratic Assignment Problem, and (iii) *power-aware inter-VM traffic flow routing*, modeled as a classic MCFP. Specific heuristics have been used to find a solution for each part.

3   System Model

We consider a data center made of physical servers, network devices, and links. Every application consists of one or more elementary software components, each deployed in a separate VM, which represents the granularity of our model. VMs are created and destroyed according to the application life-cycle management logic, which is not relevant for the model and corresponds to an arrival/departure process. VMs are classified into different groups, depending on the power management mechanisms that can be applied without incurring in performance degradation.

3.1   Data Center Infrastructure Model

We model a data center as a weighted directed graph $\mathcal{G}\,(\mathbb{M}, \mathbb{E})$, where $\mathbb{M}$ and $\mathbb{E}$ are sets of nodes and edges, respectively. In the graph $\mathcal{G}$, a node $m \in \mathbb{M}$ is either a server (leaf) or network device (root or internal node); while the directed edge $e := (m_1, m_2) \in \mathbb{E}$ represents the network link from m_1 to m_2 (with $m_1, m_2 \in \mathbb{M}$) characterized by the bandwidth capacity C_{bw}^e (expressed in Mbps) and by the traffic utilization level $C_{\mathrm{u}}^e \in [0, 1]$. Always referring to the edge $e := (m_1, m_2)$, we indicate the source and destination nodes with $C_{\mathrm{src}}^e := m_1 \in \mathbb{M}$, and $C_{\mathrm{dst}}^e := m_2 \in \mathbb{M}$, respectively. Besides, to simplify the equations in the following sections, we define the set of source and destination nodes $C_{\mathrm{node}}^e := \{m \in \mathbb{M} \,|\, m = C_{\mathrm{src}}^e \vee m = C_{\mathrm{dst}}^e\}$, $\forall e \in \mathbb{E}$, too. Furthermore, we describe the opposite edge $\bar{e} \in \mathbb{E}$ of $e \in \mathbb{E}$ where $C_{\mathrm{src}}^e = C_{\mathrm{dst}}^{\bar{e}} \wedge C_{\mathrm{dst}}^e = C_{\mathrm{src}}^{\bar{e}}$. Considering the notion of edge, for each node $m \in \mathbb{M}$, we introduce the concept of neighborhood $\mathbb{M}_{\mathrm{nb}}^m := \{\tilde{m} \in \mathbb{M} \,|\, m \in C_{\mathrm{node}}^e \wedge \tilde{m} \in C_{\mathrm{node}}^e \wedge e \in \mathbb{E}\} \subseteq \mathbb{M}$.

We denote with $\mathbb{S}$ and $\mathbb{N}$ the sets of servers and network devices, respectively (obviously $\mathbb{M} \equiv \mathbb{S} \cup \mathbb{N})^2$. Considering that the number of ports can vary from one network device to another, we use σ_n to denote the number of ports into the network node $n \in \mathbb{N}$. The resources of a server $s \in \mathbb{S}$ are defined with a pair composed by the number of CPUs [3] C_{cpu}^s and the quantity of RAM C_{ram}^s, expressed in MB.

For each pair of nodes $m_1, m_2 \in \mathbb{M}$, we define $\mathbb{P}$ as a set of network paths consisting in a walk from m_1 to m_2 with no repeated edges:

$$\mathbb{P} := \{(e_1, e_2, \ldots e_n) \,|\, C_{\mathrm{src}}^{e_1} = m_1,$$
$$C_{\mathrm{dst}}^{e_1} = C_{\mathrm{src}}^{e_2}, \ldots C_{\mathrm{dst}}^{e_n} = m_2\} \tag{1}$$

To summarize, Table 1 shows all the notations introduced in this section (we use $\mathcal{Z}_{>0}$ and $\mathcal{R}_{>0}$ for the set of positive integer and real numbers, respectively).

3.2   VM Model

Data center users request VMs to build their applications; we do not need to explicitly take into account their belonging to specific applications since this aspect is already captured by the communication patterns. Hence, our model

---

[2] Based on the proposed node classification, we refer to $m \in \mathbb{M}$ with the term *device*, too.

[3] For the sake of simplicity, in this paper, the term CPU refers to the minimum processing unit that can be set in a low-consumption state.

Table 1. Data center infrastructure model notation.

Parameter	Description
$C_{\mathrm{cpu}}^{s} \in \mathcal{Z}_{>0}$	Number of CPUs provided by the server $s \in \mathbb{S}$
$C_{\mathrm{ram}}^{s} \in \mathcal{R}_{>0}$	Amount of RAM (in MB) provided by the server $s \in \mathbb{S}$
$C_{\mathrm{bw}}^{e} \in \mathcal{R}_{>0}$	Amount of network bandwidth (in Mbps) provided by the link $e \in \mathbb{E}$
$C_{\mathrm{u}}^{e} \in [0,1]$	Traffic utilization level of the link $e \in \mathbb{E}$
$C_{\mathrm{src}}^{e} \in \mathbb{M}$	Source node of the link $e \in \mathbb{E}$
$C_{\mathrm{dst}}^{e} \in \mathbb{M}$	Destination node of the link $e \in \mathbb{E}$
$C_{\mathrm{node}}^{e} := C_{\mathrm{src}}^{e} \cup C_{\mathrm{dst}}^{e}$	Set of source and destination nodes of the link $e \in \mathbb{E}$.
$\overline{e} \in \mathbb{E}$	Opposite link of the link $e \in \mathbb{E}$
$\mathbb{M}_{\mathrm{nb}}^{m} \subseteq \mathbb{M}$	Set of connected nodes (neighbors) of the node $m \in \mathbb{M}$

Table 2. VM model notation.

Parameter	Description
$\Psi_{\mathrm{cpu}}^{v} \in \mathcal{R}_{\geq 0}$	Number of CPUs required by the VM $v \in \mathbb{V}$
$\Psi_{\mathrm{ram}}^{v} \in \mathcal{R}_{\geq 0}$	Amount of RAM (in MB) required by the VM $v \in \mathbb{V}$
$\Psi_{\mathrm{start}}^{v} \in [0, T]$	Arrival time (in second) of the VM $v \in \mathbb{V}$
$\Psi_{\mathrm{dur}}^{v} \in [0, T]$	Duration time (in second) of the VM $v \in \mathbb{V}$
$\Psi_{\mathrm{bw}}^{(v_1, v_2)} \in \mathcal{R}_{\geq 0}$	Bandwidth (in Mbps) required for the communication from VMs $v_1 \in \mathbb{V}$ to $v_2 \in \mathbb{V}$
$x_v \in \mathbb{S} \cup \emptyset$	The VM $v \in \mathbb{V}$ can be placed in a server or not (with a request rejection)
$y_{v_1}^{v_2} \in \mathbb{P} \cup \emptyset$	The network path can be selected for the communication from VMs $v_1 \in \mathbb{V}$ to $v_2 \in \mathbb{V}$ or not (with a request rejection)
$\vec{x}_v \in \{0, 1\}$	Indicates if the VM $v \in \mathbb{V}$ has to be migrated from a server to another one
$\vec{y}_{v_1}^{v_2} \in \{0, 1\}$	Indicates if the selected network path for the communication from VMs $v_1 \in \mathbb{V}$ to $v_2 \in \mathbb{V}$ is changed
$\delta_v \in \mathbb{G}$	Membership group of the VM $v \in \mathbb{V}$
$\tilde{\xi}_{\mathrm{cpu}}^{v} \in [0, 1]$	Fraction of CPU guaranteed to the VM $v \in \mathbb{V}$

for VMs includes the computing/networking resources (CPU, RAM, link bandwidth) and power-aware classification (derived from QoS/SLA requirements).

We define $\mathbb{V}$ as the set of running VMs. The VM model is described in Table 2 (we use $\mathcal{R}_{\geq 0}$ for the set of non-negative real numbers). The parameter T refers to the simulation time period, and it will be described in detail in the next section. The VM placement is expressed with parameter $x_v \in \mathbb{S} \cup \emptyset$ that indicates the server where the VM $v \in \mathbb{V}$ is placed or an *empty* value $(\emptyset)$[4] if the placement procedure is failed (i.e., rejected request). Instead, to represent

---

[4] To be more precise, with $\emptyset$, we indicate that the variable is not assigned.

the selected network path for the communication between the VMs, we define the parameter $y_{v_1}^{v_2} \in \mathbb{P} \cup \emptyset$ that refers to the selected network path for the communication from VM v_1 to VM v_2 (with $v_1, v_2 \in \mathbb{V}$) or an empty value ($\emptyset$) if the network path selection is failed (rejected request). Instead, the binary variables $\vec{x}_v$ and $\vec{y}_{v_1}^{v_2}$ indicate if the VM $v \in \mathbb{V}$ has to be migrated from one server to another one and that the selected network path for the traffic communication between $v_1 \in \mathbb{V}$ to $v_2 \in \mathbb{V}$ is changed, respectively.

To represent the VM classification, we use the parameter $\delta_v \in \mathbb{G}$ that indicates the membership group. Each VM belongs to a one and only one group (see below). Instead, the parameter $\tilde{\xi}_{cpu}^v$ represents the fraction of CPU guaranteed to the VMs by the group membership.

We assume a shared network storage because the VM live migration works only in this case. For this reason, the resources required by the VM do not include the storage requirements.

We consider the following power-aware labels:

red for very critical entities (e.g., they are currently processing medium/high loads, and/or there are tight QoS constraints on availability, processing, bandwidth, latency);

yellow for busy entities that are not operating close to their performance limit (e.g., they are currently processing low loads, and QoS constraints are largely met);

green for low-load entities (e.g., they are not currently processing anything or have a very low load, and there are negligible risks of SLA violations).

Based on the above classification, we define a set of groups $\mathbb{G}$ where each group g is described by the properties reported in Table 3. With the parameter ξ_{cpu}^g, we indicate the fraction of CPU guaranteed to the VMs. Based on this model, the parameter $\tilde{\xi}_{cpu}^v$ of Table 2 can be defined as

$$\tilde{\xi}_{cpu}^v := \xi_{cpu}^g \,|\, \delta_v = g \in \mathbb{G} \quad \forall v \in \mathbb{V} \tag{2}$$

Table 3. Group properties.

Parameter	Description
ξ_{name}^g	Name of the group $g \in \mathbb{G}$ (*red*, *yellow* or *green*)
$\xi_{cpu}^g \in [0,1]$	Fraction of CPU guaranteed to the VMs belonging to the group $g \in \mathbb{G}$

3.3 Request Arrival and Departure Process

In this paper, we consider requests from tenants, which are generated randomly; where the arrival and departure process is assumed to follow an exponential distribution. The generic request r specified by a tenant consists of a new set of VMs $\mathbb{V}^{(r)}$. This set includes the same requirements defined in Table 2.

In addition, the request r arrives and has a duration in the interval $[0, T]$. For the sake of simplicity, we define the set of all requests as $\mathbb{R}$, with $r \in \mathbb{R}$.

The proposed request model differs from other works mainly in consideration of the *time* dimension. Unlike the work in [21], in this paper, we consider the time dimension in a continuous domain where the request can include VMs with different duration times.

3.4   Power Model

We consider a multi-component utilization-based power model, which defines the power consumption of a data center according to the resource utilization of servers and network devices. According to the typical non-linear behavior of power consumption for ICT devices [22,23], we define the power consumption of a device (server or network device) as a function of resource utilization U_m, which is the percentage of CPU utilization for servers and the fraction of active ports for network devices.

We identify three different power states: (i) *standby* $-\Gamma_{\text{stdby}}$, when the device is sleeping (equivalent to the ACPI S3 state); (ii) *idle* $-\Gamma_{\text{idle}}$, when the device is switched on but no operation is being carried out; and (iii) *active* $-\Gamma_{\text{act}}$, when the device is switched on and it performs operations.

Table 4. Power model notation.

Parameter	Description
Γ_{stdby}	Standby power state where the device is sleeping
Γ_{idle}	Idle power state where the device is switched on but no operation is begin carried out
Γ_{act}	Active power state where the device is switched on and performs operations
$\Gamma_{\text{ps}}^m \in \{\Gamma_{\text{stdby}}, \Gamma_{\text{idle}}, \Gamma_{\text{act}}\}$	Current power state configuration of the node $m \in \mathbb{M}$
$\Gamma_{\text{wu}}^m \in \{0, 1\}$	Indicates if the device $m \in \mathbb{M}$ has to wake-up changing the power state from standby to active/idle due to the last execution of the consolidation algorithm (see Sect. 4 for more details)
$\Gamma_{\text{slp}}^m \in \{0, 1\}$	Indicates if the device $m \in \mathbb{M}$ has to sleep changing the power state from active/idle to standby due to the last execution of the consolidation algorithm (see Sect. 4 for more details)
$\Phi_m^{\star}$	Standby power consumption of the device $m \in \mathbb{M}$
Φ_m°	Idle power consumption of the device $m \in \mathbb{M}$
$\Phi_m^{\bullet}$	Power consumption of the device $m \in \mathbb{M}$ at full load
$\Phi_m\left(U_m, \Gamma_{\text{ps}}^m\right)$	Current power consumption of the device $m \in \mathbb{M}$ according to the utilization U_m and the power state Γ_{ps}^m

To represent the current power consumption, it is necessary to define the power state configuration of a device $m \in \mathbb{M}$ as $\Gamma_{ps}^{m} \in \{\Gamma_{stdby}, \Gamma_{idle}, \Gamma_{act}\}$. In addition, for the execution of the proposed consolidation algorithm described in Sect. 4, we introduce the binary variables Γ_{wu}^{m} and Γ_{slp}^{m} that indicate if the device has to *wake-up* (changing the power state from standby to active/idle) or *sleep* (changing the power state from active/idle to standby), respectively. Table 4 summarizes all the described parameters.

As a result, the total power consumption of device $m \in \mathbb{M}$ can be determined by a function $\Phi_m(U_m, \Gamma_{ps}^{m})$:

$$\Phi_m(U_m, \Gamma_{ps}^{m}) = \begin{cases} \Phi_m^{\star} & \text{if} \quad \Gamma_{ps}^{m} = \Gamma_{stdby} \\ \Phi_m^{\circ} & \text{if} \quad \Gamma_{ps}^{m} = \Gamma_{idle} \\ \Phi_m^{\circ} + U_m \cdot & \\ (\Phi_m^{\bullet} - \Phi_m^{\circ}) & \text{if} \quad \Gamma_{ps}^{m} = \Gamma_{act} \end{cases} \tag{3}$$

where $\Phi_m^{\star}$, Φ_m° are the standby and idle power consumption, respectively; while $\Phi_m^{\bullet}$ is the power consumption at full load.

4   Consolidation Algorithm

Roughly speaking, our target is the design of a consolidation strategy that:

- keeps *red* VMs on the smallest number of servers, while assuring enough resources are provisioned to meet their stringent QoS requirements;
- groups *yellow* VMs together on the smallest number of servers, even on the same servers as *red* VMs if enough resources are available;
- distributes *green* components among all servers, with no stringent constraints on grouping the largest number of them together, since servers hosting *green* components only will sleep;
- places VMs according to the total power consumption of active servers, network devices, and network links, in order to minimize the power consumption of the overall underlying data center infrastructure.

Despite the complexity and the dimensions of the problem and similar to works in the literature [4, 13, 20], we formulated the proposed consolidation strategy as a global optimization procedure with the aim to find a best possible trade-off between the (i) placement allocation and the (ii) network path selection.

The placement allocation identifies the group of servers where to allocate the VMs to satisfy the resource requirements described in Sect. 3.2. We want to guarantee the performance in terms of QoS or SLA and with the objective to minimize the total power consumption of servers. Instead, the selection of the network path is performed to satisfy the traffic requirements between the VMs in order to guarantee the necessary bandwidth and minimizing the total power consumption of network devices.

Due to the arrival and departure process of the requests and the complexity of the optimization procedure, it is difficult to find an optimal solution in a reasonable period of time. For this reason, the optimization procedure is solved using various methods based on heuristics obtaining a sub-optimal solution as close as possible to the optimal one (see Sect. 4 for more details). It is important to note that there is not always a solution that satisfies the constraints. For this reason, the optimization procedure tries to place the largest number of VMs rejecting the other ones.

The strategy is shown in Algorithm 1. It starts with the deletion of the terminated VMs from the set $\mathbb{V}$ calling the REMOVETERMINATEDVM function (line 5). After this step, in line 5, it is called the OPTIMIZATION function that returns the updated set of the allocated VMs in the set $\mathbb{V}$. With the updated set of VMs, the consolidation algorithm updates the power state configuration of servers and network devices calling the POWERSTATEUPDATE function (line 7). Finally, it updates the network path set $\mathbb{P}$ calling the NETWORKPATHUPDATE function (line 8).

Algorithm 1. Consolidation

Require:
1: sets of allocated VMs $\mathbb{V}$ and requested VMs $\mathbb{V}^{(r)}$
2: sets of servers $\mathbb{S}$ and network machines $\mathbb{N}$
3: set of network paths $\mathbb{P}$

4: **function** CONSOLIDATION($\mathbb{V}, \mathbb{V}^{(r)}, \mathbb{S}, \mathbb{N}, \mathbb{P}$)
5:     $\mathbb{V} \leftarrow$ REMOVETERMINATEDVM($\mathbb{V}$)
6:     $\mathbb{V} \leftarrow$ OPTIMIZATION($\mathbb{V}, \mathbb{V}^{(r)}, \mathbb{S}, \mathbb{N}, \mathbb{P}$)
7:     $(\mathbb{S}, \mathbb{N}) \leftarrow$ POWERSTATEUPDATE($\mathbb{V}, \mathbb{S}, \mathbb{N}$)
8:     $\mathbb{P} \leftarrow$ NETWORKPATHUPDATE($\mathbb{S}, \mathbb{N}$)
9:     **return** $\mathbb{V}, \mathbb{S}, \mathbb{N}, \mathbb{P}$

4.1   Remove Terminated VMs

This procedure removes the terminated VMs considering the arrival and duration time information. It returns an updated set of the allocated VMs $\mathbb{V}$ as shown in Algorithm 2.

4.2   Optimization Algorithm

We formulate the optimization algorithm as a function that returns the set of the allocated VMs. The problem aims to minimize the total power consumption of servers and network devices; while satisfying the resource constraints (in terms of CPUs, RAM, and network bandwidth) of the incoming requests as reported in (4–14).

(4) consists of the minimization of the power consumption of the servers and network devices with respect to the variables x_v (with $v \in \mathbb{V}^{(r)}$) and $y_{v_1}^{v_2}$ (with $v_1, v_2 \in \mathbb{V}^{(r)}$), respectively; while (5–14) represents the constraints.

Algorithm 2. Remove Terminated VMs

Require:

1: set of allocated VMs $\mathbb{V}$

2: **function** REMOVETERMINATEDVM($\mathbb{V}$)
3:     $\tilde{\mathbb{V}} \leftarrow \emptyset$
4:     **for all** $v \in \mathbb{V}$ **do**
5:         **if** $\Psi_{\text{start}}^v + \Psi_{\text{dur}}^v > t$ **then**
6:             $\tilde{\mathbb{V}} \leftarrow v$
7:     **return** $\tilde{\mathbb{V}}$

Table 5. Optimization parameters.

Parameter	Description
$\vec{x}_*$	Maximum allowed percentage of VM migrations
$\vec{y}_*$	Maximum allowed percentage of re-routing of network communication between VMs
Γ_{chg}^*	Maximum allowed percentage of node power state reconfigurations

$$\min_{\substack{x_v \mid v \in \mathbb{V}^{(r)} \cup \mathbb{V} \\ y_{v_1}^{v_2} \mid v_1, v_2 \in \mathbb{V}^{(r)} \cup \mathbb{V}}} \sum_{s \in \mathbb{S}} \Phi_s(U_s, \Gamma_{\text{ps}}^s) + \sum_{n \in \mathbb{N}} \Phi_n(U_n, \Gamma_{\text{ps}}^n) \tag{4}$$

$$x_v \in \mathbb{S} \cup \emptyset \quad \forall v \in \mathbb{V}^{(r)} \tag{5}$$

$$y_{v_1}^{v_2} \in \mathbb{P} \cup \emptyset \quad \forall v_1, v_2 \in \mathbb{V}^{(r)} \tag{6}$$

$$\sum_{v \in \mathbb{V}^{(r)} \mid x_v = s} \Psi_{\text{cpu}}^v \times \tilde{\xi}_{\text{cpu}}^v \leq C_{\text{cpu}}^s - \sum_{v \in \mathbb{V} \mid x_v = s} \Psi_{\text{cpu}}^v \times \tilde{\xi}_{\text{cpu}}^v \quad \forall s \in \mathbb{S} \tag{7}$$

$$\sum_{v \in \mathbb{V}^{(r)} \mid x_v = s} \Psi_{\text{ram}}^v \leq C_{\text{ram}}^s - \sum_{v \in \mathbb{V} \mid x_v = s} \Psi_{\text{ram}}^v \quad \forall s \in \mathbb{S} \tag{8}$$

$$\sum_{v_1, v_2 \in \mathbb{V}^{(r)} \mid e \in y_{v_1}^{v_2}} \Psi_{\text{bw}}^{(v_1, v_2)} \leq C_{\text{bw}}^m - \sum_{v_1, v_2 \in \mathbb{V} \mid e \in y_{v_1}^{v_2}} \Psi_{\text{bw}}^{(v_1, v_2)} \quad \forall e \in \mathbb{E} \tag{9}$$

$$\frac{\sum_{v \in \mathbb{V}} \vec{x}_v}{|\mathbb{V}|} \leq \frac{\vec{x}_*}{100} \tag{10}$$

$$\frac{\sum_{v_1, v_2 \in \mathbb{V}} \vec{y}_{v_1}^{v_2}}{|\mathbb{P}|} \leq \frac{\vec{y}_*}{100} \tag{11}$$

$$\sum_{m \in \mathbb{M}} \Gamma_{\text{wu}}^m + \Gamma_{\text{slp}}^m \leq \Gamma_{\text{chg}}^* \tag{12}$$

$$U_s = \frac{\sum_{v \in \mathbb{V}^{(r)} \cup \mathbb{V} | x_v \in \mathbb{V}} \Psi_{\text{cpu}}^v \times \tilde{\xi}_{\text{cpu}}^v}{C_{\text{cpu}}^s} \qquad \forall s \in \mathbb{S} \qquad (13)$$

$$U_n = \frac{1}{\sigma_n} \times \sum_{e \in \mathbb{E} | C_{\text{src}}^e = n} \text{sgn}\left(C_u^e + C_u^{\bar{e}}\right) \qquad \forall n \in \mathbb{N} \qquad (14)$$

The first two Eqs. (5–6) represents the constraints related to the domains of the problems variables x_v (5), and $y_{v_1}^{v_2}$ (6). It is important to remember, that the optimization procedure tries to place the greatest possible number of VMs selecting the network path that guarantees the required bandwidth with the minimum impact on the global power consumption. However, it could happen that it is not possible to place some VMs. For this reason, the domains of the problem variables include the empty value ($\emptyset$), too.

The next two Eqs. (7–8) ensure that the VMs are placed on servers with sufficient available space for the requested resources (CPU and RAM, respectively). It is important to note that it is guaranteed only the CPU fraction $\tilde{\xi}_{\text{cpu}}^v$ for each VM $v \in \mathbb{V}$.

(9) guarantees that the total bandwidth to allocate is less or equal to the link capacity minus the bandwidth of the VMs already allocated.

Instead, (10–11) ensure a maximum percentage of migrations of VMs and re-routing of traffic between VMs, respectively. They use the parameters shown in Table 5. (12) guarantees a maximum percentage of power state transitions (wake-up and sleeping) for all the nodes in the data center (servers and network devices).

Finally, the last two Eqs. (13–14) are used to compute the utilization level of the server $s \in \mathbb{S}$ as a fraction of the CPU utilized by the VMs, and of the network device $n \in \mathbb{N}$ as a fraction of the utilized ports, respectively.

4.3   Search Methods and Heuristics

To implement the optimization algorithm we used the Optaplanner constraint satisfaction solver [24]. This framework supports three families of optimization algorithms: Exhaustive Search (ES), Construction Heuristics (CH) and Meta-Heuristics (MH).

The algorithms of the ES family always find the global optimum and recognize it too. However, they do not scale (not even beyond small data sets) and they are mostly useless. Indeed, they suffer scalability issues regarding memory and performance. In our simulation, we consider the MH family (in combination with CH ones to initialize) which are the recommended choice to deliver a good result in a reasonable period of time.

In more details, the CH build a pretty good initial solution in a finite length of time. Its solution is not always feasible, but it finds it fast so MH can finish the job. The heuristic types considered in this work are summarized in Table 6.

Table 6. Meta-Heuristics algorithm types.

Name	Description
Hill Climbing (HC)	Select the change respect to the initial configuration that performs the minimum cost. It can easily get stuck in a local optimum. This happens when it reaches a solution for which all the moves increase the cost [25]
Tabu Search (TS)	Maintains a tabu list to avoid local optimum. The tabu list holds recently used objects that are taboo to use for now. Changes that involve an object in the tabu list are not accepted [26, 27]
Simulated Annealing (SA)	Evaluates only a few changes per step. The first accepted change is the winning step. A change is accepted if does not increase the cost [28]
Late Acceptance (LA)	Evaluates only a few changes per step. A change is accepted if it does not increase the cost, or if it leads to a cost that is at least the minimum one of a fixed number of steps ago [29]

Start from an initial solution evolving into a mostly better solution

4.4 Power State Update

After the execution of the optimization problem, it is necessary to update the power state configuration of servers and network devices in the data center in order to put in standby states the inactive devices. As shown in Algorithm 3, this function is separated into two parts: (i) server update and (ii) network update. The former part is realized calling the Function POWERSTATESERVERUPDATE (lines 7–15) that updates the power state of the servers in the following ways:

sleep transition for servers in the active state without VMs belonging to the *red* or *yellow* groups (lines 12–14);

wake-up transition for servers in the standby state with at least one VMs belonging to the *red* or *yellow* groups (lines 12–14).

As consequence of this step, it is possible to update the power state configuration of the network devices, too. To be more precise, it is called the Function POWERSTATENETWORKUPDATE (lines 16–24) that updates the network devices in the following ways:

sleep transition for network devices with traffic utilization level equal to 0 for all the connected link interfaces (lines 9–11);

wake-up transition for network devices with positive traffic utilization level for at least one connected link interface (lines 21–23).

It is important to remember that the VMs belonging the green group do not perform any elaboration, so the traffic utilization level of a link C_u^e can be positive only for the contribution of the VMs belonging to the *red* or *yellow* groups.

Algorithm 3. Power State Update

Require:
1: set of allocated VMs $\mathbb{V}$
2: sets of servers $\mathbb{S}$ and network machines $\mathbb{N}$

3: **function** POWERSTATEUPDATE($\mathbb{V}, \mathbb{S}, \mathbb{N}$)
4:     $\mathbb{S} \leftarrow$ POWERSTATESERVERUPDATE($\mathbb{V}, \mathbb{S}$)
5:     $\mathbb{N} \leftarrow$ POWERSTATENETWORKUPDATE($\mathbb{N}$)
6:     **return** $\mathbb{S}, \mathbb{N}$

7: **function** POWERSTATESERVERUPDATE($\mathbb{V}, \mathbb{S}$)
8:     **for all** $s \in \mathbb{S}$ **do**
9:         **if** $\Gamma_{ps}^s = \Gamma_{act}$ **then**
10:             **if** $\neg\exists v \in \mathbb{V} | x_v = s \wedge \delta_v = g \wedge \xi_{name}^g = red$ **then**
11:                 $\Gamma_{ps}^s \leftarrow \Gamma_{stdby}$
12:         **else if** $\Gamma_{ps}^s = \Gamma_{stdby}$ **then**
13:             **if** $\exists v \in \mathbb{V} | x_v = s \wedge \delta_v = g \wedge \xi_{name}^g \neq green$ **then**
14:                 $\Gamma_{ps}^s \leftarrow \Gamma_{act}$
15:     **return** $\mathbb{S}$

16: **function** POWERSTATENETWORKUPDATE($\mathbb{N}$)
17:     **for all** $n \in \mathbb{N}$ **do**
18:         **if** $\Gamma_{ps}^n = \Gamma_{act}$ **then**
19:             **if** $\neg\exists e \in \mathbb{E} | n \in C_{node}^e \wedge C_u^e > 0$ **then**
20:                 $\Gamma_{ps}^n \leftarrow \Gamma_{stdby}$
21:         **else if** $\Gamma_{ps}^n = \Gamma_{stdby}$ **then**
22:             **if** $\exists e \in \mathbb{E} | n \in C_{node}^e \wedge C_u^e > 0$ **then**
23:                 $\Gamma_{ps}^n \leftarrow \Gamma_{act}$
24:     **return** $\mathbb{N}$

4.5   Network Path Update

The change of the power state configuration of servers and network devices makes necessary to update the network paths composing the set $\mathbb{P}$ in order to remove the paths with nodes in standby mode. To implement this procedure in order to perform a fast execution, we use a reference set $\mathbb{P}$ computed at the beginning (before to start the simulation, when all the devices are in standby mode). Each time this function is called, the updated set is computed considering only the paths with at least one node in the active state (Algorithm 4).

5   Performance Evaluation

In this section, we validate the effectiveness of the proposed algorithm using simulation and numerical results. We show the efficiency of the consolidation algorithm based on different heuristics to process the incoming VM allocation requests, and the impact of the migration regarding power, energy-saving, and resource overhead.

Algorithm 4. Network Path Update

Require:
1: reference set of network paths $\tilde{\mathbb{P}}$
2: sets of servers $\mathbb{S}$ and network machines $\mathbb{N}$

3: **function** NETWORKPATHUPDATE($\mathbb{S}, \mathbb{N}$)
4:      $\mathbb{P} \leftarrow \emptyset$
5:      **for all** $p \in \tilde{\mathbb{P}}$ **do**
6:          **if** $\exists e \in p \,|\, m \in C^e_{\text{node}} \wedge \Gamma^m_{\text{ps}} \neq \Gamma_{\text{stdby}}$ **then**
7:              $\mathbb{P} \leftarrow p$
8:      **return** $\mathbb{P}$

5.1   Simulation Settings

As in [21], we consider a multi-rooted hierarchical topology that connects the switches in three layers (Core, Aggregation, and Edge). A group of servers in a rack is connected to an edge layer switch, which in turn is connected to aggregation switches at the next layer. Each aggregation switch is connected to a group of core switches in the next layer which in turn are attached to some front-end servers for connecting to the external clients. In particular, we choose a DCN (Data-Center Network) with fat-three topology [30,31].

In our simulation, we choose $k = 8$ with a total number of switches and servers equal to 80 and 128, respectively and with 1 Gbps capacity set for the links. We assign for each server the same amount of resources: 128 GB of RAM and 32 CPUs per server.

For the power values, we follow the references [16,21,23,32,33], where the edge, aggregation, and core switches have: (i) the idle power usage of 76.40 W, 133.50 W, and 555 W; and (ii) the maximum power usage at full load of 102 W, 175 W, and 656 W; respectively. Instead, for the standby power usage, considering that most of the components are disabled and only the RAM is on, the power consumption is usually less than 5 W for all the switches.

As described in [21], it has been observed that a server with two cores consumes 170 W and 220 W in the idle and fully utilized states, respectively. Since these power values have a direct relationship with the number of its cores [23], we scale up the server's power based on its resources considered in our simulations. Accordingly, the power usage of a server with 32 CPUs in idle and fully utilized states is 2720 W and 3520 W, respectively. Similar to the switch case, also for the server the standby power is less than 5 W.

For what concerns the set of groups $\mathbb{G}$ and its relative properties ξ^g_{cpu} we consider the following values. For the VMs of the *red* group, it is guaranteed the total amount of CPU, and they have to be placed with a maximum distance of 1 hop. Instead, for the VMs of the *yellow* group, it is guaranteed a reduced fraction of CPU: 0.2 and they have to be placed with a maximum distance of 5 hops. Finally, for the VMs of the *green* group, it not guaranteed a fraction of CPU, and they can be placed without constraints about the distance.

5.2   Metrics

To make an exhaustive analysis of the performance evaluation of the proposed consolidation algorithm for all the heuristics described Sect. 4.3, we take into account the following metrics: (i) *energy savings*, computed considering the power consumption of the Data center without energy savings mechanisms enabled (e.g. frequency/voltage scaling and sleep states) but still proportional to the resource utilization; (ii) *acceptance rate*, in terms of the average percentage of the accepted VM requests per seconds; and (iii) *migration rate*, in terms of the average percentage of the performed VM migrations per seconds.

5.3   Scenario

We choose a simulation time of $T = 24$ h. Unlike other works [21], in this paper, the simulation time domain is continuous. Hence, a new request can arrive at any time between 0 and 24 h. In order to compare the performance of the proposed consolidation algorithm with the different mentioned heuristics, we consider the following scenario. The mean arrival rate of the incoming requests follows the profile shown in Fig. 1. There are three areas characterized by three different levels of average incoming requests per second. The lowest values (≈ 400 requests per second) occur in the first part from 0:00 to 8:00. Instead, in the second part of the trace, the number of requests per seconds is approximately equal to 800. Finally, in the third part, the number of requests per second reaches the maximum value equal to 1200.

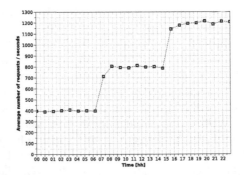

Fig. 1. Profile of the average number of requests per second.

In the literature, data center traffic characteristics at the packet level between switches have been studied, and traffic distribution such as exponential, Weibull, and log-normal have been reported [34, 35]. We choose the Log-normal distribution for the number of VMs for request. We vary the mean request duration in the range of [1, 10] seconds following a Log-normal distribution with mean equal to 5 s. All the parameters and distributions used in our simulations are reported in Table 7. With $\Psi_{\text{cpu}}^{\langle\mu\rangle}$, $\Psi_{\text{ram}}^{\langle\mu\rangle}$, and $\Psi_{\text{bw}}^{\langle\mu\rangle}$, we refer to the mean of the distributions of the resources required by the VMs (CPUs, RAM, and bandwidth, respectively). Finally, the upper bounds for the migrations of VMs, the re-routing of traffic between VMs and the power state transitions we choose 25%, 15%, and 25%, respectively.

Table 7. Configuration parameters used in the simulation.

Parameter	Value		
T	24 h		
Parameter	Value	Distribution	Range
μ_{vm}^{τ}	20 VMs	Log-normal	$[0, 40]$ VMs
μ_{dur}^{τ}	5 s	Log-normal	$[1, 10]$ seconds
$\Psi_{\text{cpu}}^{\langle\mu\rangle}$	3 CPUs	Log-normal	$[0, 10]$ CPUs
$\Psi_{\text{ram}}^{\langle\mu\rangle}$	20 GB	Log-normal	$[1, 10]$ GB
$\Psi_{\text{bw}}^{\langle\mu\rangle}$	100 Mbps	Log-normal	$[0, 200]$ Mbps
$\vec{x}_{*}$	25%		
$\vec{y}_{*}$	15%		
Γ_{chg}^{*}	25%		

Instead, the VM group membership is assigned based on the Uniform distribution probability (*red*: 20%, *yellow*: 50%, and *green*: 30%).

5.4   Numerical Results

We wrote an event simulator in Java using the Optaplanner constraint satisfaction solver [24] to evaluate the proposed algorithm. We validated the effectiveness of our energy-aware consolidation algorithm through a comparison of the different heuristics with the results obtained maximizing only the performance.

We carry out the experiments for a sufficient number of times to get small errors representing the 95% Confidence Interval (CIs). The measured CIs have not been reproduced in the graphs since all of them are small and just clutter the figures.

Figure 2 displays the average percentage of the energy savings. Considering that the proposed algorithm has the objective to minimize the power consumption limiting the degradation of the performance, the results show a maximum energy saving of more than the 50% with the LA heuristics. In general, there is a significant saving of power consumption when the traffic load is low. Compared to the other heuristics, HC obtains worst results because that can easily get stuck in local optima. For this reason, to avoid the problem of local minima, the other heuristics implement more advanced solutions. In particular, with a low number of requests, in the LA case the energy savings is stable with values higher than 20%. It is important to note how the trend, varying the request rate, is much more variable for the TS, SA and LA heuristics compared to the HC one. Indeed, these heuristics provide mechanisms to explore the search space in a better way. However, even with these methods, it is difficult to find a global minimum.

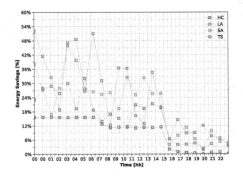

Fig. 2. Average percentage of the energy savings.

The acceptance rate in shown in Fig. 3. The difference between the TS, SA and LA heuristics are not as significant as in the case of the energy savings. The trend of the acceptance rate varies widely for the HC, too. Obviously, the problem of the local minima impacts also the acceptance rate. Indeed, for high values of incoming requests, HC presents an acceptance rate below 74% compared to the 86% of the TS case. An interesting point is the fact that TS and SA behave relatively better than LA (especially with a high number of requests). Most likely, the advanced solutions introduced by LA allow obtaining better results from the point of view of optimization (less power consumption) at the cost of a worse allocation of the resources.

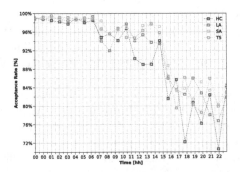

Fig. 3. Average percentage of the accepted requests per second.

The migration rate in shown in Fig. 4. The results are qualitatively significant only with a high number of incoming requests per second (the last part of the trace). With low/medium values of request rate, the differences between the heuristics are practically near to zero. Instead, with high values, SA performs better with a migration rate below 10% in some cases. As described for the acceptance rate, also for this metric the LA behaves relatively worse than TS and SA.

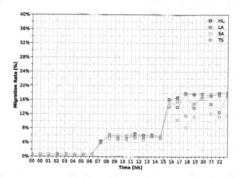

Fig. 4. Average percentage of the migrations performed per second.

6   Conclusions

In this work, we have proposed a new consolidation mechanism to reduce the power consumption in data centers. We have extended the state-of-the-art optimization problem, taking into account the presence of VMs with different roles in the overall service/application framework. The proposed approach allows to obtain high levels of energy saving, put to sleep servers that only host redundant software components.

Our consolidation strategy improves the efficiency of the infrastructure, with limited implications on the acceptance rate of auxiliary service requests. The next steps will be: (i) more rigorous integration between the server and network models, to obtain better power savings; (ii) design of a more advanced power model for network devices, considering the energy consumption for different operating rates; and (iii) detailed study and analysis of further heuristics, to find optimal allocations even with large data centers.

Acknowledgment. This work was partially supported by the European Commission under the projects ARCADIA (grant no. 607881) and INPUT (grant no. 644672).

References

1. Hammadi, A., Mhamdi, L.: A survey on architectures and energy efficiency in data center networks. Comput. Commun. **40**, 1–21 (2014)
2. Advanced configuration and power interface specification (2015). http://www.uefi. org/sites/default/files/resources/ACPI_6.0.pdf
3. Barroso, L.A., Hlzle, U.: The case for energy-proportional computing. Computer **40**(12), 33–37 (2007)
4. Stage, A., Setzer, T.: Network-aware migration control and scheduling of differentiated virtual machine workloads. In: Proceedings of the 2009 ICSE Workshop on Software Engineering Challenges of Cloud Computing (CLOUD), Vancouver, Canada, 23 May 2009, pp. 9–14 (2009)
5. Voorsluys, W., Broberg, J., Venugopal, S., Buyya, R.: Cost of virtual machine live migration in clouds: a performance evaluation. In: Jaatun, M.G., Zhao, G., Rong, C. (eds.) CloudCom 2009. LNCS, vol. 5931, pp. 254–265. Springer, Heidelberg (2009). doi:10.1007/978-3-642-10665-1_23
6. Herbst, N.R., Kounev, S., Reussner, R.: Elasticity in cloud computing: what it is, and what it is not. In: Proceedings of the 10th International Conference on Autonomic Computing (ICAC), San Jose, CA, USA, 24–28 June 2013, pp. 23–27 (2013)
7. Kliazovich, D., Bouvry, P.: DENS: data center energy-efficient network-aware scheduling. In: IEEE/ACM International Conference on Green Computer and Communication & IEEE/ACM International Conference on Cyber, Physical and Social Computing, Hangzhou, China, 18–20 December 2010, pp. 69–75 (2010)
8. Topology and orchestration specification for cloud applications. OASIS Standard, November 2013, version 1.0. http://docs.oasis-open.org/tosca/TOSCA/v1.0/os/ TOSCA-v1.0-os.pdf
9. Wettinger, J., Breitenbücher, U., Leymann, F.: Standards-based DevOps automation and integration using TOSCA. In: IEEE/ACM 7th International Conference on Utility and Cloud Computing (UCC), London, UK, 8–11 December 2014, pp. 59–68 (2014)
10. Balalaie, A., Heydarnoori, A., Jamshidi, P.: Microservices architecture enables devops: migration to a cloud-native architecture. IEEE Softw. **33**(3), 42–52 (2016)
11. Dragoni, N., Giallorenzo, S., Lafuente, A.L., Mazzara, M., Montesi, F., Mustafin, R., Safina, L.: Microservices: yesterday, today, and tomorrow. Cornell University Library, arXiv:1606.04036v1, June 2016
12. Srikantaiah, S., Kansal, A., Zhao, F.: Energy aware consolidation for cloud computing. In: Proceedings of the 2008 Conference on Power Aware Computer and Systems (HotPower 2008), San Diego, CA, USA, 7 December 2008 (2008)
13. Mishra, M., Sahoo, A.: On theory of VM placement: anomalies in existing methodologies and their mitigation using a novel vector based approach. In: IEEE International Conference on Cloud Computing (CLOUD), Bombay, Mumbai, India, 4–9 July 2011, pp. 275–282 (2011)
14. Geronimo, G.A., Werner, J., Westphall, C.B., Westphall, C.M., Defenti, L.: Provisioning and resource allocation for green clouds. In: The 12th International Conference on Network (ICN), Seville, Spain, 27 January-1 February 2013
15. Beloglazov, A., Buyya, R.: OpenStack Neat: a framework for dynamic and energy-efficient consolidation of virtual machines in OpenStack clouds. Conc. Comput. Pract. Exp. **27**(5), 1310–1333 (2015)

16. Heller, B., Seetharaman, S., Mahadevan, P., Yiakoumis, Y., Sharma, P., Banerjee, S., McKeown, N.: Elastictree: saving energy in data center networks. In: Proceedings of the 7th USENIX Conference on Network System Design and Implementation, ser. NSDI, p. 17. USENIX Association, Berkeley (2010)

17. Shirayanagi, H., Yamada, H., Kono, K.: Honeyguide: a VM migration-aware network topology for saving energy consumption in data center networks. In: IEEE IEEE Symposium on Computers and Communications (ISCC), Cappadocia, Turkey, 1–4 July 2012, pp. 460–467 (2012)

18. Wang, L., Zhang, F., Vasilakos, A.V., Hou, C., Liu, Z.: Joint virtual machine assignment and traffic engineering for green data center networks. ACM SIGMETRICS Perf. Eval. Rev. **41**(3), 107–112 (2013)

19. Zhang, Y., Ansari, N.: HERO: hierarchical energy opt. for data center networks. IEEE Syst. J. **9**(2), 406–415 (2015)

20. Fang, W., Liang, X., Li, S., Chiaraviglio, L., Xiong, N.: VMPlanner: optimizing virtual machine placement and traffic flow routing to reduce network power costs in cloud data centers. Comput. Netw. **57**(1), 179–196 (2013)

21. Dalvandi, A., Gurusamy, M., Chua, K.C.: Time-aware vmflow placement, routing, and migration for power efficiency in data centers. IEEE Trans. Netw. Serv. Man. **12**(3), 349–362 (2015)

22. Padala, P., Shin, K.G., Zhu, X., Uysal, M., Wang, Z., Singhal, S., Merchant, A., Salem, K.: Adaptive control of virtualized resources in utility computing environments. In: Proceedings of the 2Nd ACM SIGOPS/EuroSys European Conference on Computer Systems: ser. EuroSys 2007, pp. 289–302. ACM, New York (2007)

23. Mahadevan, P., Sharma, P., Banerjee, S., Ranganathan, P.: Energy aware network operations. In: Proceedings of the 28th IEEE International Conference on Computer Communication Workshops, ser. INFOCOM 2009, pp. 25–30. IEEE Press, Piscataway (2009)

24. Optaplanner - constraint satisfaction solver (java, open source) (2016). http://www.optaplanner.org

25. Russell, S.J., Norvig, P., Intelligence, A.: A Modern Approach, 2nd edn. Pearson Education, Upper Saddle River (2003)

26. Glover, F.: Tabu search part I. ORSA J. Comput. **1**(3), 190–206 (1989)

27. Glover, F.: Tabu searchpart II. ORSA J. Comput. **2**(1), 4–32 (1990)

28. Khachaturyan, A., Semenovsovskaya, S., Vainshtein, B.: The thermodynamic approach to the structure analysis of crystals. Acta Crystallogr. Sect. A **37**(5), 742–754 (1981)

29. Burke, E.K., Bykov, Y.: The late acceptance hill-climbing heuristic. Europ. J. Opt. Res. **258**(1), 70–78 (2017)

30. Al-Fares, M., Loukissas, A., Vahdat, A.: A scalable, commodity data center network architecture. SIGCOMM Comput. Commun. Rev. **38**(4), 63–74 (2008)

31. Niranjan Mysore, R., Pamboris, A., Farrington, N., Huang, N., Miri, P., Radhakrishnan, S., Subramanya, V., Vahdat, A.: Portland: a scalable fault-tolerant layer 2 data center network fabric. SIGCOMM Comput. Commun. Rev. **39**(4), 39–50 (2009)

32. Mahadevan, P., Sharma, P., Banerjee, S., Ranganathan, P.: A power benchmarking framework for network devices. In: Fratta, L., Schulzrinne, H., Takahashi, Y., Spaniol, O. (eds.) NETWORKING 2009. LNCS, vol. 5550, pp. 795–808. Springer, Heidelberg (2009). doi:10.1007/978-3-642-01399-7_62

33. Nam, T.M., Thanh, N.H., Thu, N.Q., Hieu, H.T., Covaci, S.: Energy-aware routing based on power profile of devices in data center networks using SDN. In: 2015 12th International Conference on Electrical Engineering/Electronics Computer, Telecommunication and nformation Technology (ECTI-CON), pp. 1–6, June 2015
34. Benson, T., Anand, A., Akella, A., Zhang, M.: Understanding data center traffic characteristics. SIGCOMM Comput. Commun. Rev. **40**(1), 92–99 (2010)
35. Benson, T., Akella, A., Maltz, D.A.: Network traffic characteristics of data centers in the wild. In: Proceedings of the 10th ACM SIGCOMM Conference on International Measures, ser. IMC 2010, pp. 267–280. ACM, New York (2010)

Implementing a Per-Flow Token Bucket Using Open Packet Processor

Giuseppe Bianchi, Marco Bonola, Valerio Bruschi, Luca Petrucci, and Salvatore Pontarelli[✉]

CNIT, Universitá di Roma Tor Vergata, Rome, Italy
{giuseppe.bianchi,marco.bonola,valerio.bruschi,
luca.petrucci,salvatore.pontarelli}@uniroma2.it

Abstract. In this paper we show how to realize a per-flow QoS (Quality of Service) policy based on the token bucket algorithm using OPP (Open Packet Processor), a recently proposed stateful programmable dataplane. OPP is configured as a switch that enforce a token bucket policy independently on each flow processed by the switch controlling their bandwidth and burstiness. The paper shows the design of the token bucket algorithm using the extended finite state machine (EFSM) abstraction provided by OPP and discusses the details of the implementation carried out using a proof-of-concept FPGA prototype of the OPP pipeline.

1 Introduction

There is a strong interest both in the academic and industrial community in the design of programmable dataplanes able to sustain very high throughput while maintaining a large degree of flexibility. The availability of such platforms would allow network engineers to develop network functions (NFs) directly in the dataplane. Several novel architectures for programmable dataplanes has been recently proposed such as RMT [1], Intel's FlexPipe [2] and Cavium Xpliant [3]. One of the main challenges of programmable dataplanes belongs to the lack of a clear abstraction to provide stateful processing in the dataplane. Several attempts has been recently made to include stateful processing in the switch architecture pipeline for example using atomic operations to store state variables [4] or specifying the state handling primitives as vendor specific external libraries as done in the last draft of the P4 language specification [5]. Another work focusing on this topic is OpenState [7], which differs from the previous work since inherently provides a association between the flow definition (the header fields used to identify a flow) and the state associated to the identified flow. Moreover, it rely on the use of a Finite State Machine (FSM) to describe the evolution of the per-flow state stored in the switch. OPP [8] is a major upgrade of the OpenState concept that provide an extended finite state machine (EFSM) abstraction to describe the network function that the programmable dataplane must execute. In this paper we present the detailed implementation of a QoS policy based on the token bucket algorithm. This application exploits several

© Springer International Publishing AG 2017
A. Piva et al. (Eds.): TIWDC 2017, CCIS 766, pp. 251–262, 2017.
DOI: 10.1007/978-3-319-67639-5_18

characteristics of the OPP architecture therefore allows showing the versatility of the proposed model. In particular, it is a stateful application that requires: to store a per-flow state corresponding to the number of tokens in a bucket, (ii) to compute directly in the data path some arithmetic operations (comparison, addition/subtractions), and (iii) to define a suitable mechanism to manage deletion of expired flows.

The implementation we present here has been successfully deployed for the final demonstration of the BEBA (Behavioral Based Forwarding) H2020 project, in which the token bucket algorithm has been configured on top of the OPP prototype. The prototype was tested using the CESNET academic network (>400'000 users) and monitoring the 10 Gbps Prague-Amsterdam link.

The reminder of this paper is organized as follows. Section 2 gives an overview of the reference programmable stateful data plane and Sect. 3 describes the FPGA based proof-of-concept. Section 4 describes the token bucket algorithm and discuss how to implement it in the OPP dataplane. Section 5 discusses an interesting aspect of the detailed implementation related to the management of expired flows. Section 6 concludes this work.

2   Open Packet Processor

Notable examples of stateful forwarding abstractions that provide the identification of state contexts are FAST [6] and OpenState [7]. OpenState recently evolved into the Open Packet Processor (OPP), which provides a more powerful abstraction while maintaining the core of the OpenState ideas. In OPP, Extended Finite State Machines (EFSM) are used to model stateful forwarding algorithms. Details on the OPP architecture are reported in [8]. In this section we give an overview of the architecture which is beneficial to later describe the implementation of the token bucket algorithm.

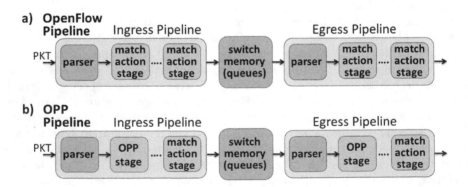

Fig. 1. (a) A typical OpenFlow pipeline architecture. (b) the OPP enabled pipeline. OPP "stages" can be pipelined with other OPP stages or ordinary OpenFlow Match/Action stages.

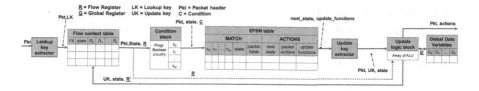

Fig. 2. Architecture of an OPP processing block

The OPP machine model extends the match-action tables (MATs) pipeline model assumed by OpenFlow. MATs are substituted with *stages*, which can be either stateless or stateful. A stateless stage is in fact an OpenFlow-like MAT. The pipeline processes packets' headers to define corresponding forwarding behaviors. OPP assumes packets headers are already parsed when passed to the pipeline, therefore, OPP can potentially leverage related work on programmable packet parsing and reconfigurable match tables [1,9]. A scheme of the OPP pipeline is shown in Fig. 1. The packets are processed by the ingress pipeline, that is composed by a parser stage and several stateless and stateful blocks, after the processed packet goes into the internal switch memory that holds the packet queues. At departure time, the packet is send to the egress pipeline that perform the processing associated to the output port. A stateful stage (Fig. 2) adds a number of elements to a plain MAT. The details of a stateful are presented in Fig. 2.

The first element of the OPP processing block is the **lookup extractor**. This element selects the header's fields that are used to build the flowkey ID. Using this ID, the flow context associated to this flow is retrieved from the **flow context table**. The extractor configuration is somewhat similar to the format of Protocol-Oblivious Forwarding (POF) element [10], as described in details in [11]. The flow context is composed by a state label, that identify the state associated to the flow, and a set of per-flow variables (called **flow registers**), which store information related to the history of the flow, such as examples the number of transmitted packets, or the timestamp of the last packet of the flow. OPP also has several **global registers** where are stored some information that shared among all the flows (e.g. the overall numbers of processed packets) and some metadata added by the parser stage (e.g. the switch input port or the packet timestamp). After the per-flow information are retrieved, OPP computes some "conditions" between the flow-registers, the global registers and the packet headers. These conditions are programmed inside the condition block. The conditions are the standard arithmetic comparison operations ($<, \leq, \geq, >, =, \neq$). The operands are selected using an extractor similar to the look-up extractor, which selects the input fields among the packet headers, the flow and global registers and the switch metadata. The output of the **condition block** forms a set of input signals that goes into the **EFSM table**. This table is the executor of the EFSM, computes the next state of the FSM starting from the packet headers and from the results of the arithmetic conditions, and select the actions to apply to the packets and the update functions that are used to update the values of the flow and global registers. The EFSM table is configured as a standard OpenFlow table and is usually realized in ASIC switches using TCAMs (Ternary Content addressable memories). The **update extractor** compute a flowkey ID to select which flow context should be updated. The use of two extractors, one for context reading and one for context update is useful for cross-state management, as discussed in details in [7]. For example, this feature allows implementing learning algorithms such as MAC learning or algorithm based on reverse path schemes [12]. Finally, the **update logic block** is in charge of actually execute the update functions and the actions to apply to the packet selected by the EFSM table.

3   NetFPGA Prototype

The OPP model presented in the previous section has been implemented using as target device an FPGA platform. The designed hardware prototype is conservative in terms of TCAM entries and clock frequency but it includes all the key OPP components and features. An OPP hardware prototype has been developed using the NetFPGA SUME [13] board. The SUME is an x8 Gen3 PCIe adapter card incorporating a Xilinx Virtex-7 690T FPGA [14], four SFP+ transceivers providing four 10GbE links, three 72 Mbits QDR II SRAM and two 4 GB DDR3 memories. The FPGA is clocked at 156.25 MHz, with a 64 bits data path from the Ethernet ports, corresponding to a 10 gbps throughput per port. The prototype can forward the packets of the 4 10GbE ports at line rate, providing a 156.25 Mpps (Million packets per second) throughput. The board is hosted by a linux workstation and a suitable device driver allows to expose the FPGA board as a 4-port ethernet NIC. The driver can be also used to configure the elements of the OPP stages (lookup/update, configuration of the state/flow tables of the OPP stages) implemented in the FPGA.

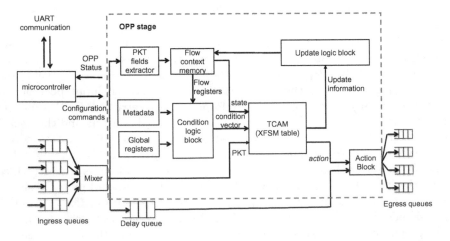

Fig. 3. Scheme of an OPP hardware prototype composed by only one stage

The prototype used for the implementation of the token bucket algorithm is shown in Fig. 3. As we will show, the FPGA has enough resources to implement several OPP stages (we implemented up to 6 stages in our experiments), but for sake of clarity we refer here to a simple implementation in which only one OPP stage is used. The OPP hardware prototype has four ingress queues, each one connected to the input of one of the 4 available 10 Gbps ports. The queues are connected to a round-robin mixer that collects the packets coming from the various interfaces and forward them to the OPP pipeline. In parallel, the mixer also stores the packets in the delay queue, which correspond to the switch memory queue depicted in the general pipeline architecture shown in Fig. 2. The OPP stage is composed of several blocks that implement the functions presented in the previous section. The PKT fields extractor provides the fields used for building the lookup flowkey, the update flowkey and some of the operand of the condition logic block. The metadata block provides other operands for the condition logic block, which in our implementation are the packet timestamp and the input port. The condition logic block and the update logic blocks implement the corresponding functions described in Sect. 2. In particular, the update logic block is realized using 5 parallel ALUs (Arithmetic-Logic Units) that perform a set of basic arithmetic and logic operations. The selection of the ALUs inputs is similar to those of the condition block, while the output can be a global or a flow register. The action block performs basic operations on the packets, which in our prototype are limited to drop/forward/flood a packet. The flow content memory is implemented using a multiple choice hash table and is implemented using the RAM blocks (BRAM) of the FPGA. A detailed description of the hash table can be retrieved in [11]. The EFSM table is implemented using very small TCAMs. That is, an EFSM TCAM has 32 entries of 160 bits. Indeed, TCAM implementation over FPGAs is very inefficient and is currently a widely open research issue [15–17]. Still, in [8], it is shown that this small number of TCAM entries can easily capture the implementation of an iptables interface. The microcontroller is used to configure the elements of the OPP stages and to perform some housekeeping task such as the eviction of the expired flows. To allow the configuration of the various elements of the OPP stage, all the configuration register/memories are memory mapped to the I/O memory space of the microcontroller. Since the OPP stages can be also configured directly from the linux workstation using the sume device driver, a suitable arbiter (not shown in figure) permit to manage the reading/writing operation on the OPP configuration memory. After the OPP stage, the packets are send to the egress queues, which are connected to the output of the 10 Gbps ports. The prototype fixes the parameters of the machine model as shown in Table 1.

The whole system has been synthesized using the standard Xilinx design flow. Table 2 reports the logic and memory resources (in terms of absolute numbers and fraction of available FPGA resources) used by an FPGA implementation that use only one OPP stage, and compare these results with those required for the NetFPGA SUME single-stage reference switch. The synthesis results confirm the trend already shown by [1]: the hardware area is dominated by memory, while

Table 1. Parameters of a stage of the OPP hardware prototype

Param.	Value	Descr.
k	4	Number of flow context's registers. Each register is 32 bit long
m	8	Each condition is in the form $var1$ op $var2$, with operand being one of $>$, $<$, $=$, and variables being packet header's fields, registers or constants
n	32	Size of packet's metadata moved between stages
h	8	Number or global registers. Each register is 32 bit long
ALUs	5	Number ALUs. Each ALU performs an operation in the form $res = var1$ op $var2$. res and $vars$ can be: global register, flow context's register or packet's fields (including metadata). op can be one of $+$, $-$, $shift$, etc.

Table 2. Hardware cost comparison of OPP and NetFPGA SUME ref. switch.

Resource type	Reference switch	OPP switch
# Slice LUTs	49436 (11%)	71712 (16%)
# Block RAMs	194 (13%)	393 (26%)

adding intelligence/features in the logic require a small silicon overhead. Notice that the reported resources include the overhead of several blocks, such as the microcontroller for OPP configuration, the input/output FIFO for the 10GbE interfaces etc., which are required to operate the FPGA and do not need to be replicated for each stage. In fact, given the required resources, a NetFPGA SUME can currently host up to 6 stateful OPP Stages.

4   Token Bucket Algorithm

In this section, we describe the implementation of a well know Quality of Service mechanism over the OPP pipeline switch, namely a token bucket based traffic policer. A traffic policer is a tool that limit the rate of incoming traffic by dropping (or in some marking) the portion of traffic not conform to a given traffic profile, usually defined as parameters of a single (dual) token bucket. A token bucket is a formal definition of a rate of transfer. It has three components: a burst size B, a mean rate R, and a time interval Q. The mean rate is generally represented as bits per second, and any of the three values may be derived from other twos by the following relation: $R = B/Q$. The token bucket algorithm is based on an analogy of a fixed capacity bucket into which tokens, normally representing a unit of bytes or packets, are added at a fixed rate R, and a maximum of B token can be contained in the bucket. When a packet arrives, it is forwarded only if the bucket contains sufficient tokens, otherwise it is discarded (or marked). If the packet is forwarded, the appropriate number of tokens, e.g. equivalent to the length of the

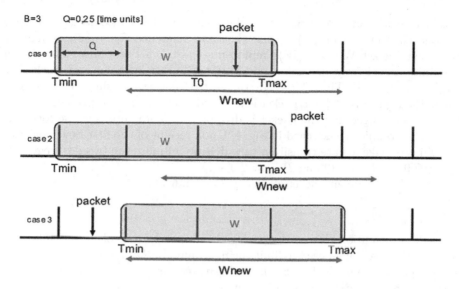

Fig. 4. Graphical representation of the token bucket mechanism.

packet in bytes, are removed. The algorithm allows forwarding flows with a rate up to the R at which the bucket is refilled, and also allows selecting the burstiness of the flow setting the maximum number of token that the bucket can contains.

The description of the token bucket algorithm cannot be directly implemented in the OPP architecture, due to two main reasons that we fill discuss soon (however, the same restrictions occur also in many others computing platforms). After, we will show how it is possible to transform the token bucket algorithm in an equivalent representation that is suitable for the OPP architecture. We believe that this is a interesting case to show how the flexibility of the OPP architecture can be used to implement different kind of algorithms. The token bucket algorithm requires to add a token to each bucket with a fixed rate. Since each bucket correspond to a memory location, this requires to allocate a not negligible memory bandwidth only to update the buckets, even if they are not actually accessed by any flow in the time window in which the bucket are updated. To supersede this limitation, the typical approach is to store in a memory location the timestamp of the last packet belonging to a flow and to update the number of tokens in a bucket only when a new packet arrives, computing the number of tokens to add, as the difference between the stored timestamp and the timestamp of the current packet multiplied by the token arrival rate. We remark that this limitation is not of the OPP architecture but depends on the bandwidth limits of memory devices. The second limitation is that in the OPP architecture the update functions are performed after the condition verification, therefore there is no way to check the current bucket level when a packet is received. For this reason, instead of computing the bucket level we compute for each flow and each packet received a time value (T_{min}) that represents the time instant after which the next packet can be transmitted. We also need to consider a second time instant (T_{max}) so that the time difference $T_{max} - T_{min}$ (namely the Token Bucket Window (W)) represents the token burst size expressed in time units. In this way, instead of updating the bucket level, for each packet we simply translate W. Thus, for each transmitted packet, we shift W by 1 time unit to the right. Instead, if a packet is received at a time instant preceding T_{min}, W is left unchanged and the packet is dropped. In more details we perform the operations graphically sketched in Fig. 4. Upon receipt of the first flow packet at time $T0$, we make a state transition in which we initialise the two flow registers: $T_{min} = T0 - (B - 1) \cdot Q$ and $T_{max} = T0 + Q$.

For each subsequent packet we verify the conditions:

- C0: $T_{now} \geq T_{min}$
- C1: $T_{now} \leq T_{max}$

The first condition ensures that the bucket has at least 1 token available. The second condition will be used to limit the maximum bucket level to B. Therefore, for each packet we might face the following three cases:

- Case 1: C0 == True AND C1 == True
- Case 2: C0 == True AND C1 == False
- Case 3: C0 == False

Case 1: Token available and packet arrival within the token bucket window. This case happens when a packet is received and both: (i) the bucket is not empty and (ii) the time difference between this packet and the previous one is less than the time necessary to fill the bucket. In this case we simply forward the packet and shift W by one token inter arrival time Q. These actions mimic the consumption of one token.

Case 2: Token available but packet arrival outside the token bucket window. This case happens when the bucket is not empty but the time interval between this packet and the previous one is greater than the time necessary to fill the bucket. In this case we cannot simply shift W by one token inter arrival time Q because this would make the token bucket exceed the burst size B. Thus, in this case we need to reset W as if the received packet was the first one of the flow.

Case 3: No token available. This case happens when a packet is received before T_{min}, i.e. when the bucket is empty. In this case we simply drop the packet. The detailed EFSM table representation is depicted in Fig. 5.

The flow memory registers R0, R1 are used to store respectively T_{min}, T_{max}. The global memory registers G0 and G1 are used to store $B \cdot Q$ and Q. The lookup and update extractors are both set to ip.src.

In Fig. 6 we show the temporal evolution of the input traffic, output traffic and bucket level for a simple token bucket with $B = 10$ and $Q = 1s$. The flow has an input rate of $4\,\mathrm{pkts/sec}$, and when the flow starts the output rate remains to $4\,\mathrm{pkts/sec}$ until the bucket is empty. This phase correspond to the allowed burst rate defined by the B parameter. When the bucket is empty, the system starts to drop packets, decreasing the output rate up to $1\,\mathrm{pkts/sec}$, which corresponds to the rate defined by the Q parameter.

c_0	c_1	state	packet fields	next state	packet actions	update functions
*	*	0	eth.type=IP	1	OUT	$R_0 = now - G_0$ $R_1 = now + G_1$
1	1	1	eth.type=IP	1	OUT	$R_0 = R_0 + G_1$ $R_1 = R_0 + G_1$
1	0	1	eth.type=IP	1	OUT	$R_0 = now - G_0$ $R_1 = now + G_1$
0	1	1	eth.type=IP	1	DROP	

Fig. 5. Token bucket XFSM.

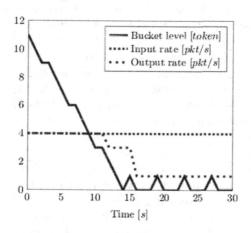

Fig. 6. Temporal evolution of a token bucket experiment.

5   Flow Expiration

The token bucket algorithm uses a flow context entry for each flow that goes into the switch. The flow context entries are stored in the on-chip memory of the OPP pipeline. Since on-chip memory is a limited resource, it is important to store into this memory only the flows that are actually travelling into the network, discarding as soon as possible the flows that are no more active.

However, due to the nature of the OPP machine model, the flow entries are updated by the OPP blocks only when a new packet arrives. This mechanism prevent to directly delete inactive flows, since the corresponding flow entries are never accessed. It is worth to notice that the OPP blocks provide a method to directly delete an flow entries, which for example can be used to remove expired flows of a TCP connection when the FIN, FIN/ACK sequence is received for the specific TCP flow. Instead, when the flow does not present an explicit termination condition (or the termination condition does not always occur correctly, like in the case of interrupted TCP connections) a different mechanism should be used. In particular, in OPP we defined a suitable "activity state" for each entry in the flow table. Each flow entry can be in one of the following "activity states": ACTIVE or INACTIVE. A flow entry is set in the ACTIVE by the OPP pipeline each time the entry is queried, and represents the flows that currently are transmitting packets. The flow entry that are in the ACTIVE state are set in the INACTIVE state by the microcontroller described in Sect. 3, which scans the flow entry table with a constant period T. The microcontroller also delete the entries that are in the INACTIVE state. This mechanism deletes all the entries that are not queried during the time interval T. The main drawback of this mechanism is that expired flows can remain into the flow context table for a period that is between T and $2T$. It is also difficult, for a general application to define the right value of T the identify an expired flow.

However, for the token bucket algorithm, a refined mechanism can be implemented. This mechanism is base on the consideration that the default state is identical to the case 2 described in Sect. 4. This case corresponds to a bucket that contains the maximum numbers of allowed token. In the sliding window representation this case occurs when the current timestamp is greater than the T_{max} value stored in the flow context. Hence, we can modify the scan procedure of the microcontroller to delete all the entries for which the T_{max} value is less than the current timestamp. When a packet belonging to this flow arrives, the OPP pipeline manage this as a new flow, but from the algorithm point of view the behaviour is the same, since both for a new flow, or for a flow belonging to case 2, the algorithm centers the sliding window around the packet timestamp.

This refined mechanism simplifies the flow expiration management and allows a faster cleaning of the flow context memory. Furthermore, it is compatible with the definition of multiple classes of token bucket policies (i.e. when the token bucket parameters are different for different classes of traffic), since the decision of deleting a flow depends on a per-flow value instead than a generic parameter as in the case of the ACTIVE/INACTIVE based method.

6   Conclusions

Programmable stateful dataplanes has becoming more and more important since they can be a optimal candidate solution to rapidly implement fast Network Functions. Programming these Network Functions requires both a suitable machine model that is able to process per-flow state information and a programming methodology that exploits the characteristics of the selected machine model. We shown in this paper an realistic example of a widely known QoS policy implemented using a programmable stateful dataplane. In particular, we show how to implement a token bucket algorithm using the Open Packet Processor as the target architecture. The paper first discusses the OPP characteristics needed to implement the token bucket algorithm and the corresponding FPGA prototype of OPP, and after presents the design choices that we did to develop the actual implementation.

Acknowledgement. This work is partially supported by the EU Commission in the frame of the Horizon 2020 projects BEBA (grant #644122) and SUPERFLUIDITY (grant #671566).

References

1. Bosshart, P., Gibb, G., Kim, H.S., Varghese, G., McKeown, N., Izzard, M., Mujica, F., Horowitz, M.: Forwarding metamorphosis: fast programmable match-action processing in hardware for SDN. In: Proceedings of the Conference on Applications, Technologies, Architectures, and Protocols for Computer Communications (SIGCOMM) (2013)
2. Intel Ethernet Switch FM5000/FM6000 Datasheet. http://goo.gl/pTl2iD. Accessed 16 May 2017
3. XPliant Ethernet Switch Product Family. http://goo.gl/mteFQZ. Accessed 16 May 2017
4. Sivaraman, A., et al.: Packet transactions: high-level programming for line-rate switches. In: Proceedings of the 2016 Conference on ACM SIGCOMM 2016 Conference. ACM (2016)
5. The P4.org language consortium: P416 Language Specification
6. Moshref, M., et al.: Flow-level state transition as a new switch primitive for SDN. In: Proceedings of the Third Workshop on Hot Topics in Software Defined Networking. ACM (2014)
7. Bianchi, G., Bonola, M., Capone, A., Cascone, C.: OpenState: programming platform-independent stateful openflow applications inside the switch. ACM SIGCOMM Comput. Commun. Rev. **44**(2), 44–51 (2014)
8. Bianchi, G., et al.: Open Packet Processor: a programmable architecture for wire speed platform-independent stateful in-network processing. https://arxiv.org/abs/1605.01977
9. Gibb, G., Varghese, G., Horowitz, M., McKeown, N.: Design principles for packet parsers. In: ACM/IEEE Architectures for Networking and Communications Systems, p. 13
10. Song, H.: Protocol-oblivious forwarding: Unleash the power of SDN through a future-proof forwarding plane. In: Proceedings of the Second ACM SIGCOMM Workshop on Hot Topics in Software Defined Networking (HotSDN 2013), pp. 127–132. ACM (2013)
11. Pontarelli, S., Bonola, M., Bianchi, G., Capone, A., Cascone, C.: Stateful openflow: hardware proof of concept. In: IEEE 16th International Conference on High Performance Switching and Routing (HPSR) (2015)
12. Bianchi, G., Bonola, M., Pontarelli, S.: On the feasibility of "breadcrumb" trails within OpenFlow switches. In: IEEE European Conference on Networks and Communications (EuCNC) (2016)
13. Zilberman, N., Audzevich, Y., Covington, G., Moore, A.W.: NetFPGA SUME: toward 100 Gbps as research commodity. IEEE Micro **34**(5), 32–41 (2014)
14. Virtex-7 Family Overview. http://goo.gl/3AI8pQ. Accessed 16 May 2017
15. Brelet, J.-L.: Using block RAM for high performance read/write TCAMs. Xilinx XAPP204 (2012)

16. Ullah, Z., Jaiswal, M.K., Chan, Y.C., Cheung, R.C.C.: FPGA Implementation of SRAM-based ternary content addressable memory. In: IEEE 26th International Parallel and Distributed Processing Symposium Workshops & PhD Forum (IPDPSW) (2012)
17. Jiang, W.: Scalable ternary content addressable memory implementation using FPGAs. In: Proceedings of the ACM/IEEE Symposium on Architectures for Networking and Communications Systems (ANCS) (2013)

Author Index

Alonso-Martinez, Carlos   3
Anyigor Ogah, Chibueze P.   143
Asuquo, Philip M.   143

Bianchi, Giuseppe   251
Blefari-Melazzi, Nicola   197
Bonola, Marco   251
Bruschi, Roberto   61
Bruschi, Valerio   251
Burgarella, Giuseppe   61

Calvo-Palomino, Roberto   215
Campisi, Patrizio   18
Carrega, Alessandro   230
Ciampini, Claudio   8
Comesaña-Alfaro, Pedro   109
Croce, Daniele   165
Cruickshank, Haitham   143

Di Mauro, Mario   31

Eramo, Vincenzo   45

Faundez-Zanuy, Marcos   3
Fontani, Marco   84

Garlisi, Domenico   165
Giustiniano, Domenico   215
Grasso, Christian   183
Grieco, Luigi Alfredo   197
Gucciardo, Michele   165

Iuliani, Massimo   84

Kuznetsov, Andrey   73

Lago, Paolo   61
Lavacca, Francesco Giacinto   45

Lei, Ao   143
Lenders, Vincent   215
Lombardo, Alfio   183
Longo, Maurizio   31

Maiorana, Emanuele   18
Malliaros, Stefanos   127
Mangione, Stefano   165

Ntantogian, Christoforos   127

Panos, Christoforos   127
Panou, Angeliki   127
Pérez-González, Fernando   109
Petrucci, Luca   251
Piciucco, Emanuela   18
Piro, Giuseppe   197
Piva, Alessandro   84
Pontarelli, Salvatore   251
Postiglione, Fabio   31

Rametta, Corrado   183
Repetto, Matteo   230
Ribezzo, Giuseppe   197
Riess, Christian   95

Salici, Angelo   8
Shaya, Omar Al   84
Shullani, Dasara   84
Sun, Zhili   143

Tambasco, Marco   31
Tinnirello, Ilenia   165

Vázquez-Padín, David   109

Xenakis, Christos   127

Printed in the United States
By Bookmasters